Sex, Drugs & A Rock Band

NEW BEST SELLER
WWW.SEXDRUGSANDAROCKBAND.COM

Donald L. Buford

Javelina Books

Javelina Books
P.O. Box 93152
Austin, Texas 78709
SAN 830-8046
Visit our web site at www.javelinabooks.com

FIRST EDITION: October 2009

This book is a memoir. Names, characters, places, and incidents are products of the author's memory and imagination.

Buford, Donald L.
Sex, Drugs & A Rock Band
1st Ed.

ISBN 978-0-9785521-4-8

Library of Congress Control Number: 2009936444

Printed in the United States of America on acid-free recycled paper.

For orders other than by individual consumers, Javelina Books grants a discount on the purchase of 10 or more copies of single titles for special markets or premi-um use. For further details, please write or e-mail Javelina Books, Attn: Premiums, P.O. Box 93152, Austin, Texas 78709 premiums@javellinabooks.com.

For orders by individual consumers, writer or e-mail Javelina Books, attn: Sales, P.O. Box 93152, Austin, Texas 78709 sales@javelinabooks.com

I would like to thank:

Amelia V. Buford, for her idea in the first place, and her support throughout it all. She said, "You can DO IT, DAD!

Lauren Goodley, for bringing my work to the attention of Denniger Bolton, publisher/writer, Javelina Books, Austin, Texas.

Jocelyn Hendrix, for loving me without boundaries, and being my biggest fan. My best to you forever...I'll never forget.

Debbie Sue Smith, thank you for your honest and blessings.

Denniger Bolton, my publisher and writing coach. Thanks for believing in me, Coach. I'll forever thank you.

Hunter S. Thompson, for his GONZO writing style that I do love the very most! For putting up with it all as long as he did.

Terry Smith, for being my friend and mentor in the days of my youth. Saw to it those days were not wasted! That they meant something. Thanks again pal...

Tony Smith the smartest man ever on this earth...and beyond.

Bonnie Meyers, I'll love you the rest of my life. I promise!

Lee Shroph, what can I say! Thanks for being my friend.

Rick and Dianna Basham, just because.

Spanky the Magic Dog, for taking care of me throughout it all.

Patty Hargrove, for showing us we COULD DO IT! No matter what. And the sweetest voice I have ever heard. A real TROUPER.

Carla (Muffin) Chambers, for making up my mind on day one!

To everyone on every page in these books. I love you all.

Laura Brewer, for planting the seed of my destiny...

Jamye Peel, for her excellent work in design and set up.

Andrea Allen, for a killer website and book cover design.

Jeannette Buford, for paying the bills as I write this trilogy.

Javelina Books, for taking a chance on me.

And to the Muse for saving my life and opening my eyes.

Thanks Again! dlb

CHAPTER ONE BOOK ONE

"I'm Home... Alive...
& Ready to PARTY"
Ψ *Let me see here...* Ψ

It's Sunday Afternoon, June 8th 2008.

I'm sitting out side of *Ryan Hunter's Studio*. In his garden! Listening to his incredible studio monitoring system...

He is listening to *"Chicago Transit Authority"*

Ryan doesn't need a big assed set of speakers in every corner of his studio. They are not needed. It's the attention he pay's to the response of each box. Every wave length in the mix counts...It is truly incredible!

He doesn't know I'm out here sitting alone. He most times doesn't. It's a real sunny day. Just beautiful under his Acacias trees.

As, I sit here. I just fade in. And, out of the music.

I found myself kinda...*Day dreaming...* The song *"Only the Beginnings"* is playing now. Every horn... Vocal... To each drum beat. Is as clear as if I'm in the room with them as they record the tracks themselves...

I'm puffing on some very fine *"Indoor"* As, I kinda drift off.

The next thing I know...It's spring 1969. I'm on the air at Radio Station KUOR. "The Voice of Freedom" 89.1 FM. University of Redlands, California. WOW!

I'm just about to wrap up my afternoon drive show. When I noticed the next DJ in the AP room gathering his print and live reads for his shift.

The cat's name is *Tad Talore...* He is from Fontana, California.

He is a student here at the University too. He is Journalism. Radio Television & Film student like me... He is also required to take this radio station class... If you want an FCC license that is. You have to take schooling in those days. And, pass a 150 question test at the United States Courthouse in Los Angeles.

If you did... you would receive a 3rd··· up to a 1st class Radio Telephone License. Without this license in a picture frame suitable for hanging on the transmitter wall. You didn't work in radio!

Not like today. Where all ya have to do is sign this little piece a paper and you are on the air.

Hey There Me Droogies... I know you must be "Kine-of-a-sewer" on fine food. See if you know this one...

What do you get when ya cross a Donkey. With a huge slice of Bermuda Onion? (*I dint know what do ya get*) Ah… Thank You… You get a "*Piece a Ass. That brings* "Tears to your eyes!"

"WHAT?"

There I am… I've just been thrown out of the "Brown Water Navy" for doing a little business that wasn't Navy business. If they had only told me that, 2 years earlier! *What a rip off*!

I'm fresh out of ol *Johnson* and *Nixon's* war. Just glad to be alive! I'm here on Uncle Sam, supposed to be minding my P's and Q's. But, what is about to happen will bring an end to all that stuff! And, not a minute to soon me Droogies!

The station and campus are about to erupt… I tain't kiddin either!

I'm watching Tad. He is starting to jump up and down as he reads the type on the AP machine. I'm wrapping up my show. *This is what I'm saying.*

"*Ok! Well I am out of here. Stay tuned for The "Tad Talore" Show. He has some new music he is going to share with you. I'll be back at the same time tomorrow with the newest music there is.*"

"Till Then… I'm Don Morison." Click… off…

As "**South California Purples**" fades out. I wave to Tad to come on in and take over… you won't believe what happens next, I didn't.

I'm getting up from the console, when Tad flies into the control room so fast he breaks the glass in the control room door. He pushed me out of the way so hard I fell to the floor. He grabbed the microphone, hit the live switch. He screamed in his best news voice these words.

"FOUR DEAD AT KENT STATE UNIVERSITY!"

"News flash!" Four unarmed students at the *University Of Ohio*! Were gunned down by the National Guard today! Under orders from Richard Nixon! Again! *Four Dead in Ohio*… We will return with more details as they become available."

I thought the cat was about to jump out of his *Skin Suit*. He is coming unglued. Totally freaking out!

I told him that he better get some music pulled, as his record is about to run out. Tad told me "That he would not be able to cover this alone, would I stay. And do a Double DJ shift with him?"

Well, I thought: I just got out of all this kinda war and noise stuff. I'm not really in the mood to join in on anything like this, not just now anyway. But, it looks like it's going to turn into a big party, so I decided to join the fun.

The song faded out, a guy ran into the control room. Took the mic, then, said the people in the main studio are *taking over the administration building,* and the radio station. "Arm bands" will be available at the student union as long as they last. "Power to the People"

I looked around for an exit sign. I remembered that there is no side, or back doors in a records vault. 3 stories up on the top of the Administration bldg…

This radio station is in its first year. It has been built over the past school year. And, is located in an old paper records vault for its sound proofing and ambiance…

The transmitter is actually in the control room with us, we can just reach over and up the wattage from 5 watt's, all the way to 150 watt's. So they can hear us in Malibu… 68 miles away. It's a *Hoot* for sure.

Out in the main studio… Where all the interviews are done… Is a diverse group of people getting locked in there with us?

There is a 2 ton fire door at the front of the studio. It has been locked and secured. We are three floors up on our own with no idea of how long this will go on. I wasn't really sure what it was all about anyway… didn't really care! But, it's getting crazier by the minute. I just couldn't leave, not just yet.

You would not believe who the eggheads went out and found to lock up with us. I knew. Tad knew. This is not going to turn out good anyway.

But, at this time… Tad is heavy into it. There is no turning back.

Tad has a secret he will soon share with me. *A Real LIFE Changer!*

Stupid if you come to think about it. I have nothing to hide from.

Ψ *"Ah, the plot thickens!"* Ψ

Now that we are locked in here with a bunch of psychos, Tad and I decide to be the engineers in charge, and lock the control room. We could listen in on what ever happened in the main studio. Watch through the big as hell glass partition that separated the two studios.

They are settling into their places around the giant oval interview table covered with microphones and headphones. There is a glass outside window in the control room. A glass outside window in the main studio… There up to high to do anything but pull stuff up and down in the "In and Out mail boxes."

People are coming from all over the campus… Bringing us all the goodies, dope and stuff we could want. We had all kinds of folks trying to climb the frigging building to get to us.

The school security force and the **R. O. T. C.** guarding the front and only door that is useable. They have locked all the rest of them. They grab anyone who try's to get in or out. So… we just settled in to have a blast watching all the shit outside on the control room TV.

The people in the main studio are... "The Students for a Democratic Society" The "Weather Underground" The "Black Panthers" The "Mexican Brown League" all the _hairy chicks_ from "POLY KI OMEGA" and, thank god! The local Chapter of *"The Merry Pranksters"* Just for comic relief! (*Wow! Is that an under statement!*)

All the *weird fuckers* are in *attendance*. Ready to spew out Hate and Loathing to anyone listening in radio land... People are running around everywhere throwing 💣cherry bombs, smoke flairs, hopping and jumping screaming... "**Revolution.**"

Most are just filled with the excitement of the moment... glad to be alive and there in this heavy duty time. Others are just looking for an excuse to tear shit up and do a bit of anarchy in the name of *their* generation.

Most of the time I'm watching all of this... I'm thinking of those **Hippy Communes**Ω and how they work. I want to invade a few of them and shut them down! I didn't know how or why. But, I just know I had to do something. That seemed like something I could do.

I'm not against the idea of a commune, I'm against the two or three cock suckers running them that have brainwashed the people into thinking they are God all mighty, when their only interest is, Hippie Nooky!

Oh well... Outside the Administration building, there are crowds of people chanting "The whole world's watching" and "Four dead In Ohio" when the vault door flew open. This guy in a Suit is spirited in... the door is shut and locked.

He is a record PR guy, from the Record Plant in L. A. He has a song with him "Hot off the press" for us to feature for the next couple a days or so. Or, just run non-stop.

Tad and I said: "Ok." off we went with the 45 rpm record... same song both sides. So we can *Burn* them out. There are 6 more ready to go. Wow! What a trip! (i.e. *Record wear is caused by the "Burn" where you cue the record before the roll*) The EXCITEMENT is hard to contain inside of us. We just wanted to start jumping around too!

The party is getting better and better by the moment! All we have to do is turn the Knob's... Play the music. Pull up the stuff from down on the ground and Party, Party, Party! What more could Two "Super Stoner's" ever want? WE ARE SET!

I looked at Tad and said: "<u>REVOLUTION</u>"... He agreed!

We knew that the "Merry Pranksters" would doctor up some drink or food somewhere along the line. We watched close for any water pistols that were hidden under a shirt. We didn't have to wait long.

Off to the control room we went with the record, to put it on the turn table to see if it was even worth playing. I was surprised to see the name's

"Crosby, Stills, Nash & Young" on the label with the title "**Four Dead in Ohio**" Seems that *David Crosby & Gram Nash* had written it in just a few hours... they ran down and recorded it.

We should play it every song or two.

I think this guy getting in here was an inside job. The song wasn't bad, so, we ran with it all that day and into the next night.

Now, these groups are starting to get on each others nerves. The Pranksters are getting bored. So we opened up the microphones and the telephones while they still worked. Went on the air with the groups stating their points of view on the goings on...

The "Weather Underground" thought... "We should just blow the shit out of _EVERYBODY_! Starting with the local Police Department"

The Panthers thought... "We should just burn down anything white, and start the revolution." They had an idea about this movement called "**Community Revolution in Progress**" (I.e. the <u>C. R. I. P. s</u>) soon it would be Whitey be doing the crying.

Of course, the Mexican group had to stick in their 2 centavos. Their idea was a bit strange, it went this way. They felt that Santana got a raw deal at Woodstock... They are going to Texas. To get the *Alamo* back for him... So he could do his next concert there. I look at Tad... "<u>WHAT</u>?"

Who knows how those mothers think! The fucking Alamo! Concerts!

Well, the *Omega* girls have whipped out their *GEETARS*.

They is a singing "Cum bye ya" Or, some shit like that in the back ground when the Pranksters went bug fuck nuts. I don't know... I wasn't paying attention.

They started tossing shit all over the studio. Jumping up and down on the table like a bunch of monkeys... I mean REAL shit! The *Pranksters* had something up there skirts they had been plotting and planning all day.

A bunch of *Turkey* sandwiches were sent up the chow line from the parking lot through the window in the control room. The *Pranksters* disappeared into the break room, doctored up those sandwiches real good just like "*The Electric Kool Aid Acid Test*"

Those idiots ate anything that came through the friggin window. As there is no *Watermelon*, or *Tacos* around, They gobbled um down.

Tad and I passed, as we knew what was going on. We want to enjoy the fun when these fools got off and got mind fucked by the Pranksters. <u>*Which they did*</u>!

Tad and I are ready for the doors to come crashing in. We are ready to haul ass out of here. We knew that if we started tossing school property out of the window to the parking lot below, that would be about that.

As a few type writers and office supplies hit the cop cars down stairs...

The two ton vault door came crashing in about 6:30 am. Thanks to the R.O.T.C and The local sheriff. Tad and I just did the Teddy Jack Eddy out the door and we were gone! So what now? What's next?

Only the Shadow knows!

Chapter Two

"Off into the Unknown!"

Everybody has their own stony cruse streets, we are no different.

I live in Redlands California, about 6 miles East of San Bernardino. Tad lives in Fontana, about the same west. That's why we are going to the "University of Redlands."

We cruse E, Street in San Berdo every night… make the turn at the very first *"Mac Donald's®"* in the frigging world. Then drive the other way to the *"Taco Tia"* for "Ten for a Dollar" tacos. Later, Taco Tia would become *"Taco Bell®."*

Tad picked me up in Redlands in his *fire engine red Mustang Mach One®*… it for sure is the pussy mobile. It never missed. Too make sure of that, Tad brought along his Rock Star brother "Red." (Figures don't it?)

He is the lead guitar player in that band *"Blue Cheer"* Or, something like that.(I thought that was soap!)

Supposed to be the Loudest band in the world… The ones that *"Spinal Tap"* copied… It was a sure thing when girls see him in the car. Everyone is gonna get *Laid*!

Before we got to E, Street… I'm sucking on a Bomber in the back seat. Tad told me of the plan he and some of his friends have. They received their vacation papers to Indo China. They are to report to the induction center next Tuesday.

This is something he felt he just could not do! He was aware of my time in country. But, friends are friends he felt. He and these guys have a great plan. But, he didn't know anything about anything… and needs my help.

Now, the last thing I had in mind is to leave this country anytime soon. For any reason! I'm just back home. I only want to *Surf* with my friends, party hearty every night, and play Rock and Roll.

But I said: "I guess I'll go"

As I haven't ever seen Europe… what the hell!

His plan is to take a tramp steamer over to London, back pack around the place for a year or two. Or, the end of the war which ever came first!

We drove over to a party at a guy named Franks house.

It's a good bye party he is throwing for his friends. Tad told me that Frank is going to take us as far as InDiannapolis. From there… we were on our own.

Seemed *Frank*… Is a race car type of guy! That dreams of winning the Indy 500. He has a souped up "VW" with a Porsche engine that we are going to leave town in, along with his roomy Joe. Frank and Joe worked at "Kyser Steel" in Fontana. They have their *vacation papers* too.

Frank is going to hide out at the Indy track, as a house mechanic year around. And, maybe get discovered there to race someday.

We are having one hell of a good bye party, when Joe pulls out a bunch of party Favors. A bag full of 4 way "Green slim acid" a bunch a speed, some good lumbo and everything's *groovy!*

I wasn't up on all the plans… But I'm interested.

The hell with it tonight! It's *fucking* party time!

It's about time too! Good acid is what it's all about. Acid today is NOT acid. I don't know what in the hell it is.

The days of "Owsley Stanley Acid" are <u>GONE</u>!

Tad and I met a guy in Frisco. Named "GROOVY" Or, so he said! He had arrived from the "Village" in New York.

He got his self Murdered for some reason or another. He dealt for Owsley. Might be what got him murdered. Who knows: Dig-it!

In Frank and Joe's backyard is the "*Fontana Drive-Inn Theater*"

The entire neighborhood wraps around the thing. Everyone has a back shed with a flat roof that has chairs on them. So everyone can just sit and watch the movie's for free!

We took the "Green Slime Acid" around 4 pm. By dark, it's coming on real good! It's getting crowded in the house… I don't know much of anyone anyway. I'm going out side for a breath of fresh.

Did I say that? A breath of fresh air in Fontana California is only found in a Canister!

The "Drive-inn" caught my attention, Roll the Movie! Everyone in the neighborhood would jump over the fence to turn up the speaker box so you could hear the movie… I climbed up on theirs and settled in to my upside down beer keg cut out into a seat.

The pictures are "Butch Cassidy and the Sun Dance Kid" Plus, "Marooned" I watched both movies as the Party inside mellowed out and died.

I climbed down went back in… there is not one person in the house. So, I found a bed and hit it!

You know. It was a longtime before I realized that those movies were not one movie. I thought they were about: two Spaced out Cowboy's stuck in Outer Space for Christ's sake!

I stayed in Redlands the whole next day and night. We are to leave on the next Wednesday morning at 5 am. So I stayed home. Packed up… And, got ready to go…

Chapter Three

"Tad's Super Pussy Pad"

Tad and Joe are doing what they do every night. Cruzing E Street.

I still don't know how Tad doe's it! But I always left the first liners to him... they never failed. This night is no different.

They had run into a <u>VW Boner Bus full of Girls and ONE guy</u>! Out of state tags and ready to roll.

So, a couple a words from Tad & a good look a RED, then off to Tads pussy pad. No shit! *<u>He has a real Pussy Pad</u>*...

Shaped like a Pussy and everything! It's unreal. Has a big assed hairy Crack for a front door.

When you ring the door bell, it oozed clear stuff and went.

"Oh HONEY, someone is here."
                        It's a big hit at Halloween!"

A few minutes later... If... you were lucky! Tad will come to the door in his "Hugh Heffner" long smoker coat. Real firkin *RED* and *GREEN*! A cigarette holder 3 feet long, with a doobie in the end. And, a *Feather* up his ass.

"Now, I never saw the feather... But, I took his word on it."

He took this VW boner bus full of girls and ONE guy. Right the freak there. Got um up inside, applied the... as he put's it "The Touch"

The "Touch" is when he would pull back that many colored beaded Curtain that divides the entryway and the living room... He swings his arm Dracula style. Then hits the Switch...

The room comes <u>Alive</u> with everything from, four foot black lights shinning through a *Huge Parachute* he stole from "Norton Air Force Base" That is so you couldn't see the black light's themselves shining on the latest, and largest black light posters printed on a black velvet background too shag carpet and Day-Glo furniture.

He has taken some of that "Lightening Bug Glow Juice"® Put it on a piece of round sand paper on a drill. Then he spins it all over the walls from the middle to the center of the Parachute.

When the black light's are on, all you see is the bright white/green glow of the Parachute it self!

But, when you turn them off! It's like you are in a *Planetarium*!

All you can see is the thousands of little to a bit larger spots of the Glow Bug juice! It is absolutely amazing! Tad is always coming up with this stuff. It seemed to make the girl's clothes just, *Fall Off!* What a TRIP!

If you are new to this life style, you didn't stand a chance! Tad had them naked with-in 15 minute's... even the Guy.

Everything about this room is *Get Um!* The stereo comes on all by its frigin self. The song is always the same... Barry White. You know... the one that goes. "*Good Love, Good Love*"... That one!

The table in the middle of the room is clear glass. When you sit down, It will light up from underneath with a, just bright enough light to see thru the clear glassware he used for smoke and snoot!

Pillows all around the damn thing... Big over stuffed kind of monstrosities Full of that Styrofoam stuff...

After about twenty minutes or so, the music would go to *Sitar*. That Guru crap! That's his plan. It sent everyone to a bedroom or two.

That is the evening.

But, not this night!

Tad rolled up two Bombers● of *RED* Bud Lumbo. About a ¼ inch thick... Each two rolling papers long... Normal Doob for the time.

Well: these girls... and one guy went bug fuck nuts.

The leader of their little pack is a girl named "Laura Brewer" (You might want to write that down on the score sheet in the back I've provided for you, as she will figure into this tale a bunch.)

You can use her for a foothold in reality so to say.

Yeah! For sure man... Reality, Dig This!

As Tad lit one of the Doobies...

The Laura girl said: "Are we going to smoke all of that there?"

Tad said: "Sure! To start with! Ain't it enough!

She said: "No, it's fine, we just have never seen that much smoke at once. Getting to smoke it... just doesn't seem right."

After they finished those two... And, a couple a more! These girls and ONE guy are floating out by Mars somewhere!

So, Tad and Joe... Along with ol" Red stuck it to um.

Showed um on their way the next morning...

That's normal for them. Like to see um come, like to see them go!

With no sleep! And, still real high.

Franks VW pulled up in front of my house in Redlands.

There I am... in the driveway waiting with all my stuff.

There are already three guys. And all their stuff in thar!

Now, I'm supposed to shove my shit in thar... myself too! This is gonna be tight. As there is no room for a mouse to fart, that would be an instant death sentence.

Chapter Four

"No Turning Back Now!"

So, we make like a baby. And, *head out* for the <u>unknown</u>!

I still was not sure what we are going to do! Or, where we were going!

I figured that I would hear about it along the road soon enough, as there was not much more to do. But, listen to the tunes and talk.

We made real good time... while we were rolling. As we are in a super souped up VW.

It's bright Orange and called the *"Rocket"*

Along about Flagstaff, Arizona... At *102* miles per hour!

Tad dropped the plan on me.

It includes the night before we left.

As, where these girls and one Guy lived! This is to be our first stop.

What he told me next. Sent chills up my spine. I wasn't ready for the idea of disappearing into the hills of *Hillbilly* mid America.

Shit! People go there and *never* come back.

As we went along he laid this plan on me. The car seemed to lift from the ground as we hit the high desert. I'm for sure intrigued! Ψ

Tad started out with a line straight out of a teen age monster gang fuck flick. These girls and ONE guy never knew what hit um.

They were used to some kinda crap growd out behind da barn in Fucka-monkee, Arkansas! Or, some shit like that... and, now. We are going to stop in their town for about two weeks. Then head for New York. Catch the steamer that would then be in port.

We are to enjoy the *Fruits* of their. And, our loins for that time... And, party down country style!

I'm listening to all of this as *Joe* kept butting in at every turn with his most nasty steel worker... "Boiler maker" point of view.

I and old Joe are not getting along very well. I'm hoping we just might lose him somewhere along the line. But, he is so dependent on Tads every move. I don't think that is gonna happen.

As we approached a *"Whiting Brothers"* gas station!

I told Frank to let me pay. As I had been this route many times... I had knowledge of how it worked... *Gas wise!*

Went this way... "Whiting Brothers" gas stations are set to be right there when your gas tank hits almost empty. Towns are not gagged by gas tanks, so most Whiting Bro gas stations are in the middle of "NO" where.

A friend in the day... Or, the night!

If you have your "Whiting Brothers" gas card punched all along the way. You get 12 cents off per Gallon.

With gas at 29.9 at the time, it was like traveling across the country "FREE."

I took $100 once. And, drove from California… to Florida on that money… We ate and partied all the way. Had change when we got to there…

You can't even get out of town for $100 now.

As we got back on the road, I had time to think over what Tad told me along the way to here.

Well about here. I told them about what I knew of this "Headless Horseman" area we are going too.

As none of them really knew where it was… I didn't either.

I remembered stuff about the area I learned from watching TV as a kid. As I told them these things, they started to see what my concern was.

I had been watching that TV show… The "Dating Game" one day while I was ditching school or some shit like that. The lucky couple won an all expense paid trip to "The Rodeo of the Ozarks" in beautiful Springdale, Arkansas.

The "Beverly Hillbillies" are supposed to live in "Eureka Springs." Somewhere outside a Bugtussel, Arkansas!

That "Silver Dollar City" that was used in 6 Hillbilly's episodes, is the amusement park itself, on the border of Arkansas and Missouri. Called "Branson" Now…

I never thought I would be headed for that part of the world ever in my life. I had no idea when we left California. We would be going any Place close to that kinda scene.

It didn't really matter anyway.

As I'm planning on jumping ship somewhere along the line, and head back to California! I don't like the Joe guy. And, I'm not looking forward to going thru hell with him around.

Tad has all this down to the very minute. That is what he told me. How can he? He has NO plan at all!

I know what is going to happen.

It's this way: either… I Go! Or, Joe is going to have to go!

God Damn… Man, I'm I glad it was him. I would have missed everything! Better him, than me, what a worm eating piece a dog shit!

Tad and I each have a ¼ pound of good Red Bud Columbian in our back packs. We each have $600.00 cash… I have. $1,000.00 in traveler's checks… So, we are ok on the cash and the dope side.

We were traveling in the post "Easy Rider" days. We seemed to find every restaurant that had the same scene inside.

Is it a girl? Or is it a boy? That kinda shit.

As I am NOT a turn the other cheek Hippie, **No Hippie at ALL**!

That stuff didn't set well with me. But, I put up with it, as we were always out numbered. And, didn't dare take a stand…

Not yet anyway!

But, not old Joe! No… Not him! He rubbed everyone, everywhere we went the *wrong* way!

Had us all on the look out all the time, what a total dick!

I was thinking in the back of my mind. This is feeling more like the *"Twilight Zone"* with every mile that passed under the VW.

It's about dark when we pass through Oklahoma, City.

How does that song go?

"OKLAHOMA CITY… IS MIGHTY PRETTY"

Well… I didn't see enough of that town to even know it was there. Seemed we are on the upcoming new thing called an "Interstate."

We have been on. And, off of that thing all the way so far. All it does is cause trouble.

On the thing! And, off the thing!

But, that is about to come to an end at the Arkansas and Oklahoma border.

As, we pass over the bridge into Fort Smith. We turned North up Arkansas Hwy. 71.

As we left Ft. Smith behind, it got so dark. I could see every star as if it were on one of those black velvet backgrounds at Tads house.

Just a sparkling RED and *Bright* Blue cascade of lights. Blinking off and on…

I've only seen that at sea! And, in the desert have I ever seen such a thing.

As we turn up the winding *moonshine* road. The smell in the air was so sweet. I thought it was the stink of Fontana and Cucamonga.

But, it's the sweet smell of "Magnolia and Honey Suckle" in the air everywhere.

It seems like something has just reached out and grabbed me.

I have nothing to go on though.

As, all I have to work with is a few smells. And, a bunch a stars!

I hadn't even seen Arkansas in the light of day.

The other guys are bitching about how tired they are. And, we should stop at the very next motel on the road. Yeah sure! A motel on Hwy 71 in 1970! I don't think so!

We are there in "Duck Hunting Central" If you know what I mean!

We drove along awhile longer. Until we saw one of those turn outs…

There is no such thing along our trip so far as a "Rest Stop." They are just a dirt turn out. And, a 55 Gallon drum if you were lucky... A tree to piss behind...

Frank spotted one up ahead. We pulled in for the rest of the night.

I was flashing on that "**Butch & Sundance**" deal.

When Frank gave me a shake and said: "Hey man... You in there..."

I said: "oh…. Yeah….. What's up Daddy-o?"

He said: "I'm too tired to drive any farther. Tad is already out. And, so is Joe. So... we gonna crash here in this turn out the rest of the night."

I said: "The rest of the night! That is a good one!"

"Man! It's 4:30 am."

Frank said: "Better get to sleep then shouldn't ya!"

There is no room in the VW for one, let alone four.

So, I climbed into my new home... my sleeping bag. And, drifted off to sleep hoping that some freaked out Rotarian would not run me over with his super fine auto botcher land rover...

I watched the stars go passed over head till I was out. I'm sleeping real hard when I look up. Thought I was dreaming... A cow has stuck her head through the gate. She is licking the bottom of my sleeping bag.

I have a "Giant Spider" sitting on my nose. An angry farmer... And, his tractor, waiting for us to get out of the way of his gate! This is no turn out, it's his property. And, we are in the way.

He didn't look like he liked us "_Easy Rider_®" long haired fagetty sons a bitches blocking up his gate. Let alone even on his earth... When he said: Are You boys Huggers?

I noticed from where I was laying. A bumper sticker someone had stuck on the VW that said "**Go Hogs Go.**" I realized he had seen that too.

He figured we were just students heading back to school.

So, I played that card. We got the flock outta thar!

Seems... He thought we looked a bit like that "**Charlie Manson**" fella.

Back on the road again! "I am hungry."

"Anybody got any idea where we might be?"

I say. "The map says we should be about there."

He points to a splotch that snakes around. And, doesn't appear to really go anywhere...

"The next town we should see is a berg called _Winslow_" "the next is _West-fork_... then we are supposed to be there."

I said: "How will we know if we have missed any of these coach stops?"

Tad said: "if we reach a town called Springdale, we went too far."

I said: "that's the town them folks won that trip too I was telling you about, now that's freaky!"

Then... as we made another turn around these Moonshine roads!

It's as if a fog cleared. There are little shotgun houses along the road.

Coming down the hill from a crossroad... Is a for real RED "1946 Ford" pick up... With 10 or 12 guys in it! If I closed my eyes, I can see the *Hoods* on their head's. The Torches and Farm Implements in their hands... Screaming... "Kill the Commie Bustards" "No Niger's going vote round these here parts!"

But, they passed without incidence.

As we climbed the hill from the crossroads, I snagged a gander at the street sign. It reads... "Archibald Yell"

Ends up at the square on the top... It's lined with these "Victorian Mansions" right out of "Gone with the Wind"

When I noticed a motel named "The Pink Bunny Motel & Restaurant" We thought we would pull in there, grab a bit a Spatchka and check it out a bit later. When Joe spoke up with a,

Hey! Looky there." "The sign! Read it!"

← "UNIVERSITY OF ARKANSAS" *NEXT LEFT* ⇐

Now! That got our attention real fast!

Off we went. It turned out that the stop light at Dickson Street and Collage Ave. (really Hwy 71) is the only working stop light in town. Hang a left. You are looking down a long midway looking street that dropped 2000 yards to the middle. And, back up again to the University campus.

I could feel my "*Future*" grab a hold of my soul. It scared me!

My face is flour White! Tad looked at me.

He just smiled... He knew. He Knew...

It's in the air... "You can't stop something when it's in the air."

I remember him turning to me saying that to me to this very day.

It's about 7:30 am when we made the turn.

I look down Dickson Street all the way to the campus. I was instantly reminded of San Francisco. Tad and I had gone there a few weeks earlier to say goodbye to some friends and check out Height/Asbury.

We visited our friends in Stockton. Went to a "Steppenwolf" concert on our KUOR radio I.D. cards... Almost got KILLED by the *Hell's Angels*. Those radio Station ID card's we made at the print shop. Got us into many concerts FREE. We cruised San Francisco on the way back to Redlands...

As we drove down the streets of San Francisco, It was plum freaking weird!

We were in a New car, eating Big old sloppy Hamburgers, listening to a wailing stereo. When I noticed we looked like a big rolling "Sub Sandwich" to all those starving Hippies that were there by the thousands with no where to go... Not able to go home because of bridges burned. Or, worst.

We hung around a week or two. Then skeedatteled outta thar! We did see Janis Joplin sitting on a bus stop bench. I stood behind her. And, took in her smell…

I would be reminded of her again very soon.

Saw the Dead at "Fillmore West" before we left town.

Did a bunch of "PURPLE OWSLEY"… A lot!

Tad was told by Laura Brewer… The campus area in Fayetteville is where the Acton is.

So, we started down the street to find the future. ☯

Chapter Five

"The Beginning of the Stoke"

We had to find Laura Brewer. And, where she lived… Get cleaned up a bit and start all that Partying I heard so much about. I'm still wondering what the girls, and ONE guy looked like. I had after all, never seen any of them.

Is it just me… what's with "The ONE guy" deal?

Turns out, the VW van was his, that was their transportation to, and from California.

They… *Laura Brewer*, the girls and ONE guy. Were visiting friends at a wedding in San Bernardino when they met Tad and Red! They said they were going to school in Fayetteville. Stop for some Country Style <u>LOVING</u> Honey!

As we passed down Dickson Street! We passed a place called *"Dennis Home Furnishings"* We have seen that place twice on the way in. So, we figured he must own the town.

We are looking for a pay phone. Found one almost at the other end. At a place named "Palace Drug Store" It's next to an "Ice Cream Parlor" named the *"Jet Set"* Owned. And, operated by a *Retired Hooker*… Across the street from a Jewelry shop named "Underwood's" Next to Underwood's Jewelry is a parking lot with a gas station on the other side all of five feet from the rail road track.

It has a car in the parking lot. <u>Totally involved in fire!</u>

I looked over at Tad and said: "This must be the place!"

He said: "Looks like it to me."

Let me run down Tad here for ya a bit.

He is the. Total ladies man…

Or, even a gigolo.

Or, "Mondo-cheesmo" If you will!

If he was to go to town on a skateboard, He will come home in Rolls, with a red head at the wheel. And, two beauticians in the back!

Tad says: "Hey… Don."

"What Man." I'm mumbling some shit about Joe under my breath

Tad says: "Don… Watch this."

I say: "Fuckin What Tad?"

He says: "*Fucking birds!* I hate the way they sit. And, wait for ya to throw a *French fry out the fuckin window.*"

He has a small bottle of Tabasco© in his hand. He sprinkles a good amount on the biggest fry. He throws a few normal ones first. To get the others all shook up so they will fight over um.

And then, when they are circling the car, he throws the red hot one and they tear it apart in mid air. *Ten fuckin birds coughing,* screaming and lookin for an *old coke* some where! Scraping their beaks along a tree and shit!

I'm cracking up like a motha-fucka! ☺

He has doctored up ten or so more and it's a total *BIRD* freak out! They know what's coming… But, they just can't let the other bird get the fri first!

Tad says… "Fuckin Birds!"

He turns to me shaking a fry at me dripping with *Tabasco* and says.

"Let this be a fucking lesson to ya me Droogies! *Never get out of the boat!*"

Oh well… I always leave the sweet talking for goods. And, services to him… Joe is inside the drugstore reading a Playboy. Frank is watching the fire.

It's for sure this is a "<u>*Headless Horseman town.*</u>"

Cause… after 30 minutes or so… The only thing to come to the fire so far is an old *1959 Ford Fairlane.* Brown… With a big *STAR* ★ on the door that read's "*Auxiliary County Sheriff Unit #1*"

There is an acorn type spotlight on the door. It was right out of "*In the Heat of the Night.*"

I rubbed my eyes real hard as I looked at the scene!

Am I really here? I still could see hoods on these guys!

A freaking fire! Now what? What's next! Ψ

The fire has progressed to a full station fire now. The station looked like it had not been cleaned up in at least 3 decades.

Well, it's getting a good cleaning right now.

As the main tank blew… with a shuddering shock wave… It almost knocked us over. Coming down the street is an old *Disney Main Street Fire truck with siren wailing.*

The Barney Fife looking cop helped them hook a leaky old as hell hose to an under powered hydrant. The place just burnt to the freaking ground. Talk about coming to town with a bang!

I must be dreaming.

Tad looks at me and say's: "This is the "<u>*Fucking Place Me Drooge!*</u>"

"Don't ya feel it?" "This is what we been looking for."

He's smiling from ear to ear. We walked over to the only pay phone we have seen anywhere.

Tad asked Joe for the phone number of the Laura Brewer girl. Joe looked in his shirt pocket. Then, his pantaloons. The, glove box and his pants pocket's again then said: "*Man, I left it on the coffee table in <u>Fontana</u>.*"

It seems like. Anything Joe is supposed to do. Or, pay for. He fuck's up every time and blame's it on someone else. Most times me. But, he isn't getting out of this one. Ain't NO fuckin way!

I asked Tad: "What do you want to do now? Wanna just move along." He said: "Let's give this place of wonder a chance. There is something so right about this place."

Hell, I'm just digging being free and alive. I don't give a shit where we are.

We grabbed the phone book. All of one half inch thick. Looked up Brewer... There are 3 pages of um. More than any other name in the book...

We spent $12 in dimes calling each and every one of them. Most didn't even understand us! We are not speaking slowly. And, slurred enough for them. None of them ever heard of Laura.

I watched Joe's lip stiffen as he realized we are now stuck in a half a horse town with nothing!

He said: "Fuck This!" Let's get the fuck out of here...*right now!*"

It's about 12:30. And, hotter than "Dolly Pardons" mini pad! Twice as wet!

All of Three cars! And, one person has gone by in the last hour.

Chapter Six

"Shelly Ford" Whitest Girl I have ever scene!"

When out of the door way of the "U-ARK" rooming house, comes...*A God-dess.*
The Whitest girl I have ever seen.
She is 5 foot 5. Just COCK stiffening beautiful. As, she walked, we are all knocked back! She is wearing a bikini with "GO HOGS GO" across the white suit in red print on her ass. With two red pigs running across her top.

She walk's up to Tad... Of course! She said: "You ain't from around here, are ya boy!"

Tad pulled her over to him. Real Fuckin close...
Whispered in her ear: "*I'll lick ya all over for a dime*"
"*If, you let us use your shower.*"
She looked at him with one of those "Southern Belle" looks!
He looked back into her big Blue eyes and said: "Ok, "for FREE then"
The next thing I knew, we are across the street, using a shower that is meant for the entire floor of 20 rooms. The place is right out of "Deliverance" Just like that rooming house they ate dinner in.

I'm just a bit dizzy... I think all of this is catching up with me. What a long strange trip it's been! Did I say that? Or, just think it?
"You know what! These fucking peanuts fucking suck!"
"Why do you keep shoving more of them into your pie hole then?"
"I DON'T FUCKING KNOW!"
Joe through the can, and all out the second floor window to the street below... What a dick!

As I waited for my turn in the shower, I took advantage of the moment. I slid over and asked this girl named "Shelly" what was the deal with this Fayetteville?

Her response was: "I don't understand what you mean... Ah, Man!"
As I held back a knee slap I said again: "where are all the kids"
I figured that school was out here. School is out in California. Most times a school town is a *Ghost Town* all summer. If it is land locked. With about nothing to freaking do at all!

She walked over to her room window. Her room is above the "U-ARK Theater and Print shop" on the corner of "University and Dickson." Her room is about the size of a good walk in closet. She has the song "Dizzy" playing on her .45 rpm record player. Pink with green flowers… And, a pie pan speaker built right in.

Next to that… Is a white dial phone with a red handle!

There are 19 more rooms exactly like this one along the outside of the building on the second floor.

As she lean's out of her window… Her <u>Most</u> beautiful ass is pinching that suit bottom all the way up. And, into each crack… She looked north to the corner.

There is this "WALL" that run's next to the only record store in town "Metcalf Records and Books" The place even has two listening booths. Old Mr. Metcalf always has one of each record opened. And, ready to be sampled.

In later years! People would just go in there and tape record the album on a cassette. Till it put him out of business! That was a drag for sure.

There is a "WALL" that hold's up a grassy area along the front of the "Christian Science Room" all the way to the corner.

It starts out at about 5 feet high at the Metcalf end. And, graduates down to nothing at the Arkansas Ave end…

It is the "Meet and Greet" spot of the entire town for many a year to come. It is where you meet up with your troops… plan the epic parties. And, events for the evening…

We still had seen no one, thought that was about it.

Shelly said: "That the "WALL" will be full of them old Hippies. And street people at about dark…"

"As, they never come out till then… They sit there all night. Play loud music. Strum guitars… *that's not so bad*. But, about midnight! They really start makin a lot of racket."

They're lying around in the grass, Making out and on that WALL doing who fucking knows what… Nobody does anything about it!"

"Just wait, they will be there! I'll suck your dick if they ain't!"

Man I'm hoping no body show's up!

Well, as it is about my turn for the shower. I left Shelly too Tad. And, hit the deal. As I walk along. I'm thinking about what Shelly had to say. And, figured that she really didn't care a shit about what I was asking her. She is quite taken with ol *Tad* there. As always… "That's a good thing!" So, I just took a well deserved break. And, settled down for the first time in 5 days…

It had not caught up with me yet. But, I know it will soon. I figured we would see what we would see at dark: 30.

We have a plan!

Now, all it has to do is get dark.

Man… it stays light a longtime here. No smog to make it dark, 30 minutes earlier.

Well, just like Shelly said. At exactly dark: 30,

There they are.

One minute there was no one at all. 5 minutes later, it's full from one end to the other.

Tad and I, have rolled a bunch of "Red Bud Doobies" to pass out down there. We jammed our pockets full of them.

Shelly said: "That besides sitting over there beaten on their Congo drums. And, singing every fuckin' song from that damn "Woodstock®" thingy. They are all long hair and no bra types that threw a peace sign or sompin every time anyone would drive or walk by."

Real bunch of Animals…

I asked Shelly if they were cool.

She said: "That they sure nuff think they are. Running around naked all night, screaming and hollering, nobody can get even minutes sleep!"

It seemed that Shelly has called a few of her gal friends. Told um of the California long haired New Meat in town! She has us all right here in her room.

A bunch of the tenants in the building she called came over to her room. They picked us out like in the line up at the "Chicken Ranch." We were escorted across the street to the WALL. _By some class pussy for fucking sure!_

I thought this would be a Good thing. We noticed as we walked up. The crowd parted. Some left. And, others just grouped up.

We sat down in the middle of the WALL. Pulled out some reefer… And, bam!

It was like we pulled up in full riot uniforms. Climbed out of a "SWAT" mobile… And, was bustin heads… They just… _Ran away_…

Now as expected. Joe flipped the fuck out. Tad didn't much give a shit. He has plans to stick about 8 inches in old Shelly there you know. Clean out her Rou hole. So to speak!

Frank is off to Shelly's. To climb into about 6 feet of floor! I'm rolling in the middle of the Fucking Street like a crazy man at the institution parade. I thought the irony was just too damn funny! Had to be consoled to stop laughing my ass off… _"Out-O-Fuckin-Sight-Man!"_ This IS! The freaking place for ME! Thank You GOD!

I crawled out of the street, up into the U-ARK lobby and sat down on the over stuffed couch on the screened in porch.

This girl named "Muffin" came over. Stood in front of me with her pussy bone poked way out so the split in her crouch stood out…

She asked: "*Got 10 bucks for the cab?*
I said: "That all depends."
She said: "On what?"
I said: "If you will stay under my spell all the rest of this wonderful night!"
She asks: "If I would buy her breakfast?"
I answered with a "YES indeed"
"Anything you want… anything at all?"
"Yes my dear, anything at all."
"OK: here's ten bucks."
She said: "You know there ain't no cab."
I said: "I knew that."
"Why did you give me the ten bucks then?"
I said: "Why not?"
She said: "I like you"

She sat down beside me. She told me she needed to show me how local women rate against those… California Hippie Chicks…

What she did the rest of the night did the trick! "I taint kiddin either"
Pass the ice please!

Well, it is for sure this place has a certain… magic about it. I still am not sure how to take it all. Just before I drift off for a few hours… I look over at Muffin. She is lying on her side, with her head on my shoulder. Her two Huge breasts, one smothering the other, are creamy white. And, so full and firm!

I asked her why everyone treated us that way at the WALL.

She said: "That when we pulled out all that *Reefer* at the same time, it set off their alarms. Most everyone on this street is from some big city some where. And, thought for sure that you guys were the *Narc's* come to bust all the summer people.

So, she had said pretty much the same deal that the Laura Brewer girl told Tad and Joe that night in California.

"Nobody ever smokes that much dope at one time, Nobody!"

So, as far as they are all concerned at this time, the *narcs* have come to town.

Now… this concern's me. I hadn't been in town 48 hours yet. And, I'm already trying to figure a way to tell the others I was not leaving with them. The last thing I needed was the tag of *Narc* hung on me!

She told me of a place over on Leverett Street. and Maple. It's called "The Deep End" It's the "Lutheran Student Center."

A cat named "Gordon Hitt" and, his sister "Cecilia" have taken it over. And, turned into a "Hippie" hang out… A "Drug Intervention Center"… and, a meeting place for "thieves and crooks!"

They are supposed to talk ya down if you be a flippin out.

Oh - oh, here we go!

One of them "*Hippy Commune*" deals I'll bet.

She said: "That this Gordon Hitt guy, is the *Guru* of the area at this time. He run's the "Underground Hippie Social" scene around here. And, all the programs that he Of course administrates."

But, let me tell you this. <u>*Smoke*</u> is hard to come by here once the kids leave town. Because, so do the dealers. There's the skad of home grown or so around most the time. It will knock your dick in the dirt. Even if you don't have a dick!

But, you have to be a Family member. Or, a close friend to get in on any of that!

Moving to fast here… will just get you shoved farther out of the loop.

She said: "After all… this is the south!" "We have our own way of doing things. Moving to fast, is not one of them!

If this is the case, Then old' Joe is a goner!

He's a speed freak that doesn't need no speed. Know what I mean?

Things are looking up, Muffin's way of cutting through the Bullshit is Very honest, so is she!

I have met my first *REAL* friend here in this "Headless Horseman" town. She not only ring's my bell. She is the only voice of reason I have heard since California!

We got up about 10 am. I don't know why. There is absolutely no one around anywhere. Wouldn't be for hours I figured. Muffin told me she had to run to Bentonville, Arkansas. Where ever that is.

I owe her breakfast! She plans to get it.

We went to her fav café up on the square. "The Red Bird Café" We chowed down on steak, eggs and hot coffee. We talked more about the place.

She said that her name was not muffin.

I said: "<u>*No Shit!*</u>"

She said: "It's Carla." She had to make an appearance at home to help her mother move. She would be back in her mom's car to pick me up. Take me to the Deep End. Then the Concert…

I said: "Concert! What concert? A fucking Concert! Out Of Sight You All!"

I must have heard her wrong.

I said: "Did she say a concert?"

Here I'm. In what I thought was a Headless Horseman town, with one stoplight. I haven't been in town 48 hours yet. And, I am going to a concert tonight. Wow! I'm impressed.

But… what kinda concert could possibly be in a Men's Gym in this here Jewel of the south.

I awoke again about 3 pm as Tad and Shelly came blasting into the room. And, stepped all over Joe, Frank and me…

She said: "Get up! Get ready."

We going to a… believe it. Or, not!

A… *"Vanilla Fudge concert"*

About this time, Muffin (Carla) came in and had ten tickets she bought at the *Student Union* about 20 minutes ago. The damn things a sell out all ready! So, here's a ticket for everyone. Two extras for whom ever we find along the way. What a girl… Everyone so far has been over generous!

She said: "Let's just start walking, grab a *Hot Doggie* on the way.

I'm liking this Carla (muffin) more by the minute.

We all walked through the campus by "Old Main" And, down the walk of Graduates, to Garland street and over to where the men's gym is.

The place is packed inside and out. But, seems there is something wrong here. It's not happy stoned music lovers. It's a full scale riot!

Muffin took a stick from the trash can. Started smashing fuckers over the back of the head saying…

"Police… Police… Let us through!"

We got past the crowd. And, inside the door… There are people trashing the stage tearing down the wall between the stage and the dressing room. Where the Vanilla Fudge are hiding out for their lives! Till the cops get here.

As you and I know… that could be days!

But, these assholes didn't know that. And, they are shitting their pantaloons… Then rubbing it on their face to hide their identity! Ha!

Here's the rub! These are not the *"Vanilla Fudge."* Or, the **Chocolate Fudge** for that fact.

They are a couple a creeps the **Gordon Hitt** guy through together. And, pawned off as the Fudge… Thinking no one would notice.

But, there was a guy there wanting to say hi to "Carmen"

Said he was an old friend.

When they brought out the guy saying he was Carmen. The cat broke up! Said: "That none off these weird-os are anywhere close to Vanilla Fudge!

Now, as tribute bands are all the rage now. I believe to this day if that cat had not known Carmen, the show would have been a success. And, everybody would have been happy anyway.

Some how, Muffin had slipped away from me. So had the others… We had shared an apple wine with a guy an hour back. And, shit is starting to look real, real good. I found myself wondering around stone-faced and floating about a foot off the ground. I took this opportunity to do some investigating on my own.

Without the Joe influence! He always kept folks on edge you know. You keep an eye on a new guy that won't shut the fuck up, knows it all, but knows nothing local. He might as well be speaking Martian as far as they were concerned! No help what so ever. People always just laughed and walked away when he was spouting his line of shit! I wanted to see him go away so bad!

Needless to say, the concert was a bust. Which was too bad? Cause, some music would have really made the night more magic! But, that was all about to change.

The acid that was in the wine I had drunk earlier was a bit ruff. Had a lot of strychnine in it as a preservative! But, without that, there would be no colors. So, the back ache is expected.

As I am sitting here 38 years later, that same back hurts all by itself with no help. Or, a buzz to go along with it! Oh well, such is life.

Where was I, Oh yeah?

Seemed that about one third of the street people here now are really just kids that lived in town… When they got to dirty… Or, hungry! They could just go home for a day and clean up.

A third are summer students and dumb ass's that flunked and had to make up courses.

Others that are showing up everyday are from every walk of life. Every corner of the country… And, beyond! All were drawn here for some strange reason like those folks in "Encounters of a Third kind" only there weren't no UFO involved.

YET! Write that down in the back for future reference.

The town just seemed to be a crossroads for every one that just didn't make it all the way to the west. Or, east coast… Run a ways that didn't want to get real far away from their homes… just in case!

And I mean… "A bunch of Vietnam vets."

Nam vets are coming in by five to ten a day.

Ok, let me see if I can explain what kinda mind set is going down. And, running this southern house of the rising sun…

If you have never seen Easy Rider!

Put this book down. And, go rent it now.

Watch it till you get it!

Then you will know what I came to find to be true. This town is being shaped by that very movie. People so young… So many hurt… And, bleeding… That movie seemed to call them out to meet and groove together before they were too old to do it. This is where they chose to live the life that movie said we had coming!

The best part is: it was a best kept secret for many years. Took the man (Wal☿Mart & Tyson's chicken) a while to realize the potential of the area… And, then totally ruin it.

But, I am telling you like it was. And, will always be in my mind of minds! Hopefully, Now yours too! If you GET it! Some won't!

As I write this book. I can't wait till it's finished. So, I can read it myself. Truman Capote said that.

I watched a commercial that **Andy Warhol** did for Coke® one year in the Super Bowl. The screen on the TV Was black. And, there was a little white dot in the very middle of the screen. In those days… when you turn on… or, turn off your TV… There was that same dot. So, everyone thought their TV Was fucked up!

But, as the white dot grew bigger… It was the top of Andy's melon, with out the fright wig he wore. Written on the top of his head was only the word… COKE… That was it. For that he got 1,000.000.00... One Million Dollar's! OH…SNAP!

I started to walk around the campus looking everything over. It didn't matter where I looked. Or, stepped… The place is steeped in history that is after all. Our country… I found myself in front of "Old Main" Old Main was the entire school in the days after the Civil war.

(I.e. *Old Main was used as the background through out the TV mini series "Blue & the Gray." Most of the filming was done in. and, around Fayetteville. And, the Battlefields that surround the towns*).

I was just sitting there on a bench grooving. Thinking how pissed off Joe was. And, how he was ready to *hit the road…*

Frank had already left. We said good bye to him in the parking lot of the "*Deep End*" just before the concert. He had just two days to get to Indy. Get settled. And, report for work.

He never made it there. He was *killed* by a *drunk driver* just East of St. Louis. <u>We would have been killed too!</u>

His VW was smashed head on into the front of a pick up truck with a Great Northern snow blade on the front. The VW was so smashed: they could not even get him out. They just strained out what was dripping. Then sent it back to Fontana the next day…

I was very sorry to hear that. As he was one hell of a good guy, He has been missed every since.

So, that left old Joe at the mercy of Tad. As Tad is his meal ticket. And, courage! He didn't have a lot to say all of a sudden. <u>*What a fucking relief!*</u> I was real tired of his nasty mouth! I, myself needed No help from anyone.

I'm on God's good graces.

Tad is in no hurry to leave. He is in a hard case of lust with old Shelly. He had never seen a girl so absolutely beautiful. I have seen Tad with women that Heffner would be jealous over! No shit Sherlock! Gospel truth!

Shelly is a southern peach no doubt, there seemed to be something in her passed no one would talk about, that bothered me a bit. As, I'm Tad's soul bro, I worried about him. And, didn't want him to go on to Europe just to save that shit head Joe!

I was noticing that I did not have to walk around with the "1000 yard stare" here. I had it when I joined the Navy, Saved my life I am sure. But, I wasn't doing it as much for some reason. I'm feeling at home.

<u>I'm 600 miles from the nearest surf, not good!</u>

But, I figured that a road trip would come along somewhere in the future. So, I just went for it. And, enjoyed each and everyday as they came!

As I'm wondering around the front of "Old Main" Reading the Graduates walk wondering where all these people are now, I noticed it was about 12:30 am, The night is young.

Even though it is dark… I can see real good! Dig it! I'm looking at the sixth step of "Old Main." There were the very first names, of the very first class. As I stepped down the stairs to the walk way at the bottom, I noticed a block with out any names. I was scratching my melon thinking someone messed up. When I heard a voice behind me!

"The year was 1889."

As, I was looking down, I heard a voice from behind me say: "That's the year Nobody Graduated! Seems' they all came down with the fever. Died off one by one… That was that for that year."

This building was used by both… the North. And, the *South*! As a signal point for their field office… and hospitals! A lamp in both towers, to send repeated messages from "Pea Ridge battle field" to "Prairie Grove battle field"

As, the school is in the center and high ground, the lamp could be seen for miles in both directions! They set up repeater stations along the way too both Battlefields.

I'm listening to this cat talk with amazement. Eye's wide with No pupils to be had! Jaw agape in wonder. When I realized he was sitting there in hospital greens. I don't mean the ones the doctors wear.

I mean the ones the Inmates. Or, Vets in treatment wear.

He is an Escapee from the V. A. hospital up on hwy 71. He is tripping every bit as hard as I am. If not heavier! If that is possible!

He has no where to go. But the WALL to mess around! And, a cubbyhole or two in a place called the "Grayhouse" What the hell ever that is.

And, some kind of Office at a thing called "The Yellow Brick Road"

That is a new one on me. "Grayhouse." What's that all about? I pulled out a joint, sparked it up. We sat there and polished off that one. And two more! He said: "Hi there! My name is Lee, Lee Shroph."

I just met about the most important friend in this town I would ever know. I just didn't know it yet. Ψ

Chapter Seven ΔTX

"*A __GURU__ with a Big Stick, OR.* "*Down the hole we go!*"

I noticed that his right arm is kinda messed up. He favors it a bit. I figured that if he wanted me to know about it, he would tell me.

We stood up and looked straight on at "Old Main." From where we were standing, It look's so Majestic. Noble if you will!

I'm taken back. I can see Ghosts in every window looking back down at us! LSD! Oh… Yeah! Good Shit in that wine.

Lee told me that the tower on the left had a clock in it. But, it was struck by lightening in 1903, hasn't worked since.

The face is just there as an Icon for the school. In the tower on the right, is where four giant horns are that broadcast the bell system. Music on Sunday morning and Holidays… Seems, that anywhere you could look was a Ghost of some sort looking back at you. With *acid*! Or, without!

He said: "That he would take me up there and show them to me sometime. When it wasn't so damn dark."

By the time we had smoked another of those lumbo Doobs. We found ourselves back at that "WALL" thingy. I was interested to see how I was treated this time. Without that damn Joe fucker along for the ride! Or, that Shelly girl!

We walked right up to a most hip looking group. They parted like the sea at Galilee. Made room for *Lee*… And, his new friend, ME!

One guy looked over, gave me one of those "Hippie Brother hand shakes." He has hair about down to his waist. Hippie Chicks swirling around him like *pretty little firefies*.

This Dummy's name is… "*WINDY AUSTIN*"

He said: "Welcome Brother. New in town? Great to have you BRO!"

Lee said: "This is. Ah… I didn't catch your name."

Now remember, back in Redlands at the radio station. I wanted a ghost name. A *ghost name*, what is that all about?

A GHOST name!

Well… I sure got one! Still with me to this day!

This is how it happened.

I opened the Redlands phone book. Dropped my figure on, of all names!

Ψ *"Donald P. Morison" 133 Lido Street… Redlands, California.* Now, I lived at, 120 Lido Street. The closeness of the place, the fact that the name *Morison only had one R*, made me say Ok!

I could say: "Don Morison, *with one R*."

Everyone would just go… Ok!

So, Jim Morrison or, not… I went with it!

For some reason, I just blurted it out. "Don Morison. With, one R."

Lee said: "I was a *fellow seeker*. And, to treat me as if I were "HIM" when he was not around!

About this time, an old bread truck painted in every color under the rainbow came down. Then up Dickson Street, with two nasty looking Redheads hanging out with tits banging together creating a ground shaking effect! Out the side door, waving and screaming up a storm!

Everyone on the "WALL" came alive! Started jumping up… And, down.

Seems… That these two girls. And, a couple a guys! Went to Woodstock # two… And, found "<u>NOSTOCK</u>." Nothing but memories… It was a farce all along. Just a Joke in Bad taste! I knew as they drove up to us. The era of the Hippie's… <u>IS OVER</u>! The summer's of LUV. Just died before my very eyes! Right there on that God forsaken corner in the Middle of fucking No Where me Droogies! Like the Cross Roads… We had heard about Woodstock #2 at the radio station in Redlands before we left. Bummer! Umm. Bummer!

They had stopped behind an old pee green Rambler® blocking the right turn lane onto Arkansas Ave.

The 8 track tape of *Woodstock*® is blaring out old *Joe cocker* butchering "A little help from my friends" Shitty Job There Joey!

But, how good can ya sing on eight hits of the "Brown acid"

"Of course… We advise against it! To each his own I always say! So, be warned about that one ok."

That's what the guy said from the stage that day at *Woodstock.*®

(*Note: See The Album. Side One. The announcements from the stage…* "The BROWN ACID")

He is playing it on an old "*Gibson's Discount Mart*" $20… *4-track machine*… With pie pan speakers out on the roof!

I'm looking at the driver of the bread truck. When I remembered something I had up my sleeve. He looked like one of those kinda guys I was gonna have to bring down. There is just a look in his eye. I knew I would be able to see it when it raised its ugly head like an alien from outer space. He is a *carpetbagger* for sure.

But, I let it go for now. And, went on with the fun… These two girls in see through sun dresses are looking for a good meal, a cool bed, and a hard dick! The payment will be memorable!

As, they are only too Horney after that long drive with a wet crotch!

I thought: "Jesus Christ, What potty mouthed girls! How fucking crude! HA!"

When I felt a tongue licking the inside of my ear!

I turned slowly. I'm looking at this glowing face. Right between two shocking blue eyes, Strawberry blonde hair waist long, perfectly straight. Framing two round firm breasts with points all up on their own.

My jaw is on the ground. I think I was drooling. And, babbling something about "Thank you God!"

When she said in the softest, purest voice of an angel "Hi: my name is "Sunbeam LSD Somebody" what's yours my darling?"

She has been watching me. She thought I was flashing back. Or, something! And, needed jolting back too reality,

Hell of the deal is. I wasn't sure this was reality either! Could this Amazon Women be real? I squeezed her very large breast's and said: "OH YES SHE IS! Thank You God!"

I'm starting to get the old "LSD dirties", in need of a shower. And a bed! I'm sure that Tad and Joe have locked up the only beds at Shelly's. The sun is topping the "Hatfield Mansion" at the east end of Dickson Street.

I have not seen Tad. Or, Joe since the concert!

The "Sunbeam LSD Somebody" girl said to me: "Bet' ya didn't know that the Shelly girl is a narc… Did Ya!

I said: "A *NARC?* Narc!"

She said: "That is a fact."

She said: "Shelly's Dad wants to be the Sheriff, most likely someday will be. For now he is not only an auxiliary sheriff with bigger aspirations, he is supposed to go to policeman school in Springfield Mo. This fall!

(*Writers note: you might want to remember this egghead. As, he will surprise you later on!*)

Sunbeam LSD Somebody said: "Man… I got the place for you to crash as long as you like. It will get you out of that Shelly's place. And, away from all that innuendo!"

The place is chuck full of run away *pussy galore. A dope store* that opens up at sundown nightly… Music… And, crazy as hell mother fuckers everywhere! *Just The Fuck like you*. Then you can FUCK my brains out when ever you like Sweety!"

I said: "Sounds like my kinda place!" I'm wondering, just what is this girl getting at?

She said: "This place has the House of The Rising Sun beat all to hell brother, everything you need is there. And, waiting!"

As she walked through the night, the lights of Old Main shined through her sheer thin Sun Dress. I can see every nook and cranny that this floating Angel has been given by a loving god.

I could have been swimming in a tank of sharks. I would not have cared. It's like. Just air is dancing around her body. I'm either really tripping. Or, horny as hell!

Or, both most likely!

We are walking to the place she had in mind for a little hugging and rolling around. We got to Arkansas Avenue, walked on down to the WALL.

As, I look over. I see myself sitting there hollering something at… Me!

I look pretty upset about what ever it is too! I can not hear what I'm saying. It seems that there is an invisible block between myself… and, Me! Wow! I'm I getting weird? I need some fucking…sleep.

About that time, I felt the cold sting of a slap across my naked left ass cheek!

A voice said: "Put on your fucking pants. And, get the fuck up! We have company."

I looked around the room. It was again about the size of a walk in closet. Had a dresser slid up against the door to keep the Riff Raff out, a broken window with plastic over it painted in many a color. And another window, open all the way, with a beautiful, PINK naked girl standing in it, Pissing out to the parking lot below me!

As she backed out of the window… she looked at me with a yawn.

In a half asleep voice said: "Who! —The fuck are you?"

I said: "We are not sure at this time! You will have to give us a minute… or, two on that one."

Nice ASS… Big Tits…

But, *NOT* the girl I came in this building with!

At least not the one I was with last time I was conscience!

Now, DIG THIS! This is the first woman I ever have seen with a *shaved smooth pussy*! Look's *REAL* tasty. There is just a bit of a *sparkle* through the last little drop she didn't drip off! She has long brown hair. And, a pair of brown eye's to go with it.

A real Knock Out! Just a real Beauty! Very well packed!

As I was putting on my pantaloons… There came a clatter to shatter the seemingly calm of the moment. I had been noticing for awhile that somewhere in the building I was in, is a record skipping. It's that song "Iron man" by Ozzy and the boy's. It's stuck on the spot. "I am iron- I am iron- I am iron- over. And, over, And, over again…

This girl… who ever she is. Opened the door that led into a hall way of room doors… And, a stairway that went up to the House Mother's apt on the kinda third floor. Seemed we were in an old Frat House turned into a Hippie flophouse.

Chapter Eight

"Rick Basham... Or, The Anti-Christ"

There is a guy standing in front of this door by the stairs hollering: "Rick, *you sick son of a bitch*! Turn that record player off!"

No answer.

"Rick... I am gonna rip the tone arm off that son of a bitch. And, shove it up your ass!

Shit! He ain't listening!

By now... There were five or six people in the hall on the verge of riot! Someone is down in the parking lot hollering up at the room and throwing rocks yelling: "Dianna! Shove a shiva in the over ripe son of a bitch! Come on, Shut the fuck up!"

I stepped into the hallway to see what it was all about. And, where I was... When out of absolutely no where like in a puff smoke is that guy Lee Shroph! He is saying through the door in a calm and, mellow voice these words.

"Rick, if you do not open this door. I am going to report you to Captain Kangaroo."

No good! Nothing, still the same... Over, And, Over again...

It is a problem that Rick has every time he would crash out after a seven or eight day speed run.

It seems that a 100 count bottle of *"Speckled Bird Eggs"* had come to an end a day or two before.

I said: "That we should turn off the power to the floor. That would make um open the door. Or, at least shut off the turntable."

Ya can't do that! The guy took a double take on me. "The power box is in his room! That ain't no Turn table. Shit man... It's a little high school girls pink all in one record player he found in the trash. It has a bobby pin needle that he made himself. He is most likely standing in front of the mirror digging out Halooseacrabs."

I asked: "what in the hell are halooseacrabs?" (I.e. ha-loose-a-crabs) These are crabs a speed freak sees under the skin of his. Or, her face. or arms. They dig. And dig. To try and get them little suckers out of there! So, they can lie down and grab a bit of *Spatchka*.

But, every time they dig. They find a few more in there.

So, Rick takes his Hook Knife. And digs... And digs! Some freaks have been known to bleed to death before they come to there senses. Or, an EMT crew rescues them.

This is not Rick's first bout with them. His girlfriend Dianna… Has taken a Plasidil 100mg Red Monster… She is on *Venus* somewhere by now. She couldn't hear a *frog hopping through a Nitro Glycerin factory*. These *halooseacrabs* are actually the bone they see. White bone… Look's like it's moving.

Too heavy for me! What in the hell could be next? Halooseacrabs!

Then I noticed that the girl I had woken up with was nowhere in sight. I heard her voice from down in the parking lot. She is mumbling some shit under her breath. And, digging up a "No Parking" sign with her bare hands.

She pulled the sign from the ground. Concrete… And, all!

Climbed to the housemother's apartment, swung that sign out the window, Shinnied down it… And, kicked in the window…

She climbed in… A few silent seconds went by as we all looked at each other with a shrug. Then, like turning on a switch… It sounded like 15 alley cats. And, 20 dog pound mutts were going in circles… like in the old cartoons! She beat the wholly shit out of the Rick guy. Nearly snatched Dianna bald-headed with one <u>snatch</u>!

The door is now open. The pink all in one record player is broken in the parking lot below. And, the morning calm is restored.

I went back up stairs. Looked in the Rick guy's room… I noticed that his hair is orange. He is wearing a hat that looks a lot like that "<u>Black Sabbath</u>" album. Pulled down over his ears…

Dianna… Is still on the bed snoring away. She hadn't heard a thing!

Chapter Nine

"The GRAYHOUSE!"

What can I say about the "Grayhouse?"

Well… It used to be a Frat House for the *Kappa Sigma Fraternity*. But, a newer, And, bigger one had been built just up across the fence from this old one. This one is soon to be an uptown modern new parking lot.

But for now, it is a flop house for students. Street people… Dope dealers and hippies. Room's rent for 33.00 dollars a month. You share a bathroom. And, lounge on each floor. With a large kitchen on the first floor that everyone used.

There is an old resident manager's room. And, a lobby on the first floor… More rooms in the back, 45 or so I think. It has a front entrance that comes from the street by 13 steps. A backdoor that opens onto the alley… And, the "White Mans' Graveyard"…

The rooms are about the size of a walk-in closet. And, come with a bed. A dresser… Maybe a chair… And, if you are totally lucky! Light bulbs… And, a lamp!

A biker named Max. That lives next door run's the place for the Bank of Fayetteville. Collecting rents for the bank so they could at least make a buck or two off the place while it was still standing.

There are steps leading to the housemother's apartment that kinda made a third floor. There are two Cubby Holes cut out of the walls of that stairway that only those in the know knew about.

They are actually the attic: Lee had made them into real nice free crash pads for all the runaways he hid out in them. He would make the rounds of the two times the bus would stop. And, grab the best runaways before someone else did.

After awhile! The word got all up and down runaway hwy. The Grayhouse is where to go.

The action is constant… All day… And, all night!

It's just off of Dickson Street on University Ave. Just a block from the WALL… Complete with a playground right next door, the graveyard. Who could ask for more? Ψ

I'm tiring to figure out how to tell Tad & Joe, that I'm staying here.

Seems that Tad. Being a real friend… seeing in the pervious 2 days that I was so loose and content. That there is No way I'm going anywhere.

I only said I would go to Europe in the first place, because I knew Tad was scared to death! But, he is the kinda guy that can hold a good front for ever. And, he has a new girl now. That should mean something.

He knew I would blow off how I felt about this place. And, go along anyway. He knew I would be for ever wondering… What may have happened? Deep inside me, I would some how blame him, without even knowing it. That's a friend!

He would have been right! I never back down on my word. When pressed: I would have given in and went. But, I assure you! I would never have blamed him.

Joe's glad to sneak out of town without me. As, he had been plotting to ditch me anyway!

He would have done it in the middle of nowhere!

That would have been a million times worst. Of Course! I would have hunted him down. And, _killed him_! In the worst of way's!

But, Hell! That's just me. Ha!

So, I moved into my own room in the Grayhouse. Room 22 on the second floor in the back by the stairs… I didn't have anything but a sleeping bag. 15… 8 track tapes. (No player) ¼ pound of that Red Bud left. A bunch of money… And, I guess a new girl friend.

Yup! That's right.

For some reason, That Ann girl likes the way I "PAT" her back!

(Hint, hint. Nudge, nudge)

Chapter Ten

"Tad is off on walk about... I'm on my own."

The Shelly girl! Plus, all of her little gal friends… Just up. And, disafuck-ingpeared! No one has seen them in a day or two. It's a real, real longtime before anybody saw them again! They went with Tad and Joe.

She… Shelly that is. Left a letter for me... with the X hooker that run's the ice cream parlor across the street… (The Jet Set).

It read:

DON… IT'S BEEN NICE MEETING. AND, GETTING TO KNOW YOU… YOUR FRIEND TAD ASKED ME TO LEAVE YOU A NOTE TO SAY WHERE WE HAVE GONE. SO YOU WON'T WORRY. OR, WONDER. I HAVE DECIDED TO GO ALONG WITH HIM. I HAVE NEVER BEEN ANYWHERE. IT SEEMS LIKE A GOOD IDEA. WE WILL WRITE YOU FROM THE ROAD GEN-ERAL DELIVERY TOO FAYETTEVILLE ARK. Tad and Shelly…

And… That was that!

I didn't miss. Or, care what happened to that piece a dog shit Joe! But, I was worried from time to time about Tad. Turned out for good reason too!

Tad and I had gone a bunch of mile's together looking for America. Look's like I have found it! Tad is going to have to go to Europe to try and find a little peace!

The plan that was made never came to pass. After all, I still have never met the people that caused us to stop in this Headless Horseman town in the first place! It felt like the whole trip was just for me! I couldn't put my finger on it. These thing's take time!

I am ready to give this ALL the time I have. The rest of my life if need be!

OK… Here we go back to the Grayhouse. I had not paid any rent in this here Grayhouse. Because I had no idea to whom, that rent would be paid. I thought that would take care of it self.

Ann told me she had lived in there off and on over a year, never paid any rent to anyone. As a matter of fact, she wasn't sure who you would pay. She would just crash in an empty room one night. And, stay till she went somewhere a few days in a row. When she would come back, someone else had snatched the room she herself had been squatting in.

But, it wasn't long. The very next morning… Bam… Bam…

Open this fucking door! Or, I'll buster down! I ain't kiddin either!

That's a giant man named "MAX" He is the biker that lives next door. And, runs the place for the "Bank of Fayetteville." The Worm Mothas!

Take my word for it! By the time we get to the next page. They gonna be crawling out from under each page before you can turn it! That's how the sneaking worms do!

As I'm coming up the street from the Jet Set, I see that guy with orange hair.

What is his name? Oh yeah! Ricky tick. Just what the fuck kinda name is that? Well… He is standing on the porch of the Grayhouse. A black guy named "ONY RAY" is sitting on the couch next to the doorway. He is a skinny tall black man. With one of those pick deals in his hair. Big as hell pilot's glass', Biker boots, and an afro the size of Brooklyn!

Seemed he is the one and only Black man from the "*Holler*" that had took the chance to venture out of that stinking place. Since they were freed back in 1863… The "*HOLLER*" as it is, has been their home.

It's the streets behind the sheriff's office. And, jail. It is below that house of bars. So, the blacks have to always look up at where they may spend the rest of their life if they don't stay in their place.

Up until the summer of love… No black had the balls to leave. They had their own stores and all that. No need for them to ever leave. They even have their own grave yard. Right there at the end of Spring St.

Dig this… It's just outside the south end of the "OLD CONFEDER-ATE GRAVE YARD" from back "IN" the civil war. Not, after it.

See what I mean? I am *Back in Time* Everything I knew. And, had been taught… Is WRONG!

Up till then. Or, so it seemed.

This place just keeps my eye's open in wonder. It's like an E Ticket ride at Disney Land… Without the long line's to wait in.

"HISTORY!"

Something I never paid any attention too before now.

Here… It crawls out from every turn at you. Like turning a page!

OK, let's go back to the Grayhouse.

He had read me the riot act that morning. And, made it real clear that. He… Is in charge around here! So, unless I was hiding a split tail under my bell bottoms! Rent's due every Friday before 5 pm. Or, else!

I NEEDED TO PAY HIM SOME RENT BEFORE DARK.

I did. And, that was that.

Max turned out to be one of my closest friends for many years to come. As Ony Ray is to this day… (I have since heard of his death a few years ago. But, I have also heard from those closer. Of their meeting and greetings, just a month's ago!) So, who knows?

Anywho… Where are we? Oh yeah.

I went down to the pool hall the Ricky Tic guy runs at the front of the Bowling Alley. I went in.

There is Ony Ray. A couple other folk's playing 9 ball. A really strange looking guy with no leg's looking like Santa Claus. He is just, looking out into space somewhere around Saturn. Or, some fucking place. I watched him for awhile. I was not sure if he was even alive. Hell, he might have been a stuffed something Ur other. I didn't know.

When Ricky Tic (from now on called… Just Rick) tapped me on the shoulder.

"Man! You have to be careful how you look at ol' Uncle Bob there. He will give you that look. And, turn you into stone!"

Laughing I said: "What's up with the old dude?"

He said: "Bob was in WW2… Korea & Nam… Got his leg's blown off in Tet.

I was there for Tet. I can see how that happened.

Well: said Rick. He's been here ever since he learned how to hobble around on those stilts there.

I said: "Why doesn't he use a wheelchair?

Rick said: "If he can't walk around in some form or fashion, he would just as soon be dead. No wheelchair for him!

Seemed whenever some new Acid would come to town. Uncle Bob would have Rick try it first. To make sure there was not much speed in it. As his blood pressure is already out the top of his head, he didn't need anymore pushing! So, Rick would swallow a hit. And, tell Uncle Bob if there was any in there. Then Bob would take his. Worked well!

Seemed that Rick was always tripping… Not a bad deal if you ask me! Especially if you have scrambled shit for brains!

Now, I thought this was a hillbilly one-horse town, with absolutely NO action at all! Well, that's right too! But, like Shelly said back when.

"They only come out at night"

I'm starting to feel at home in this magic place. It didn't take me long to figure out most of the town. Or, should I say. The only part I so far cared about.

Let me throw this in. My first Sunday… I was sitting on the WALL about the time church was out. All the straight folks would drive by the WALL To watch the Hippies run naked in the streets. To show their children the freaks! To show them what "NOT" to grow up! And, be in their lives!

Little did they know! My wife of today told me that. Load of shit! Here is why.

Now let me straighten something out here. At the first beam of daylight. Every hippie… And, everyone else on the WALL would disappear to their little cubbyholes. Or, crash pad.

No one… _I mean NO one!_ Was on any WALL at 12 noon on Sunday! Take my word for it!

The people the folks would see on the WALL. Were the students themselves. Now… how weird is that?

Just to cause trouble, the Kappa Sigma boys did the ol streak with wigs on. The freaks took it to the country.

The country… that's a laugh!

No freaks were ever seen until dark thirty. But, after that… The show was great the rest of the night.

About dark & 2… Everyone is good and stoned. Needing a snack… There is a store not far away that is taylor made for a "walk around dinner." Or, take out order. As most everyone else, myself included very soon. Had little… Or, no money to speak of at all!

This store "DILLON'S" at Garland & North Street, kept most of us alive that first summer. And, a bunch more to come!

Well, this night. We had just gone there. Grabbed a bunch of watermelons from the front of the store… We were digging down on them right there on the WALL. Busting them against the street light pole… And, diving in…

Here come the cops. The "COPS"! That's a fuckin laugh!

Now this town only has two old _FORD FAIRLANES._ They make so much noise, you can hear them coming down the other end of Dickson Street.

By the time they got to us, those melons were history. But, the trash box that Ony Ray is sitting on. Is stuff full of rinds!

So, of course! They arrested Ony Ray. And, tried to haul him off to the little holding cell they had down to the square.

But, I jumped up! And, in the middle of the street, I started yelling. Jumping up, and, down sayin. "_THE WHOLE WORLD'S WATCHING_" We all started yelling all around those pigs… Chanting so loud, those cops packed up their squad cars and retreated back downtown!

We of course, are digging the fact that "We had just made a move." And, we are still alive. ☯

About that time, the assholes at "Kappa Sigma" frat house across the street. Who had been watching all this with a bit of Carnival excitement from their balconies! Decided to help the cops out, and, started shooting from their room with a .22 rifle. And, BB guns!

A real bunch of "NeederMeyers" for fucking sure!

Chapter Eleven

"Don't get MAD… Get, <u>EVEN!</u>"

That night… We felt so bullet proof. We held what most of us Nam vets on the scene at the time called. "*Jungle Liberty*" 20 of us Snuck into their frat house from the kitchen.

We had the time set on our watches. (*What Fuckin Watches? I had mine painted on my arm…set at 8 pm. Or, some shit like that!*") We had a battle plan. And, an exit plan! It's great!

We stood one guy in front off each room on each floor. At 12 minite we pounced. Base ball bats in hand. Socks full of soap. And, so on. We wanged, and, banged the dog shit outta those sucker's for fuckin sure me Droogies. For at least an hour!

What FUN!☺ Felt GOOD!

We did some serious damage too some other wise pretty faces!

As, the years of Nixon are upon us! Myself. And, Tad tried other places for a month or two, under the auspicious that we were running around sneaking into Huge concerts free as radio station DJs saying goodbye to all our friends.

From San Francisco, To Fresno, Back to LA, Then San Berdo! We saw Janis Joplin at the Height. Saw the Dead at Fillmore West. We thought we were lucky just to get out of town alive!

There were Ten Thousand freaks on every block we drove down.

All homeless!

A thousand miles away from home! Couldn't go home because of pride or, broken bridges! Or, worst! There we were well dressed up. In a fine car, eating a hamburger, and, driving down Asbury, With the Jams Whalen, and, the windows down! With starving girls, and dudes all around us! We felt like our ride was between Two Pieces of bread!

I only mention this again… Because this is what I & Tad are looking for! Him… a place to hide from Johnson's and Nixon's war…

Me… Somewhere I saw in so many dreams in the dark.

But, I didn't let that scare me off. I almost stayed in California. As I was not ready to do anything but join my friends in San Clemente. And, surf each and everyday the rest of my life!

Get Stoned! Play music, have babies. And, "Just keep livin."

But, the very first thing I do. Is hit the friggin road.

This town reminded me of the parts of San Francisco that I loved when I was there. The place feel's like what I imagined it should.

Remember I said that Also, remember what Tad said to me 25 minutes after we arrived. He said: "This place feels so right! Don't you feel it too?"

I only wish he had stayed. He is missing so very much. Maybe someday he will read this very book! I hope so. (Tad)

The list of folks in this Era alone may be long. But, the place is full of people from every walk of life, from every corner of the country. It's like a magnet for some screwed up reason. Everyone from everywhere that tried it elsewhere found the same reasons to stay in this pure place so far away from the scene. Or, the city's a lot of us left behind. Or, so the rest of the world thought!

I like to call it… "Our own little secret"!

But, this book will change all that. Good things always come out someday. Thank God!

I am glad to be the "Humble Narrator" of this Trilogy. There is WAY too much for just ONE book to carry. It's hard sometimes to write. A tear clouds the eye.

I wish I was still there. These were the best years of my life! But, they will never be again. Not just because of the time that has passed.

There was a feeling in the air then. Like what we were doing was… "The RIGHT thing"

No Matter how silly it looked to the rest of the world.

We were ON TO something!

Something that is so elusive! IT runs through your fingers like water. You only are allowed to feel the cool wetness in your palms as it falls away and dries. You have to cup your hands to keep it on you, before it fades. The answer may be in the micro sized sparkles that dry. And, also flake into the wind as you watch.

Maybe there is something in there to find.

Who can tell?

LSD kinda helped me look deeper at those from time to time.

Still NO answers though!

Now where was I?

Hang a left right here... head down the hill.

What's that? It's a road sign. It reads: The Road narrow's ahead"

BE READY! Slow for Curves.

Good advice for sure! I feel like a Storm is coming up behind me now. A chill just went up my Spine. Something is pulling me closer and closer to a new life I DID NOT expect. Or, understand.

I don't know. I'm kinda scared now. I couldn't put a finger on it. I'm kinda dizzy.

I just attributed it to the. Excitement, And, the Mystery of it all…Ψ
What is it Frank Zappa said to us that morning not long ago?

"Come on people, Put your shoes on, we taken a walk just down the street. Let's GO! We will soon be passing a very large group of "Plastic People." Pay them NO mind. "Suzy Cream Cheese… Oh baby now. What's got into you! Wa, Wa,Wa, Wa, Waa!" Or, some shit like that there. WOW!

Here is the rundown on "DICKSON STREET AREA" At the time. *We owned it.*

Has anyone noticed? I have not said "Far-Out" one time in this story. "What's up with that? I get .25/cents. Every time I say (MAN).

On the west end of Dickson Street, Is the campus. That is. And, will be referred to as the west end. As, at that time! It was.

There wasn't much passed there but the school. And, Markham hill. From there, just out into the abyss!

The East end of town, as far as we were concerned. Was the "Hatfield Mansion" just passed the "ONLY" working Stop light in town. The corner of hwy 71 & Dickson… Except for the square… There is not much more than that.

At the North end of hwy 71. Aka College Ave… Is the 71 Drive Inn. And, "VIC - MONS" fish & chip's drive inn. A very favorite place to eat for us… Fish and chips were only 1.39 cents. 6 big as hell round hunks of batter dipped cat fish. And, about 2 pounds of fry's. A big old co-cola, And, u were set till tomorrow.

Ony Ray's old lady… Ragenna ran the "BURGER CHEF" on the corner of Block & Dickson. Don't look for it now. It's been gone for a longtime. We could get a hamburger without meat, for .25/cents. Or, free if you were with Ony.

Now as you know. Ony Ray is a Black man. Escaped from the Holler! But, his ol lady is. Very, Very "WHITE"! A big assed, "No, No" in those days! Ony is a real *Revolutionary!* That ended up being his demise in later years. Or, so we thought!

There is only one pizza place in those days. It's called "THE TOP HAT" it's at the corner of Lafayette & College. The only place that delivered. They only delivered to the dorms. And, the frats! As no one else ever called um!

At the South end of town in two places were the other munches joints in town. At the bottom of "Archibald yell" is "HOOTS CHICKEN." On the South end of Arkansas Avenue, is the *"RAZORBACK BURGER."* Plus the very best burger in the known world to this very day, "BRENDA'S BIGGER BURGER"

I name all of these eating places not for their wonderful food, which of course they had. But, that was the boundaries of our world at the time. We sometimes snuck down to the 62 drive in if we felt like a fight. Or, out to Farmington for a run on the rednecks at "THE RINK." That's where a real talent lived named, Larry Stapleton. We will get to him down the line.

Most of the time, we ate at the campus Commons. As we looked just like everyone else! And, the printing press at the "Ozark Mountain times" Or, the Deep End. Made great copies of student meal cards, and book store cards...

Most everyone had read "STEAL THIS BOOK." As it was required reading at the Grayhouse. Dog eared from start to finish. Lesson's well learned! Only thing that cat did worth a Fiddler's Fuck! Beside's fuck everything up! What a Turd. (I.e. Abby Hoffman!) Sorry ABBY. I call um like I see's um!"

There's a place Out between Farmington and Fayetteville Called "THE AMVETS" (I.e. *the American Veterans of War*). Great Private Club! Bathed in Black light, with the same posters as at Tads house in Fontana... It's the only place a few of us could go and get a bit of respect. As, it is "VETS" only! All it took was a DD-214, a discharge. Or, your VA card to get ya in.

To everyone else in the town, we are just a bunch a long haired hippies that need a haircut. Worthless draft dodgers! Even though as I would find out in later months, the place is just crawling with NAM vets!

Most of them have bought cheap land out side the town. They are all busy living green. And, growing green... If you know what I mean! They are all settled in. It's around a year before they get bored. And, ventured back out on the streets of town, to barter their wares in trade for the Creature Comforts they have missed.

I was always glad to see them along Halloween time each year.

A bunch of Nam vets were in town. Running the "Vietnam Veteran's Against the War" and, the "Ozark Mt. Times Weekly News. Mostly all the vets in town are here on Uncle Sam. Or, had just found themselves here... On Dickson Street, There are just a few places that were kinda Hippie Theme stores. As, the school kids are all wanting the clothes and stuff they see us wearing around town. But... wouldn't admit it.

So, up started popping Hippie joints Such as "THE BRAVE NEW WORLD" ran by *Mac Macintosh*. It's a Hippie clothing store, with a few posters. The clothes are mostly Crushed velvet blue bell bottom pants. And, other wild Hippie clothing like ya see in the "Stupid Hollywood Hippie" movies" Or, on the music makers, like Jimi. And, Janis!

But, let's not get out a line. It would be easy to do that, so much happened each and everyday! Down from the "Brave New World" is Cedric's "THE DREAM MERCHANT" It is the Quintessential "HIP-PIE HEAD SHOP" for sure man! (25 cents)

Everything from a *Stony black light poster room*, down to lung chocking incense burning in every corner… A counter at least 100 feet long filled with everything from *"Merry Gins."* To Strawberry papers (*a Merry Gin? Yes, a merry gin*) the most underground comics I ever saw. (I.e. *Zippy the Pinhead, Big Assed, Furry Freak Brother's ECT.*)

Next to that is the liquor store. The next stop is "ROGERS RECRE-ATION POOL HALL" (*Roger's wreck*). Next to that is the flag stand. Then, "THE HOME OF DENNIS HOME FURNISHINGS" main store…

From there East is the straight community. We never went there. Just off of Dickson Street to the north is Watson Street. Along Watson Street is a bunch of very cheap house's and duplexes. Behind all of these stores is the WAREHOUSE, *Gordon Hitts first Hippie hang out.*

Completely decorated by Ann Dixon… And, her evil twin Joyce Ledbetter! They had watched *"Easy Rider"* A few time's too many. They are taken with the *"Sunburst"* on the commune main house door.

They painted one on the warehouse door, only Ten times bigger. That for sure made it an instant "*Target*" for the straight community that now is getting a bit scared about the new folks in town. And, all this "*Freedom*" — Dig It! Ψ

Remember this town doesn't even have a local city police dept, didn't need one till now. The only two are auxiliary sheriff deputies in old Fairlanes, with screaming brake shoes. They are never anywhere they needed to be.

The campus cops are a couple a guys that stamped your meal card at the Commons. But, that was all about to change! I Believe I have laid enough track to get us though a couple a happening's. Let's get started.

Chapter Twelve

"I cannot believe this place is so FUCKING Cool!"

"THE PLANETARIUM… <u>AND, The Pottery Shop"</u>

There are two places that we really had a blast in the first days. And, nights! The WALL would be ok. Till about eight. Or around nine o'clock! But, then we would be getting off on the acid. Or…whatever. And, looking for other entertainment… Didn't seem to matter what…

There really wasn't an "Us" yet. As, I'm hanging out with most everyone… When, a crew seemed to form it self right around me… I like it when that kind of stuff happens.

Back at the WALL, Tis time to plan the night's epic parties… And, other plans. Grab any dope you would feel like doing of an evening. Except for smoke in the summer… When the kids left in May, So did the dealers.

But, home grown is right around the corner. Only problem there was. You have to know someone, if you were to get any of that! Or, make a run to Tulsa!

That's where we meet a bunch a friends with there very own TV Show! We will get into that later down the road. It WILL! Blow your mind!

I guess the night was getting on when we were trying to come up with something else to do. The crew is starting to make itself known to me.

There are 2 guys. And, 3 girls that seemed to be right where I am all the time. They agree with most everything I say. I have not noticed how weird that was at the time! We shared the same dreams. And, ideas about thing's. We are becoming a little family of our own!

<u>*The Gavence Family Travelers*</u>" is born.

Out of the need for self protection I think. And, the fact that… Safety travels in numbers.

I'm noticing that everyone else is doing it too. Soon… named houses would become a reality. We are taking over an entire town, without even trying, it's very exciting!

It's like we are in a weird experiment that some force out there is running as a game or something! We are a bunch of people stuck on a square playing board, Real Twilight Zone stuff!

Like we are all supposed to be there for some cosmic reason... So what the hell... No turning back now. I'm on board for where ever this ride is going to take me. I had decided that a week or so ago. Then something wonderful happened!

Chapter Thirteen

"Good God! What a trip...
Bonnie Meyers. Is she real?"

I noticed the Sweet, Sweet Sound of a Gibson Guitar... And, a Girl singing. She is singing that Janis song *"Me & Bobby McGee"* a great song. I swear to God... I thought Janis herself was sitting there singing.

I looked over... sitting at the other end of the WALL. Is this Strawberry Blonde/Brown headed girl. That look's like Janis. She is sitting crossed leg in a pink see through sun dress. And, nothing more! Her wonderful round full breasts propped on top of that Gibson. I wished I was that guitar just then.

Bare footed, with **NO panties** on. I am looking at my *Second Shaved Woman!* Her slit dropped to a perfectly shaped ass pushing her long, creamy white legs to each side. Her long waist length hair is draped over her guitar and shoulders framing her face and body like a cloud. Her... oh so soft sweet voice is permeating the air all around me... Causing my heart to palpitate! I felt a pain deep in my chest! I could not *MOVE!*

As I watched her playing and singing, I am frozen in the scene. She has taken my breath away so hard. I thought my heart was about to explode! I got up... walked over. Sat down next to her...

I listened as she finished up the song. Then went into *"Ball & Chain"* My heart has wings all of a sudden. My Mind is HER! I can't Break Loose!

Nobody is paying any attention to her. They all are in their own little Trippy worlds!

A girl sitting crossed legged on the WALL singing and strumming the guitar is not anything unusual. Everyone else is hocking their wares.

After she had finished the song... She looked at me. God... I'm telling you me Droogies... *MY HEART SUNK!* I was frozen within her blue eyes. As they attacked me, she moved so slow... And, confidently!

She said: "What do ya think?"

I stumbled. And, bit my lips... Afraid... I said to my self. "This girl is talking to me!"

I said: "You are very... Very good!"

She said: "No, Fuck that shit! What do you think about "Full Tilt Boogie?"

I answered: "I never liked Big Brother. Bunch of asshole! punks! They held her back I always thought."

The *"Full Tilt Boogie Band"* is much better!

She looked at me and said: "Where in the HELL did you come from…? *Don?*"

Nobody… around here has any idea of what really counts.

She is looking through my eyes all the way down to my heart.

She said: "Don, *I would like to know you! My name is Bonnie! Bonnie Meyers*." Her eyes *Never* left mine. Her hands are so soft. Her smell is overpowering me. I feel our hearts come together at her hands as she caresses mine. I'm Shaking!

Well for some reason. I'm still using the name I coined at that radio station in Redlands California. "Don Morison" That's with ONE R.

By the time I decided to stay in Fayetteville. I was already STUCK with the name. "MORISON… from CALIFORNIA"

Did she call me *Don*? How did she know that?

Anyway, I said: "Do you mind if I play your guitar?"

She said: "…No! By all means"… She handed it to me, like it's a piece of her. She said: "Be my guest."

She sat back with her knees up. And, her arms folded across them. I almost couldn't sing with the view. She held my hand in hers for just a second. I almost could not go on. Her heat… And, heart beat transferred hard into me! God Damn Man! I think I am *spotting!*

I started playing "TEACH YOUR CHILDREN." Then I went into "4 DEAD IN OHIO"

I looked up about half way though. The WALL is so quiet. You could hear a pin drop. Everyone is sitting, listening to me. It felt so weird. I could feel the *STOKE* coming up my spine. I had never before in my life felt this way. I could not explain it. In all the years I've played since. In so many bands, and so many venues…

"*I've never felt that way again.*"

By the time I had finished. And, given Bonnie back HER guitar… She was holding it out with a look on her face.

"Did that come from this Guitar?" Slowly she would look up at me. And, then look into the guitar like a drill instructor looking down the barrel of an M14, and back again.

I was "In like Flint."

If I striped! And, rubbed shit on my face in the middle of Dickson St. I could do NO wrong now! That of course, didn't sit well with "Windy Austin and the boys" from "RODEO." *A Rivalry is born!*

OK, A rumble if you will!

They are "The Town Talent" at this time. They wanted it to stay that way! No room for anyone new. Especially if they had any kind of talent!

The night passed as People sang and played songs they never even knew they knew. It's amazing.

I just don't know... every turn is something SPECIAL!

Something had just happened to me. I know now the power "Charles Manson" held over his followers.

I'm from an exciting place that the few that are here have ever been too. But, they sure had heard all about the *Wonderful Place*... Where being young meant everything! And, people ran around naked all the time. With brown skin and bikinis, played music... And, hung out at the beach... Surfed all day... Then hung out on the *Strip* in Hollywood all night... Raced cars... And, told their parents to "Stick it where the Sun doesn't shine."

Some powerful stuff for sure! They wanted in on that.

I represented that lifestyle to them.

About that time... a cat pulled up in a Green Rambler... With Woodstock jamming out the windows.

He said: "It's cool off time! Let's hit the wreak hole, Come on, let's go."

This swimming hole is in a town named, **Westfork**. Just south of town, it's said... That a circus train had crashed there back in 1938. And, dug out this giant swimming hole in the creek bed that ran through there on its way to the Arkansas River...

It has a 30 foot drop from a boulder straight down to the middle of the swimming hole and then spreads out where the train engine and following cars had dug it out.

Great story! But, so sprinkled with horse shit, its silly!

Didn't matter though... next thing I knew. I'm sitting on the trunk lid of a convertible 1963 Bellaire, Blue with white trim. It wasn't far to the wreak hole, down a few Super fucked up roads. There must have been 30 of us in. and on, that car. Ten other cars in a line following us... If ya fell off. You were a dead motha! No freaking doubt!

The guy driving has hair just a bit too short... To eager to please! I swear! I have seen him somewhere before. But how could that be? I had only just arrived here myself.

So I just blew it off to the fact that he looked like 2000 other crazy straight motha fuckers wanting to get a bit of Hippie Nooky that I had seen all over town lately. So, I just got super high... And had one hell of a great time... And left it at that!

The evening is going great till a guy that looked right out Happieville, hoisted his bottle of Thunderbird wine a bit too high, fell backwards all the way down the front of that boulder. And, broke his leg... "OUT"

It's a hell of a climb back up the cliff to the road. We hauled him all the way up, loaded him up, and dropped him off at the emergency room

And, back to the WALL. It's about 3 am. I'm starving. Dinner time! Dinner time! Bone sticking out the skin kinda dinnertime?

Rick said: "Could that be BLOOD all over your jeans there DON?" Could be!

OUGA! BOOGA! HORNY!

Did anybody say anything about <u>HORNY</u>?

BONNIE said: "I'm hungry too, let's go to my house and eat."

I'm sitting with Ann. and Joyce.

BONNIE said: "All of you! Let's go. Now, up, up, up!"

We started walking south on University Ave, passed the Grayhouse. We cut through the Whiteman's grave yard. And, down the cut to Center Street around to Hill Street up an alley,

There, in the alley… Between "Duncan and Hill"… Is the "PEOPLES GARAGE" Run by "*RACE CAR JIMMY*" & MIKE MEYERS…<u>Bonnie's husband?</u>

The shop is run out of a 4-car garage that is hooked onto a Giant Wonderful 3-story Southern House, built in 1901. The rooms are so tall, they disappear in the dark. Wonderful chandeliers hung in every room.

This beautiful house is rented to Mike. And, Bonnie for the outrageous sum of 110.00 a month! Completely furnished.… And, all bills paid.

Mike and Jimmy have a gimmick. They would rebuild only Volkswagens. Of which there are about 300 on the campus at any one given time.

Their gimmick is, they would tear your entire engine apart. And, paint every part a different Day-glo color as they put it back together. They charged ya for the job most times in dope. Or, food from your farm! Or, commune, UGGG! Communes!

That word has been raising its ugly head a lot!

Well… we went inside. There we are in this Giant kitchen. With, a smell that took me back to Grandma's at Thanksgiving.

Bonnie pulled out bacon, eggs. And all the stuff needed to make a great country breakfast.

We ate and ate till we were about to pop. The Grayhouse was not like this. This place… And, these people seemed more real. The Grayhouse is a state of mind. A nut house… A night away already felt good.

About this time I'm felling so tired. I needed a bed and about 6 hours to catch up. Bonnie showed the twins "ANN & JOYCE" and me, to the attic. Where there is a Giant bed. I don't even remember falling into it. I was out for the count. Dreamland at last! Oh Yeah!

I woke up at 3 pm. Felt like a Street Car had run through my head. I looked at the clock'

I said. "Three O' Motha Fuckin Clock!" What in the hell?

Ann is lying across my chest naked. I had my finger's inside of her Woo Woo just wanderin around.

Joyce is across my leg's doin the same to me. With a three beam ceiling fan above us keeping the Beat. And, the heat in her hand is caressing my very hard cock.

Wow... What a trip!

I think it's REAL! Pinch!

"SHIT DON! Stop it!"

That clit is Hot To Trot! *Don't pinch. Suck!*

So, I sucked on that pink devil awhile. As I did, Joyce is rubbing my balls and pinching them. Tickling the inner side of my thighs... We rolled around awhile on top of each other till I heard Bonnie's voice from around the partition wall. I stood up. And, walked to the door... My woody got there before I did.

I noticed a bathroom there on the second floor. I looked inside. There is a big old bathtub on four big eagle claws, and in the middle is Bonnie. She motioned me over, told me to slide in.

From under the water came "SURPRISE!"

Ann... How did she get past me?

Around the corner is Joyce washing her hair. I looked behind me to see if there was two of everybody. Room for 4 in thar for sure!

Well, you know what my next move was. In I went.

Bonnie grabbed a hold of me like an anchor chain. The three of them are washing me. And, stroking me... And, pumping me till I just EXPLODED!

After a nice soak... and, a scrub! We all got into Bonnie's pink 68 Mustang Mach One®.

That's right! A "*PINK MUSTANG*" Ride... Sally Ride.

Seemed that Mike built it for her while he was stationed at "Camp Morgan" A motor pool base where they rebuilt tanks that had been damaged in Nam... Not many tanks ever made it to Nam that I recall!

So, they were not very busy.

Bonnie is a Godsend. As, she pretty much opened up the town to me! Showed me the Ins and Outs of the town. Good thing too! As, the times are only gonna get stranger as the days go by. But, let me assure you. I'm mesmerized. I could not have escaped the hold the place has on me for any reason. The people I'm meeting are not the Hippies!

The couple of songs I sang at the WALL the night before. Have opened the social pipeline to me of the artist/musician people of town...

There are the street people. There are the dopers & dealers. There is the music. And, theater people… That are more in-tune than the others. And would be the people that formed the structure of the town as it was at the time…

The place has a lot to get over. 200 years of Southern "*__Ku Klux Klan__*" mind set. Or, the other side of the coin, those that believed the Civil War is still going on!

The rest of the area is still just a bunch of water headed, inbred Hillbillies. No joke!

To them… we are just a bunch of Commie clowns. That needs a hair cut. With the peace sign on our clothes! This to them is the cymbal of the "AMERICAN CHICKEN" We are just bugs that need to be squashed. Most folks that pulled that Easy Rider shit on me found out just how chicken I was… I never heard of turning the cheek. I'm a Pissed off Nam vet when they pulled that shit!

They have a different point of view after me and the other 20 or so Nam vets I was hangin out with Showed um how chicken we were. I think that's when "*__GORILLA THEATER__*" started.

We will get into that tail soon I assure ya.

Everything ain't Hunky Dory in a place where it feels so right! You can't ever forget that there was a "Pecking" order before all this "FREEDOM" came to town. And, that was about to be made real obvious.

But, it's just a bump in the road. It really put it all in prospective. I was going to have to keep an eye on the other side of town too. Cause they made the rules that we all had to follow somewhat! Depended on how you looked at it! Dig it. I thought to myself as I sat with these women… "I fucked me TWO shaved women in the same tub!" Plus a very hairy mountain girl!

I wasn't even sure which one I was in at any one time. They just HAD their way with me! It's like a feeding frenzy. Heaven! All moaning… And, laughing as they just flat fucked me good! What a way to start the day!

But, it is Hippie sunrise. I'm in the ol pink mustang, looking at a total freak out, Headed for the Grayhouse!

We parked on the side that bordered the graveyard. And, standing there with a film crew… is the town Thespian. *Mr. Larry Stapleton!*

Chapter Fourteen

"Watch out for Fairies.
In the Bone Yard"

I say the town Thespian.

Because… The guy dress's liked a fairy. You know. A *Pink winged*, floating, hopping, friggin fairy!

Ann & Joyce ran over to him like he was the fucking Messiah or friggin something! I ain't kiddin either! Like… on their fucking knees, wailing some shit about "Who's your Daddy?" Who's your daddy? Kissing the guys feet. Hell, I thought he was some big assed movie star Ur sompin. Fer Christ sake!

He said in his best Dorothy Lamour: "*Darlings… Where have you been? I've been out of my wit's waiting here! You Silly Nillies!*"

Ann said: "Oh… you punkin faced wonderful fagot! I just truly love you the very most! Enough of that you asshole, what part do I play?"

OK… now I'm as lost as you are! I ain't got a flitin fart in hell of an idea of what in the hell is going on here! But, I'm about to fall the fuck over laughing!

You know that movie that *Patrick Swazye and Wesley Snipes* made. About being Drag Queens! That's about what I was thinking as they came out in the daylight in Spidersville.

I stopped laughing long enough to here fairy Larry say: "Who's the new man Ann?"

She said: "None of your fucking fag assed business! And, Stay Away!"

I was shocked! Because she really meant it!

Ok… Here's the skinny. Seems that ol Larry here… Is shooting a "Monster" movie in this very grave yard at 10 p.m. this night… Ann and Joyce are the stars. He plays **Fagula**! Figures don't it!

He has a whole crew. Complete with cameras, dollies, grips, soundman, smoke machine and lighting. Everything needed to make a great public access TV movie. Only… That's in the future a bit. He just has a lot of Money.

I liked this more and more by the minute. How in the hell could a place like this exist, and nobody know about it! Every turn I make is something new to see and discover. People in love with life… Smoking, Fucking, Sucking, Partying. And, just flat fucking doing what they pleased 24 hours a day! I knew there had to be a catch! There has to be!

Ok... Larry the fairy took his underage over to the Warehouse to get in character. They couldn't come in the Grayhouse. They had a beef with MAX. I didn't know what it was. I looked up to the House Mother's window: there is Rick, Ony Ray & Max. Rubbing their chins... Plotting... And, planning... Or, somethin!

I had to find out more about this.

Hold UP! Do what? Hold up! You ain't all that... And, a bag a chips! What in the hell is that all about?

But not now, we have other fish to fry. But, remember I said this. Maybe something else for the notes pages!

There are people that live in the town that were making their move before we arrived. Ony Ray outta the Holler... A real honest to god fag right there in plain daylight. I was told that just a few years before, that would be an instant necktie party.

Now, speaking of Ty-dye, who was speaking of Ty-dye? I am!!

Just before my friends and I left San Bernardino, I was spending a bit of time at a HEAD SHOP in Redlands that covered as a Bead Shop and record store. If I was going to stay in Redlands, I was going to be where the action is, that shop "THE HAPPY THINGS HEAD SHOP... AND, BEAD SCHOOL" was the in crowd.

I was working there of all things. Refilling 4 track tapes... That's right! "MAD MAN MUNTZ" two track, manual shift 4 track cartridge tapes that would later become 8 track tapes. Only difference was, The 4 track tape cartridge had to be shifted between the upper two tracks and the lower. On an 8 track, it did that by it self. But alas, it did it in the middle of a song.

Well, in those days you had to record the music on the tape while it was still on the reel to reel. And, then load it into the cartridge. What a fucking hassle! But, worth the time and effort because of the fringe benefits that came along with the job.

Like this big breasted "FLAMING" Red head Named Gloria. G. L. O. R. I. A. The Good Witch of the Inland Empire! She worked there. And, had a big ol' station wagon she liked to drive up to *Forest Home Water Falls* just up the mountain from Mentone, California.

Work spells... Then throw these wax balls full of gun powder over the waterfall and Watch um blow the fish out of the water half way down.

Then make "WITCH LUV." That was my very fav part for sure man. Well, to get to the point. What a wonderful little witch she is! She taught me how to Ty-dye®. As I'm pretty good at that Ty-dyin, I thought it would be a great way at make a buck.

I still have the *$1000.00 in traveler's checks.* I have been living off of God's good graces, doing real good so far. I was a street person by choice! I'm enjoying living from the street. After where I had been not long ago! It's SWEET! For sure man. Real Fuckin Sweet!

I couldn't help but think that I was in some kind of time warp. That somewhere out there on the hwy coming here, we slipped through some worm hole. Ended up here!

"Hey! Hey! Wake the fuck up man!"

"What? What?"

There is a guy poking me in the arm saying: "You Ok?"

"HEY HIPPIE… MOTHA FUCKER!"… You OK?

"What?"

"Oh… Ok! I guess so."

He said again: "Hey you dumb shit hippie cock sucker! You can't sit in the middle of the street. You Hippies gotta get a handle on yourselves." "GET THE FUCK OUT OF THE FUCKIN STREET!"

Out of nowhere here comes Ann and Joyce. Who are Of course Joined at the hip! They Grabbed me. Told this guy that I was OK, and to mind his own! "MOTHA FUCKING"! Business… You cock sucker!

As Ann lifted his wallet!

She said: "You` come on with me honey, we are going to take you back to the hospital now."

Joyce told the guy: "He has a very bad case of "Vagina Pectoris." "And, I would be OK as soon as I got my medication."

As we went into the Jet Set ice cream parlor,

She asked me: "What that was all about?"

She said: "One minute I was right there! The next minute I was gone."

I had been noticing that either I was in the Twilight Zone over this place. Or, the WAR experience is on me too! It's like I was not here sometimes. It's hard to tell the difference. Still is!

We are walking down Greg Street from Dickson to Lafayette Street where Ann knew a guy that lived in a house known only by the name. "The Greg street house." See what I mean! Guess I'm catching on real fast.

As we are walking, it is just a little passed dark: 30. We are in front of a house on the corner. That, I swear to god looked like a fancy castle in London or some shit. But, scaled down to be a 5 bedroom, 2 story house. Wrought iron fence with gates, a hedge between the street and the fence. If you have ever been there, you know where I am talking about. Right there in the hedge.

Ann turned to me and said: "Would it embarrass you if I told you I love you?"

I said: "Do you mean… get married, and have kid's kinda love. Or, just street Hippie love?" (I had heard that from that other girl too).

She said: "I didn't ask you for a question. I asked you if I said I love you…
Would it embarrass you! That's all. Nothing more!
I said: "Ok… I'll fall for it! YES! It would embarrass me!"
She said. "Never Fuckin Mind you Moron!" I was just wondering." "Wondering what?"
"Nothing… Something I have up my sleeve."
I said: "u ain't wearing no sleeve."
She said: "Yup! That's right!"
"Oh, well, it doesn't matter. We are here."
We walked up the steps to the front door. Understand that most every house within a 10 block radius around the campus is there to house students. So, most houses had a "ROOMING HOUSE" layout.
But by this time, The University of Arkansas has built dorms. And, Frat and Suzy houses around the streets of the campus. These old buildings are now just rooming houses for anybody to rent and live in. Most are still students. But, many are full of street people that could panhandle the rent each month, not so hard to do. But still… $33 is $33. Even then!
I felt like I had been here before. Déjà Vu.
I swear to God. It's like I knew what was going to be around every corner.
We walked into the Greg street house. I could hear the faint sound of a screaming electric guitar and feel a pounding bass. Now… this lit me right up.
As we walked up the stairs to where the music is coming from… Joyce jumped out from behind a dark doorway. In her life changing beauty! She said: "Man, they gots some real ok Speed pills! Ought to keep us up all the way through the movie shoot"…I had forgotten all about that! I don't know. I seem to be floating around in some kinda purple haze or, some kinda shit. I'm feeling real weird. Head floating, 3 feet above me on a string!
As we climbed the stairs after the exchange in the hall, Ann looked at me. In my ear she said: "I know you will dig this."
She blew a deep warm breath into my ear. It sent chills down my spine!
She said: "I'm not going to tell you nothing, you just keep your eyes wide open my love."
We stopped at where the music was sneaking under the door. Ann reached out, she opened it. It was like an Atom Bomb went off. I mean just like on the cover of a Maxell® tape carton. My hair is flying backwards. Standing in the middle of this 20x20 room is a guy that I swear to all mighty Christ Looked just like Uncle Jed on that Hillbilly show! With a white left handed Stratocaster over his shoulder, a two speaker stack of Marshall's® behind him turned to 11.

Next to him is a little short stubby red headed round man with a 4-foot beard, Banging' out the bottom on a White Fender Bassman, through three… COUNT UM! 1- 2 -3! Dual Showman bass amps on 11…

They are cranking out "HONKY TONK WOMAN" off of the new "Rolling Stones" album. I think they must have recorded that album after their short time with "GUY TERRIFFICO." They sure sounded Country Rock there for awhile.

These two guys didn't have a P. A. system there. But I tell ya, they sang over those guitars. In the corner is a set of Ludwig® drums. As I am a drummer from age 6, (Instrument of choice to this day.) I had to sit in.

They didn't even stop the music. They just looked at me, went right into "Heart Breaker" Good ol' Grand Funk Song.

Ann and Joyce are not to be found for awhile. I just banged the drums till they came back.

When I left with them… Those guys hadn't missed a beat. They were still playing as we walked back out the front of the house. Was I dreaming? This place is too good to be true. I thought: What Next?

Well, Anyway. The 4th of July, is coming up soon, I haven't had a 4th in years. The 4th of July is my absolute favorite day of the year! As I was raised in California, Fireworks● were few. And, far between! By the time I was 11. Cap guns and, sparklers were it.

At least up till then, we had every kind of ground works there was. From Waterfalls of fire that stretched across your clothesline. Clothesline! What the hell is that? Too Fountains that shot so high, for so long, you thought God was comin Ur something! The few years I was in Texas with my mom. I saw Bottle Rockets go against the law. (Circa: 1964)

I'm noticing Fireworks● stands everywhere. You might say… I was not paying attention when it hit me. Shit man. I'm trippin so freaking hard. I could see the color bars flowing out of my eyes.

Ann opened the manhole covers that were my eye lids.

She said: "Knock, knock, Open up! You in there? Testing 1- 2 -3!"

I said: "Ain't they open?"

I could see just fine! I had not been *dosed* in a longtime. Let's see, I think it was that night in "Kookamungkee". That ol Joe, playing tricks! The Son of a bitch! What a _DOG_!

We walked over to the Warehouse. Where fairy Larry is waiting to go over the shoot… I'm thinking… I should do ok in the thing. Because, I don't have any idea what the hell he is talking about. I'm so freaking stoned, I just followed them all over to the Grayhouse parking lot.

We went into the graveyard. And, did the thing… It was the old. Two _naked_ girls deal. Where, Ann. And, Joyce Are lying on a Tombstone slab,

Crying over a *dead* guy they just buried.

When out from the shadows comes... Oh no! It's Fagula!

Girls run.

Fagula follows.

We Chase Fagula...

Fagula catches girls. Bites their necks...

We catch up with ol Fagula.

And, shove a stake up his ass.

Oops... Almost gave away the ending.

"I mean. Through his heart!"

I *never* give away the ending.

As all the cameras shoot in layers. Layers?

In all my years in media production since then, I've never heard that term. Hell, it was 10 years before I even saw the movie! That was at ol' Larry's funeral. He had died of Cornholia. That's what he called it! Cornholia... That shoot took all of 30 minutes.

As we were stumbling out of the North gate of said graveyard. That guy with orange hair... Rick. Is at the planetarium waiting on us to arrive... He and Mike Boyd got that Pink Floyd record *Inter Stellar Over Drive* They are playing... "Destroy the fucking whole Universe."

Ann took my hand and away we went. Don't look for the Planetarium or pottery shop. They are long gone. Along with the road they were on.

Not one bit of proof that they ever existed. Or, that a road ever ran there. But, what fun while they were there! Many a fun hour spent makin and breakin pots. Crashing the Universe too!

There is an Open air mall just east of where the first two Barnhills were. Below the dorms half way down Garland from Maple. Kid's have no idea it ever existed.

As we walked up to the door of the Planetarium! Inside, I could hear "Inter Stellar overdrive" Pumping out of the sound system. Playing real loud...

We walked in, there is Rick Basham and Mike Boyd Taking turns blowing up the Universe with the star pointer. Every time Pink Floyd hit a high note. *Blam*... Lights out! End of time, Flash of Black light! Great stuff! Right out of "Rebel without a Cause.".. bet you thought I would say. Right out of "Star Trek®" didn't ya!

Rick and his ol lady Dianna are sitting on the top of the projector globe. They are chanting. "Stick it in your ass, because you have no class" over. And, over again... Mike is crawling around like a viper on the floor. Using every chair as a slither point, shooting with the star pointer...

Mike has no teeth on the bottom of his mouth. He would put them in upside down to scare all the girls and little children! Here's the run down on Mike B. He is in this story till the end. So, might as well hear about um. Mr. Mike Boyd. A 5 foot 5, skinny, Southern Rebel looking... Wild man! With crazy as hell blue eyes... And, long stringy blonde hair receding in front!

His mother lives on what at that time was the south end of town, in a big ol wooden house on a creek. Mike didn't have many friends till we all came to town. He was a fish out of water most of the time. He just stayed home. Where he built the Largest Comic Book Collection I have ever seen. I am sure he is very rich from them now.

But anyway, Mike jumped out from the underside of a chair and grabbed Rick by the foot. They both fell out of the booth onto the concrete. And, knocked themselves colder than frozen turkeys! So, we kicked them out the door, started the album over. And, went to town playing the game till they came too...

About 20 minutes later, That "Sunshine LSD Somebody" girl came running in totally naked.

She said: "She is being chased by a bunch a Razorback football players." They had got a hold of her. And, _ripped_ off her clothes, she slipped away. When we looked out there... It was Rick and Mike In stolen uniforms. The campus is a great playground for anything, Like _Disneyland_ for Weird-os.

Anyway, the next thing I knew we were waking up from the acid stupor on the roof of Old Main. Remember the guy with the strat? He is the janitor at Old Main a few nights a week and let us in. I don't remember a friggin thing. But, there we all were. Looking ragged with a Bad case of LSD dirties! All Naked! Smoking a J... That's right! _NAKED!_

Well, Seemed that Ann had done some kind of talking to MAX. We moved to the House Mother's apartment at the very top of the stairs with Lee's cubby holes on each side that day. Rick and Dianna's room at the bottom of our stairs...Now, I know what you are thinking. You have been here just a little while and already moved in wiffs a chic ya just met! Well, it wasn't like we were moved in together. We just now had the best room in the place. I mean with Ann and me. And, our little daughter Joyce! We needed more room. Yeah right!

Ann went to her home in Monett, Mo. the next day. And, came back with everything from furniture, to a killer stereo, a bunch a records, and guess what else? A "Harmony" Guitar!

Wasn't much, I played the hell out of it for a week or two.

I was sitting there listening to the guy downstairs talk to that dude with the convertible. You know... the dude with hair just a bit too short for the time! I grabbed my shirt, took off for the WALL. I wanted to see what this guy was up to. Didn't take long! Seemed he was up for another run to the *Wreak Hole*. And, is looking for a crowd to have some free acid and a swim…

We all were just about to jump in the car, when a guy we never met walked over and said: "Hold up, Let um go! I got something to tell ya about that guy there."

So, we sat down on the WALL and said: "We gonna hang here, See y'all later, have fun!"

After they disappeared down Dickson Street to hwy 71 south, this guy said: 'You don't want anything to do with that asshole, my sister is a meter maid in Springfield, Mo. She smokes. So, she's kinda cool."

She said: "She saw that guy at *Policeman school* in Springfield just last month" She was wondering what he was doing here!

This new cats Name is… *John Polamasano*, from Springfield, he too had come here to make the scene after Nam. He became an Instant member of the *Gavence Family Travelers* right off the bat!

Now, I know what you are thinking again. Hell… How do you know he ain't a cop too?

If you are a Nam vet… or, a vet of any war you know your Brothers in Arms the second you see them. They have the same *1000 yard stair* you do. This information turned out to be a gold mine in the next few months, but not for the guy in the convertible. He has been made. Now… everyone in town is watching him! Not the other way around. He didn't even know what was going on.

Things are coming together real nice I thought. We have an edge here in our favor!

That in it self… Brought the score too… <u>Cops 0 Freaks 2 </u> Not bad for a **Headless Horseman** town. I was thinking I made the right choice by staying here and not moving along with Tad and that other guy. What was his name? Oh… that's right. Shit Head. Ralph. Biff. Something like that. This could never have happened in California. *Never!* I'm intrigued for sure. You could not drag me away at this point. A free trip to Malibu would have been the only way, and that would have been a hard decision at this time. Just didn't enter the picture. Only a ROUND trip ticket would be accepted! Just one more day I guess. One more *Wonderful* day after another!

We went over to Bonnie's for breakfast and back to the Grayhouse to crash. "SWEET BABY JAMES" is warbling out on the stereo as I drifted off to la la land. Ya know, I totally forgot about the acid about 3 am. Bad acid… Or, was it like when ya take a *Vicadin*. If you hurt all over, you don't get a buzz, you just get out of <u>pain</u>.

Isn't that the same thing?

The day is hot when I rolled over and noticed I was alone. There is noise in the lobby: it's about 10:30 am. And, already 95 degrees! Just as wet. Outside the window there is a bunch of people talking about how the place was not legally rentable by Max. And, everyone was going to have to register with the rent man or else get the fuck out. One day... And, Out! Well, what can I say, It's *Hippieville* remember! How do you tell 3 floors of people to just move? <u>*YOU DON'T!*</u>*...You run for your life!*

So, we did what every good house full of *bum* squatters would do. We ran the guy down the road through the graveyard with sticks, rocks, firecrackers● and shit. He didn't come back for <u>2</u> months. But, that's another part of the story, we will hold up on that.

There is another girl that every swinging dick in the area is after. Her name is *Sarah-Beth O'Sullivan*. She drive's a gold Plymouth Duster. In the encyclopedia under *"Daisy Duke's"* there is a picture of Sara-Beth. As, she invented them years before anyone else!

She has *4 skateboards* in her trunk at all times.

Ann said: "Sarah Beth! Got Ur boards?"

She said: "Surf's up baby!" Let's go *Surfin!*

This got my attention right off. I looked at Ann.

She said: "Man, you gonna like the hell outta this. We are going to **"Finger Bowl Beach."**

She had in her trunk. Three skateboards with steel wheels. And, one her brother made out of shoe skates and a hunk of oak. I grabbed that one right off. I didn't know where "Finger Bowl Beach" is. But, what the hell, let's go!

On the North end of Razorback Stadium! There is a parking lot shaped like a finger bowl. It's where Razorback and Maple St meet.

Now... you will not believe this. But, Sarah Beth has 4 ski ropes hooked to the inside of her trunk. She would open it and drop them out. You grab a board and go *"Bust Your Chin Surfing with Me"*

So named... because most people forget to let go of the *friggin rope* when they do a <u>chinner</u>... <u>hold on sucker!</u>

Every steel wheel board is flying up in the air, more than on the street. Many a chin was <u>split wide open</u>. When the fools forgot to let go of the freakin rope... Funniest thing I ever saw on a skateboard. Wow! What fun...Ha, Ha, Ha, Ha! *<u>Hillbillies On A Fuckin Skateboard</u>* is funny enough!

They just kept hooking on! Couldn't give in! One right after another had to show how bad assed they were. I loved it. The more they hit the asphalt, the faster she went. She is relentless! So beautiful, your pride keeps you from given in. Every time a guy would go down, she would just laugh and laugh and laugh!☺ I saw a guy go down on the same split chin at least 5 times before they took him to the school infirmary.

That was when we called it a day.

The guy that went to the E-Room! Broke his jaw in three places... Wore a cast and wired teeth for the next 7 month's. What an Idiot!ಠ When he could finally talk... He saw Sara Beth on the street. He said hello to her. She FLIPPED him off! And told him to "SHUT THE FUCK UP!"... Asshole!

Well, the 4th of July Came. And, went! The big forth I was expecting was not so friggin big. The Fireworks show at the Country Club Went off an hour before dark. So that sucked! We went out and shot up the town with bottle rockets. And, had Shoot out war with them as we would pass each other on Dickson Street...

About the 3rd week of July, Ann decided that we needed a Van. I asked her why she was not in summer school. She had not gone to school since I had been there. That I had noticed.

She said: "Well, I thought id spend my school money on something I need more, A *Van!*"

Seemed that the money her family had was really hers. She did what ever she wanted. Anytime, she wanted.

Now, here is where the new guy feel wears off. And, real life starts. You ain't a new comer no more! Ya live here now. That kinda stole some of the *romance* I thought. But, I was just not watching for what was coming next. Wow.

We went down to this car lot on college. There... sitting on the lot. Is a "1969 Dodge" split window cargo van, BLUE. That had been ordered by a company that went out of business before it arrived?

It has 8 doors, a slant 6 engine you could crawl into to work on. And, the engine cover was the middle seat. I guess I wasn't really paying attention to what was going on. Because, I can spot a plot a mile away before it can drop on me! Ann was for sure up to something. But, Hell... now we had a van. *All paid for.*

Here was the price for this brand new special order van. *$1,550.00* right off the showroom floor. With 21 miles on the odometer!

She told me. "You just look right in it.

We drove back to the Grayhouse. We unloaded a bunch of stuff we bought at Penny's Department store on the square. We had about 100 packs of Rit-Dye®. In every color from fuchsia to lime green, rubber bands, string, wood clamps, Laundry soap, Cloth's pins. And a bunch of cloth's line.

We moved it onto the second floor of the Grayhouse. And, opened the "TIE-DYE FACTORY" We went back to Pennies and bought a bunch of T-shirts with a pocket on them for your smokes... and, went to work...

We had 4 guys & Chics in one room doing the first tie. Then a couple a girl's in the kitchen, boiling tubs of water for the dye. 6 showers on the first floor with a Naked girl in each one doing the rinsing for the next... Or, final color... Then... off to the laundry matt for a <u>free</u> dry. Nobody charged for dry then. And, a wash was just 10 cents.

We made 110 shirts the very first day.

Now, we had to sell um to buy more stuff. Remember I mentioned "THE BRAVE NEW WORLD" We walked in there with ten shirts. *Mac* bought them all at 10.00 a piece. Resold them to the kids at 19.95...

He ordered all we could make. We were off and running! Didn't last long though... Most everyone got tired of doing it after a week or two. I sold the whole deal to *Mac* for 500.00. And, that was that! I was smart enough to register the Company. See Coach... I was listening!

Driving around in our new van... We ran across a kid named Steve Burris. He was walking down the road like that guy in *Chainsaw Massacre*. We picked um up. And, a 30 year friendship was born. He took us over to his Mom's house at "Stone & Hill" Streets. Where he lived with his Hippie mother, two sisters', three cats... And, a bad assed dog...

We were surprised to see that Rick. And, Uncle Bob were there. We went in.

Rick said: "Welcome me Droogies! It's *witches* night to night. We be a having a Bewitchin party! Join in!"

Rick passed me a bottle of Thunderbird. I drank. And, passed it...

Rick said: "Thirsty are yee?"

I said: "Tastes good!"

Rick said: "There's 5 hits of 4 way blotter in there. Oughta kick you in the boo boo real soon, I figure you drank a hit Ur two!" or three.

I said: "So much for a good day's sleep."

We are getting in the party pattern. When, Uncle Bob changed the mood. The kid Steve is walking around whispering to a cat's skull he had boiled clean. His mother Lonnie has a dog skull with a candle in it. I thought... What's next? Where do we go from here?

Out on the front porch where *Uncle Bob* is standing, is about 6 feet above the stone walkway below? It is *steeper* at the other end. Rick. And, I. Walked out there just as Uncle Bob, in his deepest wisdom, hobbled off the end of the porch, knocked himself colder than the Road Runner after a 200 foot cliff fall to a flat rock like a splat!

Hell… We thought the fucker was dead. I thought Shit! We gonna have to explain this to the cops. Then I thought… _**What fucking cops!**_ There ain't no cops! We better pick um up!

So, we picked Bob up. And, took him back up on the porch and sat um in a corner, tied um in. Bob always did the unexpected when tripping. Most do! But not with a flair for dramatics like Bob!

The Porch light burned into the night. With, its lead framed colored glass globe that Lonnie made. _It became the only light after awhile._

As the sun rose, we listened to the first "Crosby, Stills & Nash" album till we were ready to crash.

Ann said: "Can we crash here?"

Steve's mom showed us up to an extra room. We did some heavy fucking. And, crashed out for awhile…

We still had the House Mother's apartment at the Grayhouse, but we stayed there at Stone & Hill House about a week In and out. The place is a lot of fun. We hadn't tired of it enough to go back to the Grayhouse just yet.

It's the end of July now and things are starting to become routine. We had got us a dog we named "_SPANKY_" After Spanky of our gang, because he had a target eye. He is a dog like "Chuck" in "Up the Creek." Smart as a whip… He doesn't think he is a dog. I'm the very first thing he saw when he opened up his eyes. We are together every minute for the next 5 years. If you were looking for me! It's. "Don and Spanky!"

Chapter Fifteen

"The First Gavence Tribal Rock & Art Fair"

Something new needed to happen soon! Everything is going like anywhere. I woke up at about 4:30 pm. On the side of the bed that looked out south of town.

Off in the distance is a big assed grain silo at the feed store. In my haze, as the downing sun gleamed upon it. It look's like a tower at *Woodstock®*. I looked back in the room and rubbed my eyes. On the stereo came the song by *"It's a Beautiful Day"* "GIRL WITH NO EYES."

Painted there on the powder blue wall is a "Girl with No Eye's" in the corner of the room. I looked back out the window. And, the way the light was hitting the silo, I could almost hear the music of "The Who" coming from that tower. And, low and behold.

I had the greatest idea of my life… up till then. And, it's gonna be a hoot ta boot.

"The First Gavence Tribal Rock & Art Fair"

Well… Seemed that Steve's mom had a thing for this guy named Tony Smith… Tony. And his brother, Terry Smith! Had been working for a Jingle Factory in Memphis… And, playing in a blue eyed soul band… Tony is back here to stay, this Terry guy will follow soon.

Now, I have this idea that we should put on a "Rock Concert" to end the summer of fun and love before school was to start in a few weeks. There were enough bands in town to play, everyone would for sure come! Everyone looked at each other and it was like a bell went off in my hazy head. "THE FIRST GAVENCE TRIBAL ROCK FESTIVAL" is born.

Ok, here is where things started getting kinda weird and stuff starts to go wild. This is just what I was waiting for. "Battle!" What fun this will be.

This is not just a concert I had in mind. I'm ready to slap out at my first *commune*. And, put the thing out of business.

Now, I needed more info. And, some troops that won't ask too many questions right off the bat! I was about to meet a whole bunch of people I would never forget. Seemed the minute I said anything about this plan. People came out of the Woodstock woodwork to be any part of it.

A guy that used to do liquid light shows at Fillmore west... Named "Magic Bill" has all his overhead projectors, Gallons of colored oil's and mineral waters of ever weight known to man! We have three bands ready to play with that guy "**Windy Austin. And, Rodeo**" **Headlining.** They are a bad Joe Cocker knock off, but the town band.

We put together a trio. Those guys jamin at Greg street house that night... And me! Called ourselves "*TIN WHISKERS*" For the little whiskers that grow on solid state mother boards!

Four other bands signed up too. All with the understanding... That we split 55% of the gate... That is for the bands. The concert... is *On*!

Went this way... The "Butt chunks"... The "AMF"... (What ever that meant) "Harbor Rat's"... Windy & the boyz... And, us so far, it is still pre "Morison & *Smith*" days. Don't Even Know *Terry Smith* yet.

I feel at this time, we are in need of a mind "MAP" of the old Dickson Street. If you were not there, you will get a kick out of this. Imagine that you are standing on the corner steps of the University of Arkansas southeast corner at Arkansas & Dickson Street. Right across the street from the front door of Kappa Sigma Frat House, And, catty corner from the U-ARK Theater and rooming house...

OK, now you are standing at 12 midnight in the middle of the blinking red light .that's right, right the fuck under the sucka. You see the only working red light in the entire city at the other end, blinking now. Because, it get's switched Off by a deputy at 6 pm by hand!

After midnight, the street has almost a Disneyland look to it. Not any more of course. But then it had a Magic that would grab your soul. And, like a fast acting chewed up valium. It is intoxicatingly wonderful. I swear, sometimes I felt like I had just stepped out of my own body and would just float to the other end. (I.e. that may have been LSD or shroom induced!) Sometimes it was a drug that brought on the scene. But, I tell you all it was pure Magic that first summer and fall. Every where were people that were sure that what we were doing would mean something. Not just the movement of minds everywhere at the time of stone high enlightenment. But the fact that we were sure we were right! "It is in the freaking air. And, you can't stop something that is in the air." Gorge M. Cohan said that.

Now, I had been to San Francisco and L.A. and, Indo china all in the years of the famed, "*SUMMER OF LOVE.*" I missed that sucker! But I for sure heard all about it from Over Seas Radio. And, a little known cat at the time... Adrian Cronauer.

Hold on here! I want to get something straight here Right freaking now "*I HEARD ADRIAN CRONAUER SAY: "GOOD MORNING VIET*

NAM!" One fucking time! I was there from his first day, to his last. I drove my ton and a half passed the American Armed Forces Radio building to the Navy Headquarters at least ten times a day fer Christ sake. Dig it! Where was I? Oh yeah.

Dickson Street. Just the name lends a feeling of the south. There is nothing more you could imagine here in this "Headless Horseman" Town. When the Dickson Street Train flies through at 3 am... Everything feel's like a small earth quake. From the Grayhouse up to the Cross...

Rick said: "There seems to be a cure for everything these day's. They are working on a cure for premature ejaculation... I hear it's cuming quickly": WHAT!...We all fell back!

"First Gavence Tribal Rock Festival" even sounds like a great show.

Let's see... You are looking east at 12 midnight as the road drops about 2000 feet. And, rise's again to another 2000 or so feet at the other end. Before it fades into Mt. Sequoia and out of sight passed the old Hatfield Mansion...That's the one!

After about 10 pm most night's in the summer. There is very little wind. The trees all touch all over town. If you were to fly into Fayetteville, You would notice, that the only thing you would see is the downtown square Courthouse and post Office. Parts of Dickson Street!

Highway 71 aka Collage Avenue... I have a post card I bought at the Pink Bunny Motel the first day I was in town. It has a picture looking from Archibald Yell to as far North as the flash camera could see. (ABOUT HALF A MILE) Both side's lined with stately Mansions, all trees touched, 2 lanes just a bit wider than *two Model T FORDS*, so they could pass.

It read at the bottom "Most Stately Avenue in the South."

Boy that sure didn't last long. Dickson Street faired a bit longer but not much. So here is a run down. Wow! Get ready for to have your mind blown. Or, at least know where we are talking about at anytime. Because there's none of these place's anymore. Wal❄Mart... And, Tyson have taken over. And, Destroyed the "Charm" that was... *FAYETTEVILLE*, ARKANSAS.

There's a mist that forms down Dickson Street about ten pm. The very few lights make the steeple on the church at the other end look magical. It's a scene that has to be experienced! As you look east, the first thing you see is the Christian Student Center, hooked on that is the WALL.

Next to that is Metcalf records and book's next is the Entrance to the. *U-Ark Bowling Alley*, on each side of the entrance to that building is the *Pool Hall that Rick Basham* runs. Across from that is a Student clothing store, up stairs is a *Hair saloon* and a meeting place for "The Northwest Arkansas Riding Club." And, a Ballroom room for hire.

Across the alley from the U-ark building is the "Jet Set ice cream parlor. Hooked on to that is the Palace Drugstore. That is the start of a small strip type mall, even though they didn't exist yet.

That parking lot to the corner of Dickson & Greg had a few shops. And, a Piggly Wiggly store. A few more stores were between Piggly & Palace Drug. Along with a laundry mat!

Across Greg Street is a place that is for sure the biggest joke I had seen till then in this town. Behind a little restaurant on the corner was this old yellow boarding house, in the basement of said house is the "_Yellow Brick Road_" it is an old basement apartment with one bedroom with a step up bathroom dug into the dirt, a ledge about four feet above the bed was about 3 feet thick and was lined with mattresses. There is a double bed against one wall in the corner and the door led into a rather large living room, then left into a dug out kitchen.

Nice little basement apartment for sure. But, it was a drug Intervention Center. Dig it man, a Place where ya go if you are freaking out on drugs. This place figures _heavy_ into this story for sure.

There are two jerk super longhaired Assholes running the place In the name of Jesus Christ our God and Master, Over scene by Lee. Most times they were higher than the suckers they were supposed to be helping! Sometime's our friend Lee Schroph runs the thing. That is the only time it is a REAL thing!

Well, you know what our next move was, as far as this place was concerned! But we will come back to that. Now back to the Dickson Street run down…

Next to the restaurant there on the corner was the Swinging Door, then the "Library lounge" and the "Brave new world." The Library lounge is a private club and open all night. _Dickey Pool_ named it that so when students ran to big a tab, they could write home for money to pay for a book they lost. Make the check payable to the "Library." Pretty smart! He would become the "God Pussy" of Dickson Street. In years to come!

The _Swinging Door_ is owned by a cat named Bob Bogart, its a little beer joint with a very small burger grill and a couple of 25 cent pool tables. It wasn't anything yet, but boy that would change real soon.

Then of course the Library Lounge, Next to that is a stairway up to some rooms that housed the Hookers and Drug dealers of the time. With front and back doors, it is an easy stop for both. No big deal… Just good sex… And, fair drugs.

Next to that is the Brave New World, then the liquor store. There is an alley that runs around and behind the block to the "Warehouse" A place where Hippie street people looking for a free meal, and street musicians hung out.

Across that alley still moving east is "Dennis Home Furnishing's Main store, all Redwood and birch building soaked in diesel and Cottonseed oil preservative. It seems to be a local hillbilly method of paint.

Still moving east is a Restaurant supply, then Future site of Fayetteville elementary. Then the Church and you are at College Avenue. That's the left side of the street. Now, back to the west end again looking east, to the Corner of Arkansas and Dickson again is The U-ARK Theater and rooming house, Next door to that a real Apartment complex fenced in. Then *Underwood Jewelers* and that gas station that burned down. Across the street is a bar with a band area out back named "Gorges Majestic Lounge"

Might wanna write that one down too!

Then there is the Train Tracks and The Train Station. Step across the tracks. And, there is the *Ice House* "Home of the ever famous "*EAR*"! Behind that ice house is The Campbell Soup Company, you heard right! Every TV dinner made of chicken, is made in that building from feathers to the final dinner. We will get into that "Fuck Story" later I assure you!

Across West Avenue is the Ozark Laundry Company. Then, the only place that was open 24/7/365 in all of Fayetteville, the Yellow Cab Stand! In front is the only Cigarette, Candy, Pop & Rubber machine's, We never knew the price of rubbers though, we never used um.

It was very busy all night: I don't recall many cabs going anywhere. And, there were only two cabs anyway. Next to that is a small little Frat bar named the "PUB" It is a place Hippies, or, longhairs generally didn't venture into unless ya wanted to spice up your evening, we did it often! But most turn the cheek Hippies avoided the place for sure. We (Nam Vets) loved it. They had toasted sandwiches that were just like on the base, only 25 cents.

A parking lot is next. It is where all the delivery trucks parked to load up at the Holsom Bakery for the next day's deliveries.

Next to that… and, all the way to the corner of East Street are little shops and office suites then a gas station named "Big Daddy's" at College Ave. Dickson Street alone embodied all of the same charm and coolness of every place I could imagine jammed into one. This street would astound most people. And, be a nightmare for any developer. Stretching out like tentacles on a giant squid is all the streets that were our Soho. The names and place's changed faster than any where I had ever seen.

A common saying in the town was this *I LEAVE TOWN FOR THREE DAYS. WHEN YOU COME BACK… EVERYTHING HAS CHANGED! Happened all the time!*

Now back to the concert "The 1st Gavence Tribal Rock festival and Art Fair" Three days of fun in the country, camping, swimming, food, art booths of ever kind, Killer bands & Light show's non stop for three solid days.

It's the Woodstock of the Midwest! The whole deal was just about ready to go. We have formed a small group of ready and willing Groupies to help in every way.

Uncle Bob picked us up, took us out to the commune on Hwy 16 west in his *Studebaker Hawk*. We sat down with the cats that ran the place and sold them Hook line and sinker on the idea. Oh what fun we is a gonna have!

There is one chicken house that was not up to par for the Tyson people, who had come to the aid of all the farmers and ranchers that were about to go broke. It is up by the road and built by the original owner of the property About 50 year's before. It had not been used for 30 years or so for a chicken house, but it was used as a shop and a garage for tractors and such. I looked at it and of course saw dressing rooms, a staging area for the bands, workers, food venders and such at the event.

The top had a bad roof, but under that roof is a sub floor made of 4x20 pieces of oak and strong as hell. To hold supplies. And, other stuff from the farm days 30 or so years ago

So, we actually helped the real farmer, who is being ripped off and abused by the cock suckers running the commune. Calling themselves "The Leaders of the Revolt" and living a Green life style. All the farmer wanted is what these assholes offered in the first place. A bunch of free slaves that want that country life and in return will help with the farm for Free!

When all these Assholes were doing is pulling one giant Con! The ones I just had to bring down! We were paying real close attention. To make sure only these so called leaders took the heat. And, No one else would even know what happened. They would just have fun!

Here's how it went, Te He He!

It's a thang of beauty… That took on a life of its very own! The story is still told around a pipe. Or, a campfire to this day! It's part of our heritage 40 years later. But, nobody till now knows why!

I'm the guy that came up with the idea. I still don't know what it was all about! It started out as one *Monster* that grew into a complete fiasco! But what FUN! OK! Let's get fucking started having the FUN! Here we go.

We turned the top of the chicken house into the stage. The flat top is 120 feet long and 60 feet wide and just flat as all get out. It has power boxes every 25 feet Just under the wood on the inside of the building, Both 110/220 volts. It has a giant load box to carry all the equipment that was once there, even an Arc Welder.

There are lumber piles and small junk piles everywhere, so pickins was good as hell. There are at least 30 one room migrant worker shacks all in a row at the far end of the site. You know, this was actually starting to be a ton a fun and hell… It might just work even though it's to be a savage burn on the three guys in charge of this commune.

It's looking like it would be fun anyway for those not evolved in this BURN. All I know is… I'm having a blast. We (Ann, Joyce & I) had started staying at the Stone & Hillhouse in an upstairs room where all this started. We all still had rooms at the Grayhouse, but we were heavy into this and having a blast. We needed to stay close to keep all this on track.

It's a week or so before we planned to have the concert. The first production meeting is tonight. With the people we had picked to do certain things and those with bands, arts booth ideas and questions.

There were folks that wanted to provide the Light Show, the sound, food and even dig the San-a-Cans. The only ones missing were the three guys that thought they were in charge. They are to busy telling all the people at the commune how great they are! And, how they prayed and prayed for this concert deal to come along and save them all. Plus, their way of life! How the "Powers that be" answered. By having Uncle Bob have a flat tire in front of the place a few months earlier. That is when they fixed his tire and invited him and his wife to share bread with them, see their wonderful Utopia. That's how Bob knew where we could do the best good. As they were just waiting to get it!

So, we all sat around that night and listened to what all the people had to say. Told them we would formulate a starting overview the next day, and go over all the notes and Ideas. Put them in some sort of order by the following night, around 8 pm. The meeting closed with some good acid and weed. We all hit the streets to get out the word.

The WALL is packed as always. As we walked up everyone was talking at once about the same thing. "The Concert" Word is already out and we hadn't said anything about it. It's about 11 pm, the night is still young, the acid is coming on and we are feelin the little horns coming up on top of our heads. We needed to get into some shit now to get our minds off the commune deal for awhile. What happened next is a classic to this day me Droogies! You just can't make this shit up, I dare ya to try!

Now, Ony Ray is sitting on Mr. Rock's Box watching all this crap going on, he was just biding his time, he has bit of a problem, but he wants to wait till the prize joker of them all showed up and got rambling on over the rest.

That suckers name is *Danny Rocks*, Swear to god! Hence the name of the trash box… "Mr. Rock's Box"… Danny told everyone… That spot is his and his alone! So Danny of course, wants his throne. Ony Ray is sittin on it and wouldn't budge.

Across the street at the U-Ark theater, the last show is about to end. Soon… the folks will be coming out into the street. Ony Ray told Danny that he was up on the roof of the U-ark. He was rolling a joint, rolled up the bag and dropped it down on the marquee three stories below. He could see it sitting there unopened, but he could not figure out how to get down there and grab it. He had tried a long stick. All kinda stuff. Too no avail… did he (Danny) have any ideas?

A small crowd had moved over to where Ony and Danny were talking about this. A bunch a folks had some pretty good ideas. None as good as Danny's though. Just ask Danny! The question finally came up "what do I get if I get it for ya?"

Ony Ray said: "I'll split it with ya."

Danny asked how much is there.

Ony Ray said: "Oh… I don't know. An ounce or two I guess."

Danny said: "Let's go!"

He… and about 30 people started up the U-Ark rooming house stairs and out to the roof over to the ledge above the marquee.

Rick. Mike. Ann & Joyce are looking at me.

Ann said: "You know what's going on here?"

I nodded… YES.

We just sat across the street and watched from the U-ark bowl balcony. I couldn't see the inside of the marquee, so I ran across the street and took a look down. For fucking sure, there it is. Sitting there on the Marquee surface just inside the light box area, still closed and looked sealed.

As there was very little pot in town at the time, No one! Especially Danny, was gonna let that stay there. So by the time I had crossed the street and back up to the balcony, the people started coming out of the movie. Danny is climbing down a rope. He slipped. And, went through the glass partition above the sign and on down the rest of the way…

Glass is flinging everywhere right on top of ten people or so. Covered everyone… Cut the shit outta Danny in many places. But, he grabbed the *Marijuana* on the way down. He is real proud of that.

He ran across the street like a dog that just stole the carcass. Bleeding all the way… Sat down, opened the bag, looked inside and started *screaming Ony Ray's name*!

In the bag is a Long… Black… Stinking Turd!

Everyone looked for Ony Ray. He is doing the "Teddy Jack Eddie Shuffle" all the way up Dickson Street. And, laughing like a loony bird!

We are rolling on the balcony. The cop is on the scene. What a trip! *The Merry Pranksters are alive and well. In Fayetteville, Arkansas*

Thank god! 😀

After that excitement settled down, we went back to the Stone & Hill-house to party frickin hardy the rest of the night. I had been laughing so long and hard at what happened, I hadn't noticed just how high I was. We are so fucking Stoned. We are farting multi colored smoke! Laughing so firkin hard, Our Sides hurt! We keep falling down every ten feet or so. You could hear us walking along as far as two blocks!

As we passed the Graveyard, I saw at least 7 Ghosts walking along with us partying down! That's back when one or two hits of good smoke had everyone on the floor laughing out of control, Remember those day's? When a kilo was $90.00, the Mexicans would just run the entire plant through a chipper. You got every part of the plant, even the dirt. Dig it, I took out a saw onetime and sawed a kilo in half. Inside the thing was a low top tennis shoe. A note inside the shoe read "FUCK YOU GRINGO" shoe was worn out.

We started to discuss if this thing we had started would stay a fun joke on a bunch of assholes trying to run peoples lives. Or, if we weren't creating a Monster that would come back and bite us in our collective asses. The thing is taking on a lot of people and ideas that we had not planned on. People actually thinking this was for real! We are getting a bit afraid we are in to deep. We planned to have the thing on the following Friday, Saturday. And, wrap it up Sunday.

See! It is really taking on a life of its own! I asked Mike: "how many people do you think will come to this thang?"

He said: "Well… there are only about 300 or so people in town student wise. And, about 100 freaks and street people… Not counting the people that live here."

I said: "How many of those would you expect to come to a Hippie Commie Rhythmic Ritual like this?"

Ann spoke up, she said: "I would imagine _none_!"

Joyce rang in, she said: "You know, If word gets out… a lot could go wrong, how are we gonna keep this thing just local?"

I couldn't see how anyone around here would care about what we had planned, except the local kids. And, us!

Now Remember, the commune is on Hwy 16 west, half way between Tonitown. And, Siloam Springs. That's a winding two lane moonshine road that has so many hairpin turns and cut backs, it takes 5 hours to go 30 miles as the crow flies. It's the last place we figured anyone from anywhere would try to get too. Let alone find the damn place. If not for Uncle Bob, I would have never even seen the place. As, it's on a curve where you have to look the other way, You never even look down that drop off! But it's the kinda place. That if you ran out of gas, you would hear the Generator before ya see the house, just like in Texas Chainsaw Massacre☠

There is nothing appealing about this rundown, Wore out farm in anyway. Only when it's dark does it have any charm what so ever! Fortunately, the wind is most time from the N.W. and blow's the stink of the 100s of dead chicken's the other way. So we felt like we were ok to proceed. Te He, He!

We planned to have Uncle Bob run us out there on a layout run. To place the markers for this and that… and get started… 5 days to go. We had a lot to do just to pull off this *Commune Killing Hootenanny*. Did I say that?

Now, time for a bit of Spatchka me Droogies. Soon comes the Dawn. Most times morning is 3 pm or so. 7:30 am Comes early. It's a 2 hour drive to the commune called "*The Family Called Us*" So: we had a bite to eat, did some heavy fuckin, and called it a night.

The next morning, we waited on Uncle Bob to take us out to the commune. He didn't show till later. Ann and I went down to the court house to get tags on that Dodge van she bought with her summer school money. I was still trying to figure out why she did that, and why she put it in my name.

I didn't mind that. Tony had asked me why? I couldn't answer him on that. It bothered me a bit, the fact that Tony asked bothered me even more. Cause Tony's mind works so fucking fast, there must be a reason why he would waste time on that.

Tony's the kinda guy that ya give a coat hanger to. And, tell him what ya need. He will invent, and, produce it right there before your very eyes. He is the greatest wonder I ever knew. Must have had an IQ of at least 250! He asked: "Why Ann would put that truck in your name? It might be a good idea if you find out just who that girl is. And, what she really wants!" I said: "Well… I know her dad and mom live in Monett, Mo. He owns a chicken hatchery. And, her mom runs a private Employment Agency in Springfield. She has a sister that lives in Joplin. But, that's about it!

He said: "What about that Joyce Ledbetter girl, where does she figure into this deal? And how come the both of them are everywhere all the time? And always willing to get into or involved in what ever at the drop of a hat? What's in it for them?"

"How is it a rich girl at the University of Arkansas from Monett, Missouri? Is best friends with a Nobody girl from Bentonville named Joyce Ledbetter. That has a Hillbilly family as the only thing going for her.

Lee says: "YEAH!" "That's right Morison… How can you be so tight with the two of them, they follow you around like you are some kind of *Guru* here from California to save us all."

"Shit man. You are starting to remind me of the guys out there at that commune that we are trying to sting! Just who the fuck are you? And, where are you really from?"

By this time, I was looking at Tony who was looking at Lee.

I said: "What in the fuck are you talking about? I could care less about any of this family shit. That crap is for kooks and Assholes that didn't have any home life at all. And, will grab onto anyone that can show them that lead figure." You know: "Someone who can pull everyone up by the boot straps every time shit looks hopeless!" A father figure if you will... The force that was not present in their early home years.

You know... They say that you have your personality by age 7. If that's true! WE are all Fucked! Because, my only want in life at 7 was cartoons at 6:30 every Saturday morning! Mighty Mouse... Bugs Bunny. Donald Duck. A Giant" bowl of Alpha-bits buds... And my favorite,

"*THE SOUPY SALES SHOW*."

Now that guy is funny, years ahead of his time. I loved ol "Black Tooth" the very most. Pie in the eye anyone? Don't open that door. *Smack!* Anyway, Said Tony: "We should keep an open mind. And, an open eye on those two big boobed, tight pussy, creamy white girls. There is something about them that is a bit shaky!"

Now... you can imagine what I am thinking. These guys' are talking about my girl friend and her evil twin! I don't know what they are up too if anything at all. I really don't care! The sex is REAL good. They are both Gal-Pals. They make my dick twice as hard when you watch the two of them walking up to YOU! They also will leave you wanting more as you watch them walk away. Good God, I'm spotting!

Give me that bottle a wine!
"It's got acid in it!"
"I don't care!"

As I'm about to drink it... The phone rang. It's Uncle Bob. He isn't going to be able to come by. We should go on by ourselves. So, we went out and got into the van.

We have since named it "*Smoke*" I don't know why. But at least they didn't name it "*Puddin*" or, some shitty name like that.

As we were driving, we were still trying to figure out what our next move should be. I'm driving through Tonitown. With the 4 track blaring. And, Joyce is flying around in the back. We hadn't had time to do anything to the Van yet. I was thinking about what Lee had said earlier about the family thing.

He said: "We are getting close with this Gavence Family thing."

I said: "There ya go again."

He said: "Is it so hard for you to see? Are you still so fucked up in Nixon's world that you can't even see what you yourself have created? Is it that transparent?"

LEE has never raised his voice over a monotone since I have known him. I felt I should listen. I shut up! I'm starting to realize that Lee mean's a whole lot more to me than any friend I have met since arriving.

There is something about the guy that make's you think everything is ok! When everyone else is losing their minds... He Is the VOICE of Reality! When something need's investigating. Look for LEE!

They don't give ya 13 "Purple Hearts"... If ya ain't someone pretty special. Or, the "Bronze Star"! Along with the "Congressional Medal of Honor"! He has those. And, many more! _Real True Blue Hero stuff_! (LEE)

I don't remember him every talking about them. But, I have seen them framed in his in his office at the Yellow Brick Road.

Now, Rick. And Mike, Along with Joyce are sitting there in the back of this striped Dodge van with nothing but a spare tire to hold onto for dear life. I looked back. And, they were all jaws agape.

Rick spoke up and told Lee: "Man... what in the hell are you tripping on?"

Mike said: "Rick! You asshole! It's as clear as your face. If we are going to have any respect in this town... we are building."

He is looking around pointing at everyone nodding his head for all of us to go... "RIGHT ON MOTHA _FUCKAS_!"

He went on: "Like it... or, not! We have to form ranks."

Mike looked at Lee... and, they both in harmony sang.

"All hail! "The Gavence Family Travelers" 1970"

Chapter Sixteen

_"We are what we hate...
How did that happen"_

We had become the very thing we had vowed to destroy. This was not what I had in mind! We drove on a mile or two. And, I turned around in a parking lot of a restaurant in Tonitown. Hi class Restaurant I'm told. "Mary My-strees" I have No idea how to spell that one. Sorry... Mary.

It seemed that they are famous for their Pasta Sauce, spaghetti and wine. People came from all over the world to try their spaghetti and sauce meal with the Tonitown wine that had also been grown and made there. They even had a Fair every year at the end of August. Population of Tonitown at that time was 201. It's a German town founded in 1700s Ur some kinda shit like that!. Its spot on hwy 16 was its claim to fame as it were. A stage stop in the olden days.

I said: "Really? I'll remember that."

The Plot Thickens"!

We drove back towards hwy 112. But, I didn't turn there. We went on east to a hunk a shit town named, Springdale. Where we turned right on Hwy 71. And, went back to Fayetteville to the local _"Gibson's Discount Store"_ Later, to become the 2nd Wal☃mart in the friggin world. We Are going to Monett, Mo. The next day. I want to check out the _8 track players_. And their 8 track tapes.

They are to get there first batch of both today. But, had not come in yet. So, we went on to the commune and would return later.

We grabbed a bite at "VicMons" on the way out of town. I still have those travelers checks. I'm ready to break another one. But, later I guess.

It's around three o'clock when we arrived at the commune. Everyone is gathering eggs, and feeding the chickens. The guys we left to dig san-a-cans are hard at work.

We got stopped at the main gate. A gate that lift's and drops' like at a German road stop had been built and manned since we left.

We cruised Down to the main house where the three guys lived with the farmer and his wife... We have a meeting with the "Powers that Be" they told us that everyone is very excited about the idea, that they had given their permission for the commune workers to take a few hours off each day from their work and help with the presentation.

On their time of course!

They had decided that the "Family Called Us" Would need 75% of the gate to allow this to go any farther. And, 50% of all concessions. And, the art fair booths.

There was _no_ gate planned… It is a free concert! We didn't bother to mention that of course. I looked at Lee and Tony. We both could see that someone had heard of the upcoming festival. And, now was couching them. This is working right into our plan!

Chapter Seventeen

"They have taken the bait! Concert is... <u>ON</u>!"

Now... if they wanted to take advantage of us poor little *Hippie boys*. They will have to wait till we have about wrapped it up to attempt to take complete control. And, that's what we wanted to happen next.

So, we went about our business of getting *FUCKING WASTED ON SOME OF THEIR WONDER BUD! Marking* out areas for this and that... And, working on the stage... Playing with the brush hog... Clearing the crowd area...

One of the bands has come out to see what kinda stage we had come up with.

The stage... *"CHICKEN COOP"* looked down on a natural bowl that dropped down about 50 feet to a grassy knoll. Real Woodstocky!

"WOW! Is that a gun in the bush over there? Red Team go! Red Team Go! (Oh... Ok... sorry!) Then it hit's some trees, to a creek at the bottom. Where a tractor road went out to the "Tyson®" chicken brooder coops.

The top of the site is the road itself. Where the traffic makes the hairpin turn... It is 22 miles west to Siloam Springs, and Oklahoma.

And 21 miles east to either Springdale or Fayetteville! Rogers-Bentonville... In the middle of the run to Springdale is Tonitown. Its 3 miles west of the hwy 112... And, another 5 to Springdale city limits... It's the only road in either direction! <u>Clog up</u> that road at any point! And, nobody's going no where!

We knew that these commune guys had made some big assed deal with somebody and it was gonna be them that would have to explain why there really was <u>NO</u> concert at all. Never was gonna be!

They must be Nuts! NVTS... Nuts!

Or, something! What concert? We don't know nothing about no concert! *Who's having a Concert?*

Then they would be left holding the bag. Trying to explain just why they took bribe money from mob guys to put on a concert that never happened! Looking good! Like domino's falling... One after another! No dope outlet here!

Only thing wrong is. That's the problem!

No matter how hard I think about this, I can't put my finger on what the reaction is going to be.

We for sure have it all covered... I hope! I think.

We returned to town, went by the WALL. Ann was not there, along with a bunch of others that are, most of the time. Seemed that the "Windy Austin" guy... Wants to play as the "Headline Band."

Ann told him that he would have to talk to me. Or, Rick!

But he said: "*Its headline!* Or, No bands at all!

I said as I walked in the door: "What do you mean... No bands at all?

Windy says: "If we don't play. No body will. It's just as simple as that!"

They didn't even know we had already decided they were to headline. And, on the other bands too...

But we played along. "What, other bands do you have in mind?"

He told us a bunch a shit about some bands that really sucked.

But, we said. "Ok" Tony's freaking out!

He say's: "Don... Excuse me but... *WHAT FUCKING CONCERT*?"

Not to worry... Got the Curry...

There is a Radio Station in town that has just started up. Called "K K E G"... They have two disc jockeys. *Ogre*... And, *Ears*...

They are the station owner's sons. I think? And, they live next door. They are the only ones who would work for free! Their dad got those call letters for the obvious reasons. The other Radio Stations in town are AM. Call letters of K H O G... & K F A Y... Get it? They played *Twang* Country.

We talked Ogre and Ears...into playing Rock & Roll one day at the WALL... The only time the radio station is on the air. Is when they were playing with it, so, the first play lists started in our room at Stone & Hill.

It is the most powerful. And, number one radio station in the four state area now. And, with very good reason too!

Well... Ogre...and, Ears... Decided they would do a remote from the concert. That's right... The concert! What concert?

This thing is starting to grow legs. If Teeth appear, we is Fucked!

Somewhere along the story, I'm going to have to make a long story short. Because, it's taking up time from other things that are happening!

...At the very same time!

We are starting to hear around town about a "*Midwest Woodstock*" planned for the last week in August. Near Fayetteville, Arkansas. On a "*Magnolia* Mansion" Grounds... off hwy 16 west.

50 bands... A film crew making a movie of the entire event...

Wavy Gravy is gonna host the affair.

James Taylor Is the first act.

Talk of Bob Dylan too! Could be... You see. *Dylan's* back up band. "The Band" lives in Springdale & Rogers.

We are hearing all this on the street. And, we started none of it.

How can this be happening?

Runaways at the Grayhouse from as Far away as New York & California… Here just for the event. And, more in route… Saying they had heard about it on the road hitch hiking… Everyone is coming!

I felt that old sinking feeling working its way down my spine…

When Lee said: "We have to get the fuck out of here… fast! They're going to hang us!"

I said: "They ain't gonna hang us!"

Everyone gave me the fish-eyes as I said: "They gonna hang those three bastards at the commune! Dig it! The Place went Nuts!"

This is getting better by the freaking minute. We couldn't have planned it this well. It was just falling in line. What fun.

Chapter Eighteen

"It's Mother Fucking...
<u>SHOW TIME!</u>"

Ok... The next day I'm walking down Dickson Street. I'm going to the burger chef to see Ony Ray about the guy he knew from San Francisco. He had talked about this guy before. Named, Lightshow Bill, A real guy! Not a figment of his imagination. He is ready to do his thing. I had not met him yet.

He said: "As a matter of fact, that guy over there is the very *Lightshow Bill.*" Shoving a Burger...a Coke... Fry's & Pie in his mouth at once! Afraid someone will steel it! "He ain't doin well since he left the Haight!"

He said: "My stuff is all out there. I'm ready too!

I said: "NO fucking shit! Man. I saw you do lights at Fillmore. At "Blue Cheer!"

He said: "Yeah Man! I remember ya!" I chocked on my burger bite!

We all broke up when he said that. I Said: Sure ya do!

I asked Ony: "Where did you find Bill there?"

He is working at "Hatfield Cattleshack" as an Engine Rebuilder.

I looked at his bare feet. They looked all chewed up. And, smashed out of belief!

Ony Ray says: "He does all his engine block work barefooted too!

I said: "No shit man! Is that goop on his toe there?" What toe?

Bonnie Meyers drove up in her pink Mustang. She has a big assed set of speakers in the back of her car.

She said: "My old man hooked them up to a power amp. And, the 8 track in my Mustang!" She has about 100 or so 8 tracks, and a battery charger in the trunk to hook the 8 track too. *She would be tickled PINK to provide the tunes for the building.* And, getting ready for the next few days!

If we want her to that is.

I took her hand in mine. And, kissed it softly... Then... in my arms, I dipped her back... Then, French kissed her hard!

<u>*I'm not sure. But, I felt her snap inside*</u>. She just melted in my arms. I looked her in the eyes as we broke from our kiss. She looked visibly moved. And, she had this... *Scared look in her very blue eyes!*

What a great girl. She drove out there. And, parked her mustang at the bottom of the stage... We ran wires up to the speaker stands that had no speakers of ours. And, as far as we were concerned, never would!

Put her speakers up. And, cranked up the battery charger... Then the 8 track... We proceeded to get the got damn place rockin! And, man if the fucking place didn't come a fucking live.

Before that... It's been all... Bang, bang, bang, saw, saw, and saw. Now... there is Rock and freaking Roll reverberating from every mountain side and we are just rocking the fuck out! I freaking tell you! It was... "Far out MAN!" Chills, Hair standin up! That's a lot a standin!

Something happened to us all right there. Right then, I can't explain it to this day 38 years later. I still get goose bumps when I think of that moment.

I have played live in front of 20.000 people. And, the feeling even then was not as strong. Or... as deeply felt...

At least 100 people in one place were touched at the same time. The song was "ARE YOU READY" by Grand Funk Railroad. That car stereo that mike put in Bonnie's car... Freaking wailed.

I've heard. And, owned a few "BOOM CARS" in my time... But, what ever Bonnie's old man did, I've never been able to match.

There were no Boom Cars then!

This damn joke is turning into a real thing. And, we couldn't stop it. Couldn't even slow it down! There is some cosmic power in control now. And, it didn't matter who intervened. Cops...or mob guys! Down hill motion cant be stopped!

We are right on that too. The damn thing is _snow-balling!_ Its Thursday night, we are in a bar with a TV. We saw before our very eyes, on the news from Joplin, Mo. This story! What a total freak out... we are floored.

GOOD EVENING. Topping the news tonight...

A WOODSTOCK-LIKE ROCK AND FOLK FESTIVAL IS PLANNED FOR THE WEEKEND OF AUGUST 21ST THRU 24TH. In N. W. ARKANSAS! GROUPS FROM THE LOCAL AREA... AND, AS FAR AS NEW YORK CITY WILL PERFORM BEFORE THRONGS OF YOUNG PEOPLE FOR ONE LAST FLING BEFORE SCHOOL STARTS NEXT WEEK.

State Police Captain... JIMMY NELSON, OF THE ARKANSAS STATE POLICE TROOP L. TELLS THIS REPORTER AT NEWS TIME THAT... 25 EXTRA POLICE OFFICERS... ALONG WITH LOCAL CONSTABLES AND SHERIFFS OFFICER'S... WILL BE ON THE SCENE TO SEE TO IT TRAFFIC CONTROL IS RESPECTED. AND, THE PEACE IS KEPT FOR ALL."

THE CHIEF SAID: "THEY WOULD NOT BE ON SITE. AS, IT IS BEING HELD ON PRIVATE PROPERTY OWNED BY "Hansen farms" AND UNDER LEASE. UNLESS THERE IS AN EMERGEN-

CY! WE WOULD NOT BE ABLE TO INTERVENE. THE EVENT PLANNERS… THREE GENTLEMEN IN CHARGE OF the PRO- DUCTION AT THE FARM SAY: "THEY JUST FELT THAT THE KIDS NEEDED A LITTLE FUN BEFORE THEY BUCKLE DOWN AT SCHOOL" MORE AS THE STORY UNFOLDS. I'm. Brent Brock- well, KJOP, Joplin TV 3

Now, those guys are not us. They are the <u>three guys running the commune</u>. They had taken full responsibility for the event. It was like we never had anything to do with it.

Now, we had a clear path to do what ever we wanted. Without taking the blame!

But, the story on the TV took us all by surprise. We had no idea that the word was out that big. A sheriff's deputy told Rick, As many as 100.000 people may be on their way, and should start showing up anytime now.

I had been noticing that the town was getting crowed, I just blew it off to the kids coming back for school. And, this is true Of course.

The dorms and rooming houses had been filling up all week. The rents were going up as of September 1st. They go up from Sept 1$^{st.}$ to may 1st. Till there dirt cheap again.

I was also noticing that the trees are changing colors. I have never seen anything like this before Ever in my life. I could actually feel the season starting to change… *Totally new experience!*

It was kind of a strange feeling. I could feel the "Bite of the Hawk" Never knew what that meant before. The summer had been a total gas. But, man it sure went fast! You know, I actually felt a sad wave go through my body with that thought. Is this the end of my "Summer of Love?" Will this be it? Is it all over but the crying?

It's the Day before the concert.

Most all of the work that was going to be done at the event, has been done.

Stage is ready, light show is all set up except for the screen. And, this light show is the type used at "Fillmore West,"

First used in the factory. By Andy Warhol… in, New York City!

And Used again in both Fillmore's.

You know… four. Or, five overhead projectors, and, some different weight colored oils. And, mineral waters… A big assed screen… Or, two… 100 police lights crossing the screens… And, you got one hell of a great light show.

All the booths are in place and manned. *Two giant vats of chicken and rice*… One full of burnt meat something, that Ann… And, Joyce made.

Two coke stands… That Coke a Cola brought out… And, the _Fucking Pig Farm_. Believe it. Or, not!

All in place and, ready to go at 10 am Gate time in the morning… We had a _big ass wrap party_ the night before. Cooked a pig… And, drank a keg of wine… And, a bag of LSD!

About midnight, I and others drove back to the Grayhouse for a bit, and then back to Stone & Hill about 3 am.

Rick had scored a 100 count bottle of bird eggs from a pharmacy friend of his in Winslow. We popped a couple a piece. Around 6 am we were climbing the fucking walls. Couldn't sit still… So, we made like a bunch babies! And, headed out for the farm…

On the way out there… We saw that our plan was going to work.

I am holding that piece of information for the end of the Gag. So, I don't blow it for you. Let's just say that we knew something that nobody else even had thought of. Not even the heat! Not Nobody!

We are grinning from ear to ear. Like when a dude buys a Christmas present for his girlfriend. He's so proud: he just can't hold it in.

We wanted to savor the Flavor! When the noose tightens and chokes the three dudes to death in their own greed! And, everyone from the farmer on down to the commune workers they are ripping off. Would see them out of their wolves clothing… And, see them for the _shivering cowards_ that they really are.

If they don't hang um high, I'll be surprised. We just had to make sure our exit strategy was sound. So we come out smelling like the proverbial rose. So, we went about doing very little till the gates opened. We had built our own hide out office in the van. We are taking up our posts all over the event to make sure everything went according to plan… and, didn't get out of hand.

On the first day, Around 2pm!

What we knew was about to clog up everything. The shit is about to hit the fan! Hit it very, very, hard.

Check out what happened next!

Ok. Here we go!

The stage is only playing tunes from Bonnie's car. The crowd is chanting to get started. Not, one band is on site. According to the phone, all are in route. So, we just kept playing the car stereo. And, serving food… Having a pretty goodtime…

Over at the farmer's house, are people that had motored in from Tulsa through Siloam Springs. They were not the kind of people I would expect to see at a Rock concert. More like the back room of a court house some-where. Or, some shady mob boss office. They are decked out in the _Docker_ type pants and arrow shirts. Pilot's sun glasses shined shoes. And, blue ball caps.

Parked behind the house is a stretch limo, for sure there's. I let all the air out of the tires on the side they were not able to see. Just for shits and giggles.

By this time, the highway is jammed with people walking from as far away as 10 miles west.

See… We never thought of parking. Wasn't supposed to be more than 100 or so people there at any one time… It was estimated at 5.000 or so were on the farm grounds right now.

And hundreds, If not thousand's… Were on the way still. The sides of the highway on both sides as far as the eye could see, were every kind of cop under the sun! Searching everyone coming and going… But, here's the rub!

Our event is planned on the very same weekend as!

You guessed it.
THE 55TH ANNUAL TONITOWN
WINE & SPAGHETTI FESTIVAL

And not one car! Or, truck. Would be able to get past in any direction for the next two days…

The trap is sprung! No bands could show up. No sound systems. No nothing! Just a light show… Good food. A loud car stereo… a pair of great speakers… great tapes. A few folks on acoustic guitars… HEAVEN!

And! "That's about it!"

A ton of pissed off cops. And, a bunch of business men. But for some reason, the thousand's of people that are there. Are having a great time. And, the farmer may actually make a few bucks!

Chapter Nineteen

"The Commune... THE FAMILY CALLED US is DEAD!" And, gone!

Most of the workers stayed on. And, went to work for the farmer...

Everyone lived happily after, except the three guys. They just were not around any more. (*Hell Me Droogies... That was too easy!"*)

We had a blast in the long run. And, we were the hero's after all. That Windy Austin guy got what he deserved... <u>NOTHING AT ALL!</u>

He is still mad over it to this very day! What a guy!

So, what's next? Oh yeah! *"The Ozark Mountain Times Strike"*

Now, that's a real hoot! The truth is always stranger than fiction! Hell, we even have a pot picking story a coming up... way up!

That's really surreal! The 1st trip to the surf... And, back...

All aboard! The Fayetteville express is about to leave from track #13. All Aboard!

Well. As you might imagine, There were mixed feelings about the outcome of the big concert that never happened. Windy Austin and the boys are all pissed off.

They said that the damn Tonitown Deal screwed up absolutely everything!

Windy said: "Hey... were going to play at the shell. Along with the other bands that couldn't make it to the concert"

I asked: "What in the hell is The Shell?"

The shell is a where they hold the graduation event. And for film orgies, and, concerts Too!

But, we will have to come back to that. It's a week or two away yet.

School is about to start. The town is coming alive. I found myself sitting on the WALL watching car after car after car Turn the corner at Arkansas and Dickson Streets.

Most times, I can count. One... Or, two cars every two or three minute's! It's that many. And, a whole shit load more now. I'm walking from the commons to Dickson Street. A guy in a multi-colored dyshieky carrying a giant walking stick saw me sitting there for a minute.

As he walked up to me, He stopped and looked at Spanky.

He said: "Are you tired, my brother?"

"I noticed that your gate changed as you climbed the hill. You are a meat eater, are you not?"

I said: "A burger and fries are ok with me. But, a good meal of all the right stuff is real good too, when it presents itself!"

The guy leaned in close to me. He said in my right ear: *"You are weak. And, worthless"* At this stage of your pitiful wasted life! Your aura is so gray, I am expecting rain!"

I'm getting a bit tired of this freak putting me down!

When he said: "Here my brother, take this walking staff to help you on your way. Use it as a crutch, a reminder if you will… Of our meeting! When you leave the red meat of defenseless animal's behind you. And, eat only from the fruits and vegetables of the field. You will soon be not in need of thy staff."

"When that day comes, pass the stick on, I leave you now my brother. May piece be with you all of your days! No-Mass-Day!

What the hell ever that means!

In all my days in Fayetteville, I never ever saw that man again! Nor, did anyone else, But the staff is a wonder to behold. The artwork on it is beautiful and seemed to never fade. I never became a Vegetarian.

I kept that stick. Till we were in Aspen Colorado. And, on a hike in Woody Creek! At *Hunters house…* I left it against a tree. Up where the *"Monument"* is now.

As I didn't even know who Hunter S. Thomson was then. I think the guy with the staff was my guarding angel. Showing up again… He did that a lot in those days. Sometime's I saw him, sometimes not.

I walked on the rest of the way to the *WALL.* Wondering if that really happened! But Of course, I was walking along with this far out staff of life in my hand. So, I guess it did.

I arrived at the WALL to find no one there, that wasn't unusual. As it is still daylight. You no how it goes. "They never come out till after dark." I went up to the Grayhouse. There sitting on the front porch is five or six folks passing the pipe around. Talking about the concert… or the lack of!

I walked up and said: "Howdy Y'all. What in the hell is going on around here…ANYWAY?"

Rick said: "Ann is upstairs looking for you." **Spanky** and I climbed the stairs to the apartment. There she was. Sitting with Dianna… They had just returned from Dianna's mom's business in Springdale. A place on Emma St. Named "*BYRD'S NEWS STAND*" It's the kind of News stand where you could get a Hamburger. And, a Newspaper!

Dianna and Ann had returned with a box of Hamburger patties, and a bag of buns, a couple of bags of fry's. It's starting to Look like it's gonna be a Hamburger dinner for all.

I wasn't sure if Mrs. Byrd was aware that Dianna was walking out the back door with all that stuff. But, I wasn't bitching!

The topic of conversation was:

The Grayhouse is getting a bit crowed. We should move somewhere else. I still have $900 in traveler's checks. Now, the House Mother's apartment was alright. But, getting kinda small!

The Gavence family is growing by leaps and bounds. We have created the same monster we wanted to destroy. But for some reason or another, it was all working out ok! There's a couple of new faces that have come along after the concert deal. A guy named Terry Fields. And his toady, Wayne Faulkner!

They showed up in a RED Torino and, a BROWN Ford Fairland. Somehow they had managed to make someone think they were our kinda folks. As we found out later, they were both Heroin addicts from Little Rock. They Were HOT in that place. So, they came here to get in on the action. And, hide in the crowd. They are a bad element on the rest of the new family. And, these country fuck's Had no idea how to look through people like these two IDIOTS!

But, I'm outnumbered, they became family members. The fact that they both had cars… And, dope. Impressed a few people… But, I didn't really care for either of them from day one. One of these guy's will become a close kinda family friend, and unfortunately stay's in the story to the very end.

The kind of guy… you hate so bad! You like 'um!

I'll be watching him for sure!

Chapter Twenty

"ROAD TRIP!
A Surfin' Run Is Needed"

I went in the room. Grabbed a burger... sat down.

I said: "*LOOK* at you freaking fools! Here we are, a family called the Travelers! Here we sit munching Hamburgers while Dianna is FREAK-ING out about having to go to her fucking sister's wedding!"

I'm for sure getting some... WHAT THE FUCK you talking about looks! I said those word's that set our generation off every time.

"ROAD TRIP"

Let's all load up. And, make like a bunch a babies, and, head out to Pen-sacola. We need to run Dianna down to her sisters wedding so she won't have to be away from old Ricky Tic there.

He looked at me with a Thanks bro look! Her Sister is marring a Navy pilot At the Navy base there.

As I was stationed there, I know a bunch of people. We can do some surfing. And, Dianna can see her sister get married. I can show you all around the place.

Ann said: "Joyce and I are up for it. Most everyone in the Grayhouse should maybe... Take a short out of town run anyway. But, before we go, we should drop a bunch of LSD." She crawled across the floor taking off her clothes as she crawled! We sat there watching this. Dicks getting hard... And, pussy's dripping. She crawled to me, grabbed a hold of my Willy and started rubbing dick. And, balls in a very wonderful way. Every-one is freaking out wanting to know what she is going to say, so they too can do the big nasty!

She squeezed my Willard so hard as she said: "How about you and I getting married. On the 4th step of Old Main! "We could have a big assed parade down Dickson Street at sunrise. From College Avenue to the steps of Old Main. And, then all go to Stone & Hill house for the reception."

I hit the freaking floor... Laughing my ass off!

I said: "Get married!...You....Me....Married?"

"I don't fucking think that *EVER* is gonna happen"

"Oh, come on Don, We all dress up in our best Hippie garb."

I said: "Don't call me a Hippie! You know better than that."

"Oh... Sweet baby, you know what I mean. What a way to end the sum-mer. Get married! With a Honeymoon in Florida!

Well. The acid is coming on REAL strong. It is real good stuff. Lots a colors… we are doing our thing at the WALL. And, on the campus, we were in groups of ten. Or 15!

When John Polamasano said: "It's time for everyone to meet at the other end of Dickson Street at Big Daddies."

With me and Ann, in the open back seat of someone's convertible. John on the front hood in full regalia… Top hat… Too spats! Plus, that most colorful walking staff!

There are at least 30 cars and vans in the precession. Everyone's car stereos are tuned to, "Clyde Clifford's" "Bleaker Street" from KAAY, Little Rock, as loud as they would go!

We all came up Dickson to the old service road that ran between Old Main. And, the Engineering Building, It ain't there no more… We parked the entire length of the road from Maple, to Dickson Street. In both directions! Around to the front of Old Main we went. We had at least 30 guitar players. Playing *"I had a dream last night."* Figures don't it!

And, that Country Joe song just for fun! They all ended up with "Goin' to the Country" by Canned Heat.

The Universal Life Church Minister… and lead guitar in the band AMF… As the preacher! His Reverent: Don Brown

What I didn't know was this. You did not need a Blood Test. Or, a license! For that fact, all you need is two witnesses' and, a trip to the County Clerk's Office the next day… and, SURPRISE!! We are "REALLY" married.

That's how she is going to explain the School money she blew! I now had wife # ONE. Short marriage though! As you will soon see! Less than 9 months. GOD DAMN! How in the Hell did I let this happen?

Talk about the weirdest "Surfin` Safari" I ever went on. I've been on a million or two at least. I was about to go surfing with a bunch a Hillbillies.

I know a guy in Pensacola (*John Vote & his DAD*) who lives at the beach. And, has an old 2 story fishing shack we could stay in, about twenty miles out the highway from Pensacola. Going towards Alabama…

The place didn't even have electricity or anything else for that fact. Just an old pot belly stove, so you could heat the place at night, Cook on it in the daytime.

There is no shiter in the place. Just a crapper on a DUNE just outside the backdoor… It's up about 6 feet above the ground. So, it won't back up. Has a small fence around it. When you are in there, you looked like a king! Or, Queen! On the throne! Everyone could just watch ya take a dumper. Or, a Tee Tee. Bonnie loved that! She would do passages from Shakespeare. And, Sonnets, I sure do *love that girl*. (Bonnie).

I have surfed this place many times. When I lived here in the Navy...

But, I didn't mention what kinda place it was to the others. As, I wanted it to be a surprise! Oh boy!...What a SURPRISE!

The upstairs is where ya slept I guess. As, there were no beds, the place came complete with a floor that didn't look to good. The slats that made up the floor didn't touch. So... as someone would walk around up thar, the sand would rain down on everyone below.

We made sure we all were on the same floor at any one time, if that was indeed a good idea now that I think of it! But Alas, I'm going to Surf. Fuck. Surf, Eat OUT. Fuck. Party... Fuck.

Ann said: "Don?"

"Yes dear"

"You said Fuck Three times!"

"Well: I like fuck the best!"

She said as she spread her legs: "*FUCK ME NOW!*"

I did!

I was looking forward to the response from everyone when we arrived, it would be worth a full roll of film for sure. I could already see the Grand Accommodations that most everyone was seeing in their third eye. Kind of like the cocaine episode in the freak brother's comic. Ann, Joyce and I had the van to sleep in. THANK GOD!

They expected!

You know. Nice beach house. With, all the creature comforts and plenty of them! But, the place was meant for fisherman that would bring everything they needed with them. Not, a bunch of Dope Smokin Weird-Os, looking for a good time.

As Dianna would be staying with her sister on the base, we were on our own till after the wedding. We are planning to stay about a week and return to Fayetteville. But, we almost didn't make it. So, we loaded up our Van. And, Terry Fields Brown Fairlane... And, off we went. Like a turd of hurtles! Off into the unknown...

Rick is driving the Fairlane. I'm driving the Van. Coming up the rear like a bat out of hell is a *Pink Mustang Mach One*®. It's Bonnie! My heart started to race. I had not noticed how much I already missed her...

My Heart skipped a beat! I'm so glad to see her screaming up behind me. She has been chasing us for about three hours. And, finally caught up... I had asked her if she wanted to go. But Mike needed to do a bit of work on her Mustang first. She drove at 122 miles an hour to catch up.

Said she: "Didn't even have the peddle to the floor."

Joyce and a few others that had been crammed into the van, Jumped in with her. Off we went. Up in the Fairlane are Rick and Dianna. Terry Fields and Wayne Faulkner… And our Cereal Killer, "*Steve Cooper!*"…

NO!!… We did not know he was a cereal Killer!

Steve had been all fucked up when a car ran over him. He was 8 years old. Half of his skull and brain were ground off by the back wheel of a car. As, he crossed Dickson Street, chasing his brothers, but, didn't look when he crossed! Really FUCKED him up! The car rolled 2 blocks, grinding off Steve's head. Before, it stopped in front of the Bakery.

We stopped for coffee about half way there. Even though we were speeding our brains out, I noticed a bit of a slap was needed before we hit the road again. I wanted everyone on the same page as we drove away from this *Twilight Zone* Diner in the middle of NO where.

So, I laid a sad story about my Grand Ma Houser on um. I had everyone's attention

When I said: "Not long ago, when I came back from country… I had to go see my grandma for sure! Or, get my ass kicked next time I see her. If I do that is. She is very old. Her… And, her little dog "*Pepè*" do almost nothing but Garden. All day long!"

We pulled up in her yard to see an ambulance leaving with her in it! We followed it to the hospital. Went in. and, waited on the Doctor's report!

I tell you what me Droogies. You could hear a pin drop in that diner. Everyone in the place is listening to me, even the kitchen staff. It's dead quiet!

I went on: "The doctor came out and said: ok, you can see her now."

As we walked in, I asked the Doctor what had happened. He told me they thought she had a Heart Attack. Just ask her.

Grandma is very glad to see me as you might expect.

I said: "No grandma, don't get excited."

She said: "Oh Son… don't worry about that asshole, he don't know SHIT!"

I asked her what the problem was.

She told me: "Well… I was gardening with my little dog *Pepe*. When I stood up too fast! Woe Daddy! I had *Real Bad* chest pain. I couldn't stand the fuck up son! The neighbor called the cops. And, then all of this!

Turned out….. I was standing on my Tits!"

The place is Dead quiet still. It is like they were waiting on more when… The whole place came alive at the same time! EVERYONE got it at the same fuckin` time. They were slapping everyone on the back. And, LAUGHING, LAUGHING, Laughing!

They wouldn't let our 3 tables pay.

I said: "That joke was worth dinner on them!" "That's the funniest joke I ever heard" They all said.

I said: "NO... It's TRUE!"

Dead quiet again! Then, Bust out laughing all over again! Truth made it even funnier. You could hear all three cars retelling and laughing all the next hour up and down the highway! I'm noticing how much I was enjoying this! I was in Kitty Cat Heaven!

Well... I'm just a bit worried about that deal where they had thrown me out of the state of Florida. Just a year earlier, I had just got out of the Navy. And, had bunch of money... I wanted to pick up my surfboards and the stuff I had left behind when they transferred me to Nam. I had left it all with a girl named. Now dig this one. Antoinette Josephine Galatiota. Now, that is one hell of a mouthful. I was a few days AWOL staying with her and her sister and mother.

I was on a 30 day leave there at the end of my shore duty. I stayed a few days to long. Well there you are! Freaking making it with Mom in the morning, Sister at noon, the rest of day and night with Toni!

It was hard (that's what she said) to remember what fucking day it was, or even the fact that I was on leave from the base. I looked out the living room window one Sunday. And, Wham! Bam! There is a shore patrol truck just sitting on the corner behind a tree trying to look cool. But, the glint from their by-nocks caught my eye. And, my attention!

I grabbed my bag, looked at my leave orders and noticed I was three days out. I escaped out the back door of the garage and down Navy Boulevard to the base. Hauled ass over to the OD headquarters... And, turned myself the fuck in! If they had picked me up, I would have been a deserter. As, I had nothing on that was of Navy issue. By turning myself in, it showed that it was just a mistake. As, it was! After all! I enlisted. Why would you go over the hill, if you enlisted?

Well... that is what the Captain at the Captain Mass thought too.

He said to me as he was about to give me my punishment. "Are you the son of Warrant Officer William M. Buford? One of the only survivors of the U.S.S. Arizona, and one of the finest Warrant Line Officers in the Navy, RET?"

I looked down at my UN-shined shoes and said: "Yes."

He asked: "Does your dad know that you are here for AWOL? Bet not! Well: if he were here, I know what he would do. Son... Or, no son!"

He looked over at the Quarter Master, Ordered him to escort my young ass over to the base barber. Have my head shaved "Hi and Dry" and, watch me pack my sea bag. Then escort me to NAS-VT4.

Put my ass on a C-130, bound for Travis Air Force Base. And, send my ass to the "USS Agra Holm DD-86" Off of the coast of Vietnam. For duration of the war! Or, two years... Which ever comes first! And, down the stairs we went. And, that my freaky friends... Was, THAT!

My head is spinning from how fast all this took. I was in the brig all of 3 minutes. And, on that plane by the end of the day shift... One stop in Houston... On to Travis!

There I meet up with 60 other Holding Company outlaws, Just like me. We were all in the same boat. Some even had just left the big house in Kittery Maine. It's life... Or, the Brown Water Navy.

The fucking what? What in the hell is the "Brown Water Navy"

Well, I for sure know what in the fuck it is now. Sadly!

We landed at Tan Son Nhat Airbase. Deplaned out the rear ramp... A bunch of nasty looking Marines met us.

They said: "You Cheese Dicks for the Agra holm?"

I said: "Yup, That be us!"

The sucker started laughing. And, said these words: "You assholes are in the Marines now! Seems your dumb-shit ship Captain done ran Ur ship up a sand reef. AND, ripped out the bottom... She is getting towed to San Francisco for repair. As we need an entire warehouser shop keeper crew, you are it. So, get ready for a crash course in how to do it."

I said: "Well...I am a *Shop Keeper*. See this here striker badge here. (I.e. strikers badge. That is the insignia that is in your stripes. It denotes your billet.)

He said: "Yes, what about it?"

Well... "Notice it has a quill trough a keyhole. And, those are First Class Stripes...You Is looking at... Cheese Dick Corporal!"

"First Class is the same as a staff Sergeant in the Marine's! So cut the shit. And, show us to our gift shop."

As he was talking, I looked at the others. They were all lined up behind me like I was a Mama Duck. And, they are the little ducks! They, As I. Were scared to Death! We made a great team. And, most all of us came home. We took care of.....

Hey Don!...Hey, Don.

I said: "What, what? Oh"

I rubbed my eyes.

Ann said: "Where the fuck ya been?"

"Oh, shit. Where are we?"

She said: "Just outside of Pensacola, You been driving about 10 hours now. Want me to drive awhile?"

I said, "No, I am ok."

She said: "No man, you were just driving asleep man! Pull over, I am taken over, I'll wake ya up as we come into town."

I thought a few minutes or so of Spachka would do me good. So, I climbed in back and hit it for a few.

Now, I am a *Surfer!* The second… The smell of the Gulf was in the air. I was up like a rocket.

"Hi! You look wide awake." (kiss)

I said: "Can't you smell it?"

She said: "What?"

I said: "The ocean!"

"Well… now that you mention it, I do smell something."

She had never been anywhere near the water, except for a lake or two. I told her that was the smell of Surf. Warm water… Toe's in the sand, with a drink in her hand.

Pull over… I am going to drive. And, catch up with Rick. And, Bonnie! Before they get too close to town… Cause John Votes house is 20 miles before Pensacola. Here… on the Alabama side. I wanted to let John and his dad know we were here. Going straight out to the beach house before we took Dianna to her sisters…

I had already called him the night before from that truck stop out there. All was ready. Down to a few old surfboards he had lying around the beach house. We should just go ahead and use them and get moved in. He would see us when he got there. I was getting more excited by the mile. I had been 5 months out of the water… I couldn't wait!

We pulled into John's driveway. No one is home. We drove on down the trail to the beach house.

I said: "Start unloading, I'll be right back."

I grabbed a ten foot *Hobie* three stringer leaning against the front screen. Out I went! 3 foot, Clean… And, fun. Wow, did that feel good! Breaking left just the fucking way I like it. It was like I never left. One great ride after another.

After about 2000 or so great rides… I looked up at the beach. Everyone is just watching me. They had never seen nothing like that befuckinfore in their freaking lives. All they could say was "Look at Um Go!" I grabbed a few 1000 more good glassy nose rides. And, headed in…

They surrounded me. It's like I had just won the "Maui North Shore Open" or, freaking something. How the hell do you do that? Or, I could never do that! Or, how can you just go out there after so long and make it look so freaking easy? Shit like: I wanna be next, Show me, I gotta do it! That was Bonnie… She took to it like she had done it all her life. What a wonderful girl she is. Joyce liked to float around and catch sun. Ann did some mean body surfin!

Everyone else really enjoyed it too. We are having an absolute blast.

No one is thinking of Dianna's sister's wedding. Or, Fayetteville either. We are in heaven. John and his dad 'Willy' took all of us gigging. And, fishing in their john boat… Nobody even went into Pensacola but twice. Once to drop off Dianna and get supplies. And, again to pick her up!

It was real hard to get me to start the trip back to Fayetteville. Especially, as we had a stop to make in of all places, California! I had promised to go to California one of the nights we were in FT. Walton Beach visiting a life-long friend **Bill Duhon**. Along with him and his new wife Kathy!

We go back to a few life threatening situations on stinky creek. Some-where along the Parrots beak, And Snoopy's nose… in a stony answer... to a question! I said: "California."

Shit… I need to go there and get one of those Crosby, Stills and Nash guitars with a freaking bird on it!

Bill said: "What the fuck you gonna do with that sucka. You don't even know how to play one of those critters!"

I said: "How fucking hard can it be?"

He said: "You are one hell of a dynamite drummer, you will destroy a piece a wood like a Guitar!"

I said in a drunken slur: how dare you imply I can't hold my Booze?" I'll show ya! Hey John: "Give me that Geetar over there." I proceeded to play "House of the rising sun" "Cowgirl in the sand" And, a few others I was pretty good at. He was impressed.

I said: "How ya think I met all these great looking legs ya see running around here? With a bag a dope, Nope! The ol guitar did the trick!"

Chapter Twenty One

"Bonnie has a vision...
I felt it too"

One day not long ago. I was thinkin. I am gonna start me up a band Ur some shit like that. Hell... I can do it. If I just find a partner, cause I hate being up there alone.

Imagine. Rock Star, Me For Christ sake! Well it's worth a shot.

Now... all I have to do is figure out how. Got any ideas?

John said: "Better get a gimmick Ur something like that."

Bonnie is looking at me talking like she is seeing through me into the freaking future! She got up with this stony look on her face, her hands over her mouth.

She said: "Shit Don! I can see it as clear as day!"

I said: "See what?"

Nothing, Nothing...

She grabbed me. And, kissed me REAL hard! YES! I can see it all. Well, This Fayetteville is a long way from Rock and Roll town! But, who knows what's gonna happen next.

Ann was watching Bonnie kiss me there, she was not amused!

Ann. And, her twin Joyce said: "Hell: let's all pile in the van. And, just fucking go!"

I want to meet your mom and dad anyway.

We got three weeks to go, what the hell.

I said: "What about money?"

Ann pulled out $3000.00

She said: "Will this get us there and home again?

I was up. Away we went.

Dianna. And, the rest went back to Fayetteville. They made the turn at Hwy 59. At, the Texas border...

Bonnie turned off 50 mile's earlier. Before she drove off into the morning, she took me behind some trucks. To say goodbye for now...

She said: "*Don, You don't love that damn Ann girl!*"

Before I could answer, she is chewing my bottom lip, saying she felt funny watching me drive off with the Bobbsy twins!

She said: "Please come home Don! — Please... (Kiss). Come home! *PLEASE... COME HOME!*"

She is crying now. HOME! What did she mean? HOME… WOW. Home!

She said: "*I have seen the future Don, You are IT!*"

She is licking my face. And, sucking on my lips…

She say's: "*I have some plans I have to get started. Please Don, Come Back To Us! Don't stay there and forget us! We love you so very much, Please don't forget us! I pray you too come home to us, I will be waiting!*"

Now, does she mean them? Or, HER!

She just burned rubber north with tears in her eyes. I felt like something had just been pulled out of me! I am VERY confused, to say the least! You know, it's a long way from Pensacola, Florida. To Redlands, California! With a stop at my mother's house in Bacliff, TX I hadn't seen her in 5 years.

It was Corpus Christi where I enlisted.

In Orange, TX is where the rest turned north up Hwy 59. To go back to Fayetteville! We cruised down to Bacliff to see my mom… But, she was in Rockport. In south Texas, She didn't know we were coming.

So, I grabbed the two boards I had there in the shed. We hit the beach in Galveston. Saw some old friends. Grabbed a new dope supply… We spent the night. And… off we went on our way to California the next morning.

As we passed through Austin, We stopped off to see our old friend Paul Rosenberg at the University of Texas.

I noticed how much I liked Austin. I remarked that I would like to spend a bit more time here someday. If I was ever back this way. Little did I know just how soon? And, how deep into Austin life, I would become before very long.

We were starting to see those Whiting Brothers gas stations now. I was starting to feel kinda at home for some reason. Might be because… all my life, I have made that run From Texas, to California. Winters with my Dad in California… And, summers with my mom in Texas and all… Along Santa Fe, New Mexico, We picked up this guy named "Wildman" and his one armed old lady, "Roberta."

We stopped for them merely because the Wildman guy was carrying a guitar case. All we had in that van was the 8 track deck we bought at Gibson's Discount back in Fayetteville. The Double album of George Harrison's "All things must pass."

Along with "Credence Clear Water Revival" Someone playing guitar in the back would for sure be a treat. Not just for that reason. But, I wanted to play it too.

Turned out… The guy was using it for a suit case.

He said: "It also helps us get rides."

After all I stopped… Didn't I?

I was about to dump um out of the van in the middle of fucking nowhere at 2:30 am.

When Ann said: "Come on man. They ain't got shit. We are going their way anyway. So for Karma's sake… Let um ride along."

Ride along my ass! Eat along. Drink along. Smoke along.

When we got to Redlands, My Dad… (*He is so fucking cool!*) He felt sorry for um, and got um a cab to their destination in Riverside.

As they were getting in the cab, the guy drops his Trucker's Wallet. And, at least 30 $100 dollar bills fell out. They fanned across his lap. He just looked up at me. I just shut the door. I never even mentioned it.

Along the way after a very long winter in California that was NO fun! Ann. and I were starting to get on each others nerves. It wasn't looking good.

After six months or so at my Dad's… Lake Arrowhead… San Clemente and Redlands again… She and Joyce flew back to Monett Mo, and Bentonville Ark. I guess that was that! <u>Short and sweet!</u>

Chapter Twenty Two

"I am going back to Fayette-ville! I'm not sure why."

While I was in California! I tried to find Tad a hundred times at least. That is when I found out about Frank Getting Killed. No one, from his Mom to his brother RED had heard from him in over a year. That's when it was we left! I was worried for sure. Who gave a shit about that toad Joe?

I sold the Van to a friend. (That will come back to haunt me in book 3 somewhere) *I bought that guitar with the bird on it.* A plane ticket for me and Spanky! It was back to Fayetteville the end of March.

Guess who's there to meet me. Joyce Ledbetter! Weird…. Ain't it!

You would have thought Bonnie would have been there to pick me up for sure. Well… Bonnie isn't even in Fayetteville at this time! She is staying with a "Movie Director/Producer" in Bella Vista. Bella Vista, What in the hell is that! Writer/Director guys name was *Jimmy Varney*… Or something. (I.e. Ernest P.)

Joyce said: "New millionaires hide away up on the border above Bentonville for Wal ✱ Mart & Tyson's execs."

She is working on some sort of Mission. She won't tell anyone what it is. She has been real secret about whatever it is.

She said: "Bonnie says that if she speaks of it, it won't happen." That's the last we have seen of her. She asks if anyone has heard from you at least 100 times a day when she is here!"

What did you do to her Don?

Nothing!

I asked: "Where is Ann?"

She said: "Who knows. —Ahhh— *who cares!*"

Wow, what in the hell had happened in the last 6 months! Fayetteville didn't even look right.

I had called Joyce at her mom's house in Bentonville. I was surprised she was home. She had not been back to her folk's house in years. That told me that she and Ann were not together. That looked real oblivious now. Ann is most likely in Monett, Mo. I Called Joyce from "Love Field" in Dallas… I was about to climb on the very last plane ride I have ever taken. Now, let me tell you something. I have flown off the end of aircraft carriers in a C130. I've flown out of Military air bases where we almost ran off the runway a few time skipping incoming fire. I've been in "Dustoff" choppers. And, a few "Slicks" too! Under fire, picking up wounded. As I was catching a ride back to Tan Son Nhat.

But, in all my days of flying, I have never had a brow raising plane ride like the Bonanza Airways plane. (That too would be in the cross roads soon) This airline flew out of Dallas. To Ft. Smith, and then on to Fayetteville… Last stop Joplin, Missouri. Then they head back.

They are old parachute planes. They had about 6 of them. Nothing else flew into the thing they called an airport. Here's a later note. The wife I am living with today. Ended up running that very airport! Go figure! There would be other things too.

Well, as we flew out of Ft. Smith, The plane made a stop that wasn't on my ticket. They landed on a DIRT runway in Van Buren. All I could see coming up a dirt road throwing a dirt cloud as long as the road itself. Was a green Lincoln, There was a wind sock at one end of the Dirt runway. And, a small building painted red and white checkered. And, man that was about it! The landing was hard, through us all over the fucking plane. The plane turned and taxied over to that little building. This guy got on. And, away we went. I didn't know it at the time. But, later when I met the guy again, I knew he was the guy on the plane. This was years later of course. From the side of the street I was hanging on. Don Tyson didn't show up a lot! That's not to say I never saw him Shit faced. And, puking out behind the Swinging Door from time to time… Ya saw just about everyone there after awhile.

We lost cabin pressure as we took off from that dirt runway. Had to tree top all the rest of the way to Fayetteville. Thru an early spring thunderstorm in that area, a thunderstorm is a bitch! You take a roller coaster ride into Fayetteville anyway. But, I was sure I was a dead man. I could hear my dog Spanky barking from the cargo hold just under my feet.

All the barf bags are full, even mine. I'd never thrown up in the air ever before! When I got Spanky from the Pet Dock… He was hiding in a corner, and Nippin at me. He pissed all over the 100 dollar carrier I bought. I just left that right there in the room. We went outside to wait for Joyce. I had no idea what the hell I was gonna do. Or, even why I came back here!

Like I said: "It is like a magnet."

All I had to go on was Bonnie's eyes as she drove away that morning. And, what she said before she went.

"Don… please come back to us, we love you"

That was good enough for me. Bonnie. I'm here! What's next?

It's about 6:30 pm. Almost dark. I had been gone from town about 6 months I guess. It took that long for Ann to drive my folks crazy.

They had a John Birch Guy come over to the house while we were there. I knew what was going to happen next. Ann heard them talking to my Dad. And, Avon in the living room… She opened the bedroom door and listened for a few minutes. When she heard what the Bircher was preaching, She flew out the door, down the hall and attacked them. Hit the one guy over the head with a big assed brass bed warmer my step mom Avon had next to the fire place.

Knocked that sucker into next week!

The cops said: "They were taking her away."

My Dad… The smooth dude said: "We were just visiting from Arkansas. She didn't have no manners. Like that ol granny on that hillbillies show. We were heading back to Arkansas the next morning. She wouldn't even be in the state no more.

Now, I don't recall saying anything about leaving at dinner. But, I assure you. The next morning it was. Ann and Joyce on the plane! Or, everyone out! Including me!

I was laughing my ass off thru the whole affair. Those John Birch guys had never seen anybody like Ann.

Hell… Dig this! While we were in California, We went to the "Fontana Drive Inn" and saw that student revolt movie. "*The Strawberry Statement*" She was so involved at the end where they are getting Tear Gassed in the student union! She was beating so hard on that van windshield. She almost popped it out!

So, I'm back in Fayetteville. With a sleeping bag! And, not much more than the first time. Accept a brand new guitar.

As I said before: "Leave town for a few days and when ya return everything has changed." It had.

The place is full of young people as far as the eye could see. Every corner I turned Were more kids, more cars, it's a different place. I would find this normal in later years. But, now it seemed strange. Almost like, I shouldn't have returned.

Joyce asked me where I wanted to go. She lives in Bentonville now and would be going home soon as I was set. As, she is in her mom's car!

I said as we drove down Dickson Street: "Take me to the Grayhouse."

She said: "Good idea, Rick and everyone are there. I already told um you were in route."

I could bunk in with Rick & Dianna is what they told her. They were waiting with GREAT anticipation on my arrival. That made me feel better. REALLY folks! I have NO idea what is next! *I almost feel LOST!*

We pulled up to the Graveyard parking from the back.

She slid over to me and said: "Don…. in all the time I was with you and Ann. I never got to do this!"

She slid the seat back down. And, crawled on top of me, and, kissed me like nobody's business. She pulled off her top and her giant pink nippled tits fell out on my chest! She straddled my now hard as a rock cock. And, _fucked me hard as she could!_

She rolled over onto the back seat and pulled me down on top of her hard! She reached down and shoved me in again. She was hot as a pistol and not done yet!

The windows were gone with steam, that station wagon was rockin me Droogies! I had been with Joyce before in a pile of bodies. But, never just her and I! She is a very different woman alone.

After an hour or so, she said they were all waiting on me and she needed to get her Mom's car home.

She said as I got out of her car: "Don, I have waited for that since I first ever saw you. That Bitch Ann. Just got to you first! I was never her twin. I just could not stay away from you. I hope you don't hate me."

I leaned in and kissed her cheek. Whispered in her ear… _That was something I too have waited to do ever since I first saw you my dear!_ We just never could get away from Ann long enough to do it!

Please Joyce, _May I call on you again soon?_

She swooned. And, drove away blowing me a kiss, saying with her lips, YES! She made the right at Dickson and I was alone in the dark street with my whole future 100 feet away and waiting!

I walked up the steps to the Grayhouse. On the porch is Lee. He is whittling on a Voo Doo Doll. He is going to put a spell on the chic he wanted to snake.

He said: "Well, where in the hell you been?"

He had been in the VA Hospital getting more skin graphs most of the time I been gone.

I said: "Lee… Man, you are the first I have seen except for Joyce." He said: "Yeah, I noticed the car a rockin over there." He reached up and grabbed me. And, pulled me down right to his face and said: "Don't ever do That Again! I will take a giant Shit on you! You scared the fucking shit out of me! DON'T DO THAT AGAIN! Hear me?" Damn, that was intense Lee! I live intense Don! Don't fuck with me! What's it all about Lee? Just watch it! Don't Do That Again!

We went to Rick and Dianna's room. He told me they had moved upstairs. You know, into the House Mother's apartment? We went up and knocked. But, the door was ajar, in we went. Nobody is home. It looks like there were more than just the two of them crashing up there. So, I didn't bother to settle in.

I went and found an empty room in the back, kinda moved in with my Sleeping bag, back pack and new Guitar! I was tired. Spanky stunk from the plane ride. So, I and Spank hit the showers for a clean off. It seemed that most every room was taken. But, I wasn't seeing anyone. A stereo or two is on. I could smell the toast someone is cooking coming up the back stairs from the kitchen everyone shared.

Spanky and I went back to our room. Rolled a big one… Fired it up… I stared playing "Teach your children" and smoking the J. Two girls I'd never seen before… Great looking freshman girls… fresh in town! And, away from home for the very first time… they are in the building slumming.

When they heard me playing, they just walked in my room and sat down. No panties on these two beauties. And, a very tight pair of Daisy Dukes on! So, fucking tight, I could see right through Christmas! And, into the New Year!

Moms Mabley had nothing on these two. They asked if they could stay and listen.

I said: "HELL YES!"

And went into "Cowgirl in the Sand."

About half way through the song… My door flew open. In came Mike Boyd. With him is Rick. And, some, biker looking dude!

Mike said: "Put down that guitar. And, come upstairs, *now!*"

It was like I hadn't even left. No welcome home! No where ya been? No fuck you ass hole, nothing! As I went upstairs to Rick's apartment. Lee stuck his head out of one of his cubbyholes, Climbed out and joined us in Rick's room.

The biker looking fella said: "Who the fuck is you?"

My gaze moved from him, I didn't answer him. Just gave him a fuck you look sucka! I looked at Rick and Mike.

I said: "What in the hell is going on? Not even a Hello. Or, freaking nothing!"

Mike said: "What do ya want? A tickertape parade or something?"

We got bigger things to worry about! Besides you coming home. Where ya been anyway asshole?

Ya see… Mike didn't go to Florida with us. Rick and Dianna had just returned themselves. Seemed that everyone that went on the Florida trip was just themselves returning to town… Looked like I hadn't missed anything at all… Yeah sure, Bullshit! Just wait!

I did feel like time might have stopped here while I was gone! I seemed to miss the cold as hell winter. Here I am getting ready for another summer of love Part Two. Things are looking up!

I was trying to figure out what in the hell was going on. And, why this biker dude was stomping around the floor like he was waiting on news about a new baby or something. Seemed to be real pissed off about something...

As I and Joyce had come up the street earlier, we saw a girl named Debbie sue coming down the Grayhouse steps. She had something in one hand that looked like a big jar of weeds. Turned out to be some of that home grown.

Seems around here... Homegrown came jammed down inside a Mason® jar. You didn't buy a quarter pound. Or, a half a pound like you would everywhere else. Here... if you are lucky enough to know someone that grows. You can buy yourself a "JAR." Didn't matter how much was in it. As, it held as much as the guy could jam in there with a "Little Leaguer baseball Bat®," Take a bat, And, start with the tip of a 2 foot long, 7 inch around bud Partly dried, of "Confederate Crimson Red!" And start shovin!

Or, Some of that wonderful "Cherokee County Christmas Tree" and start to jam it down in that Mason® Jar in a swirling motion till you can't get anymore in there. Then *Can* it, the same way you do preserves.

You know... Wax and all!

Set the Mason® Jar in the hot water so it will vacuum seal. Just the same way... Now you have a jar of primo-primo bud Daddy! And, I ain't fucking fooling either!

You can take a case of those Mason® Jars, put them in the pantry, and break one out at different times of the year. It's just as fresh as the day it was bottled. Just a half an hour or so in the room at temp... And you have perfect knock your dick in the dirt (even if ya don't have a dick) Kick ass smoke.

There is never a shortage of smoke in the years to come. But, let's not get ahead of ourselves here.

James Taylor is playing "Sweet Baby James" As the room erupted into a fire storm. I was just starting to drift off. I was startled back to reality! Dianna had put up a thin real sheer pink piece of material. About 4 foot by 6 foot across the archway. That framed the window seat that stuck out over the porch roof in the Housemother's apartment.

As I jumped up, the red light on the other side had me thinking the fucking place was on fire or some shit.

When the biker looking dude said: "That's it! I can't just pace around here! I gotta do something!"

Mike... Who is pacing in the other direction! They would say "Bread & Butter" as they passed each other like those ants in the cartoons.

"Well, there is only one move we can make at this time."

About this time from outside the window and down on the steps. That Debbie Sue girl was hollering something about how she had just fallen in the street and sprang her ankle something fierce. I saw this happen out of the corner of my eye. But, I didn't think it was real.

She was coming up the steps and fell backwards into the street. There is a bad step 3rd step that will trip you if you don't know it's there. She had that jar of weed in one hand. A Dr. Pepper in the other… And, a Doob in her teeth and a mouth full of Double Bubble… Bubble Gum!

She rolled backwards and back to her feet all in one motion didn't spill a drop of either thing in her hands or teeth! She sprang her ankle and stubbed the shit out of her toe. Would someone please *RUSH* to her aid! About that time, Tony came from the first floor and grabbed her around the waist, carried her to where we all are.

I could feel and hear someone park their ride real hard out the side of the building. Hard because, they hit the freaking house… The entire building shook. I was starting to get the feeling that something was real wrong.

Tony and Debbie Burst into the room with a bang! Started to holler… Tony looked at me. Then over at Lee!

Lee said: "Yup! That's him."

He came over and stuck out his hand for a shake. When I shook it… He pulled me up, and gave me a Welcome Home Brother hug.

He said: "God damn man, Thanks a lot for leaving me with the concert aftermath to deal with! Welcome home man! Really! Glad to see ya."

Debbie still in his other arm with a what in the hell… Who is this Bozo?

She said: "Put me down!"

Now, Lee is all smiles. And, Mike was still pacing. This biker dude is really in the dark now.

He says: "Tony! — Tony!!! Who the fuck is this dude?

Tony says: "Oh, I am sorry… this is Don Morison. Don… This is my little brother *Terry Smith*.

Don just got back from… He looked at me as if he was not sure just where I was back from.

He said: "Ah….. This is Don.

"This is my brother from Memphis Terry."

As I am shaking this guy's hand, His mind is not on me. It's on what Debbie Sue has told him and Mike. Somebody is gonna die. If he gets his hands on the sucker that is!

I said: "What in the fuck is going on here. Would somebody please fill me in?"

About this time a set of car lights pass across the dark side of the room. Mike and Terry run over to the window to see who has just pulled in. Its Rick in Mike's brown Ford station wagon he lovingly named *"THE SNAKE*ç. He is waving his hands around like to say. Ok, let's go.

Lee speaks up and says: "where in the hell do you turds think you are going!"

Terry says: "Man, if we don't get movin, we will never catch up with them. They will be so far ahead: we will never know what happened. They could be killed! Who would even know?"

Well, I am still trying to get some kind of handle on this thing. I ain't got a flippin fart in hell of an idea of what's goin on. So, I just sat there as they kept going over the pros & cons of the deal. But, still I had no idea what it was all about.

Lee looked over at me and told me that this guy named *Tim Copland*. Had taken Terry's girlfriend *"Jocelyn Hendrix"* and, Tim's girlfriend *"Karen Addams"* and, ran off to California. The Karen girl's dad is a bad assed truck driver named Big Ed. He has already loaded up his truck and hauled ass for California. Going the same way they will have too, and he knows everyone along the way, it's his route.

Twice a month he makes that run. So, they won't get far! He will have the sheriff hold on to um till he gets back.

Terry said: "Not if I can help it! Fuck that sheriff! And FUCK big Ed. God Damn IT. I am gonna FUCK THAT SUCKER UP BAD! I'll go catch up with them myself!"

Mike says: "Hell yes! Let's go! Right freaking now!

Lee says: "For geet a bout it!!"

Mike says: "OK! But, Thanks for thinking about it though!"

Jocelyn, Karen, Tim & Wayne-o. Or, some shit like that there. Who in the hell are these idiot's! Sound like a Folk Singin Band Ur sompin!

Well it seemed, that this Terry cat had been working for some second rate record store in Memphis. Doing the *"Pepper Jingle Factory"* when they needed him, that wasn't doing it.

Tony is having a ball in Fayetteville. Why stay in Memphis while the action is in Fayetteville? Or, so it seemed. Not only is he right. But, like that Devil's Mountain in *"Close Encounters of the Third Kind"* The place is a destination for Thousands of runaways. To every free life style tribe going in this wonderful time...

Terry had just returned from Memphis. And, was crashing at Tim's house... Looking for an opportunity to come along... Me the same! I know this... I have never been able to explain it any other way! The years we were together as first friends to the end of life to this very day, to business partners and traveling troubadours. Were the best years of my life! We are a dying breed.

They didn't make them like us anymore. If there was an end to Country Rock, we are there. If we weren't, I tell ya! You could see the End from where we were. We were in Austin when the great Willy/Waylon movement was going down. It won't be long before we invade that rolling tale. We were not outlaw country! But, we were not Eagles. Or, Rock either. We were just us. "*THE MORISON SMITH BAND*"... But, it took a few years for that to come about. Right now though, there seems to be some Magic about to happen right about here I think. That's where we are heading now. So, please stay seated while the ride is in motion!

I'm not sure who this. "*Jocelyn*" And, "*Karen*" are. I have no idea who "Tim" is either.

Remember I said: "If you leave Fayetteville for a week or two. Or, even a day for that matter. Everything is different upon your return"

Well, most all the people we have dealt with up to this part of the story are about to drift right the fuck out of this story! Some! Not many. Come back and forth from time to time.

Lee is still trying to talk some sense into Rick, Terry and Mike. I'm ready to strum a bit on my New guitar with a Fricken Bird on it. So, I whipped it out and went to Strumming "*Cowgirl in the Sand*"

Terry and the others went down the stairs in a huff! I was just sitting there playing and singing to a couple of Lee's run a ways of the week. I had this cute little *14 year old with NO panties on* from...What's the name of that town? Oh yeah, InDianna. Or, Ohio, or, some place like that. Hell, I can't remember. So many came and went. I'm back in town for less than 6 hours and already the drama done started.

I heard a car peel out! It's Mike's Ford Station Wagon, "The Snake¢"Rick is drivin. I knew that. Because, Rick only knows two speeds! Stop! And, floored! The guy ruined every car any of us ever had. But, for some reason... We always let um drive. He could get from Fayetteville. To Ft. Smith, in 28 minutes! In 1970 that was one hell of a fast time! Nobody could beat it. He is even faster on his bike.

Mike's wagon has arms and legs hangin out of every hole. Right out of a movie script. Or, a Freak Brother's Comic! Off go the good guys! Ha! Right!

But to my surprise, Up the stairs comes Terry. He has a guitar case in his hand. He walks into the room, lays it on the bed. And, pulls out with the care of a Gibson ... A Yamaha something or another... But, to him and me... these are the finest Guitars there are! Up until now anyway...

I had that old Harmony I banged on till I got this one with the bird on it. The Harmony® was better used for the local *Archery* meets than a guitar. I am deadly with the thing. I could stick a sharpened drum stick thru a hole in the back. And, wipe ya out from up to 100 yards. Or, more! I still have that old sucker... Those sharpened drum sticks hurt like a bitch when I got ya in the ass. Go in at least 4 inches! Go right through a *Heckler*!

Terry was a bass player. I was a drummer. That's what I liked the very best most time's. I still love to sit down at a great trap set. The more drum's and percussion goodie's the better. But, guitars were easier to carry around with ya in a war zone. So, a *Guitar* player I became.

Terry's excuse is. "The guys up front got all the chics"

Tony... his brother was the vocalist of a *Blue Eyed* soul band they were in while in Memphis.

Tony could sing like no one else I ever heard! He could not sing at all! But, he had more soul! And, Rhythm! He has the best timing I ever heard! That made up for the other. He always laid on a stone hard harmony when called upon. Or, when he heard one missing in the root scale...

We got all prim and proper as our rock year's evolved. And, believe it or else, it did. To the point where we both found our reasons for saying "*BRING IT BACK HOME*"

Bring it back home is what you say to the band. When they are getting way out there in the middle of a song Live on stage... You're jamming along for 30 or 40 minutes.

When ya say: "Its time to "Bring it back home."

Terry sat down on the end of the bed.

He said: "I heard you play "Cowgirl in the Sand" Was that from the "4 way street album?"

I said: Yes! Do you like Crosby, Stills and Nash?"

Now, I'm wondering... What is this cat getting to here?

He says: "I don't play by music or nothing. Just what I hear..."

"Me Too!..." Was my response!

"Ok, what in the hell we have here?"

He went into "Down by the River" I started playing the second guitar part. We didn't even know what a first and second guitar part was. Terry's style is to play full bodied orchestral chords, on a full bodied, thick Bassy guitar.

My preference is a lighter wood, dreadnought, bright guitar. I play with a bar chord and open chord chunky electric acoustic style. Some what reminiscent of "Stephen Stills" We even speak in Harmony for Christ's sake! We were a Duo from that night on!

The Jocelyn... Tim. And, Karen deal seems to be on the back burner all of a sudden. After about 4 hours of nonstop playing of a 100 or songs we didn't even know we knew. We decided that we were just going to have to be some kinda duo! Or, band... or something!

Write songs…Get famous… Because, there is no doubt!

We have something going. It is like we are meant to meet right there! "Right Now" This very night! Something is happening. Is this the reason I'm here in the first place?

After that meeting, Nothing! But, music mattered. For the next 9 years. I mean… *Nothing Brother!* Every waking minute… Of, everyday was music, music, music!

As we played more songs and people came and went. I was *Rushing* so fucking hard! I had not noticed till now. But, I have this weird feeling! My heart is kind of fluttering: the room is quiet now… In the DARK corner, is a girl kind of sobbing!

I went into mode. I played "*Guinevere*" to her as she sat in the dark. Her sobbing lightened.

She said: "I knew it! God… I fucking knew it!"

She stood. And, the candle light glow of the room. Caught her shape as she parted the sheer silk curtain that covered the alcove… She stepped into the full candle light. Her soft strawberry/blond hair shining from the candle glow…

MY GOD! My eyes are about to jump from my head! I am crying Giant tears the full length of my face. My Heart is racing… Hair on end!

I ran to her… ITS! *BONNIE!*

She had returned from Bella Vista when Joyce called her. Told her I was back. Before midnight she was sitting in this room!

She is standing there quivering looking into me!

She say's: "*I knew it as if it meant my LIFE!*"

I am Lost in her eyes. I can't stand there looking at her shaking. I took her. Pulled her in my arms… and, kissed her for every kiss I had longed. For over 6 months now. We just held each other in the alcove way for what seemed like hours.

Lee is watching us. With, a very happy, contented look about him!

I felt so very warm! As I kissed her, Again, And, again, Bonnie♥ Bonnie♥

I kissed her again. And, Again!

She took Lee. Terry and myself over to her Party apartment on Lafayette Street…

I said: Wow, Bonnie… This is cool."

We went in.

She said: "Play for me!"

We played an hour or so as she just stared at us with a tear every now and then coming down her cheek. She would just smile at both of us.

She said: "I knew! I swear to God… I saw it before the two of you even knew the other existed! I knew it all along. There is just something in the air! You can't stop something that is in the air."

She walked me to her car.

She asked. "You want to go back to the Grayhouse?"

We did… There we played at least another 5 hours.

Now, that Rock concert deal Tony and I pulled. Would come back to haunt us sooner than we thought!

That Windy Austin guy still was holdin a grudge from that. He would bad mouth us as a couple a "*GEETAR*" Strummers… Down to the WALL, On our "*Crosby, Stills and Nash Geetars*"!

Terry and I. were sitting on the WALL the next night, doing our thing with a crowd of 25 or so. When the guy "Bob Bogart" Walks up the street from the "Swinging Door." Sits down on the WALL… And, listens…

He watches the response from the small crowd.

As we are taking a smoke break there…

Bob says to Terry: "You guys know me. What would u need to come down the street and play this stuff in the other room from the bar? Away from the pool tables… And, noise and all?"

I said: "Well, how about beer and a burger or two"

He said: "I'll do even better than that! I'll even give ya $20 a piece! And, you can put out a kitty jar too."

Hell, we are off and running with our first gig! We weren't even trying. That's when you know it's meant to be!

Now, everyone that had been in town for 6 months or more was kinda getting off in their own little families. Just like I predicted they would.

There is this house. And that house springing up all over town,

Terry and I. Play our first gig together that night. March, 22nd 1971.

We are off! And, running! It feels good too!

Tim, Jocelyn & Karen… Along with some strange idiot named Wayno… Or, some shit like that! They returned a few days later. They never even went to California. That was a ruse.

They went to Houston, Texas. And, almost got killed! The girls almost got *Raped*. So, they came back home.

Lee. And, I knew they would.

Karen lives over in a house on the other side of the tracks. The Jocelyn girl is the daughter of a Horse Doctor (dvm). Out in Farmington some where.

Tim lives up on Nob Hill. Rich Kid!

It was a while before we saw those 2 girls on the street again. But, we had other things to do. And, music to play!

We became the very first live music on Dickson Street. There is a wooden sign to prove it. Over both 4 at the "Swinging Door" it reads.

Don (Morison) Buford & Terry Allan Smith"
First live music on Dickson Street. March 1971

There is live music in the Library Lounge. But, we are the First live music "ON" Dickson Street. And, the First one's that drew the "OTHER" crowd!

The few clubs that have live music... Catered to the School Crowd... We had the rest of the town in our corner it looked like. We are the "VOICE" of the STREET! Even if we don't want the Honor! It has already been decided by them to be!

Bonnie said: "You can't stop something that is in the AIR"

ᴧ Ψ Writer's Note Ψ *

Dealing with time is hard on a guy. So, much has happened!
To try and put all of this into just one group of steps in the road,
Is near impossible! The mortar over-runs the cracks. Time warbles. And,
skews.... There is "NO" map to follow. Just Faces. And, Memories" ψ

Chapter Twenty Three

"This... Back and Forth, Is driving me Crazy!"

The Music changed to *"GUNN'S & ROSES"*

I noticed that Ryan is watching me from the screened porch. The client he has been working with has just left. He noticed I was out there under the trees. He has a "What are you doing?" look on his face.

That look takes me back to the Grayhouse. The Housemother's apartment. Tony is turning to me with that look! You know... He's got "That look"

He gets this little wrinkle over his left eye. And, a smirk on his lips, starts to twirl his moo - stash.

He looked at me and said: "Hey man! Were ya been?"

"I been talking to you for 30 minutes now! I don't think you have heard one word I have said!"

I said: "Sorry man, I think I was somewhere in the *FREAKING FUTURE!* I swear! It was clear as day! I mean, even in color!"

Far-out man!

"Oh well, I'm sorry. Now, you were saying?"

Terry and Mike have run to the cab stand for smokes, how about you and I run through that *"Cripple Creek"* song again. We did that for about another hour or so. And, then put on the "All Hail Marx and Lennon" record. *"Firesign Theater"* Then, smoked two bombers.

Firesign is some the funniest shit I ever heard. The cover of the album is a picture of "Groucho Marx" and "John Lennon."

After awhile, we all know every word and phrase so well. We could recite any part on demand. Even do entire passages at parties.

The Grayhouse is filling up with a lot of real strange people. It is nothing like Last summer. There are so many new faces in town that we kinda just disappeared into the crowd. Like *Ghost's*! All of a sudden, everyone looks just like us! We needed our own section of town to rule.

Our own HOUSE!

We pretty much all live at the Grayhouse. But we knew that was gonna change soon. There are just too many of us here now. Something has to give. But, all of that is about to be on the extreme back burner.

There is Revolution! And, *Craziness* in the air! I could feel it! I knew music was about to take a hold of us. And, take us somewhere! Where is another Story for sure! The calm is about to Erupt again!

It isn't getting Hot yet. Even thought the trees are getting green. It's warm at night. The Noise coming up the stair's got my attention! It sounded like a mob coming to take someone to the Gallows Pole!

Tony looked at me and said: "I am so Fucking Stoned! I can't even see your face."

I said: "Yeah! I know. I'm high as a Giraffe's ass… right fucking NOW!"

He did Retort: "I do believe, all *HELL* is about to break loose in here, in less than 30 seconds."

He is so sure about that, he is actually counting down from 30. He continues: "A kind of Ruckus like you have NEVER seen Partner! He stood up and took a DEEP breath. Watch this my FRIEND! He looked at me again, motioned me up and away from where I'm sitting.

Tony is counting down from 29. To one…

When the door on the second floor blasts open!

About then, an entire Army came through into the stairway. The first two through the door are. Bonnie and her childhood sidekick "Zelda"… There are at least 50 people coming up the stairs behind them.

Bonnie. And Zelda, Are wearing "Chrome Helmets" carrying white M1 rifles they had stole from the R. O. T. C. Armory. Bonnie, is dressed in Army gear. Zelda is in a waiter's uniform she ripped off from the Holiday Inn where she works as a maid.

Tony and I just fell back. Looked at each other and said at the very same time: "OH SHIT!"

We hit the fucking floor… As, Bonnie hit the floor right on top of me! Zelda jammed a chair against the door. Then jumped behind the couch and took up a defensive position.

Bonnie yelled at Zelda: "If we don't make it through, we fought a good fight!"

Zelda yelled back: "Give um Hell! *Chicky Baby!*"

Spanky jumped out the Housemother's apartment window, to the roof below that topped the porch. He and the Grayhouse cat "Super" both hit the street for their hidey hole out under the van that Racecar Jimmy had parked in front of the old storm dug-out at the street level of the stairway. They both were lying under the Van looking out at the fun.

About this time… 30 or so assholes dressed in Army uniforms are kicking the shit out of the door. And, yelling some kinda shit about. How Bonnie and Zelda… Are, under House Arrest!

Just as they said that, every bad assed motha from the WALL is there, pulling them back down the stairs to the street. Everyone is just kicking the wholly shit out of each other.

The Sheriff is in his car at the corner of the Graveyard and the alley. Watching all of this, laughing his ass off… That was the first time I saw Sheriff "Bill Long" as actually seeming to be a Sheriff that really didn't want to get involved too much. It just made for more work. And, he didn't want that to happen.

So he… And, his HIGH deputy just watched till the fracas settled down. Then, they just drove away laughing. Kinda like the cops in "POR-KY'S." He didn't notice I was watching him and his deputy more than I was watching the fight. His reaction to all of this was more important to me than the excitement below. So, as the fight moved down the street and over to the train tracks out of our view… I took this time to Debrief. And, Kiss Bonnie all over her face!

They are not sure what was going on either. There is some kind of riot up on campus, about something that had to do with some news paper! Or, some shit like that! "The Ozark Mountain Times" Hell I don't know!

Tony said: "What the fuck do you two have to do with it?"

Bonnie has her head against my shoulder saying: "Oh… NOTHING!" Zelda is busy putting the chair back in front of the door. Bonnie is finding a new hiding place just in case they double back.

"After all, they were after us weren't they?" Bonnie said.

I said: "Who knows? They came in and got dragged out before they could say anything. Like their Hair was on fire. And, their ass is catchin, that old scene."

Never a dull moment that's for sure! Strange, Weird, Good people!

About that time came a Bang on the door.

"Let Me In! It's Renee!"

I said… "WHO?"

"Renée!"

I said: "Renee……. Renee is not here!" Chuckle, Chuckle…

Zelda went over. She opened the door. And, in ran this, Beautiful. Tall… Thin. Cotton White Girl in a Purple Beret. A black turtle neck sweater… Holding up two! Count um! Two Giant breasts that should pull her over front ways! She is all of 5 foot 5 and 105 pounds. Wearing a pair of black leotards so tight, you could tell she shaved that there pussy! The lip's split and swelled as she spread her legs and held her rifle over her head!

Those leotards sucked at least a foot in side of her as they clamped down on the return. Down to a pair of bright RED Hi Top tennis shoes… With, bleached white laces, a hunting rifle… And, a bullet belt over her shoulder. Long blonde hair to her waist…

As she JUMPED from the spool table she had mounted on her entrance. She turned to look at us. Her waist long perfectly straight blonde hair caught the light as she flew around to proclaim.

"It's a Fucking STRIKE!"

Tony yelled! "What kinda strike? Calm down, tell us what is going on here!"

Bonnie and Zelda are keeping watch out the window for the enemy. Renee went on to tell us this: "We were all up on campus today passing out "The Ozark Mt. Times" When the ROTC. Plus, the new campus cops took all of our papers…"

Then, rounded us up and said: "That we would no longer be able to pass out our, Moronic, Stupid, Peacenik, Pinko paper on campus No more!" Then they through us in their new campus police cars and dumped us out at the WALL.

Told us: "Never to come back!"

I said to myself: New Campus Police Cars!

Tony looked at me and answered: "Yup, Look's that way!"

How did he hear me think that?

He went on: "This is the kinda shit I was telling you about. If you let these people get under your skin… They got ya!"

Tony went on to say that he felt that they should just pass the paper out around the campus and on Dickson Street. Then there would be nothing they. Or, anyone could do about it.

About that time, Lee came into the room.

He had slept through all of this in his cubbyhole. Rubbing his eyes, he demanded an explanation as to all the freaking noise! Renee and Zelda told him what was going on.

He said: "The Hell with that fucking high school Harry Crap! Take all this noise somewhere else! I got to get me beauty sleep before my operation at the VA tomorrow. So, Shut - The Fuck up."

Well, it's not as easy as that, the whole area is up in arms over this. This is something the fine people of Fayetteville have never seen before. The night is just getting started! Before the night is over, there will be hell raised all over campus.

The Journalism building will almost be a thing of the past. Seemed this guy "Bill Aires… Of "*The Weather Underground*" is pissed off because the campus leaders. And, the V V A W (I.e. Viet Nam Vets Aaginst The War) told him and his little toady Scott Vanartsdale. (*I think that was his name.*) To FUCK OFF!! And, get the fuck out of our town!

The Bill guy said: "<u>You Hillbillies ain't got NO balls!</u>"

Well… we showed him a thing or two! That's all I have to say about that for now!

It is said that the Scott guy, would try and blow it up! That would bring the FBI to town along with the "Rabbit!" The days of Speed, Beads and Weed are almost over!

Just one Fast summer! And, so much changed! But, the fun is just beginning. We could not see it yet… The future is coming at us like a 747 into a High Rise! You are standing on the 181 floor watching it come at you at 545 miles an hour with your morning cup of well deserved coffee. There is *NO* way to get out of the way. Or, escape! It show's that everything you think you know is… WRONG!

The Helmets and stuff Bonnie and Zelda were wearing were stolen after all. Along with a lot of other stuff! The M1 rifles were just wood. They didn't work. So, they didn't get in any trouble. The school just took um back. And, that was that!

About sunrise, I asked Tony: "Did that all really happen?"

"Shit… You got me man!"

We were sitting on the WALL. When up walked Terry and Mike. Terry say's: "What happened here?"

I asked: "Where you two been?"

Terry said: "Getting smokes from the cab stand!"

I said: "All fucking night long? You left 7 hours ago! The cab stand is two blocks down Dickson Street. You two missed everything! It was a hoot! No-doubt!

Tony said: "I'm still not sure all of that happened."

Allow me to make one of the many observations. I will notice as the years wear on here in Hillbilly heaven. I have never seen as many shaved women in my life! As a matter of fact, I have never seen one till here. Seems though, the shave thing is a thing here in town. Out at that Commune we busted up, those women had so much hair under their arms. And, on their leg's, so much hair on that old pelvic arch! I thought there was a "RENT SOME MORE HIPPIE HAIR" stand some where on the Farm.

Mike said: "Guess who is back in town? Tim and Karen."

Terry said: "The Jocelyn girl is back in Farmington. Karen and Jocelyn are grounded forever, Debbie is too." That set Tony right off. As he is getting to like that there Debbie girl,

Well, everyone is pretty burned out from the long night. Ready to crash out awhile… No such luck! A girl named *Shannon Star* came in the room. Had a big bottle of Dexies, a case of ice cold Coors (bootlegged) beer, a bag of Steaks from her dad's farm. With, charcoal and more!

She said: "Let's go to my house and party this Saturday away!"

I said: "Saturday?" I thought this was Thursday.

She said: "It is! Get It?"

That really screwed me up!

"No, its Saturday all day unless it rains!"

Zelda spoke up with a. "That's right! Then it would be a Rainy day!"

Shannon lives up Markham Hill. In a Fire engine red two story house. You can't see passed the front of it. It is over grown with Honeysuckle vines. Super private back yard with a stone fire cooker in the middle...

I don't know about you. But, I can't eat a whole bunch when I am on a speed run. This of Course... The next 3 day's became.

We had our guitars. And, all of a sudden we were figuring out just what our next moves should be. Music... And, band wise.

We are writing songs that we would not remember the next day. We are speeding so freaking hard. Only one song stuck. The last one always does...

A song we wrote on the only guitar that still had any strings! As we broke most of them playing "Only the beginnings" Over. And, over again! Every time we played it. It was louder. And, harder, till we had two strings on Terry's Yamaha... We wrote a song with those two strings called "The Freeway Blues" We sang that song all day Sunday, when someone said: "The bottle is empty!" "No More *Speed!*" *"Ever heard a cattle stampede?"*

There is a bunch of people there by then. Once the food, drugs, beer and music ran out... So, did they!

It was just Terry. Rick. Shannon. Mike. And, me!

Shannon asked me: "If I would like to stay the night."

I looked over at Mike... He is nudging me. Winking for me to notice him... I did. And, declined...

I said: "I'm so nasty. All I want is a shower. And, my sleeping bag!" Mike smiled. The rest of us left for the Grayhouse.

On the way there I said: "The Grayhouse deal is not gonna work out for us music wise. We have a lot of work to do!"

Terry said: "Says WHO?"

I say: "Shit Terry! I don't know! Seems like the thing to do, don't it?"

He said: "I guess so!"

Rick found Dianna.

Spanky and I hit the bag for a bit of good old Spatchka!

As I hit the bag and floor. Spanky came into the room, Climbed inside the bag too! I don't know where he had been for an hour or two. He stunk to high heaven. The sucker is a fool for a pile a cow shit! Just has to roll in it till it is gone! I was too tired to care and so was he.

Snooze away we went. Ah, PEACE AT LAST! I remember as I nodded out wondering: Well... ol Spanky... ol buddy boy! I wonder what will happen next.

He said: (Now this is a dog talkin folks) "Look Man. You worry to fucking freaking MUCH! Just GO with it… Now, Shut up. I'm a tired doggie me ol Droggie!"

The Ozark Mt. Times, Weather underground. Students for a democratic society news paper thing went on through our speed run. That's how interested we were in it! But, on the last day of the Strike! All the students, plus others that had been striking and protesting had gathered on the steps at the front of the Engineering building.

We are all spread out from the street that is no longer there, to the top of the steps as the school photographer took the shot of all of us flipping off the camera. There is a guy that had chained himself to a big old tree in front of Old Main, and us on the steps.

Both pictures made it into the Razorback Yearbook that year, take a look for yourself. The guy on the first step in the middle is me with Bonnie and Zelda on one side of me. And, SURPRISE! There is Ann. And, Joyce on the other! Mike. Terry. And, all the rest are behind us. Yes, I said: "Ann. And, Joyce!"

They too are back in town. And, doing their part to make as much trouble as they could… They are very good at that!

Chapter Twenty Four

"The band is getting in shape... Even the <u>Groupies</u>!"

Well... after a day of sleep. And a shower or two... Or, three... To wash off the speed run... I emerged from my back room at the Grayhouse. In the hallway are Terry and Mike.

Terry said: "It's about time! Looks like we gotta Gig!"

I said: "A what?"

Mike said: "You a Rock Star already Ur something?"

I said: "I don't get it?"

He said: "You isn't gonna turn down the first gig are ya?"

I asked: "Where is this gig"?

Terry said: "At that new place called the *EAR.*"

The Fucking EAR.... Whose great idea was that?

Terry said that: "Tony was in there talking to the guy that ran it. He said that we could have all the donuts we wanted. And, a dressing room in the back."

I thought... <u>A dressing room</u>... <u>Donuts</u>... <u>Coffee</u>... *Hell lets go!*

We grabbed our guitars. And, down to Dickson Street we went.

As we turned right at the WALL. Everyone noticed us walking down the other side of the street. They knew if we were going down Dickson with our guitars, there must be a reason. So... about 20 of them followed us down... We picked up 30 or so more as we walked.

I stopped at the entrance. We just fell back laughing with a... *"Right On Man."*

Now... this is too freaking weird! The freaking place has a Giant Ear for a doorway.

I said: "Where in the hell did that come from?" Remember how I have said a few times: "If you leave for a day or two..." Well, we hadn't even left town. It happened again, everything had changed.

I turned to the group of folks that had followed us there. I told um to: *"Fan out,* come in a few at a time, it will look better to whom ever is running this joint."

As Terry, Mike, And, I walked in. We were surprised to see that these were an old set of walk in freezers in this part of the ice house. They had been turned into a pretty nice little night club.

Nice stage with lights. Great PA system for such a small room... With a bar... With stools, about 20 tables and chairs... With nice table clothes with candles in the middle, an area in the corner with donuts! Coffee and such… Kinda dark and cool! In the back is a dressing room and office. I thought: "What the heck! Let's play!"

It is about time to see if we really have anything going here. The place is filling to standing room only. The guy running the place is wondering why all these people are here for just a sermon. I'm Jazzed to see what we will sound like on a real p.a. system. See if we can even do it! Kinda Scary when ya think about it!

All that you had to do to enjoy this place… Is listen to a sermon or two that really weren't bad! They didn't try to shove it down your throat. They just left it up to you. And, left it at that…

After awhile, we would just take a smoke break in the dressing room while all that was going on. The smell of the pot was drawn up the ceiling into a dryer shaft to the roof two stories above you.

Ok, we are playing at the Swinging Door. And, at the EAR! We are starting to get a following. That really pissed off that Windy Austin guy. If that was indeed his real name! I've known him for almost 40 years. I couldn't tell ya if it is!

I said to Terry: "We need some more songs and stuff. Folks are gonna get tired of the 30 songs we know."

In the audience, are two girls that looked about 14 looking right at Terry and me all night long. As we closed our set for the night, these two girls came over, asked if we would come to their house with them for some dinner. And, a bit of Heavy Duty body slamming. And, Hard FUCKING! Next thing we knew. We were in a duplex on Watson Street eating chicken and rice. Drinking Thunderbird with ACID in it…

These two girls would not tell us their names.

They said: "Just call us The Boogie Girls from Tulsa." Turned out… These two girls are runaways form Tulsa who had rich parents. They were floating in cash and were having fun. When they ran out of money, they would go home.

I said: "You two are 16?"

They said: "Would it matter?"

I said: "If not, we are out of here! Two runaway girls. Over a state border, Getting hard fucked in every hole on their bodies by two guys in a house in Fayetteville! Ten minutes will get you 10 years!"

Terry said: "Let's go!"

The two girls produced driver licenses that said they were both 17 and going to school here. They were playing some kinda trick on us. That made us feel like maybe these girls were cops! But, after doing them and their drugs all night… We didn't care no more.

About the *crack - a - dawn*, I'm laying on the living room floor in front of the door doin her for the 4th or 5th time. When a big girl about 300 pounds pulled up and went into the other side of the duplex. We named her "The Cowgirl in the Sand"

She had a 1959 black Buick "Invicta" parked out front. In the light of morning it looked like the *Bat Mobile*. A couple of guys walked up, started breaking into it. We made some noise. And, these two walked over to the door where we were naked still hooked together.

And said: "Wanna smoke a joint?"

We have just met Freaky Pete. And, old Weird Bob. Lucky us!

Coming up the street is another character named Fuzzy Campbell. 250 pounds of rip-off trouble! The whole… "You got it! We will get it" crowd had been out all night.

This Headless Horseman town is growing up way too fast before my very eyes! I had seen this happen before, it wasn't good. Now that the *RABBIT* is here too, trouble is just ahead! Word of this wide open place has spread near and far. Students… And, street people are coming up like weeds. I thought about Tad… I sure wished he was still here. This is his kinda town. He is missing so much. Everything we were looking for… Is here!

Chapter Twenty Five

"Bonnie take's over...
This is for real!"

*"Old Mother Hubbard, Went to the cupboard. To get her poor doggie a bone!
But, when she came there, the cupboard was bare! So the poor dog had none.
She went to the bakery to get him some bread. But, when she returned, the poor
doggie was dead! She took a King dish... To get him some Tripe! When she
returned... He was smoking a pipe!*
  Hey! Wait a minute! How can a Dead Dog smoke a pipe"?

Stan Laurel "Saps at Sea"

While we are at Bonnie's house. Not her party pad. The Duncan
House... I'm watching the TV... I didn't know anyone else that had one.
Every house in town built their party rooms around the best stereo they
could come up with no matter what it took. After that, there is no money
or need for a TV.

I'm rolling on the floor laughing my ass off at this Laurel and Hardy
movie. Saps at Sea... When Bonnie came in... Turned off the TV...

Asked me: "Are you and Terry really serious about the music thing? Or,
is it just a dodge to get chics?" Cause if that's the deal! It would be a sad
thing. She would not really want to get too involved with it.

Now to say the least... I'm looking at her with a, <u>What in the hell are
you talkin about </u>look on my face. I noticed she has a stream of tears running from her eye's.

I said: "<u>Are you crying?</u>"

She stood up. Turned her head... Then wiped her eyes...

And said this: you and Terry have something that is very rare in this
world. Not just talent... *which of course you both are over-flowing with.* But,
there is something I feel when you two guys sing and play. Everyone feels
it... I've watched their faces. People are in a Trance or something when
you two play. I have never seen anything like it. I feel like something is
pulling me from my toes to my head as I listen to you both and watch your
faces. It's like you two have played together all of your life. You both know
what the other is going to do next! It's fucking UN-freaking canny. For
god's sake! I love you both so dearly. I want to see your dreams come true.
Don't fuck up and let it pass. Get to work as soon as you can. There are a
million lonely people out here just like me that need you both!"

I could not believe my ears! At NO time in my life has anyone told me I was Special. No one ever sat me down with tears in their eyes to convince me to stick with it no matter what. I'm moved for sure. I could have blown it off too. She is just high. But, she isn't! I could see in her Piercing blue-green eyes she was speaking her heart. I didn't know what to say! For the first time in my life! I was speechless. Sigh. I just looked at her, she is so very beautiful. *I'm so fucking LOST in her eyes!* I could not let her down! NO WAY!

I had to ask myself Of Course. WHY, does she care so much? WHAT, is it about all of this that moves her so much? WHERE, does she see all of this going? WHEN, does she think we will get there? Everything about this says: *"Watch out for steep grades ahead!"*

Well… We are a hit at both the Swinging Door. And, The Ear!

The next night, Bonnie had gone around. And, asked a bunch of folks to meet her at the Ear for a mini concert by a couple a guys that will be recording stars soon. If she has anything to say about it!

Tony saw me walking from Bonne's house.

He walked up and said: "Everyone is looking for you at the Grayhouse. Some kind of band meeting or something!"

Now I am thinking… "What freaking band?"

So, I said: "Band?"

He said: "Yeah! Fuckin Band Man! The Morison Smith Band"

In total disbelief I said: "The what?"

He said: *"The Morison Smith Band"* What do ya think?

I said: "Do you mean… "The Morison & Smith Band?"

Tony said: "They had talked about that too. But, it was to wishy washy."

Whose idea was Morison Smith? It sounds like one guy.

Tony said: "That's Fuckin Right! Like… Which ones pink?"

I said: "Oh yeah…I get it." I didn't of course.

I had no idea what the hell he was even talking about! But, I was willing to play along.

I said: "Who thought up this name?"

Tony chirped out: "Bonnie! Hot damn! Can you believe it?"

I say: "Yes, I can believe it."

But, when was this idea hatched?

Tony: "After you went wherever it was you went last night."

Well… that could not have been true. The only time Bonnie has been missing since I got to her house was… *Hey,* <u>how did I get to her house?</u> What was I doing there? What happened to the Boogie Girl's? Something is NOT adding up here!

Tony Said: "No! While you guys were busy writing songs at Shannon's"

Bonnie was running around checking out some kinda stuff that seemed real important to her.

Ok, ill fall for it! What was it that was so important?

Tony says: "That's the weird part, she wouldn't say. Her answer when asked was: she is on a Mission! Next thing we knew you guys were. *The Morison Smith Band!* *Which one's pink? Get it?*"

By this time we are at the *Grayhouse*. Climbing the stairs to the House-mother's apt. everyone is here. Even Bonnie... She was still at the house when I walked this way. How did she get here so fast? I sat down to see what this was all about. Everyone is looking at me!

I felt the weight of their stares! It's scary! What the fuck is going on here?

Mike came over and said: "Well,...I guess that's that! Anything I can do to become part of this band You can.... *PLEASE*... You count on me!"

What FUCKING band?

Terry said: "Blowing my mind too! These folks are not going to take No for any answer. We even got *Groupies!*"

The talk is every where. We MAY be a freaking hit! I guess we are the people's choice, without being asked! Now, it is our Responsibility. To support, and, speak for these people in this Headless Horseman Town!

Was this the Fayetteville Tad and I came to just a short time ago?

I felt UNEASY inside, almost upset stomach time. I tell you all me Droogies. I was shook up! They could see it in my eyes.

Bonnie said: "U'all Shut Up! We are Scaring this Loverly man!" She moved to my lap. She is blowing cool breath over the back of my neck. Why is she so concerned? What's next? My whole body is covered with the chills bumps Bonnie is making. If I could only make her mine! But, she is a married woman after all! Has a full life already. No room for Innuendo. Sad! But, true.

I looked over at Terry. Who is sitting in the window seat scratching Super the Cat behind the ear?

When he said: "Well... I guess we should decide on a direction and work on it."

I said: "We should do what is the easiest. Sounds the very best... We are not sure what that is yet.

When mike said: "That we should get on our way to the Ear. Hit the Dressing room to get ready! We have two shows to do by midnight."

I say: "two shows? What do you mean two shows?"

He said: "That's what the ad window in front says. Shows at... 8 & 10 on stage... *The Morison Smith Band!*"

What band? It's just Terry and me! Didn't matter... Away we went.

This is our second show there. Hope we do as good as the other.

On the way down the street!

I said to Terry: "Let's just do the songs we know. And, fake the rest. Ask for requests, and then fake those."

Terry said: "Ok! Try to keep it in G# or A#." Good country keys.

We turned into the big ear door, then down the steps through the door. The place lit up! There are at least 50 people there waiting for the first show that is to start in 20 minutes. We hit the dressing room to hide out. And, <u>freak out</u>!

We looked at each other as if to say "What in the HELL is going on here?" We both shrugged at the same time like two Wild. And, Crazy guys!

I said: "We can tell jokes between songs to stretch it out."

Terry says: "What jokes?"

I said: "Shit man, I don't know... *Just freaking fake it!*"

When we heard Bonnie get on the stage...

She said: "Ok: We got um! It wasn't easy! But, here they are.

"The Fantastic!. . . "*Morison Smith Band!*"

The place erupted into applause like Crosby Stills & Nash were here or some shit! We walked out. There is a mini trouper spot on us all the way to the stage. We sat down as the crowd calmed down to where you could hear a pin drop.

We went into "Longtime Gone." We finished the first show. Then a guy got up to preach. We hit the dressing room. We walked through the crowd that had filled the room through our first show. People are reaching out and grabbing our hands saying: "That was so Fucking Great!" All kinds a shit along with: "What are you doing in this place?" It felt almost *Creepy* for freaking sure!

We got to the dressing room. Looked at each other and freaked out. I felt like puking, Terry just sat there, put his head in his hands.

Then looked up at me and said: "Did that happen? Have you ever felt that before?" We have taken NO drugs of any kind. We are damn near tripping on what just happened! I'm in a *haze*. I couldn't tell if it was real! Or, was I dreaming! But, we couldn't be dreaming the same dream. Could we?

Into the dressing room flew Bonnie.

She said: "<u>Sign here!</u>"

The last time I did that. I was in the Navy the next day! So, I had to take a look at what she wanted us to sign. It was a contract to play at an upcoming concert.

Out at some Christian outdoor campground on a river just west of town… Real money… and, everything! Wow! Outdoor Concert! Some little town named. SAVOY, ARKANSAS. Sponsored it every year!

Savoy!…Oooo! Twilight Zone stuff! Plus there is something there that would effect me deep very soon! Real HEAVY duty shit too!

It's time for the second show. We've come up with some kind of song list. Most of the same songs again though! This time there were more people out there. Between shows the crowd has their Donuts and Free coffee. Then out they go… They are gone. These people are not here to have Donuts!

"They are here… Too hear us!"

Chapter Twenty Six

"Oh my God! Then it happened ... Bonnie is right!"

We went right into. "Almost Cut My Hair" Then into "Ohio." We were telling some story or another to seg-way into the next song when this Very tall, almost *Gothic*, Patty Smith, looking girl. With, straight shiny waist long coal black hair, dressed like a *Beatnik* stood up. And, asked if she could sit in on the next song?

Terry looked at me then asked: "What song do you want to do?"

I asked her: "If she knew *"California Dreaming"*

She didn't even answer… She just came to the stage.

I made room for her at the microphone I was using. So, I could hear her close. So I could be sure to Harmonize with what ever she sang. So we didn't look so bad!

We started singing… Within seconds, the chills are running up and down my spine. I had to stop. Terry is looking like his jaw is about to hit the ground. The place is pin drop quiet. No body moved! Everyone is watching to see what will happen next.

Rick… of all people… Stood up and said: "Something is missing! *I know what the fuck it is too.*"

I was so glad he did that, I was lost. Even though we were about to get OUR *Dennis Wilson*… Right there on the spot! The Magic was unmistakable! Cosmic.

Mike stood up and said in his best Firesign Theater: *"Give that man a Guitar and this blue work shirt. And, let him tell it like it is."*

Applause rang out as he worked his way through the dense crowd to the stage! Terry made room for him at his microphone.

The girl's name is Patty! Or, *"Peppermint Patty"* We had perfect three part harmony that was missing just one thing! Rick saw what that was, came up and added the thing that it took to make our Harmony *Ring* like a bell for Christ's sake!

A "Monotone"

Everyone felt the shiver of the *Cosmic* Vibrations from this four part LIVE PERFECT HARMONY! That, before their eyes had just fallen out of the sky to them here on earth. It didn't matter what song we sang. The result is always the same. Unbelievable! Bell Ringing… Harmony!

What a magic night!

There is just no end to the wonder of this place I had stumbled into just a short time before. I thanked GOD for guiding me back to this place. And, for my good fortune, we sang way passed the midnight close time. We still had an over crowed room at 3:15 am. That's when the pastor called it a night.

They don't pay you for playing there. But, we were filled with so much gold that night, it didn't matter!

"The Fantastic *Morison Smith Band*" is born.

That is all that matters for the next nine years. I cherish every memory of those days. I was truly: "Living the best years of my life."

The next corner is right ahead. See it? That's the sign post just ahead, the Way-Out Zone! God I'm having fun! Plus, I'm about to fall *Head Over Heels In Love!* I just didn't know it yet. I already thought I was in love. They made over $600 in donations that night. We helped keep that place open for some time. Till, we our selves moved along. Never made a dime there! But, that didn't matter. It was ours! *OURS!* I like that.

After the pastor ran us out… We hit the WALL for a few minutes. Up came Lonnie and Steve. They are just floored by the last set.

I said: "Oh… You heard that?"

Lonnie said: "I had an idea you would be a hit." After we sat and sang "Our House" along with her smallest daughter one Sunday morning. That little girl could sing the entire song all the way through. This little girl is only 4 year's old, Never missed the Harmony. Or, lost the timing…

Lonnie had been listening to us from her witches den. She felt like there was some kind Magic afoot! Big Buffy St. Marie girl for sure… But, she wasn't going to say anything to spoil the spell. She is still a little biffed over that bogus concert we pulled. I mean the entire event was planned at her house, she never even knew the real deal.

That was how we wanted it for anyone involved. If anything went wrong over the damn thing. Tony and I were ready to take the fall! The rest could just claim Tony and I were a couple a "Carpet Braggers" from up north, trying to cash in on the San Francisco type scene that was going on here. I have to admit. That the streets are starting to look a lot like the crowds myself and Tad had to deal with back on Height-Asbury on our good bye trip before we made the trip to this place.

I guess that if you had just come here. It would for sure be your foothold in reality someday. When you explain to your grandchildren how it was you hoped you died before you were 30. Boy, ain't ya glad that one didn't come true! I was noticing that Pete Townsend is not advocating the old ways, when it came to his famous statement so far back when! Hell, Did I say that? How fucking profound!

The difference between the Ear… And, The Swinging Door is like night and day! From God will save you, to have another beer on me!

Terry looked at me and said: "I'm encouraged by the way the night went." It seemed to make that little sinking feeling in the pit of his stomach ease up some. For a 17 year-old cat, he is very serious from time to time… Almost like. What it is they say? "A moment of clarity in an otherwise scrambled world." Or, as he is also famous for saying "Somewhere in this song, is a moment of silence." I still am not sure what he meant by that! But, what the hell, it leaves the folks out there scratching their melons. That's always a good deal…

We had wasted the rest of the evening. And, thought we should hit the road. When Mike and Rick pulled up out front… Mike's car is a 1966 Ford Fairlane station wagon. "The Snake.ς" It's Gold. I think. It's so dirty most of the time. It's hard to tell.

Mike said: "That Peppermint Patty wanted us to come by her house the following morning."

I asked: "Where does she live?"

Rick said: "She shares a Duplex with that Allan guy. With the great stereo over at the Intersection of Leverett, And, North Streets! Hers is the one in back. With the front door at the driveway side of the house Dig It MON…. Ok! IRE, IRE!

Terry said: "That's over by where Debbie Sue lives. Terry. Spanky, and I. Took off over to the Grayhouse, where we were sure everyone else is by now. As I stepped out onto Dickson Street, I dodged back as a car went by. I looked at it and thought I saw the Girls in the thing! You know, the Debbie Sue girl. And her sidekicks. Jocelyn. And Karen! They were all against the windows looking back at us. I turned with a what do ya know about that! Look on my face.

As Terry said: "Wasn't that. . .?"

I'm shaking my head: "Yes… I do believe so."

He said: "Oh well"…We walked on to the Grayhouse. And up the stairs to the porch,

Sitting there is John Polamisano. "What's up Doc?"

John said: "Well, I was upstairs till they got so far out there. I was getting scared to turn my back on any of them!"

Any of them? I asked.

John said: "That the group up there is waiting for something to happen. Ur, some shit like that!"

"What shit?" Says Terry.

John stands up… Gets right in Terry's face… Like he does to everyone… And say's: "How… in… The… Fuck… Do I Fucking Know? <u>You Fucking Moron</u>! *Go find out for your self.*" Then storm's OFF!♣

Now, John is for sure Hyper for a freaking Pothead!

John stomps the shit out of his own hat and says: "I can't understand people I can't understand!"

That is profound revelation # 44. We have them all the way to 100. Dig it! Profound Revelation # 21: "If you push something hard enough, it WILL fall over!" So, with that in mind… Terry and I left the John saga at that for now! We figured, if he wanted us to know what was wrong with him. He would have told us!

Turn's out later though, he had received some real bad news. And, was going to have to leave town for awhile… So, we didn't see John Polamisano again till he came back with a map to a Treasure, and a girl named Carmin. This you will not believe. Later on that one me Droogies!

Terry, Spanky and I. Turned the loop at the stairs and climbed to the second floor. At the top are Marty and his friend Don. They are coming down from the housemother's apt. They are laughing their asses off!

Marty slapped me on the back and said: "That Rick guy is in rare form today. What in the hell did you do to him? I was in the dark! I had not seen Rick in a bunch of hours. Terry looked at me, I looked at him and said: "what in the hell is up jack?"

We could hear that song from Woodstock playing. What was it…? Oh yeah…? "Going Home" That is one long song! <u>Sucks</u> Too!

As we went closer to the stairway, it felt like the floor was undulating in some heavy duty earth quake Ur some shit like that there. The place is yawing and pitching up and friggin down like a ship at sea fer Christ's sake. The walls are moving and it wasn't because of acid this time! They are really fucking moving! The steps are hopping up and down like frogs in a dynamite pond. Lee kept sticking his head out of his cubbyhole like a Clown in a box…

Lee is trying to tell us something. Something like, "a Warning" or, some shit. We heard a crash, boom bang! Lee didn't stick his head out again. He pulled back in like a scared turtle.

Ony Ray came up behind and gave us his Shiva.

He said: "You suckas gotta do somethin man. Throw a net over um or some shit man! The guy has totally lost it. As, I was walking up here, he was mooning the street! He gonna gets us in Dutchy, he don't cut that sap happy crappy out padna!"

I was awe struck… Rick and Ony Ray are real good friends.

Terry is starting to back down the stairs to the floor below. I grabbed um and said: "Hey man, where do ya think you is a goin? We is a goin in!" As we started back up the stairs, it sounded like all of *Hitler's* Nazi storm troopers stompin the goose step up there.

I actually felt plaster coming down from what was left of the ceiling. Ten Years After is jamming away. It is so fucking loud at the top of the stairs: my ears are starting to bleed!

WHEN, BLAM! BOOM! Out the fucking door comes Rick in hyper drive. Grabs me and pulls me up the rest of the stairs without even moving from the door and shakes me like a rag doll.

Rick Sticks his nose right to mine and at super high speed sings. "Goin home: dee dle de de... "Goin home: dee dle de de! Over, And, over! And, over again! Then he plays the break air guitar style! By the time he had finished the break. We are Screaming and Jumping. Up and down. With the craziness! As, Rick tripped, fell backwards all the way down the thirteen steps to the second floor landing! Jumped to his feet in his best Evil K. Throwing the peace sign saying: "I am ok! I am... OK!" Ran down the rest of the steps... And, out into the street hollerin... Ony Ray...You son of a bitch! FUCK...YOU!

As he turned down Dickson St, and out of sight, the record is still screaming as we hit the doorway. Rick has 15 or so of Lee's runaways dressed up in Nazi uniforms he stole from the drama building the night before. It has something to do with a *fantasy* he has had since he was little bitty baby in Nashville. To this day, I don't believe he has ever been to Nashville.

Terry cranked down the stereo and asked the girls what in the hell was going on. This bulked up dyke came over and lifted Terry up about four inches off the floor, then asked: "What in the hell is it to you buddy?"

Terry said: "Just making sure you are all not getting hurt by Ricky Ticky the big bad wolf."

Is that what you think is going on in here? We were just about to kick the shit out of him, when you two pussies stuck your big nose in it!

I said: "Well, I see everything is ok here, we will just see you all later." We cleared the front door of the Grayhouse as the Dyke tripped down the 3rd step. And, broke her arm...

That damn third step is always getting someone. It looked good on her. Things are for sure starting this day out way cool. Tears of Laughter are BLINDING me! Terry and I are rolling around on the sidewalk next to the print shop just Laughing, Laughing and Laughing!

We are about to split a gut when, up walked Muffin and her Girlfriend Alice. Both in see-through sun dresses of the day. Blue... I have been noticing that the girls here wear sun dresses that have the buttons in the front! I wondered what the difference is.

The four of us sat down on the WALL to talk awhile. I asked Muffin what the deal is on the buttons.

She says: "Well, I'll have to show you. *Not tell you.*"

We stood up and crossed the street to the bench at the top of a 6 foot retaining wall that run's along Arkansas Boulevard. Her friend Alice was keeping Terry company on the Grass.

She sat me down on the bench. She unbuttoned the front of her sun dress. Her giant Creamy White Melons fell out in my face! I had to hold them up with my face Of Course! She has pulled my jeans down around my ankles. Sat down on me with her oh so sweet fresh shaved lips. I'm very hard by now and slipped it right in.

She did one hell of a grind on me for about 15 minutes till I shot like an oil well! She stood up and buttoned the front up and said: "See, from the back nobody saw nothing." I think I will ask a couple of other beauties I know the same question.

She also answered another question I had earlier: "Why do the town girls look so clean, as apposed to the commune girls."

I heard a new term I had never before heard before. "HIGH MAINTE-NANCE!"

She said: "We are Earth Hippies… with no shame! We are Women that want a hard dick whenever we are ready! I can't speak for every girl here. But, I can tell you this Don: *I LOVE BEING A GIRL! I love watching your dick get hard when ever I come around you!*"

I said: "WOW. I love you Muffin!"

She said in my ear, in a soft cool voice: "Carla, My Love…Carla"

Chapter Twenty Seven

"Let's get real here! I like this tube of Tooth Paste!"

It's time to talk about getting out of the Grayhouse. Things are not anything like before. It is kind of a drag at the Grayhouse. So, we went out on the street. Took off walking to the *Piggly Wiggly* to grab a bite of something sweet…

We are talking about the concert that Bonnie has booked for us. It's out in a town along hwy 16 WEST. Almost to "Lake Weddington." The area was built up back in the days of the W P A… (i.e. the **Federal Work Program of America**).

They went around in work gangs for the government. And, built State Parks… And, Camp Grounds for a small wage. They sent the money home. And, lived in the camps as they worked their way across the country…

Well, there is a big horseshoe in the road about two thirds of the way there. It's a little town called Savoy. At the time all it was known for is the little ol church house. Outdoor Worship… Along the riverbed and dam, A Concert grounds plus this show. There's an old Mill with a water wheel. And, a dam built on that part of the river. Great for swimming and all kinds of fun!

Nothing on either side but pastures… Wall to wall houses now I am told! You and a friend could hike a mile or two up the cow trail. Then float down in your inner tube to the dam, and then do it again. We will revisit that tranquil scene a bit later.

Now, we walked over to this place I told ya about called "*The YELLOW BRICK ROAD*" We had a little Dope dealing concern working out of this place that was meant for the other side of the bill. I Thought, what a better place could you stash and deal a bit of fortune from. But, a drug Intervention center full of long haired Red and Acid freaks.

I had a bit of the green. Terry has a small health improvement pill company working from the site. I stashed my goods behind the mirror in the bathroom. Terry had his behind the spice rack in the kitchen. It worked out great. Close to everything. And, safe as in your mother's arms!

I asked Terry where he thought the girls were heading when we saw them.

He said: "I don't know, I thought they were grounded for life. Let's check into it a bit later to see what's up."

Tony is in LOVE with that Debbie Sue girl I think!

Terry said: "I think so too."

The Karen girl lives just down University Avenue, you know.

"Yup!"

Debbie Sue… lives on Weddington Road just off of Garland by Dillon's.

Isn't that over by Peppermint Patty's house?

You know I think it is: "We can have some fun over there tomorrow."
Then get a "*BIG SLUT* with *SIDEBOARDS*" from *SANDY'S*©.

Oh man, that's a great idea!

We didn't know it at the time. But, that area is to become *Our Turf* real soon. It is just flat going to be belong to us! That's just all there is to it! "You'll see."

The "*Gavence Quarter*" we could call it!

Damn Right! Too Freaking COOL! Seemed different over there!

We are about half way down Leverett Street, heading for Peppermint Patty's. To see what it is she has on her mind… if anything!

We have not seen Rick since he fell down the stairs and ran out after ONY RAY. So, we will just have to tell him what she had to say later I guessed.

Terry said: "See that duplex up there?"

I said: "Yes"

That is where a cat named "Too Much Ted," lives.

I said: "Too Much Ted! HA! HA! HA! What's that all about?"

Terry went on: "Well, you know Race Car Jimmy right?"

"Yup!"

He and Ted have this side of the place. Ted lives here all the time. And, Jimmy is back and forth from the Duncan house.

We turned up their stairs. On the porch to our very surprise, is <u>Rick</u>! Passed out cold at the door, half way in and half out… Ted is dragging him in before his landlord sees him. As, he is there collecting the rent from the basement apartment. We helped him get Rick in the door.

Ted said: "What in the hell happened to Rick, Terry?"

"Hell buddy, we don't know? He came flying out of the Grayhouse a bit ago chasing Ony Ray down Dickson street."

We are a long way from Dickson, man.

Ted looked at me with this weird grimace. "Who is this guy you got with ya Terry?"

Terry says: "Oh, yeah. This is Don Morison."

"Don."

"Ted."

We shook hands and I said: "Have I met you somewhere before?"

He said: "I met you at Bonnie's house at the car shop office."

Now, let me tell you all! This guy looks just like the *Schweppes*® Effervescent man! He is the last Beatnik in Fayetteville.

I said: "Beatniks in Fayetteville, How fucking cool."

This *Headless Horseman* town had a past I was not aware of I guess.

Ted cruised around in a very fine sports car with no top most of the time. He drove an MG I think it was. He is about to cruise a bit, do we want to go? Three in a two-seater, I don't think so.

We smoked a big old bomber Ted had. A shot of tea and we were back walking down the road towards North Street. A bit farther down Leverett… We passed the Big Red house of Gordon's sister *Cecilia*. The place stunk like a shithouse of garlic all the way to the street. We walked on past at a higher pace. Passed *Skull Creek* to the intersection of North and Leverett… Peppermint Patty's is on the corner. Across we went, into Patty's pad for some talk and *smoke*.

Now, just what could old Patty want we thought? I really didn't know much about her. She is from some where over north of St. Louis. Spoke with a heavy Northern accent. Dressed in black most of the time, had long, long *coal* black hair to her waist. Thin girl with super Red lips and Huge tits! Swear to god! Looked like she was wearing lip stick, She wasn't! I do believe she has a thing for Terry. I know she doe's! She loves him more than he even knows. But, she wouldn't mention it for some reason. She just stared at him as we all sang. Never paid any attention to the rest of us!

She put on some music she wanted us to hear while she asked us just how into this group deal we really are. Or, was it just a lark, to pick up girls! I'm getting tired of everyone thinking the only reason we are doing this is to get *pussy*! When I was 14 it was to get *pussy*! Now, it is real. I seem to be getting PLENTY O` pussy without the aid of music, I think!

I was surprised at how serious everyone is getting about this band thing! Maybe just a bit to Involved! No FREE lunch says I, What's NEXT!

We talked, smoked. And, sang a few songs.

When she looked up and said: "OK! I really like you guys. Even that Rick guy! By the way, where is he?"

I said: "Long story. He's hung up, he will be here soon."

She said: "No matter. My girlfriend… And, roommate "*Trixy*" has graduated. She moved back to St. Louis. I am in my last year at school. I would like it very much to be in a real Rock group, than be an *Opera Star*! She could go back to that. If ROCK doesn't pan out!

I wanted her to get to the point. I already knew she wanted to be in our crowd real bad. As, she has been hanging around behind the scenes even before she sang with us at the Ear!

Then she dropped something on us that we were most not expecting.

She said: "Terry, Rick and I could just move right the fuck in there for *free!*" All we had to do is come up with our own food most of the time. Then we could practice when ever we wanted.

She has TV. A Stereo… two bedrooms. Nice living room and a big assed kitchen where we could play music and party hardy.

"Real *Guy Terriffico* kinda stuff man!"

But, here comes the *Big Butt!*

She has to head home for Spring Break to St. Louis. She promised Trixy she would. We would have to crash out wherever until she came back.

That was ok, I was still at the Grayhouse and so was Terry. Rick is crashing over at Ted's. He got threw out of the Grayhouse. Thrown out of the Grayhouse! What doe's that tell ya?

Tony had moved out of the Stone & Hill House. And, moved in with Tim on Mt. Sequoia… So, we were ok till she returned. This is gonna get us out of the Grayhouse.

It is starting to get dark already. The day had gone by fast. We went over to *SANDY'S*. And got ourselves that *"Big Slut with Side Boards"* we had promised ourselves. Bonnie picked up the tab!

A big slut with side boards is a big Mac kinda thing. SANDY'S made theirs with shredded cabbage. And, added tomatoes with a piece a cardboard wrapped around it (the side board). A sandwich… Fries and shake is all of $1.21 plus tax.

But, it is getting harder to come up with that much money as time went on. But, we didn't mind! It was all part of the experience. We are all living on the street so to say, by choice! We are longing for our own Shelter. Full of our people, and, be able to do as we please 24 hours a day! But, we are having too much fun for that just yet! A few more weeks of hanging out, then we will buckle down on the music thing.

Still, everywhere we turned, it's music this, music that! We need to make like a baby, and head out! Cause some trouble to get our night going good.

So, we finished off the big sluts and made for the WALL to get the night started. After all, it's *Friday* night!

Terry looked at me and laughed. "Nowadays bucko, every night is Friday night!"

Then he said: "It is Friday night, isn't it?

I said: "Hell, I don't know! Ha Ha. Too much, FUCK IT! I feel as Dizzy as a blonde!"

Terry says: "Would you like to DANCE?"

"Why… yes I would! LA DEE DA!"

We danced all the way to Bonnie's Mustang®.

I noticed that hours had gone by. This end of town is kinda different then Dickson Street. Plus the 10 blocks around it seemed like another place… kinda.

Back when I was about 13 years old. My dad and I were batching it in West Covina, California. (1963-65) it was my middle school years. High school was just around the corner. I was feeling my oats for fucking sure man!

My dad was so fucking cool. We had a house with 4 bedrooms and three baths, a ranch style home in the suburbs! My dad was all the rage on our street and so was I. We two were FREE and wide open Party Men! When he wasn't in *Las Vegas* all weekend. He was throwing Block Parties around our pool and patio. It was the years of the English Invasion. I am a Surfer. And, a Drummer! So, I already had hair longer than the Freaking Beatles fer Christ sake! Bleach Blonde from surfing.

I was the Drummer in a Surf Band named "*THE KAHUNAS*" I was set for sure. Girls hanging out all over the place, my dad's girlfriends buying us beer and Grass! It was Teen Age Heaven! I felt a certain feeling then, like all of a sudden. I was now only old enough to pretty much say or do what I want!

But, Sex, Drugs & Rock and Roll had a hold on me! I felt like I had "Come Aware" When I watched the Beatles on the Ed Sullivan Show that night in our living room. I KNEW! That's what I am GOING to do with my life. You know. I also remember a little dude that danced and sang in the act before the Beatles. That little dude became *Davy Jones* in the Monkees! He told himself the same thing that day! I think Millions of us did.

I was feeling that way again these days! It wasn't like it was when I first got here. In those days (did I say those days? See what I mean!) It was all exciting! Just being somewhere that felt like I was making the scene! But, it was small and compact into just a few streets of safety, like Height-Asbury. Or, the Village in New York City!

It became called on the highway from sea to shining sea as little this and little that. Soon, that would stretch in all directions of the compass! It was even "LITTLE AUSTIN" for awhile.

I looked at Terry as we hit the street. I stopped and turned around a few times.

I said: "This is OUR part of town! We need to *lay claim* to it some how."

Terry said: "Well, it's a ways from Dickson, I like that! Nobody would bother to walk all the way over here to find our place if we had one."

Boy was he fucking wrong! Sheeish! As we got almost to Dickson Street, Our friend Paul Rosenberg, Soon to be "Senator Rosenberg" was coming up the street. He was headed for Dickson Street to hang out. So, we climbed on his convertible. We turned at Maple, hit Wilson Park and smoked a big assed J of some real fine Paul had brought back from school in Austin!

It was the start of *Spring Break*. About time for a strange trip called "Gaybellie" Back then students stayed at their schools and partied, not like today. This was a three day art and music festival held at the Washington County fairgrounds for students & friend's only!

Your student card got ya in and out! You name it, it is there ready for you to dance too, eat, join, or, what ever you could think of. The next two weeks we had to fake it till Patty got back. LET'S PARTY! Two weeks. Two weeks hauls ass by I tell ya. AZTEC partier! AZTEC partier!

We cruised out of the park up to hwy 71... As, we went by Mt. Nord Street, We saw Rick and Tim walking up from the Mt. Nord house. They climbed in, off to Dickson Street. We turned down Dickson Street towards the WALL, there is Tony walking up from the Holsome Bakery with a bag full of fresh bread. He climbed in the car, we backed up and headed east UP Dickson to the Cross.

Up on *Mt Sequoia* in front of the Christian Science camp grounds on the summit, is a big assed **Cross** all lit up, You can see it for miles. It seemed to be at the top of Dickson Street. But, in fact it was way up there and around the bend. We spent a lot of time up there. Smoking dope and tripping. We drove around the loop on the top till we passed the Cross a few times. We saw a lot of people and got way, way Stoned!

Tony and Tim have moved into a way cool little apartment in the basement of an old as hell house with the old lady land lord up stairs. It didn't last very long as you might expect. But, it was a place for them to meet up with and put it to their girlfriends Debbie Sue and Karen.

Jocelyn is living off and on with a girlfriend upstairs at the Lafayette House. Bonnie has a Party room on the first floor by the front door. Why she had that place there, plus lived with her family at the Duncan house I never knew! But, what the hell! To each his own! So, at the time, the only ones not affiliated, Were Terry and me! Patty has designs on Terry there. So its time to party for Spring Break like everyone else.

They all looked just like us now! So, who knew? Paul had to see someone at the Cross in about 15 minutes.

Tim said: "Don't go far for long!"

I said to Paul: "Hey man, I'll cruise along with ya…if that's ok?"

He said: "Let's go!"

He is meeting his friend for some secret reason.

As we left, Terry grabbed me and said: "Don't leave me here, Come back! *I got a plan.*"

Paul said: "We'll be back in about 30 minutes with something to add to the festivities."

Tim and Tony have a night planned for us all that will blow our fucking freaking mind! I ain't kiddin either! I was hoping to run into some slick Hot chic before the night was over. Man was I gonna get hit hard by cupid. I didn't know it yet!

This is going to be the start of a time that would change everything. I had noticed that their partner in crime. Jocelyn is not here. What the HELL kinda name is JOC? I had seen her just a few times in passing here and there.

Absolutely Beautiful freaking *LOOKING GIRL!* There is absolutely *NO* doubt about that! But, alas she has a Rich boyfriend! I am about as Rich as *PEPPY POPPER!* My wallet is not only EMPTY! I lost that sucker and my other stuff in it a month or so ago! I have been a GHOST for awhile now and loving it VERY much! I suppose I'll have to do something about that soon! But, shit on it for now!

Paul says: "Let's get moving then!"

We walked out and up the trail to where the street is. In this part of town, everything is like *Anti-Bellum!* Or, some shit like that. Pre civil war stuff… This is the part of town where the GREAT Hatfield & Broyles feud was for over 100 years. This is where the south made a stand and lost in some real big ways for sure. This was the Fayetteville of the past. The rest of the town grew around the school and the square.

The Sheriffs Department is in an old stone castle looking building over looking the *Holler.* Next to a giant old Court house with a steeple and a clock in the top. You could hear that bell all over town.

Paul said: "He has to get out and go with this cat at the Cross for a few minutes. So… would I drive and just wait there till he returned? It seemed like when it came to dealing with people, that I might have a bit of trust in, it was our crowd people hung with. The rest were out for what they could get.

We met Paul through Ann and Joyce back in the first days. What was that Gerry said: "*Well the first days are the hardest days, don't you worry now my friend.*" We rounded the loop at the Cross until the guy was there. Then, we parked next to a Bright Orange VW bug. I was sitting there smokin a woofer and digging the scene.

Chapter Twenty Eight

"Jocelyn... The whole world is Beautiful!"

Ψ I looked over to my left... Sitting there in the VW... Is this absolutely beautiful girl! As our eyes met... I saw a Spark of Bright Green-Blue light reflect back from her Ψ eyes to mine Ψ

I felt my *Heart Pound*. And, skip a beat. Or, 50!

My jaw is in my lap. I'm sure I'm pale white. I just could not look away! The smile on her face is as fresh today, as it was at that very moment! I felt Dizzy... and light headed! I'm shaking all over. And, sweating profusely! My throat is swollen closed. I almost can not breathe.

The joint is burning my index finger when I came to! I felt a Tap, Tap on my shoulder. It's Paul.

Hey man: "You alright?"

I said: "NO!"

He said: "What's wrong Don? You look like you have seen a *GHOST*"

I turned to look back at her. She is going around the corner in the VW.

Paul said: "What did you do to the guy in the VW?"

"What? What guy?"

He said: "That dude was about to pull you out of my car here and kick the shit out of you till I walked up! He told me to take care of you, as you must be too stoned to be out in the open alone! He is a guy named "Don Garamin" He had a few classes with me in high school. No one to mess with I think!

I said: "Fuck that asshole, I'll kick his ass!"

Almost got my chance later, we will come to that soon enough!

Oh well, back to Tim and Tony's house for the big surprise.

She drove off and away. When we returned to Tim & Tony's house... Terry noticed that I was in some kind of Trance.

He said to me: "What's wrong with you?"

No Answer.

He asked Paul: "*What happened to old Don here?*"

He said: "Well Terry... to the best of my knowledge. He told me he had just seen an Angel. No... He said, The Angel!"

I only saw that spark one more time in my life out of three. I saw this spark the very first time Bonnie and I met, or should I say in that kiss when I felt her snap. This lightening bolt ⚡belongs too. Guess Who?

This time it's like my eyes are burned from looking at the sun to long! Her image is burned into them. All I can see is her! I can't loose this flush feeling like niacin burn coming over me every five or ten minutes. My knees shake so hard I almost can't stand!

I went on with my night trying to not think of her. But, all I could see was her eyes and face. Those wonderful puffy lips! What was I gonna do now. She has a boyfriend! This shit only happens to fucking ME! Oh well, PARTY TIME! There is a good Party here! If I say that all night, I just might live long enough to see the sun rise! OH GOD! I'm hit hard man!

Back at Tim & Tony's house! Hold up a minute. I need to tell you about Tim.

Imagine this in your mind of minds! Really! Open up your mind like you did before you got old. Look at this guy I am going to describe. If you have ever read a Furry Freak Brothers comic, this guy looks EXACTLY like Phineas Freak. If you have not, here is a run down.

This guy is about 6 foot even. Weighs about 101 pounds… Has fuzzy stringy mousy brown hair puffed out in the back. And, a stupid as hell set of bangs that Karen talked him into on the front. A pair of pop bottle bottom glasses. Big ass ears… And, a hump in his shoulders! Kinda guy you would expect to have a slide rule in one back pocket. And, a triple beam in the other!

With Tony and Tim in the same room, The I.Q. is about 250. Tony is one of the smartest men I ever known of course. But, he has Horse sense. Tim is way out there on Mars some fucking where when it came to responsibility! Cheech Marin said: "Responsibility is a heavy responsibility, man!" He was fucking right! When Tim walked, his hair would stand straight out behind him as if he were moving at 100 miles an hour. Which most times he was…

He has this idea that the house they lived in is Haunted. Which of course it is! Every house in this area is Haunted by something or another. Hell, Rick burned out the front foyer of the Mt. Nord house. Because he thought he saw a Dracula figure looking down at him from the top of the rounder stairs that took you to the tower top on the front of the old Mansion. It is a $25 a week rooming house at this time. He lit up the fire to burn the fucker out of the house for scaring his girl friend Dianna. When they all returned from Pensacola… guess who was pregnant?

She was not doing well that way. So, she moved home with Pearl and Homer at the trailer court they owned outside of Springdale. And, worked at the News Stand in the day time… Then drove her Bonneville over to see Rick nightly...

We are all kinda scattered out from that Florida trip. But, like after the big bang. Our planets are coming back together to reform the GAVENCE FAMILY.

Last summer seemed 10 years ago. It's so very different! Speaking of, What happened to? I went to the post office the other day and checked General Delivery. Guess What I found there waiting for me! A letter from of all folks… Tad and his new wife… Shelly! UN BE FUCKING LEAVE A BULL!

They lived in London for 5 months. And, now live in Amsterdam. They run a sex shop and theater downtown next door to a hash bar. I was worried about Tad, RIGHT! How stupid. He is in his element there.

This place would have been to slow for him. Remember Joe? He is in a *Turkish Jail* for the rest of time! Couldn't happen to a nicer guy!

OK, we are sitting in Tim's living room listening to the Moody Blues. Tim has a real nice stereo. It's made from a Public Address System, more than a stereo. That's one reason why I liked um. He has two Voice of the Theater® A-7 reflex folded horn speakers. So big you can climb into them from the back.

He has an ORANGE® 500 watt per channel amp in stereo phase through a Harmon Kardon 24 band EQ, With a *Dual*® 1200 direct drive turn table and a new fangled thing called a *Cassette Deck*.

Every great album you could think of from. "Blodwin Pig" to "Quick Silver Messenger Service"… He has this stereo set up in the dining room of the basement apt they live in. and, could only crank it up when the old bag up stairs was at her sister's house in *PettyGrew*.

She is gone for the entire spring break, Lucky deal for sure. "Days of future passed" is sounding like the group is in the dinning room. Everything in the living room is dancing around on the shelves and such when *Zap!* The stereo shut off and grey smoke with the smell of ozone is heavy in the air. Now, what pray tell could have happened?

Just as the guy in the Moody Blues hit that friggin high note at the end of the first day passage, the whole damn thing blew sky high! Flames were shooting out of the amp as we entered the room. What in the hell did you fucking do! I didn't do nothing man! The guy was singing and BLEWY! I think the heat pots are blown! No, it's the damn heat sinks… The fucking WHAT? The friggin HEAT SINKS! Do you do dishes in THE HEAT SINK? What in the fuck are you talking about?

I let them argue as I turned to see what everyone else was doing. I could have sworn I saw something move in the back porch area! A misty looking thing kinda! I looked all around the room. And, there was nothing there. What in the hell? I could hear someone in there. But, nothing! REAL-LY! Someone was moving around or something! Even though I was right there in the room, I still could hear it! Sounded like it was behind the wall of the porch pantry! There is a thumping sound behind there. I knew of course that there was nothing back there but DIRT! It looked like there may have been a door there once. But, not in a longtime! Still, something was back there!

"DON... HEY FOOL!"

"What!"

Tony said: "Are you hiding out or something?"

I said: "No man! I thought I saw someone in here!"

"That's Porky!"

" Who? PORKY!"

We call him that because of the lack of any thing else to call him! If ya get a good look at him, He's a fat ol Floater! No telling where he came from. Just hangs around.

"Sure! Bullshit!"

"Well you just saw him didn't ya?"

"Well, I saw something, yeah! But, I didn't see it working here!"

Do you know what I mean! Digit!

Tim says: "Well, something is about to start in here. Your presence is required!"

Tony says: "Ah, Don, is there something bothering you? You look out there all ready! You Ok!"

"Oh Yes Tony... I'm very alright I think. I feel like a pin cushion. You could stick a thousand pins in me right now and I would feel nothing at all."

As the smoke cleared... Tony, Tim along with Mike who had just arrived was all over it. Tearing down this and that and this and that... I knew they would have it figured out soon, they always do.

I see the headlights of a car come into the room from the parking space in the street above. The lights cross the walls and back out... It's a VW.

All of a sudden I felt this RUSH come over me! I ran over to the door and looked up the path. It's a VW alright. It's blue and carries the daughter of the old blue-hair that owns the place. She has come by to feed the cats. Good thing the stereo is on the fritz. I felt that rush melt away. I realized what I was feeling. But, she has a boyfriend and that is that! Now let's get back to the evening.

About this time the lady took off. At the very time she cleared the street, the stereo came back on with a super loud! "*POP*" That shook the building, out rang Grand Funk Railroad's "Heart Breaker" at about 500 watts. We started to dance, jump up and down. Roll around on the floor and freak out. When Tim jumped up and said: "IT'S TIME!"

He ran off into the bed room. Came out in a Wizard's suit Complete with the pointy hat and all… A crystal ball on a silver plate with 15 communion glasses around a crystal gravy boat in the middle with some sort of blue fluid! Now, I wonder what that could be.

He took us over to the big as hell Walnut Dinning room table that is at least about 200 years old for sure. We all sat down around it. He went over and put on this tired as hell sitar music from the mid 60s, came over and sat down crossed legged on top off the table sort of in the middle. Started to pray some weird deal in tongues… Then filled each communion glass to the top with the blue stuff...

He sat one in front of each of us, as there are that many people here now. Bonnie and her sidekick *Zelda* have dropped by. It's looking like something Cosmic is about to happen. There is *Magic* in the air for freakin sake. I could feel it like I was tingling. I'm still Dizzy from the Cross. God! What is wrong with me! This is just too much!

I guess it's about seven or eight o'clock by now, not daylight savings time yet, but the days are a bit longer. The sun went down in the front window as we drank from the glasses.

Tim said another few words: we went back to the stereo and waited to start to get off on the blue stuff!

We are all talking at the same time about every fuckin thing in the fucking world when I get up, go over to the turntable and take that sitar crap off, then replaced it with *Firesign theater® "Please Pass the pliers! Or, please don't crush that dwarf"*

Bonnie is lying across my lap in the middle of the room. Laughing her ass off till she is about to pee her panties, she ain't wearin No panties! Not just Tee Hee laughs. Big HA, HA uncontrollable, back slapping laugh's. So am I. It is incredible!

All of a sudden I noticed I'm getting off real freaking heavy! The walls are breathing. There is a ringing echo in my ears. A deep rumble from inside of me… There is a Strawberry Blonde beauty laying on me. *LSD* in me! Turn on, Tune in, Drop out! Yes… Sir!

Bonnie is squeezing my thigh harder every time she gets tickled! I will most likely have bruises there in the morn! I hope… Hurts so good! Man, I don't know what kinda Acid this is, or if that is what it is at all! But, it for sure is KICKING my ass!

Bonnie is almost crawling up inside of me. She is clutching on to me so hard, she is REALLY getting off! HARD!

I looked over at Tim. He is looking back from his perch on the table scratching his *Goatee*. He looks like the RED DEVIL! He is looking at me smiling saying with his eyes. Get ready Motha Fucka! You ain't seen nothing yet! I swear I can see horn's growing from his forehead right before my freakin eyes!

As we are getting off. More and more… Laughing our ass off at everything that moved no matter what it was. I realized that this is some very, very heavy acid, I mean real fucking good and clean. Not much strychnine, so the colors are kinda strange. But, I'm seeing more shit than I have seen since the last Owsley I did not so long ago.

Laugh, laugh, I thought I'd cry. It seemed so simple to me. Cry, cry, you want to die, cause life ain't what it used to be.

Bonnie had stopped squirming around across my lap, she is pushing her head into my lap harder as she is getting off harder by the minute. Not laughing so hard now. She has begun to cry a little. I can feel her crying inside of me! She is hugging my waist tight as she turns her face to look into my eyes so deep, I could feel her inside my head. I'm felling almost scared inside. I'm shaking a bit I'm noticing. She looks at me deeply for another minute or two.

And, then she said this: "*Don*"

I knew not to speak. As she said: "*I do believe that you are in love…right NOW…like you never thought you could ever be! I know it feels so funny when you feel her around you. You don't even know who she is! Even if she is not there, you see her in every crystal spark in the corner of your eye as you turn to see who is behind you.*"

My eyes are open so wide at this point, they are about to fall out of my head.

As she said: "*I saw it in your face when I walked in.*"

I said: "What did you see?"

She said: "I didn't see you in the middle of the action as the center of attention like always."

I retorted: "Center of attention! What do you mean?"

"Don't get freaked out Don. You are an Entertainer. It's your job to entertain everyone around you all the time. We look to you for it. Those of us that know a trooper when we see one… Also, know a second hand story. When we hear one!"

Listen Don… She squeezed my hand tight to her cheek.

She said: "*I feel very close to you when I am with you, or not!* When you went with that Fuckin Ann girl to California… It almost *broke my heart!* Not that you went with Her, Because, *I saw a vision that night*, it was all about what we are doing right now. Or, what I hope we all will do very soon! I can't lie to you… I am very much in *Love* with you. There is NO doubt of that."

She went on: "*I would like you to be in Love with me!*"

She drew in a large breath of air as she choked a bit on the tears she has running down her face!

She says: "*I know you are not in love with me.*"

Bonnie has a way of shocking you into the real world with the things she feels strong about. She will wait till times like this to confront you, she knows then she has your full attention.

She said: "I feel a love between us that is wonderful to behold."

She felt a kinship with Terry too.

She said: "That Terry and I playing together is inspired by the muse of melody. Even though in the future, many others will come and go, it will always be you and Terry as the center of the group that counts."

I was lost in her eyes and could not turn away from her stair. I was recording every word she is saying into my memory from later closer perusal!

She went on: "I think I know who has stolen your heart, I'll leave it at that for now. But, I'll always hug you, kiss you, and love you as much. No matter what happens… As long as…*I Live!*"

This is a real drama trip coming up. I always trip on the kinda mood I am in when I start to get off. Bonnie always shook me up when she looked into me with those piercing eyes. She is so serious when she is talking to you! Five people or a hundred in the place… when she talks to you, it is like no one else is there. We have a very special love, everybody knows it! We don't even care!

Bonnie grabbed me as we were about to move our trip out into the street. She pulled me aside, kissed me so deep and hard, I could feel her all the way to my toes.

She blew a warm moist breath in my ear and whispered: "She lives upstairs from me from time to time, her roommate leaves about noon every day. Come by my room around 1 pm tomorrow. I'll tell ya if she is up there. Then she kissed me deeply again. Her lips are trembling. Warm. Soft and so sweet! I swear they taste like a sugary sweet honey. Her tears are salty and soft to the tongue. Every part of her tastes like woman!

WOW, I'm Tripping my ass off!

Ok, we are all standing around in the living room about to head out to the *Cross*✝. We thought we would just walk up there, as it is just around the bend from where we are. Good place to start the evening out.

Everyone came by there of an evening if they had a ride, maybe she would come back. About that time I stopped kidding myself. I can feel it! I am in LOVE! It's quiet in the place, everything is turned off and we are walking out when... Bang, crash, bam, shatter, blam, crackle boom.

We looked back towards the dinning room. There is flashing light in there again. We thought the stereo was blowing up. But, that is turned off. We all ran back in there and to our amazement, all of those communion glasses had been thrown hard as hell at the stone fireplace in the corner of the room!

Now, I thought someone was havin fun with us. But, there was no one in there, No one! We are so freaking high by this time. We all looked at each other and just like in Animal House. We went screaming up the landing to the street and freaked out all the way to the *Cross*. ✝

There is a bunch of people there, not her though. As we got closer I noticed that Rick was sitting on top of the Cross. He had climbed up there while he was just starting to get off. He is tripping so hard. He has to hug the thing to keep from floating away or something! I'm walking around like my head is 3 feet above my body and is a balloon tied to string from the collar of my shirt. The Cross ✝ is pretty Huge. As, I stood at the very bottom of it looking up, it looks limitless.

Sitting on one side is John Palomisano. On the other side is Jerry Montgomery. A Nam Vet kinda new to town. Picture Jimmy Buffet in camo. That's Jerry! Super ego! That didn't set well with old John! He's flipping bird shit at him.

Below this Cross is a shit load of trees. Then another street... Then, more trees, another street. More, trees then a long drop to the bottom a couple a hundred feet below. Then, a big old water tank...

It is IN those trees just below us. It hadn't been used for water in years. It's a crash pad and a devil worship deal we were told. Didn't know though, we didn't hang with those people anymore. To freaky for us!

Well, an hour or so had gone by. People had come and gone. We were still sitting around up there watching the town lights twinkle and the stars pass over when that guy Gordon Hitt showed up.

You won't believe what happened next.

Chapter Twenty Nine

"And Now... Here he is!
Gordon Hitt!"

I guess we are the people that he could not bullshit. Or, hypnotize. So, he had to show us just how cosmically special he was. What he was about to do, is still discussed to this very day. Around the pipe, And, Campfires!

Is it real? Or, is this just a part of a ribbon of time. That, lattice of coincidence that hangs over these kinds of random scenes!

I just looked up and shook my head like it would go away. And, the boogie would be gone when I looked back. Yeah! Sure! Dig this!

Gordon Hitt walked back to the front door of the office of the Christian Camp Grounds about 200 feet behind us. He started running as fast as he could. When he got to the stone wall around the Cross,

He fucking............*JUMPED!*

He spread out into a perfect swan dive. "Head up to the gods!" As my Phys-Ed teacher used to say. It would have pulled all tens if it had been diving competition. He fell with such graceful calm. Then he just disappeared into the trees below. As we watched with jaws agape!

We heard limbs breaking! His! And, the tree's I would expect. Crash and boom all the way till he hit the water tank and bounced up into view again. The full tone of a well tuned timpani drum from the top of the old water tank, along with a PERFECT "Lindy flip" fer Christ's sake!☺

He kinda just hung there in mid air for what seemed like… 15 minutes. Then, he spun around and dropped out of sight again. Rolled and crashed all the way to the bottom we figured.

We figured RIGHT of Course! What a mess.

Rick is so freaked out, he almost fell off. He is hanging on like he too is about to fall. They put sharpened spikes in concrete up there to stop the fuckin birds from sitting there and crapping all over the thing. We had to bend them over weekly. Or, have a perforated ASS! Tore up a lot of jeans there…

We didn't hear no cops coming or anything. So, we just went back to Tim and Tony's. We piled into Paul's car and *Bonnie's Mustang*® headed to the WALL to see what kinda trouble we could start down there.

Bonnie dropped us off at the WALL, took her car back up to the "Lafayette House" parked it. Grabbed some weed. And, walked down to the WALL with Zelda hand in hand… They stopped for some Kissing on the corner. I don't know. Zelda has some kind of spell over Bonnie! I don't like it either!

Tim is higher than the rest of us. He took a bit more than the rest. He is way the fuck out there on some kinda Jesus based rage. Where he is sure he is the Jesus. He needs to go and find some Razorback Hog kinda fuckers and show them the real way!

It didn't take him long me Droogies!

Tony said: "He should stay here with the rest of us so he would not get in trouble again!"

Didn't work though, a few minutes later he was sitting naked in the middle of the Dickson Street, chanting something about how we all needed to find the light."

He said that a couple a hundred times, jumped up and cleared the WALL. With one jump, headed for Old Main… Neesh-keet!

The WALL is packed with partiers looking for some crazy shit to do. Everybody is tripping hard. Seemed there is a bunch of this "Clear Light Blue Window Pain" acid in town all of a sudden. It is so fucking trippy. Everyone is on the same trip and looking for trouble.

"DOUBLE FUCKIN TROUBLE!"

I always like to abide Of Corse! I'm ready to start some serious shit too!

We came up with a secret code word for when… and, if we needed to pounce on some poor UN-knowing son of a bitch out here in the streets. Terry says: "SHIT IN THE HAT, pull it down over your ears."

I said: "What in the fuck is that supposed to mean?"

He says: "I know, it's more than one word!"

"What is it man?"

He says: "It's the FUCKIN *Secret Pass Word Ass Hole!*

Mike B. says: "We is Trippin here Remember! Give me a fuckin Break!☹"

Oh… Ok, now where were we?

The horns on our heads are all up and sharp! Bonnie and Zelda came back to the WALL in these "Boner Springing" nude, see-through, leave ABSOLUTELY nothing to the imagination. NUDE colored leotards…

They both are wearing feathered hats. Have multi colored boas around their necks. *Barefooted, Naked, Beautiful Strawberry/blonde Women* with absolutely NO inhibitions at all! Wonderful, God sent Creatures of the night! How! I ask, *HOW I'm I so freaking lucky to be here?*

What did I do right to be allowed to exist here with all of these Outrageously Wonderful FREE people? Is this what this Hippie thing is all about? Did I say that? I didn't say that! I didn't even think it….. I think! Therefore: I am! I think? Therefore: I must be, I think.

Tony said: "Tim is too FUCKIN high to go off by his self, He will just get hurt again. We need to kind a go up on campus and look around for him, see what kinda shit we can get into while we are looking for him. At least, we could find some cool make out spots up thar."

I knew what he and Debbie Sue have in mind! I looked around for Karen. I had not even thought about her since Tim ran off. She is pacing around being consoled by Bonnie and Zelda. Don't worry Honey, we will find him! Just have fun till we do. You stick with Zelda and me till then.

Somehow we all kinda got split up into groups of two and five. We kinda started playing grown up hide and seek. Terry and I, along with Mike, John & Jerry were looking for some shit to get into. Looked like the five of us were sneaking for some reason…

Bonnie and Karen, Along with Zelda… And, now Sarah, Are playing spades in the middle of the service road behind Old Main. That's right! Tripping, Playing freaking Spades! Go figure!

John came running over, grabbed me by the t-shirt and said: "I spotted a bunch of guys in a class room, just off of the main building at the Sports Center. I think they might be Razor Back football players. But, I'm not sure."

His face is pure white. His brain is squirming like a toad. When I grabbed um and told um to calm down a bit. He pulled free.

Turned with a shot and said: "Let's get them Bastards! I have a plan….. Now Dig This Me Droogies."

We all huddled around as he laid it on us. This is the actual plan as it was.

He went on: "We sneak up in the bushes, then form a single line at the windows where they are sitting. At, the same time we jump out and provoke them so they will burst out. Then, chase us all over the campus.

That outta be good for some real laughs! If we get caught… we can have fun rescuing each other! It will be a real HOOT!

I said: "Shit in the Hat, Pull it down over your ears. Is that right?"

He said: "Yeah… some shit like that will do! Don't bother me with that whimsical bull shit!"

Terry and I looked at each other.

We said: *"Whimsical Bull Shit!"*

He said: "COME ON! Let's fuckin Go!"

So Terry, Rick and I. watched through the bushes a few minutes to see what they are really doing. Looked like they are deep in Foot Ball player must do school work.

We stepped out of the bushes, slowly moved towards the windows. And, took up our pre picked positions till the light caught our image...

As they looked up one by one at this Rag Tag group of Mysterians assembled outside their class room windows in the Dark, they would for sure freak.

But, they didn't move!

It's like they are frozen in the head light's of a 54 Chevy pickup or some shit. So, I pulled out my Brand new Deer Knife and held it up to the light so the outline sparkled at them.

I said in a full mid toned voice: "Hey Mother Fuckers, ya want your shit packed?"

A Dead quiet few seconds went by as we looked at each other... as they did.

Then like an *explosion*. They came out of that room like Mad Hornets. We jumped about ten feet in the air, came down in the full reverse run position, and took off like Road Runners in a blast of FIRE & SMOKE, With 20 Giant foot ball players chasing us at Full Tilt Boogie!

They're getting kind of close. I Hollered: "SCATTER"

We went off in twenty five different directions all at once! Not bad for five guys ya know! 25 directions at once... Try that sometime. It's hard on the ass, let alone the brain! We Left them standing and circling up the wagons in front of the Engineering Building scratching their melons!

From the bushes we started throwing anything we could get our hands on at them. The girls are still sitting there playing cards! They didn't even notice a thing.

Tim comes out of nowhere, looking like he is about to Cross some finish line. Dig it! He looked like a stick figure with long stringy hair flowing behind him in Giant oversized tennis shoe's like in a cartoon! His arms in full swing from head to hip! 8 foot stretch between steps on the ground, if he ever touched the ground that is!

Great Googalee Moogalee! This is some fucking good LSD!

As Tim ran by us, he is in a full soul arch. He ran out of the hedge. He just flew across the service road like his feet were not even touching the friggin ground. Wow! *What a Race!* Behind him coming up fast, is his own shadow in the Sodium light as he runs under it.

His shadow caught up with him, then passed him by till it is stretched out ahead of him... and, gone!

In that shadow is a vast number of Tims running in order of Red, Blue and Yellow. I'm reminded of that scene when I am working with multi leveled video sources now! The trails behind him are all the way back to the football guys. They are reaching out to grab at them thinking the shadows are him! This allows Tim to gain some ground. And, for us to catch up just like the cowboys that have been waiting for the bait to run the good guys through the pass, to find us there ready to fall upon them. Then just wipe them out!

We are catching up when... *Tim stopped like Rocky Rococo was standing in front of him in the way. Tim jammed on his brakes. And, stopped on a dime... Unfortunately, The dime was in Mr. Rococo's Pocket at the Time!*

The football players are coming up fast, we are just behind. We had no idea that Tim had stopped and turned to take them all on! They came to a stop at the 1927 section of the student grad walk. Tim is just standing there as we snuck up behind these creeps and got ready for the old T-bone play when he said: "Stop! Stop! Stop my Children!"

He went on: "I say to Thee this day that I have COME! In the morn ye shall find total Salvation and truth in thy ways! The path you seek will become clear, that you should line up for Slaughter you fucking Squealing fucking Pig Fuckers! Thee are a walking testament to why thy Mothers should have demanded your Daddies wear their Jimmy Hats! So, on your friggin knees you Sons a Dog Fucking Bitches!"

He then stood in a cross stance, bowed his head like he had just been Crucified! He had them going there for a minute, till their slow minds caught up to what he was saying! We are laughing our ass off in the bushes.

By this time, Tony has come running. And, told us what Tim did to get them after him, and not US.

About mid-way from the sports center, they had started chasing Tim after he mooned them at the Planetarium. Called them all sinners of the highest degree... And, then pissed on the picture of coach, giving him the finger! That was all it took to get um real Pissed! Kinda like Ozzy pissing on the Alamo fer Christ's sake.

Now, Tim is headed off campus to Dickson Street. After he would hit there and down the street, every freak on the WALL would be all over their ass.

It is different here. The freaks... And, Nam vets. Not Hippies. Are the street people! The freaks are mostly Nam vets. And, would be murderers that couldn't bring themselves to do it unless provoked! Looking like a Hippie in the South was all you needed, to start any number of fights! Wow, Dig it!

We went to places all over the area Hippies did NOT go for that very fear! We thought it is our duty to bring the Hippie cheek turning mind set in the area to an end! When we got restless, that is what we did. Got our ass kicked too! But, we sure changed their minds in the long run. Before long they All looked just like us.

Although this scene has my head spinning like a TOP on a motor bike. I mean, Saturday night is alright for fighting, ain't it? Elton says so! We just could not leave it at that! The others are trying to figure out if their ass is on fire. Or, is all this the most outrageous load a shit you ever seen?

What in the hell are you fucking talking about! I'm just about lost! How about you me Droogies? Where is this all going? Anybody know?

Now, I want all of you to pay very close attention to what I have to say! Don't be blinded by these Razor Back football players mistrust of you here weird-Os. They just don't understand your urges!

God Damn It! Who's urges are we talkin about here?

I looked over to see who it was that had stopped the noise. And, had everyone paying such close attention… Or, I don't believe this!

It is a Cocker… with Red and White spots sitting on the middle of the WALL. He has a Red bandanna around his neck that made him stand out from the other 50 mutts and cats named… Acid, Or Hash… Some kinda Stupid crap like that. At least it was just pets. In later years, these same freaks would start naming their children these names!

The Cocker has another dog sitting next to him with a Blue bandanna on.

What the FUCK… The other dog is… Spanky! He has an Ammo Belt around his middle. A flag that says *"Foot Ball players Eat SHIT!"* waving from his tail… He is pacing back and forth behind the Cocker.

Every time the Cocker says something Profound! Spanky jumps up on his hind legs and starts to get the crowd all riled up! Then, when they calm down the Cocker continues.

Now… this is a dog talking here.

He said: "I think you should consider the fact that you should not just let these asshole Football players get away with this shit! It doesn't matter where. Or, what we doggies are doing. These football butt holes are always fucking around! Soon, these fascist assholes will think its OK to just come right the fuck up and kick the shit out of any little cutie pie doggies in the streets like me and old Spank here! Remember this… Me brother dogs… And, Kitty Cats… *"Stray dogs that live on the highway run on three legs!"*

As he said that, he turned and did a slide to stage right.

Then Spanky came up and said: "We are available for Weddings. And, gatherings of any size." Then he rattled off their phone number and they all started firing off their M16s in the air.

About this time, Bonnie is pulling on the back of my shirt.

She said: "What in the FUCK is going on here… Anyway?"

I said: "That Spanky. And, his new Buddy Rex there… Had riled up everyone to go off and do…"

Bonnie is looking straight into my eyes. And, holding me by the shoulders saying: "Snap to... Come on sweetheart. Snap too."

I stopped and looked at her. Then I turned my head in what seemed a complete circle.

Then to my surprise, I noticed that I was the only one there except Bonnie! Spanky is sitting at my feet, Sound asleep!

I stood up and looked down Dickson. And, back up it to the campus. Nobody, nowhere! It is so quiet: "I can hear the Dickson Street train all the way in Springdale, coming this way!" That train runs at 5:30 am. It was just after midnight a few minutes ago.

Bonnie said: "You are pretty fucking stoned ain't yas? YES... I do believe you are toasted! What to do? Ah! I know, just the FUCKING ticket!"

She has her arm around my shoulder walking me over to her place at the Lafayette house. I had been there looking out into space for over three hours! Now, this is good acid. Nobody even fucked with me. Or, I don't think they did. I would like to think that Spanky, with his M16 would have taken care of me.

She said: "Sure. Shhh! don't worry about it Sweetie. I think he took real good care of you!"

Spanky is allowed in anybody's house. Or, place anywhere. He is always super clean. Unless, he had just rolled in a pile a cow shit. Everybody loves him as much as I do. When we would get somewhere, they would answer the door and say: "Don and Spanky are here! Come on in you two and have a J!"

Most dogs are parked outside by a tree. But, Spanky is one of the crew and he knew it. He would stand behind anyone of us at anytime no matter what! When I would find my spot to sit wherever we are... Spanky would sit. Or, curl right in front of me no matter what. That way... you had to go through him. To, get to me! *That was not a good idea.* He is a real gun toting bad ass if ya fucked with him.

We got to Bonnie's pad and went in. The sun is just starting to come up. It seemed that old Paul has left us a little surprise at Tim's house. There were fifteen of us there when the night started. He had promised a surprise. It is two racks of REDS he had scored at the Cross that evening. That's 14 REDS to go around. So, everyone would have great days sleep. And, be refreshed that evening.

Bonnie had grabbed mine, as I was not there.

Tony said to Bonnie to give me mine.

She said: "Hell y'all! I'll give it to old Don alright!"

Tony said: "Right! Where the hell is Don?"

Last time I saw him, he was at the WALL with Spanky, playing some game. I'll go down and get him. I'll be right back. Of course, we never went back there.

We were inside of Bonnie's pad on Lafayette. She went out to the bathroom, started a big tub of water. Then to the kitchen for a pot of Tea, She came back into the front room. I was going thru the records. Nursing a cold coke and looking for a record to put on. She turned on the air conditioner, locked the front door and disappeared to the little kitchen in the back.

She hollered out to me to come in the kitchen, I went in there. Standing in front of the kitchen sink is Bonnie, wearing nothing but an apron. I have a heavy affection for Creamy Skinned Women!

Now, at first I was not shocked by this Beautiful Woman to be naked here in front of me. I had been skinny dipping. And, in a few tubs with Bonnie before... She is always a perfect LADY in such matters. So, I didn't expect anything out of the norm.

I said: "Bonnie... You are a beauty to behold. Is that tub a hint?"

Well, we both have a very bad case of LSD dirties... You more so! Peee you! I think you Must have rolled in the cow shit this time. I looked myself over and did a pit sniff! Not that bad.

All of a sudden I noticed that. I have a tee pee in my pants! There is this new rush of *Horny* coming over me as I watched Bonnie make the Tea. In the background is the sound of the tub filling. And, the stereo in the other room... Bonnie came over, poured a glass of Tea for us both and sat down.

We just looked at each other kinda goofy for awhile. Then, drank the Tea... She stood up, came over behind me, lifted my nasty ol t-shirt over my head. She tossed it in the clothes pile where her nightly wear was also laying. She turned me around on the chair, reached out and slowly pulled me up by my hands. Then reached down, unsnapped my jeans, slid them down and off.

I was really surprised at how aroused I am. We sat back down. She showed me what Paul had left for us.

I said: "Wow, That is the surprise! Out of sight!"

She reached across the table, sat the RED on my tongue and one on hers. Gave me a sip of Hot Tea to wash it down, she did the same.

I found that we were kinda walking backwards to the tub. She is kissing me all the way there all over. Now, what did she have in mind? After all, as I remember, I had seen the Light at the Cross that evening! I was thinking of what I would have to do to find out more about her. I knew who she was after all, boyfriend too. But, that is about it. I needed more information about Jocelyn.

But, what is it that old Stephen Stills says: "LOVE THE ONE YOUR WITH!"

Well, that is how Bonnie is looking at it! I'm just so tired, so hung over and on the edge. All I really wanted to do was kick back! But, not Bonnie! Nope! Not Bonnie. She knew that the minute she showed me where Jocelyn lived. That would be how they say... That!

She was not wrong either.

She climbed into this Absolutely Wonderful warm and bubbled up big assed out of sight Tub. She pulled me in.

Then I started to notice that the RED was kinda hitting me. Soon I would be a Goner! Reds always hit me hard. Most times within the first hour of taking it. There is a certain amount of speed in the acid. I was still waiting for that to turn off when. Bonnie started to wash my back real slow. From the top of my spine all the way down to... well you know!

I'm lying back in the middle of her two Big Full breasts with the Pinkest Nipples I had ever seen, standing out at least a foot. Sitting between her legs as she started kissing the back of my neck! Now, Jimmy is gearing up to start drilling for oil or sompthin! He has broken the surface from the arch I'm in from the chills running down my back.

I swear that water is warm, almost hot kinda. But swear to God: "I can feel Bonnies heat and her chills through that water right into me." It is unbelievable! Tell me Droogies, what would you have done?

I've slept with a bunch of girls and women in this town over the last year or more.

One girl told me as I was taking her home, that she is out to set some kind of a record for the most Dicks in one full day me Droogies! She is about 18 and ½ going on 15. Tight little red beaver! Right there in your face! What the fuck ya gonna do?

I asked her this: "Well, how many so far?"

"53" she said! With a Huge grin on her face, and who knows what else!

I said: "BOOGIE! Or, what's your name again?"

"Cassandra!"

"How many did you say?" I thought I was hearing things!

She said: "FIFTY FUCKING THREE Man."

I said: "FIFTY FUCKING THREE! That can't be right. Who do you think you are trying to fool honey?"

She pulled out a list of Signatures of each and every guy that had Poked her so far this day. It read like a Who's Who for Christ's sake. Everyone I knew, except me is on there! Some guys TWICE. And, THREE times!

One of them is John Polamisano. I don't think that guy is even human! He's a throwback to the Ice Ages, where he climbed off some freaking

Space Ship and froze in the preverbal fucking ice! Man, for a country guy Italian family type dude with a strong Hell's Kitchen New York accent. It's hard to believe he is from Joplin, Mo. Or, that his family goes way back to the days of the, Shangertanglia Family in Springfield!

Which Springfield? Take your pick! Bet there's one in your state too. That way it will feel more like you are in this story with us. A foothold in reality so to speak! Ha ha ha! I feel that as the reader, you are. I swear I saw you last night on the WALL with Danny!

Oh well… I told that girl that, number "FIFTY FUCKING FOUR" was not going to be me!

Bonnie said: "SHUT THE FUCK UP YOU WEIRD O. AND KISS ME YOU FOOL"

I guess I had been *Rambling* on Ur some shit like that. I was right back in Bonnie's arms in the tub. She had turned me over, pulled me close. We are stuck in a full deep embrace. From the way she had me pinned. I'm about as far inside of her as I can physically go!

Our tongues are as far down each others throats as we can stick them. The bubble soap has popped to clear water. Her body is dancing like a dream in that water. Floating up and down on mine, rubbing together like a couple of eels in heat! *I'm coming down fast! But, she is miles above me!*

We got out of the Tub and worked our way over to the kitchen table. She reached out and shoved everything off to the floor. She climbed up on the table with her elbows in back, did her best Bunny pose, and then slowly spread her legs. Her womanhood pulsated. Opening and closing as her face and body. Twist, and beg!

I could see all the way through Christmas into the New Year! Her breasts are heaving with every Hot breath she took, I'm UNDER HER SPELL! She has definite ideas on what she wants in the next hour or so. I'm just pretty much along for the ride! Good thing too. I'm Jelly in her hands by then! It didn't matter what I did, for the next how ever long. I am HERS! That's all there is to it! I don't know who taught her all this stuff. But, listen to this!

Bonnie climbs on top of me and slides me in as she says: "Surprise, I didn't know how to tell you! But, I am just a bit *KINKY*! So, hold on to your balls, because I am taking over this flight! Now, take me to the Captain"!

There is a whip in her hand, a pair of high heels on her feet. She says: "You gotta get down and dirty to see what these things look like after a bit of fire. Or, a small explosion!"

I said: "What are you talking about?"

She said: "I'm just kidding."

She kicked off the heels and climbed back into the bed where she had body flipped me. She still has that whip though.

She said: "You look like you could explode yourself, after you do that, what good will you be to me! I need some slow roll and boil! This may be our BIG night!"

I'm so fucked up. I'm no longer able to keep up with her. She is a Power Dynamo when it comes to sex. In a hurry she is not!

But, time is running down for full frolic, the reds are taking their toll on us both after an hour or so. After a lifetime of pleasure that she is right about, after that night everything changed, Everything! We lay back.

About three thirty pm, I woke up and looked around the room. Bonnie is in the kitchen making something. I just propped myself up on the pillows, thinking about what I could remember of how I got there.

If I remember correctly, we were all to meet back at Tony and Tim's place. Then we were to all get together, jam over at Stone and Hill house to see what we were going to play at that concert out in Savoy Saturday next.

Bonnie came back in the room, She climbed up my legs to where she is laying right on top of me. She has me in a scissor lock and is kissing me. When, she lay back.

She said: "Don, like I said at Tim's last night. I wish you were in love with me. I wish that more than anything in this world! The girl that has taken your soul is living with another girl. Her roommate leaves for class everyday around noon. I don't think she actually lives there. She just crashes there when she can't get a ride back home. Or, she needs to hide from some asshole following her around.

I said: "Ok, where does she live?"

Bonnie had a few tears running from her beautiful Blue-Green sparkling eyes as she pointed over her head and said: "Right above us!"

She chocked a bit and said again: "Right above us. That's right!"

I pointed: Right up there⊠?

The walls are very thin around here. Bonnie makes a lot of noise when she makes love. Not moans and squeals, there are those too. But, she likes to talk about stuff while you are shoving 5 pounds a meat in her woo hole!

Like: "Do you know that the capital of Georgia is Atlanta?" "Is it?" I wasn't sure!

"Sure is" She said! "Do you know what they are famous for in Atlanta?"

I said: "PEACHES!"

She said: "Nope... they are famous for that wonderful elixir...

CO- COLA®!"

I said: "Is that how they say it there?"

She said: How the fuck would I know, I ain't never been there."

We lay there in each others arms naked awhile longer. She held me so tight I couldn't breath.

She said: "*I love you.*" In soft sweet breath in my ear, "*Forever. And, forever! I don't care what happens ever! You just never know what will happen next, I'll be there when it does!*"

Let's see here. We slid through the shower, and then get dressed. All the while I was scratching my melon like I was missing something. Ur some shit! Bonnie runs over to me and jams a glass of Tea in my hand, an English muffin heavy on the butter, then she handed me a Bird Egg.

She said: "Eat the food first!"

"Ok Mom" I retorted.

You know what: I don't believe that Bonnie had gone to bed at all last night. I asked her, she said she just sat and watched me sleep till I started to move again. What is it you can't remember? I don't know. OH, SHIT! I was supposed to be at band practice last night, wait a minute, that can't be right! They must mean tonight! SHIT let's go!

Bonnie has already opened the door and shook her Mustang keys at me and said: "You drive."

I'm amazed: "Wow! Me drive, come on… you mean it!"

You see "Nobody" drives her Mustang®… Nobody!

She threw me the big assed Mustang key holder that had a little key on it… Away we went like a turd of hurtles!

We burnt rubber around to Dickson Street. Bonnie yelled at Zelda who is walking up Dickson to go to Bonnie's house: "Hold up Zel! We will make the corner."

Before her echo cleared Dickson… We are back around from Lafayette. SCREECH! The big ol Mach One® came to a halt! Zelda slid in, we is flying down Dickson again. Zelda is giving Bonnie this look as to WHY I am driving her car!

We approached University Avenue to make the left turn. When Bonnie grabbed the wheel… We went up onto the campus at speed Right thru the NEW red light! That's right, the New red light at the intersection!

Blew through that sucka like it was butter… the girls are up and sitting on the back seat. With Their long hair billowing in the wind! The streetlights are dancing off of them both as we drive under one after the next!

Zelda is a big girl, not fat. She is a "BIG" girl! That's all there is to it. 6 foot 2. And, 125 pounds of walking German Workmanship for sure. She could make a statue hard just by walking by! Huge giant firm up turned breasts that fell out of every thing she wore!

She looks like that big ol wrestling girl on the WWF. I felt like that ZZ Tops song. Where they are cruising in the car with a redhead in the front and two beauticians in the back Jack! God dang, I'm flying freaking fucking flipping high ass a camel's ass! It's the scene doin it to me, not the fucking "BIRD EGG" I forgot all about that! This stuff doesn't happen to people like me!

I am stomping that peddle to the floor on our way out to the NEW bypass. Over the NEW bypass bridge and out HWY 16 West.

We are cruising out to that outdoor church thing we are to play at in Savoy. Bonnie wants to get a look at it, she has an idea.

I looked over at Zelda and said: "Bonnie is pretty good at this stuff isn't she?"

Zelda said: "I couldn't say. Until <u>You</u> came along, she never even thought about this shit."

What shit are you talking about there Zelda?

All this band shit.

What band shit?

She seemed upset.

She said: "Look Don… Just do what ever you are going to do! *Fuck her good.* And, make her fall in love with you. Hurt her! Go ahead…You Men always do whatever you fucking want anyway."

I lit up a Bomber as we cruised in the cool, cool breeze of the country night. Like it is in some kinda wonderful movie or something! My face is all aglow as is Bonnie's! Zelda knew we had been fuckin all night. Just by how healthy red… And, CLEAN we are!

I didn't notice at first how jealous Zelda got when it came to Bonnie. I would have been more in tune to her abilities! She taught me down the line NEVER to under estimate her. Or, ANYBODY!

Does this happen to everyone? Or, is it just me? This is Hollywood Movie stuff! The kind of stuff that never happens to a guy like me! These are Dreams that most time's NEVER come true! But, Here I am!

Women that are so far out of touch to guys like me, they just float by you. And, out of sight. I am driving a Brand New Mustang Mach One with two Beautiful Amazon women into what ever is next! HELL YES BROTHER!

We got there just as the moon is coming up. I looked over at Bonnie, who is back in the front seat now. She is smiling from ear to ear. Her aura is so clean and bright blue! I could see it cushion her from the air that is flowing over her. We pulled into the place.

She hopped out and said: "Stay here for a minute."

She snuck off into the place, looked a bit here and there. Went over and checked the power supply. Then, the size of the stage and how many folks would the place hold. She wrote all this down in her book. Off we burned back to town. Turned south on that NEW by pass, over to Hwy 62 then to Stone street, over to Hill.

This is a way I have never gone. Because, it was not there 2 months ago! Soon Wal❋Mart would take advantage of that!

Up the steps of the house and in the front door, I was about to say how sorry I was we were late, When Bonnie grabbed me and pointed to everyone else with a "They all just got here too look" I looked over at Bonnie and said: "You knew that didn't you?"

She reached back and pinched me on the cheek of my ass.

She said: "The fun is over now. Get to Fucking work Future Rock Star!" Over to the group I went.

She sat down and waited her turn to talk. That's when she brought up our trip to Savoy. She ran down what she felt we should be aware of and what to expect, we are all very impressed.

Tony wanted to know what the fuck happened to me last night. Nobody could find me. Bonnie and my eyes met and sparkled. It is our Secret Smile we share the rest of our time together.

Ok, where were we? Oh yeah! Everyone had their guitars out and their spot in the room to sit for the evening. Singers, players and groupies... Along with Steve, And, Kin! Dinner is on the stove. And, the Beer is very cold. Watermelon, out back later and a few left over Fireworks for around midnight.

We whipped out paper and pencil. Bonnie became the secretary of the night. She kept track of the songs we sang. She dumped the ones that sounded like shit!

She said: "Only play the ones that feel good while you are playing them. The Hell with the others!"

It didn't take long to put away the first set. Now, it's dinner time... Out to the kitchen we all went. Even though I'm speeding, I'm starving! The food is just wonderful. I put it away but good!

A new guy in town showed up as we were working on the next set. He had some new stuff called "PARTY TIME" malt liquor. About, 105 proof... He had two ice cold cases of the stuff in assorted flavors!

What the hell is this shit? He looked over and said: "University Party! Things are gonna change around here Hippie."

I looked at him with fire in my eyes and said: "I ain't no fuckin Hippie!"

Terry looked over at Tony and said: did he call Don a Hippie?

Tony said: "I do believe he did Terry!"

Terry stood up as did Tony to move way back to the back of the room.

Lonny said: "Why are you guys backing off?"

Terry said: "Well, that was the wrong thing to say to Don. So, out of the way is where to be" As he moved. So did her and Steve. The rest of the room went deadly quiet, like you are freaking deaf or sompin!

Rick spoke out, he said: "Oh, Shit! Now you've done it!"

I walked over to this guy. Climbed up on the coffee table and into his face… Flipped him HARD on the tip of his nose with the tip of my finger.

I said: ☠"Don't! Ever call me a Hippie! *I am not a Hippie*"

He said: "Oh yeah! Then what the fuck do you call your dorky self? You look kinda Slap Happy to me motha fucka!"

My eyes are about to burst out of my head when he said: "Nawh, Nawh. I'm only kiddin!"

I said: "To me my draft dodging friend. A HIPPIE is a cat or chic living with the fucking pigs, eating shit and garlic, having babies, and getting fucked ten times a day by the assholes that run the friggin place."

He said: "YOU! You are that guy that put on the Bogus Concert isn't ya!"

Ψ *Writers note… Remember I said: "That thing would come back to bite us in the ass!"* Ψ (Yup! I said that!)

Well, he made a double take, ran out the door and down the street yelling: "I know someone that is looking for you cock suckers… Real bad!" "Enjoy the Party Time…It's on me. Let me know If I can get ya's cases wholesale. Be back later"… is echoing up the holler as he made the turn at Center Street. You could hear his footsteps as he ran.

This is strange. As he had driven here! His motor cycle is parked in front of the house. So, why did he run off? What in the Hell is going on here? Who wants to see us real bad? Not Good!

About that time, we realized that the *Party Time*®. Is, really PARTY-TIME! The freaking walls are Breathing, Melting. And, turning all kinds of weird colors! These things are full of "ORANGE WEDGE" "OWS-LEY SUPER ACID!"

It is referred to as S T P… Not LSD.

The high is very intense! You would peak over. And, over again for three days, or, more! I had not seen any of that *Great acid* since our stop in San Fran. I mean, we slugged down those party drinks. They tasted like different flavors of fruit punch! Ice cold… And, good as hell!

So, we felt we were <u>doomed</u> for sure. Plus, who ever wanted to get their hands on us would have us at their mercy. We had to make a move fast! Who do you think came to the rescue?

No… Not Bonnie… (Shit!)

It is of all people… Lonnie! Steve's mom the witch!

She had a concoction potion #8 that tasted like total shit! But, it would reverse all the effects of that STP. Best part, it will make the speed better and make you bulletproof! "Anybody want some?"

We looked around at each other. I took the bottle and opened it. The smell would knock a *Buzzard* off of a _Shit_ wagon!

She said: "No shit man, there is buzzard shit in it!"

Lonnie… Have we talked about her in detail?

She is one Tall Drink of water my friend. As, beautiful as all the other most bitchin women I have met since I have been here. Come to think of it! There are only Beautiful women everywhere you look! I like it here! *A Lot!*

Her new boyfriend said: "He is a warlock from Nashville."

I said: "That a new music group?"

He said: "Not the Dead man! I am a WARLOCK!"

I say: "Oh, I get it! You Is a BOY witch. Is, that right?"

He said: "Lonny, where did these *bozos* come from?"

She said: "They are my very own Rock & Roll Band! Ain't they neat?" I won um. On… *MTV*… Good Acid! No Fuckin Shit!

Ψ *Writer's note. Now remember this me Droogies. "We are. Young, Dumb & Full O Cum! We have hair down to our ass at the time. The kind of hair that swings around as you turn… And, then frames your face in Youth. And, Confidence"* Ψ

Debbie Sue says: "_BOZOS!_"

She is sitting on the arm of the sofa next to Tony.

She looks at Tony and says: "That asshole don't know where he is… Do He?"

Her eyes are full. And, round. I have never seen her so Happy. Or, so High! Did I say that? Or, just think it? Shut…up Don! OK!

Tony says: "Well… Watch this shit" Rick & I… Did our world famous DOG SNIFF! All up & down that sucka! Ha! What fuckin fun!

He… Sat Down! Smart on his part… The abuse would have been EPIC!

Chapter Thirty

RIZZELSNORT ☯

It seems a shame to shut down this wonderful acid. But, the group felt something not good may be afoot!

Bonnie said: "She had see that guy at Gordon Hitt's house over on 71. She didn't know what he was doing there. He left so fast! Looked like he was giving Gordon a bunch a shit for stealing his bicycle… Or, some shit like that! I didn't like him then, I don't like him now!"

She reached over to Lonnie. And, took her #8 on the tongue, kissed Lonnie's hand… And, said: "Thank you!" She kissed her lips next. YUP!

Bonnie is one Unbelievable Lady! We all took the stuff. Sure enough! We never got off on the STP! But, better safe than sorry!

Well… The air is so charged with electricity you can feel it. The speed isn't bad either. I still think we might have got off a bit! But, we are so stoned anyway. Who Knew?

We are just about to wrap up "Teach Your Children" for the third time. When, Uncle Bob hobbled up the stairs.

He said: "I cruised the WALL looking for you guys. There seems to be some real ruff guys down there talking you guys down as a bunch a butt holes suckers for ruining that concert awhile back."

I looked at Bob… I said: "I think I have seen that one guy before somewhere."

He said: "Which one?"

"How many are there?"

Well, there are four. Or, maybe five of them at the WALL on Harleys, in black leather jackets… It says something about "*Galloping Gooses*" on the back. And, under that in the rocker panel it says. "OAK PARK, IL."

I looked at Terry who is scratching his head.

He looked at Tony and said: "The Gooses are a New Orleans club. Isn't they Tony?"

Tony said: "Last I checked!"

I asked: "Are you fucking sure about this Bob?"

He said: "Sure as I'm standing here now. They said to a bunch of girls that were defending your honor! That, Things are going to be different around here now. The brains have arrived! Pass the word!"

We all looked at each other. Stood up and said at the same time! "Let's get um!" Terry reminded us that this is "Our" fucking town! Nobody, no matter whom, is gonna change that!"

Chapter Thirty One

"Who's a street gang? US! Ain't NO way!"

OK… Bonnie is looking worried. Zelda is shaking her head too. Zelda says: "That's not what to do! Let's get um like we did before on those Kappa guys!"

Bonnie says: "Oh, you mean the ol… scouting teams deal to see just what we are dealing with." "*BATTLE!* I love this job!"

She said: "Exactly! Now, here is what we are going to do."

I have not seen Jocelyn since the Cross. No one had. She is stuck in Farmington. Her Dad ain't cool yet. She appeared to be grounded for some reason. Too friggin bad! I'm itching to see her again. But, I wasn't sure yet what I was going to do about it!

Out into the night we went. It's Covert Ops time. My favorite game for sure… Even in the Navy I loved that game. The Navy, the Navy. There is something in there. This puzzle is taking on more meaning by the minute. The Navy! What did that have to do with any of this anyway? I keep seeing that Navy Prison in the back of my eyes. And, that fucking guy, Oh well, let's go! Off we went.

We decided to go on a run around town in three cars, take a look around to see what we could see. We hauled it out to the cars. And, then jumped into Bobs Studebaker Hawk… The, Snakeç… and, Bonnie's Mustang… Bonnie is talking to Zelda. Next thing I knew. Zelda jumped into the Hawk. And, off they went. We all passed the WALL before going off in different directions. We are to meet back at Stone & Hill house to debrief around 10 o'clock. Or so!

Terry and those guys went out east Hwy 45. They had a lead on where these assholes might live. The Hawk is to cruise the main drags for their motor scooters! Bonnie and I would terrorize the entire area for the Dastardly Bastards!

Bonnie Threw the Peace Sign Salute from her heart to Capt. Uncle Bob! Did the same to the Snakeç Then we headed up west Dickson. Down the back road to Garland, Then, over to the Razor Back Burger for a Cherry Coke…

We pulled in… Parked…

The Hop came over. Took our order… Then, was off in a flash… We still had the top down. It's cool with little spots of ground fog. Plus, a full moon over the mountain... Bonnie is looking at me with this Devil & Angel look in her eyes.

She said: "I love to watch you Squirm! What say... (kiss) when we get our cokes...(kiss kiss) I spark up this fatty here. And, then you and I take a ride west of here just a few miles?"

I say as she is biting my bottom lip: "Oh yeah! What ya got in mind." She replies: "A little fact finding trip. You up for a ride in the wind in the Mach Dragon One."

I said: "Lay it on me baby!"

She said: "*Hang The Rich!*"

Then burned rubber four blocks down 6th Street! (HWY 62 west)

We passed out into the darkness. The stereo is playing "Darkness Darkness" as we flew passed the 62 Drive-in!

I watched the AMVETS go past in a blur! I looked over at the speedometer... It's at 102 miles an hour! The TAC is just floating a bit below the red. Like nothing out of the norm is goin on! She grab's 4th gear.

Like an after burner... We are going faster! I'm wrapping around the passengers seat like a snake. Like Rick taught me. Dark... Two lane country road, Full of Blind curves... Banked MOON SHINE curves.

When she laughed like a Demon! She looked at me. And, her eyes turned Bright Red just in the middle! The outside is bright blue-green to yellow sun flairs from the whites!

Hot damn! An *E* ticket ride... What's next?

We flew off the fucking ground! "*OFF THE FUCKING GROUND!*"

At least 4 feet. Sailed 1000 at least!

She powered down then said: "What's wrong man? You afraid of a little speed?"

In my best Cheech & Chong I said: "What man... You got some speed Man?"

She said in her best Cheech: "Ah what... Ah... No, Man! I ain't got no speed man!"

I said: "Oh. Ok!"

She said: "But, you know what I do got man? I got a joint man!"

Then she pulled out another bomber. And, hit the Ciggy lighter as she calls it. It glowed bright Red in the Moonlight. Her face is lit in warm Red and Orange as she dropped the speed to 70, then lit the Doob.

I saw the turn off to Larry Stapleton's house fly by. Now, I'm in virgin territory.

I said: "Just where in the hell are we going?"

Right then, the Farmington city limits sign went by. I felt the Shiver! OH GOD! I know where we are going. I haven't been this scared since I

~ 171 ~

was a little boy waiting on an ass kicking when my DAD got home. Bonnie took my hand.

She said: "Don, you are shaking. Calm down!"

I could see in her expression. She is very moved by my emotion. I felt like I could cry! I am flat Scared! Breathing fast… Sweating… Confused speech… Heart palpitations… I feel like I am about to *"Freak The Motha Fuck OUT!"*

As we entered Farmington, She dropped it down with a screech to 25 miles an hour exactly!

She said: "Don't ever go over 25 in this town. Speed trap!"

She said: "See that big white house we are coming up on at that curve. The one that looks like we are going to drive right into it?"

I chocked to clear my throat: "Yes."

She said: "You're True love lives… There."

"No shit!"

"Yup! Right there!" Ψ ψ ♥

As we pulled off of 62 onto Rhea Mill Road. We passed her drive way on down to the High School parking lot. We went by the house at about 1 mile an hour. The Mustang's header pipes are booming. And, thumping the air into submission… You know if anyone is in there. They, feel it.

She backed up onto the high school parking lot. Turned off her lights… But, not the engine, she knew that you could feel it even better from this far away… "*Exactly.*"

Bonnie! Wow. What, a gal-pal.

We watched the place for a few minutes.

I looked at Bonnie.

How in the hell she knew. Nobody knew, it just happened, it's weird! It just happened. How in the hell can you know about it. And, be so fucking sure. "Bonnie… who, are you really? Are you my guardian angel?"

She said: "Shut up! Watch the house. Not, me!"

That is the "*Farmington Animal Hospital*"

Her dad…

I broke in: "The guys name is Jimmy Hendrix"

She said: "That's Dr. Hendrix."

I said: "How do you know that?"

She said: "I take my cat and dog there all the time. I see her and her sister "Juli" out there working every time I go there"

I said: "So, are you saying. I should just go up there?"

She did retort: "No. No, not that. Do you think you can find this place now?"

I said: "You know it. I feel like it's home for Christ's sake."

We pulled out. I could feel the chill go down my spine. I'm squirming around and couldn't hold still. We are just barely moving. The headlights are lighting the west side of the two-story house. There in a window that looked like it was in the middle of a stairway is *Jocelyn*. She is looking out to see who is creeping around the place.

You know. The 50 dogs or so that are there, never even barked one time. That, I found in coming years was UN-heard of. There is more of that *Magic* in the air.

Bonnie stopped at the driveway. I just sat there looking up at her. She knows Bonnie's car. But, did she see me? She waved a beautiful "See you later" wave. I had a little tear running from my eye. Bonnie wiped it off with her finger at the stop sign.

And said: "God… you are in love heavy Don. If I had a camera here… I could take your picture for the Encyclopedia of Love cover."

I say: "Why did you bring me here Bonnie?"

She said: "Because *I love you too*. I want you to be happy."

I've never known if Jocelyn knew it was me that night. Because I like to think to this day that she did. So, I have never asked. Not to this day!

We drove back to Fayetteville.

She looked over at me. And, said: "You aren't going to pass out on me or anything are you?"

"No… I'll be OK."

She said: "Don. Let, me tell you how it is that I know about this."

Zelda and I were sitting on the other side of the VW at the Cross. I saw you and Paul pull out from Tim and Tony's. So, we followed you guys to see what was up. When you parked… And, Paul went off with the other guy. We noticed who was sitting in the VW. I was about to get out and come over to you. When, you turned and saw her! We saw her eyes meet yours. We saw a beam of bright blue light that went to each of you. Zelda looked at me. I at her! We nodded at the same time.

Zelda said to me: "He just got hit hard! There will be no getting away from what I just saw."

I said: "It hit her just as hard."

Zelda asked me if I was gonna be OK: "I told her Yes! Ill live with it, you never know."

Don, The guy she was with saw it too. That's why he drove off. Didn't come back… That's also why we never saw her again. He just took her home. And, "So, when you came into Tony's house, saw me there looking out the window to the street."

She didn't wait for me to finish the sentence.

She said: "That's right my beautiful long haired man! I already knew. That's also why I fucked your brains out all night!"

Now, let's hit the WALL and see what's what. What about the looking around we were supposed to do? Hell with it, Just fake it! Follow my lead.

I said: "Yowsa Boss! What ever you says Boss!"

You know… when, you and Paul drove off from the Cross. It was like we were not even there. There was nobody else there but us. That's how I knew."

I said: "What about last night?"

Bonnie said: "Like I said… Just a smile between us in passing."

I told her: "I would also always love her! No matter what… As, far as I am concerned, she is my saving grace!"

Then I leaned over. *And, KISSED HER!*

Before she got me first!

Everyone is at the WALL, talking up a storm. Seemed that Mike is not wrong, these assholes lived out Hwy 45 east on a hairpin curve in front of a Graveyard Out in the hills! We are all gonna head out there, *LET'S GO!* When, Danny came over, he said: that those guys were going back to Oak Park for two weeks. Then, move here for good"

I asked how in the fuck he knew all of this.

Danny said: "They gave him 20 bucks to go by and feed their Spider Monkey. (Sidney) Bad assed monkey!"

So, now we had an inside spy. We didn't see them again till we moved in with Patty. Good thing too. We didn't have time to mess with those psychos right now. We need to get ready for the concert. Raise some money. So, we will be ready to move into Patty's. When she comes back in a week, or so…

All of a sudden, I saw that it was getting kinda late. Where did the night go? I'm kinda worn out. The speed is no longer. Spanky is lying on the ground snoring! So, we just went over to the Grayhouse to our room to go night, night. It is good we still had it. I'm sure I could have gone home with Bonnie again. But, we had cleared the air on that. We are moving up.

She went home to *Duncan House.*

It is the first time in days I'm in bed before the sun comes up. The floor in my room is hard. Not like Bonnie's King size bed. But… it is not enough to keep Spanky and I awake. Off to la la land we go. What a fucking night!

I'm wakened by a *Slam! Slam! Fucking BLAM* on the side of the building just below my window. I looked out.

There is Tony and Terry. "Let's go get FREE Chicken!"

I said: "Where is Free Chicken?"

I looked at my watch, it said: 11:45 am. Then it says… "Don't bother me again!"

Man it is early!

Knocking on my room door at the same time is Carla.

I hadn't seen her in awhile. She has some Sweet rolls in one hand, a pitcher of ice cold milk in the other, a towel over her arm. That is about all. I said: "Well, well, well! I Ain't seen you in awhile." She says: "That's right! I been in Rogers, working at the Country Club."

"Oh! Is that right?"

I'm stumbling for something to say. When she came in, shut the door. She sat down Cross legged on my sleeping bag. She is for sure revved up about something. See, she is kinda dripping there on the ol sleeping bag. Looks like something is boiling down there!

I'm still fumbling for something to say. I could hear Terry and Tony coming up the back stairs to see what is holding me up. When, Muffin just leaped over on top of me. She, is holding me down, riding me like I'm a Bucking Stallion! Which of course…I am! Dig it.

She had locked the door with an ice pick, she would not budge. She had me down on the sleeping bag. She reached around, grabbed my dick. Said: "Use It. *Or, Lose It Buster!*"

I have my hands around her waist. I stopped her for just a minute.

I asked her: "You are hotter than a pistol inside, what's wrong with you?"

She told me: "A guy came into the upstairs apartment. Had some pills in his pocket, passed um out to three or four of us. They are Spanish fly."

I asked: "How do you know that?"

As her cervix swallowed the head of my *Jimmy*… and, would not give it back! She clamped down on it so hard! I thought I was gonna have to haul out a water hose. And a bar a soap! To get us apart!

She started pounding up and down so hard. She knocked the breath out of me. I'm hollering "HELP!"

Terry. And Tony are laughing their ass off in the hall. They sent her in here! They went down into the street so she could sneak in behind me. She didn't know what to do! She is so Hot! So, what the hell, I got the scratching job!

It didn't matter what I would have done. Carla had *RAPE* in her eyes. I had never been raped before! Didn't think you could Rape a man. *SHE RAPED ME GOOD!*

Who ever spiked these girls, Must have been a crazy. Because you don't spike Beautiful girls with Spanish fly. Then, leave them alone! You _FUCK_ their freaking socks off of their *friggin pink* feet!

That's what Spanky said as we woke up from the coma she put me in! It's 2:30 pm now. Tony. And, Terry had long disappeared.

It's Sunday ain't it, what are we supposed to be doing?

Carla said: "Man. I should have seen that one coming for sure."

She said: "I owed it to her. For running my best friend off with Tad! She… And, Shelly were very close. I could tell she missed her." You seem different Don. What's up?"

As I'm pulling on my pants, AGAIN! I noticed that Spanky is looking at me shaking his head.

He said: (*Now, this is a dog talking folks*) "Man: you are a piece a shit!"

I asked: "What's that all about Doggie?"

Spanky said: "You just let that girl come in here. And, Jump on ya! You should have heard all the huffin and puffin that girl was doin on ya. How disgusting! Next time you get *Raped*, how about cracking the door so I can go lay in the hall! Or, hit the kitchen. Or, some shit like that. Next time! OK?"

Wow…What a bitch!

Listen! Let's just face facts as they are! *I LOVE WOMEN!*

Everything about a woman just makes my blood boil. If I am sitting minding my own business, a woman walks by wearing little or nothing. Or, even dressed in a skin tight evening gown… Or, an Eskimo suit! All it takes is a woman's smell to set every nerve in my body off at once!

A naked woman is all it takes to make me putty! I had not yet met the woman that could steal my heart completely. I'm so moved by Jocelyn! It makes me Dizzy! I have never in my life been making love to a HOT pounding woman. And, saw the face of another! I thought that was all for them romance novels on the shelf at the airport.

But, even though Carla is pounding my poondalenny! It is Jocelyn standing in the stairway window I saw through the whole deal. I could not get her out of my mind! All I could see is her face. When, our eyes met at the cross. I'm not in LUST! I am in fucking LOVE!

I'm trying to figure out what it is I'm forgetting. If, anything at all… Or, what was I going to do with the rest of this Sunday.

Bonnie and Zelda drove up behind me. Zelda grabbed me, pulled me into the car. Bonnie shot off around Ark Ave. Then, over to Lafayette to her Party Pad! We got out. Went inside, there is Tony. Terry. And Mike, Plus, that FREE Chicken I had heard so much about a bit earlier. I'm as hungry as a Minor! I dug in!

As we ate and talked over the day!

I said: "Oh, thanks for the *Nymph-o* you butt holes. Why didn't you just fuck her yourselves? She would have fried both of your snuts! That Amazon woman was down right HORNY!"

Bonnie said with a Chuckle: "What are you talking about?"

Terry said: "That he got Raped! By that Carla girl… You know, Muffin?

Bonnie said: "It was…you she raped? What do you mean dear?"

"Oh, nothing!" Ha ha ha.

She is talking about it down at Rogers Wreak. She didn't say who though! I thought there might be some New meat in town. She looked at me. We both smiled that new *Secret* smile.

Tony said: "She looked a bit too Hot for his liking. But, I'm in love too!"

That wasn't nothing new! All you had to say was: "Debbie!"

He would jump Ten feet in the air. Then, just float back to the ground like a feather in a deep sigh!

I thought I was in LOVE in the past. I thought I knew exactly how it felt every time. It was never before like this. I'm still shaking when ever I think of her. All I can think of is what she is doing right now! Is she, sad? Is she, lonely? Oh Man! I got it *bad*.

As we finished this wonderful Dinner that Zelda and Bonnie had prepared for us, to make sure we all were there for what was next. Bonnie took the floor. She has the whole week lined out in her book.

Chapter Thirty Two

"We have a Director now...
Guess who?"

What book?

I said: "Bonnie has kind of been our manager for awhile now. That's OK with everybody isn't it?"

Everybody replied: "Shit yeah!"

Everybody agreed that Bonnie had Great ideas. She is a mover and a shaker. Very good at this kind of thing!

Born for it is how it look's to me say's Terry! Everyone.

Welcomed her aboard!

What she is going to lay out for us is way cool. It is what we needed. We are so caught up in the *Moment*. The *Music*... And, so deep in Love! We needed someone that had our best interest at heart. Then we could concentrate on the music. She is a *God* send for sure! We all *love* her very much. You can have a Director... But, if you don't listen to them, what good is it? We took every word from her mouth as <u>Gospel</u> Did whatever she said!

She said: "Ok you guys, everyone comfortable?"

She passed out note paper to everyone. Told us all to listen to what she had to say. Keep notes. And, ideas on the paper there... Then, after you hear what she has figured out here. You can add your thoughts. And, ideas to the stew!

I just watched her talk. I'm looking at her move. Working the room like a *coach* at half time. I knew she would take good care of us. The others needed to hear this. I am looking into Bonnie's eyes. As, she continued to lay out what she thought we should do.

As I'm looking at her, she turned her head still talking about the subject. And, also saying clear as day in my brain. "*I love you dearly Don!*" That flipped me out a bit.

What she had planned for the next few days till the concert at *Savoy* is. To, have us do a TRY OUT show at the Ear. Friday night. She is already getting responses from her phone calls.

She turned her head as she was talking. And, pointing to the sheets she had prepared on the punchboard. When she looked straight at me...

As, she kept talking, I heard her say inside my head again. "I love you Don. I hope you have a wonderful life with your soul mate. She feels the same way as you. She can't understand why she is Dizzy when she sees you. You will be together very soon. I love you forever!"

She turned her gaze back to the room. She never missed a word.

Just who is this…? Bonnie Meyers?

All of a sudden I'm right there in the room. Deep into the conversation we are having.

She said: "That we should "SPECIALIZE"

We said in unison: "Specialize?"

What do you mean?

She said: "As far as I can see. You, guys are the *walking doubles* of "Crosby, Still's and Nash" With Patty there as your Neil Young."

At the show Friday night, How about you do what I am calling a "*Tribute Band*" type deal.

Now, dig it! *Tribute Bands* are all the rage today. But, in 1971, it is never heard of.

I said: "This is a good idea."

We got all the songs we need. Plus, we can do some of their solo stuff as *spot light songs.*

Bonnie said: "GREAT!" Then it's settled. You guys are now…

Crosby, Steal the Cash & Run Tour 1971

We all stood up cheering. And, hollering…BONNIE, BONNIE!

She says: "OK! OK! SHUT UP! Dig it! You are still *Morison Smith*. But, this will be a publicity Gag!"

She said: "Let's do it!"

I said with a Hoot! "*FUCK YES!*"

I grabbed Bonnie. And, *kissed* the shit out of her… She grabbed Jocelyn and *kissed* the shit out of her! Left Jocelyn pink faced!

She looked at Jocelyn and said: "Sorry"

Jocelyn said:…OK!

We are off and running. In, a Real direction!

We love you Bonnie! This is like a dream! Coming true…

Crosby, Steal the Cash & Run

"It's so fucking far-out! It just fucking might work!"
Hunter S. Thompson 1968.

We are all spread out around Bonnie's apartment. Debbie Sue has dropped back in with Karen. They are going to Tim's house in her mother Phyllis's car.

Tony said: "I'll join them!"

Rick is in the shitter, doing whatever Rick does in the shitter. (Ha-loose-a-crabs)

Mike had poured out 5 Christmas trees on the coffee table. And, is separating the little beads on the inside… Clear capsule… One, color Green is the speed. The, other RED is the sedative that is in there to take off the edge. White, as a buffer… Hence the name _Christmas_ trees… They are amphetamines. Pill that is Light Blue… With, Green speck's… Are Byrd Egg's, _Dexedrine_.

Mike said: "It's the EDGE I fucking like Man!"

He would save the other for when he got home to his moms after 4 or 5 days with us. So, he could crash off of his speed run in his own bed. Made sense to me!

I heard a toot, toot outside in the street. Rick comes flying out of the bathroom, out into the street. His Honey Baby _Dianna_ is here finally! She has been havin to work at the news stand a whole friggin bunch. Rick felt that _Pearl & Homer_ were trying to keep them apart! _He wasn't wrong!_ Debbie Sue told me that _Jocelyn_ is stuck till tomorrow in Farmington. She asks me if Bonnie and I had gone to her house last night. I just _smiled_ and walked back into the room. I was hoping that she had made her way to Debbie's house. Oh well, back to business.

"Who will help the widow's son ✋ _"_

When I walked back in the screened in porch. Bonnie is sitting in a _Giant_ wicker chair that swings under the eve. She sits up. And, motioned me over there, She sits me down in front of her. And, then started to rub my shoulders…

She said: you feel like crying don't ya?"

I said: "Well, not that bad, I hoped she would come over with Debbie Sue."

As she finished with my shoulders, she wrapped her arms around my chest and squeezed a bit.

She said: "I need you to come in here and do some work. I have us ready for a song list, let's go do that. I have something I want to show you that will brighten your night."

We stood up, went hand and hand back inside. She cleared off this huge wire spool table in the middle of the room. Moved Terry and, me over to it… Note books. Guitars… Everything! In the middle of the table, she laid out a big *old round mirror*. She went into the bedroom. She came back with an eight ball of *crystal*.

Now, me Droogies! That was the day for crystal. As it was not this crap of today made out of fucking *Drain-o*. This is *pharmaceutically* Pure Hydro Chloride Flake. And, almost *clear!* Looks like *ICE* on the mirror.

I looked over at Butch. (Terry)

I asked: "You ready?"

He said: "OK… Sundance… *Let's jump!*"

She had a 100 dollar bill. All rolled up. And, ready to go.

She turned toward the kitchen and said: "I have a case of Coors ice cold in the fridge. Plus, for late night… *Fried chicken*… And, **Gasoline!** For Monsters! And, Madmen! Late night snacking!

So, let's see if we can have something by sunrise. I will keep the *fires* burning. And, do the <u>line</u> makin. You… make me a two set show *for Friday* night.

Two shows. Same, songs… Change the line up around. Close with "Ohio" fade into "Find the Cost of Freedom" get up. And, bow! That should REALLY do it.

So, get to work! I'll bring everyone a beer! *Do a line.* And, kick it in the ass!

We all saluted our <u>*Commanding Officerette*</u> Terry slipped that *Yamaha* into first gear. And, my *What* ever it is, with the *bird* on it.

Flapped its wings… And, away we went.

We hit the rafters like the <u>*Rock Stars*</u> we are going to be. With, her wonderful direction! Is this really happening to me?

As I passed the Hundred Dollar bill to Bonnie, I swallowed a bunch a *Crystal* down my throat.

I said: "Wow! That ought to do it!"

About this time, I felt my legs start to get hot: the hair on the back of my neck is standing straight out. I could actually feel my hair growing! I felt my Heart go from 58 beats a minute. To, 152 beats a minute. I grabbed my guitar. Went into " Marrakesh Express."

I'm banging out the first opening guitar part. As, Terry faded into the song… Away we went! We is a cooking like a *Motha Fucka*. When Rick. And, Dianna came in the house. Rick joined us.

Dianna has an ice chest full of *Boone's Farm wine*. About 15 bottles, a box of Ham Burger patties, and, a bag of fries. In her car she has. Twelve dozen boxes of eggs. She brought from the "News Stand"

The stuff she brought is for the *Big Assed breakfast*. She is going to be cooking after about 4 am. She looks at Bonnie: "If that's Ok with you Bonnie."

Bonnie got up. And, kissed her cheek, and, said: "I will help you any way ya want… _Chefette Dianna._"

Now, Dianna is in a lot of turmoil these days. _Pregnant,_ Trouble with Pearl & Homer over her love for Rick. Stuck working the News Stand and the Trailer Court… Rick can't even ever help her as Mom & Dad don't want him around.

Classic Teenage Love affair for fucking sure! She is so full of love for him. And, all of us, It is almost sad sometimes. We love her so very much! She Laughs, And, smiles when she is with us. (Dianna)

Working under these conditions could become habit forming! All we need now is a _Naked girl groupie_ to sit at the table here. And, swoon!

"Damn you're good" says Terry!

All the way from Ft. Smith… After, a 4 hour tour… In Europe yesterday… Here are: "_Coco and Wanda_"

They have just come up the back stairs for your _Entertainment_ & Fun tonight!

We strummed them in the room.

Coco… is the tallest black man I have ever seen. Now, I don't as a rule go around talking about a guy's Johnson mind ya! Like…Never!

But ladies… this sucker drags the freaking floor. And, is 6 inches around!

Wanda. His wonderful & sweet girlfriend… Is, about 4 foot nine inches tall in her stocking feet… They didn't mind when. Or, where they would just go at it! A crowed room… Or, a quiet _vestibule!_ Even a _Downtown_ Bus bench…

She looks like. Betty Boop, sitting on King Kong's Giant dick… spinning around on the head of his dick as she holds onto a ceiling fan, Spinning on high fer Christ sake, It is UN-fuckin be leave a bull!

First thing she did when they got sat down over by the fire place that is full of roses. Was, take off all of her clothes…

Very Nice compact little 23 year old with firm upturned tits that looked like they were being held up by a bra. Without the need of one!

I Mean they just stood out there. And said: _HI THERE!_

She made it a point of showing us that her pussy is only as big a round as golf ball from clit, to asshole. When relaxed!

But she said: "Notice that it is very elastic"

As Coco shoved that thing through the roof of her mouth! Swear to God!

She could. And, did pass for 14 year's old… She is in many a _Porn video._ And, a lot of old 8mm stag films. As, the _virgin_ school girl! Getting, busted for the first time nasty assed movies!

She would sit with her back against Coco. With, her heels up against the cheeks of her ass! And, smile at all of us! As, we *tried* to Sing & Play!

So… there is our naked girl.

Coco seems to share my liking for fair skinned creamy soft round. And, firm women that are very Caucasian! God! I'm spotting!

She smelled like Honeysuckle & Cinnamon. Her scent filled the air!Only smells I have ever liked better so far in my life are *Jungle Gardena* & *Jocelyn*. They are one in the same.

This is shaping up to be one hell of a great night.

Bonnie came back in the room and sat down crossed legged at the table. She sent chills through me. When she touched me under the table. She is trembling as she says: "Man… I'm speeding my fucking ass off for fucking-freakin-flipping-freaking sure! See what I mean?"

I took her wrists as I was trained in Nam. She is going a bit TOO fast. Her Blood pressure is REAL high!

I said: "*Calm down*. How's the list coming?"

She is squeezing my hands almost off.

She says: "This is it Don. Give me all you have my love! Nothing less!" Your time is… *NOW*!

I kissed her forehead. She calmed enough to go back to work.

That Crystal will <u>KILL</u> ya! If ya ain't careful!

Chapter Thirty Three

"The Rabbit is here to Stay"

Bonnie wrote down that song.

We went into *"Long Time gone'* next to *"Guinevere."* It *IS* her favorite that we did up till then.

I pulled Bonnie over to me real close. I sang *"Guinevere"* as a spot light song to her. She has tears in her eyes when I'm finished. She wrote it down. I guess it is *"Our"* song.

She said: "Will…you cut that out! Ok, back to work!"

About that time, Tony, And, Debbie Sue, along, with Tim, And, Karen are back. They had Cruised the liquor store. And, brought back 5 bottles of the *Bubbly* stuff… And, an ounce of some <u>Red Bud Columbian</u>. This is the way I thought it would be in The Big Time. But, here we are In Hippieville! A *Headless Horseman* Town a million miles from Nowhere!

Terry sang "Black Bird" as a spot light song. Bonnie wrote it down. Rick. And, Dianna have slid up to the table. So, we thought we would sing something next that rang like a bell with Rick. So, we went into "Sweet Judy Blue Eyes" We are wailing thru the break as we brought It Back Home! And, then smoothed into "Wooden ships"

More folks have arrived as we have been singing. Most live in the House. Some heard us from the street and were all sitting on the screened in porch. Bonnie has turned off the a/c. And then opened the windows… Big tall Southern home windows, with lace Creased curtains in them. Along with the soft cool breeze that is gently moving the curtains as the sweet smell of Honeysuckle in the air and on Wanda. Pass's through. I'm feeling like… *"Far-Out Man."* There… I said it! Happy now!

I would have been freaking out if a rush lasted this long any other time. But, I felt like I was in the middle of a *super climax!* Non stop, for hours as we played. Making the play list for Friday night… Plus, the concert on Saturday…

Bonnie added that' "She is working on a spot for us at *"Gabillie"* on Sunday afternoon. The last day of Gabelle… And, spring break. The, night is passing real fine, when it's time for a Midnight snack.

It was looking like we might be the next thing in town. That would for sure piss off old Windy! Don't get me wrong, there are some big named bands in the area. Like, *"The Cates Brothers Band."* Or, *"The Band"* themselves! Along with *Ronnie Hawks!* These guys all live here. They play the

"*Library Lounge*" a few times a year.

The Cates run "*Ben Jacks Guitar Center.*" You, could drop in there for some picks. But, find *Ernie & Earl* in the back jamming with "*Bob Dylan.*" or, "*Joni Mitchell.*" Even "*Willy Nelson*" fer Christ's sake!

You didn't bother them. You just Thanked God you were lucky enough to have come by. Then… hope they don't stop playing. Or, throw you out!

The girls have made up this stuff that *Debbie Sue* is real good at preparing. I had me a Coors beer. Then, some of her *Butter Beans and Rice* till I about popped.

The mix of pure crystal, Wonderful Columbian, Plus, Boot Leg Coors… Along with the vibe! And, people. Is all it took to keep me so very mellow!

We have the first show all wrapped up, we are about to start working on the second when.

Tony and Debbie said: "This is a very special week ahead for the <u>Gavence</u> family. This entire week is a BLUE MOON! Started tonight, Ends Saturday night! So, this Union has the blessing by the *Muse of Music.* And the "*Grace of God!*"

We all said: "Here, Here!" Then tipped our glasses!

Bonnie lined up another round from her purse then said: "Enjoy that. Because, that's that!"

It's now about 5:30 am. Most folks are home fuckin! As we wrapped it up for the night. *Dianna.* As, promised… Had that great breakfast ready… then off to bed.

Bonnie said: "We can get back in the *RABBIT.* After, we all get some Spatchka!" I'm too tired to go back to the Grayhouse.

So I stayed at Bonnie's. We crashed hard till 5 pm.

$$\Psi \text{ We slept!…Till 5 pm! } \Psi$$
When I woke up…

Bonnie said: "It's later than I thought."

She needs to go take care of a few things. Lock the door if you leave before I return.

I took off for the WALL after she left. I sat around there awhile talking with Ony Ray and Rick. Terry. And, Tony came out from the U-Ark Theater building. Came over to the WALL…

I'm looking down the street to Palace drug store. I saw Lee Shorph going into the *Piggly Wiggly* parking lot, then disappear.

I said: "I'll see you guys later, I have something I want to talk to Lee about."

He has crossed the street. And, then he went into the *Yellow Brick Road*. I followed him in, and we sat down in the kitchen.

There is a NOTE BOARD in the living room. Where you can post messages to friends... Or, just post stuff.

Lee said: "I saw your girlfriend in here a little while ago."

I said: "My Girl Friend... what are you talking about? He said: "That Jocelyn girl!"

Are you not melting to get into said young ladies pantaloons? Real fucking Horashow, me Droogie?

Have some respect! I say.

He said: "Don't give me...NO... shit, Store Keeper! I see how you *melt* every time anyone even says her name! Jocelyn! See what I mean!"

You got it really bad don't ya? I thought you would enjoy a lot more of this *"love anybody"* life style. A bit longer than you have. You were the last person I thought would get stung so fast."

I told Lee that: "It's so freaking weird! I didn't even see it coming! Blam! I'm in love!"

Shit Lee: "The girl has a *boyfriend*. Named Don Garimin. He has money. A car, He is good looking. Plus, he is a local boy. And, most important here *LEE*! He has... *HER*! Her Dad's a D V M ya know!"

"Bonnie took me out to her house. To sneak around the other night! That's what it felt like I was doing... *Sneaking around!*" I'm walking in circles. Ripping out my hair! Looked like Lee was talkin some freaked out acid head down!

I said: "Shit man! She can't even get out of her own house. I'm just dizzy all the fuckin time. My whole body shakes. When I imagine touching her. Or, holding her close! Breathing in her breath! Those Lips... Those, *luscious soft Lips*! Oh... My God! I fucking cant stand it! Change the freaking subject!...*CHANGE THE SUBJECT!*"

Lee says: "Shit Don... calm the fuck down. I know something you don't. Ya know, I have liked you since you. And, Tad first came to this town. Speaking of that asshole... Have you heard from him?"

I got a letter general deliver from them in Amsterdam.

Lee said: "Amsterdam!"

"Are they coming back anytime soon?"

I said: "No...I don't think so, they are real happy there."

Lee says: "Tad is a great guy."

I say: "*He sure is.* I miss um sometimes."

I said: "But... Not that *Joe* asshole! He is in a *Turkish Jail*." The dog dick!

Lee said: "Too fucking bad. Nobody deserves that! Nobody!"

I said: "Yeah, I guess so. God dang it Lee... What I'm I gonna do? I am so fuckin messed up! What am I gonna do?"

Lee said: "Don't worry... all is groovy!"

Sitting in the middle of the table is a stack of 4x6 index cards for the note board. Lee is smiling at me. He has a plan to see if there is any hope at all. Dig this Me Droogies!

I reached out and grabbed one of the note cards. I started doodling on it. I messed up 10 or 12 of them. Then, I had a great idea. I'll post an ad for the _Perfect Girl_. I'll describe her to a T! Then, she will see it. Pull it down. Then, give it to me. Then I'll know if I even stand a chance. I took up another card. And, if memory serves me well, I wrote this.

> *"WANTED!*
> *A girl most Beautiful,*
> *About, 5 foot 9 inches tall.*
> *Creamy white soft skin, Sweet red lips.*
> *Eyes so deep... They pull me in like a magnet.*
> *A beautiful soul of lavender, and, lace... For lifetime love affair!*
> *Apply in person at Yellow Brick Road.*
> *5 pm tomorrow. My Heart calls to yours!*
> *I saw the same light as you did." Ψ ψ*
> *Post Number #3301*

Hey Lee... I thought I would leave it with an open type date. You know, tomorrow comes everyday about this time. Lee read this.

He said: "I am going to post this and see if she reads it. Man, with a note like this, you may get a ton of answers."

I only want to hear from one, any others need not apply! If it's meant to be! She will know this is written to her.ψ

I said: "Lee. Are, you coming to the show Friday night at the Ear?"

He said: "What show?"

Bonnie has us playing two shows there Friday night. To try out our new show, The C. S. C. & R. Tour 1971 gag... For the concert Saturday night in _Savoy!_

Lee asked: "Where? "

I replied: "Savoy. Out on Highway 16 West... You don't have any fucking idea what in the hell I am even talking about do you?"

Nope!

Well. How about I have Mike pick you up at the Grayhouse Friday afternoon... And, bring you over to the Concert Pre Party at _The Lafayette House_. I'll have um pick you up Saturday morning too if you like.

Lee said: "I have to go to the VA Friday morning."

I said: "I'll wait till you is ready Brother. Call Bonnie's. And, we will get ya from the VA too."

Lee grabbed the card from my hand. Cleared out about 20 hunks a shit posted on there. Then he posted mine. All by itself!

He said: "Here is what I know. That, you don't. She came in here wanting to know if she could work the shift tomorrow night for Zelda. I asked her what is wrong with Zelda. She said that she had someone coming to town. She would be in before her shift again Saturday. Two things going on here! Bonnie has something to do with Zelda asking Jocelyn to take her shift... Number two... Jocelyn wants to be here the entire evening, in case you come by. I think the idea is so her mom will let her stay out late. That way she can run to the WALL and back a few times.

"Being a Drug Intervention Center and all! I told her she could. That would be fine. So, you make damn sure you come by here between 6 pm. And, midnight! Because I know she hopes to see you here. Or, at the WALL sometime before her mom comes to get her."

Did she tell you that I asked?

Lee replied: "Come on man!"

I say to Lee: "Thanks a lot Lee. You can be sure I will be here with bells on, my friend." Thank you my Brother!

He said: "Now... get the fuck out of here!"

Thanks again Lee!

Man I felt good! I danced all the way back up to the WALL! When I got there...

Tony said: "Been *swimming* Don?"

I said: "What?"

I'm soaking wet. I was so freaked out, I was sweating profusely! I got the chills as I sat there, Got dang! Get a hold of yourself. Shit! You're acting 13 years old! Did I say that? Or, just think it?

Terry said: "No, You said it!"

He went on: "You need to work on that. Now, it's OK as it is just us. Better work on that man. You *NEVER* fucking know who is listening."

Mike said: "*YEAH!*"

Mike has parked his car at the bank across the street from the WALL. We went over and got our guitars. Then, started through the first show... About half way through we had a pretty good crowd going.

This long blonde haired girl had curled herself around Terry like a snake. She had about three feet of tongue in his ear. He didn't seem to mind. This girls name is Ronda. She works at the *Deep End*. And has had a crush on *Terry* for awhile now. She grabbed hold of him a few songs ago and she won't let go. So, Terry being the gentlemen he is. Picked her up, sat her down in Mike's car, took her home then drilled the socks off of her for three. Or, four hours! Before, he could get her to let go. Even then, she had to be pried off of him.

It was like she had staked a claim or something! Cheeesh! Although, I didn't see Terry complaining! He got her room number at the dorm and dropped by for Tea and Crumpets a number of times in the next few days.

I still say that *Patty* has plans to tie his cock around her. And, never let go. She sure can't take her eyes off of him when we play. She doesn't pay any attention to the rest of us. She never gets out of time.

Ya know. She is a real good looking girl for a Yankee! In later years, when I would see *Pat Benatar*, I would think of *Peppermint Patty*. She is just a foot taller though. Dressed in black, Lace, and, flowing capes with lace shawls. And, Razor sharp, 4 inch black leather heels. Long, before *Stevie Nicks* ever thought of it. With of course… creamy white, soft supple skin! _A treasure to behold!_

I do believe that is why we are moving into her house. And, why she is in this group. She sings so pure and clean. What more can I say. It seemed that most everyone is getting hooked up. But, me! But, even though there is a good chance I would never even make it to say hello to *Jocelyn*. I was content with being able to give it a good old try.

The fact that Debbie Sue, Karen… And her are best friends. Makes me think I could at least stand some kind of a chance. I'm telling myself, that even if she didn't know I was alive, I would still have given it a good ol try. Who was I kidding! If she rejects me, I will just fucking die! I'm scared to death. And… intrigued at the same time!

I'm so turned on, my pants are wet! I can just feel her in my arms.

From behind me comes a voice: "Man, leave it alone!"

"What?"

"Earth to Don! Earth to Don. Come on man, snap fucking too! Where is *John Palamisano?*"

"He is at *Mt. Nord* house… Fucking the shit out of Zelda!"

Him: "That's a lot a fucking."

ME: "She is a lot of woman!"

I said: "If anyone can please Zelda. It's Wildman *John Palamisano!*" Him: "No doubt my friend!"

"Tell him to come by the shop in the morning for his check."

Me: "He will be there, not to worry!"

Then, he was in the street. And, gone…

I asked: "Who was that? What time is it? Where is everyone?"

Here comes Bonnie. Hot damn… I was so screwed up!

She asked: "What guy?"

Me: "Ah, looking for John, who the fuck was that guy… Anyway!"

I'm sitting there alone now. Everyone has taken off. There I'm. Out of nowhere came a voice.

"Don… Don"

I look behind me. And, there she is! Looking in my eyes with a come hither stair… Got Damn! I jumped to my feet. Took my eyes off her for one milla-second! And, just like that…*poof!* She is gone. Just dissolved into the air! Oh my God am I fucked up!

Bonnie stopped the car and said: "Get in." She is going to the *Duncan House* tonight to see Mike. Her, husband… I could stay in her apartment on Lafayette if I liked. It's better than the hardwood floor of the Grayhouse.

I got in. She took me there and walked me into the front door. She held me a minute. Said: "I should just lock the front door, turn out the lights. And, go to bed. We have a big day in the morning."

Morning, it is about morning now!

She said: "You know what I mean."

She took off all my clothes. Tickled my… balls, and, a few other things… Gave me a good night kiss, threw me the key to the door, blew me one more kiss, and then left into the darkness. Her Mustang burned rubber around the corner and out into the night. I laid back and thought about the day. Smoked a J and I was out for the count.

About 10:30 am. Bonnie unlocked the door and crawled into bed with me.

"She said: "Wake up sleepy head. We got people to do. And, things to see! Come on! Up and at um!"

She hit the kitchen. I hit the shower. She handed me a cup of good as hell hot coffee. With a Bird egg as a chaser! Bonnie… Yes my love.

That was some clean crystal. Do you think there might be some of that around for Friday night? Why, do you think you need it?

No… But, it's going to be a very special night I think. Most especially if you have planned it.

You really have faith in me. Don't you Don.

I love you Bonnie. I don't care what you do. I would be there for you no matter what would happen. I would have left this town long ago if not for you.

Don…

Yes dear.

What will you do if all of this falls to shit? What if she laughs in your face? No band. No girl! What will you do?

I said: "Bonnie, I have not even thought that could happen. I have made no plans for my feelings if the whole deal falls apart. I have never felt the way I feel. So, I don't know what I would do. Why do you ask?"

She hesitated for a second as she gathered her thoughts. She reached out and kissed me on the lips she said: "Never you fucking mind! Come on. We gotta run."

I asked her what we were off to do.

I have a plan to get some spot filters from the Theater Dept on campus. I need you to keep um busy while I give the guy a blow job for the jells!

Blow job! What are you talking about?

She said: "I'm kidding… You keep um busy. Ill grab the jells… Ok?

Ya got it! Then we have to go by the bank. They are trying to get me to open an account for some new stock I bought.

I never thought about it. But, it appears that Bonnie is a *poor little rich girl*. She never talks about it. She just shares everything she has, with everyone she knows and loves! We are very lucky to have her in our family. No matter whom she is. Rich. Or, poor! (Bonnie)

Writer's Note.

Everyone in this story in my opinion, Deserves their FIFTEEN minutes of FAME! Some have passed. They are not here to let you know who they were. Some folks in here deserve MORE than 15 minutes! They deserve hours of Fame. My intent… Is to detail every part of their performance in life as it was… During these most enlightened times. A chronicle… If you will! A scrap book of the time… I feel so a part of these people's lives. It would be a disservice to them to not get it right!

These people were. And, are very animated in life… Everyday that went by was a testament to the way we were. I love them all forever! These were the best years of life! For sure! Ψ

I told Bonnie that I would just take it in stride. I guess if all this did in fact *Fall to Shit!* In truth! It would have most likely made me reevaluate my tenor in this here old *Headless Horseman* town.

I'm trying just not to think about it. Makes me a bit too shaky, it didn't matter anyway. In a few days, it would be going the way I hoped it would. Or, that would be about it!

Chapter Thirty Four

"The Countdown is on!"

Now… we have only 3 days to get a whole bunch a shit done before the booked three-day weekend we were working towards, starts up. To, see if what we were doing is meant to be. Or, not! I don't think I'm alone in my thinking. All of us knew that we were about to make some life changing moves. After, this week, If there is an after, that is. Would decide a bunch of shit that had to happen to make all of this work…

I had to remind my self to look at the *Big Picture!* It would be easy to get lost in the love I'm feeling. You know, drop everything and just follow all the little animals! I have a better idea.

Take all of this. And, make it *ONE* big deal. Then take it one step at a time. Just watch and see what happens. Don't make the whole thing bigger than it is. As, the fall will only be harder if we wait!

It's a long way to the bottom… When you don't know exactly how high you are in the first place! Or, just where the bottom is!

I think the Girls had the same idea. They had been making sure they were wherever we are all the time.

In my book, that is what we were all trying to make happen. Not a gang like today, where everyone is from a bad unresponsive family! No MOM. Or, DAD! But we were.

We didn't look at it like we were going to become this big family of Smart Streetwise people that you could not *FUCK* with! But, that's exactly what we became. That old *Safety* in numbers thing again I guess. We worked hard at making sure that everyone in our group had everything the others did all the time.

One for all, And all for one… That is what made us different. If one ate, we all ate. If one didn't! We all didn't. It was that easy… cut and dried.

About five pm. We all met at Bonnie's on Lafayette. Seemed that is where we would launch this super group. We are not a bunch of guys that had never done this before. Each of us had a music background from as far back as the first Beatle song we saw and heard on the *Ed Sullivan* show.

All of us knew that was exactly what we wanted to do. For all of us, many bands, and, singing groups were in our recent passed. All a learning experience! This is the *BIG BREAK* we all are waiting for. Not just to be ROCK AND ROLL STARS. But, a full affirmation of our talents, and, dreams for our lives!

We had met all the people that felt the same way we did. There is no way we could let that get away with out a complete trial run. The chance on that EVER coming again was bleak at best! So, it's all the way. Or, nothing! As Bonnie and I got to her Lafayette pad. Every one is on the porch except one. I asked Debbie: "Where is Jocelyn?" She said: "We will be hanging at the WALL. And, the *Yellow brick* road later."

She had indeed talked her mom into the trip to town to work a bogus shift at the yellow brick rd.

While I had Debbie Sue here, I asked her a few things.

I said: "Is *Jocelyn* hooked up with that Gariman guy"

She started to answer. I interrupted like a fool and said: "Because you know, I was just wondering!"

She sat down laughing. Her laugh could stop an execution! I was starting to sweat a bit. My face is white I guess. She stopped laughing and put her hands in mine and said: "*JUST WHO IN THE FUCK ARE YOU TIRING TO FOOL DADDY-O?*"

Then she said something that not only shocked me! But, showed me I was dealing with not girls! But, young WOMEN who know exactly what they want. They are pretty sure know how to get it too!

Debbie leaned over and softly put her hand on my shoulder and squeezed, she sent a chill through me. Because, I wasn't sure what she was going to do?

She said: "I'd bet, you would EAT a MILE of her shit. Just to see where from it came!"

Wow! Did this wonderful young woman just say that?

She looked at me. And of all shit… She SLAPPED THE SHIT OUT OF ME! Not one time, twice! With a giant smile! And a Lollypop in her mouth, she said: "Get Ur shit together bucko!"

I asked: "What about the Farmington connection?"

She said: "I've said enough. Dig it, You will see!"

Then she left Out of the room with a Ha Ha! What a CHUMP!

She said "By the way. Thanks to you and Terry for making this happen…"

I said: "I had nothing to do with it! It's all of you."

I was tearing up. She came back and gave me a reassuring hug.

She and Karen are off to the WALL. The rest of us went to work.

We would see them in an hour or so.

Bonnie cracked the whip! "Back, to work. After all, practice makes perfect! I'll make Tea."

She is getting more stuff together than we thought. She is VERY good at this. A REAL business woman! We were rank amatures! That was very obvious for sure, Except for Patty that is.

The voice of reason had not been expected. You can't see your *Yoko Ono*. If she is not in the script yet! I had to put all of these thoughts into some kind of a formula.

SLAP! God Damn It! What in the fuck is going on here? I came up out of my chair. Bonnie had just knocked the shit out of me from behind. I looked around the room to see who was about to die! I noticed that everyone was sitting looking at me. The room is dead quiet. You could hear a pin drop! Bonnie is looking at me shaking her head from side to side..

Terry said: "TIME!"

Tony said: "22 minutes 52 seconds flat!"

I said: *"WHAT ARE YOU ALL LOOKING AT?"*

Dianna walked over. And, picked up my guitar from the floor where it had landed about 15 minutes ago.

She said: "Really Don!"

OK, why don't we call it a night? You guys are not going to get anything done with him fading in and out. Then sitting there talking to himself for 23 minutes…

We sprinkled water in your face and all kinds a shit! Nothing!

Rick said: "Come on man. What's it gonna be!"

Bonnie: "It's worst than I thought!"

It seemed that everything I had just been thinking about. I was living out loud. Like… Did I say that? Or, just think it?

Rick said: "Come on you guys, we are not getting anywhere. Let's hit the WALL, take a break and get some street life into the mix!"

I had dropped my guitar and just dropped my arms and flaked out into space for 23 minutes. Here's the rub. When, I used to do that. It was a Nam flashback. Or, some nasty shit like that there. Now, it's different. Am I starting to heal?

Rick came over. Grabbed me by the shirt and turned me around, got in my face and said: "Get Ur shit together Don! Tell her how you feel TO-NIGHT!"

What are you fuckers talking about? *Mike Boyd*… who has been sitting watching all of this as he always does is ready to chirp in with his 2 cents!

He said: "You are scared to death of this…Jocelyn girl, why?"

I said: "I don't know man. I think I am going fucking crazy. Every time I try to talk to her, all I can think of is black jokes!"

Coco jumped up with Wanda stuck to his rather large shaft: "Oh Yeah! Like which ones?"

I said: "I don't know, I forget."

He said: "How about you start with the one where you is a geetin you ass kicked!"

I asked: "Would that be funny?"

CoCo said: "Ha Ha Ha! I'll be fucking laughin! I'll be crackin up Jack! You some kinda whoopy bull shit motha fucker if you is sacred o that skinny little white chic! She be looking *ALL* over you every time she sees you butt. You no sees her jack!"

Wanda, being the perfect lady says: "You mean... You ain't fucked her yet? I'm ashamed of you! You is losin you touch Man!"

I turned with a snap... "What the fuck did you say?"

She did retort: "You ain't deef is yee? DID YOU FUCK HER YET? She says: "Coco... Is this guy for real?"

He says: "Wanda... I don't know. Looks like a puffy bitch don't he?" Mike went on to say: "That I should just go out right freaking now. And, get this thing straight. Or, forget about it. We got bigger fish to fry!"

I said: "Mike... Don't you think I know that? I am possessed! I want to be with her so freaking bad. I HURT!"

Mike says: "Ok, that's about it I guess, let's hit the WALL."

As we were walking out, Bonnie kissed my ear and said: "Moving right along now, don't trip over your heart Don!"

She laughed all the way out! *AS WE CLEARED THE DOOR WAY*, Bonnie stopped, kissed me and said: "Kill the Rich!" I love you...asshole!"

"My Asshole?"

"No... You're an asshole... Never mind!"

We are walking up the steps to Lafayette Street. Bonnie and I hand in hand. She is chuckling under her breath but couldn't hold it in. she is squeezing my hand so hard, I thought I may never play the violin again. She is swinging my hand chuckling when she sang out. "I know something you don't know." Then she started to skip off ahead of me and caught up with the others. I was dragging my feet down West Street. When, *Dianna* came around behind me. She started pushing me down the street.

Come on Don, *SHIFT IT!* She reached up and kissed me on the other ear.

Whispered: "I know what you are thinking!"

I said: "No you don't!"

Even softer she said: "YES I DO!"

"OK, what?"

She said: "SCRAMBLE!"

What?

She said: "Scramble! That's what you are thinking! Let me tell you this now, your aura is bright red and yellow." Plus. . . She motioned me closer and said: "Your... FLY... is *OPEN!* HA, ha!

Down the street she went to the others. And, they all started laughing at me.

I have noticed in the passed, most of my life. If you made fun of me, and laughed at me, It was a pretty good bet. You… Or, I were about to get a few black eyes.

But not this time… I stopped in the street as they kept walking and laughing their ass off at me and my problems. When I noticed I'm smiling watching them walk. I was so full of this *New way of life*. All I could do was watch them walk and realize how much I was in love with each and every one of them. In, one way or another! Now, I would do pretty much *ANYTHING* for these new wonderful people that have allowed my sorry ass into their lives, with no strings attached!

We passed Watson. And, onto Dickson over the tracks, we walked passed the Yellow brick road and my heart started racing. I skipped across the street to look down there to see if I could see her.

Nothing! We walked on to the WALL. Went passed the record shop. Sitting at the other end of the WALL!

SHIT! IT'S HER! *Jocelyn!* HER! *RIGHT THERE!*

I turned around. And, ran back down Dickson, Rick came up behind me. Tackled me,

He said: "Oh…. NO… you don't! We are getting this thing squared away right fucking now! You chicken shit!

Sniff. Get up! Sniff. Sniff. Shit. Sniff. Pee You.

He said: "What the FUCK stinks?"

He started spinning around in the street. Looking for the smell, God damn it! That is BAD man! Then he stopped turning. And, looked right at me! I'm sitting on the street. I looked up.

I said: "I just *SHIT* my fucking *pantaloons* man! I really don't want to go back over there at this time! If that is OK! With, freaking you that is!

Chapter Thirty Five

"The Rosa Rita® Refry Affair"

Those Rosa Rita® refries are a Motha Fucker man!

Rick asked: "Why did you Shit your pants sucka?"

I said: "Oh… Like I planned it!"

Well, what then?

I said: "I've had to shit since this morning. But, that Acid had me all stove up man! When I saw her… It all just let go."

I looked back up the street to the WALL.

She is laughing so loud. I could hear her down here. She is pointing at me. She threw an orange at me. It was the finest pitch I ever saw. It came straight down from a perfect arch. And, hit me right in the friggin head. From 30 yards! Good thing it was just an orange.

Well… we snuck around the power company. Over, the back way to the Grayhouse, And, into the shower I went.

There is someone else in the shower next to me. *SHIT*, it's *MUFFIN!* It sounded like she is <u>chopping wood</u> in there man. So I just crept out the side door. And, back to my room.

Lee is coming down from his cubby hole. He saw me. And, started to laugh: "Rick just told me what happened. Too much man, I knew it was going to be EPIC. Are you all right man?"

I said: I guess so, there she is. And, I shit my pants! How the hell is that going to look?"

Well, he said: "Her brother John is coming to pick her up, he is a great guy. But, he has that "Don't mess with my little sister syndrome" going in him! He is a big ol fucker too. Have you ever seen her dad?"

I say: "No! But, I've been told some tales about him for sure!"

Well, John is every bit as big as his Dad.

"Lee?"

"What?"

Are you warning me not to go back to the WALL?

No buddy!

Then what?

I want you to go over to the YBR and, get some grass from your stash place.

What stash place?

He said: "You know, the one behind the medicine chest in the bathroom."

I say: "What bath?"

"Stop it Don. You don't expect me to run that place. And, not know what is going on… Do ya? You handle yourself well enough. I don't worry about you! Or, the fact that…Terry has his hid out behind the spice rack. You know if anyone else was to do that, I'd kick their ass!"

I asked: "Why is it OK for us to do it then?"

He said: "Don, I don't know what it was I saw in you when first you arrived here. But, we are not just BROTHERS IN ARMS! I feel that we are friends too. You never treat me like I need your sympathy! You are the only one that never asked me the *bloody* details about my arm here. You are always there with a ride. You don't even have a car. Come on… who else even thinks if someone else would need a ride somewhere. If, it didn't include them."

Got damn Lee, do you see thru everyone you meet?

Almost he said. He reached out with his BLOWN UP ARM. And, squeezed my arm and shook my hand with the other.

He said: "I know you are going to be very happy my friend. Now, go get me a bag a dope out of your stash. I can't go over there. I need a smoke." I said: "OK!" And, looked at him… He is smiling like the *Cheshire Cat!*

I looked up at the House Mother's apartment window. There is Lee. Watching me walk down University Street to Dickson!

Terry and Mike hollered out for me to cross over to where they were. I did.

They said: "You been crying again?"

Come on you guys, cut it out!

All of a sudden I noticed that *Jocelyn* is not there.

Mike said: "She done left Ur ass! Couldn't figure out why you ran off."

I said: "I'll bet a dollar to a donut! You told her why asshole."

Bonnie saved the freaking day for you again sucka.

Oh yeah, How did she do that? I'm feeling about as low as a *tick turd* when he said: "She said you called Rick a No count Motha fucker. And, he chased you down the street kicking your ass all the way to Watson Street."

Well, so much for that I guess. I went down to the YBR to get some smoke for Lee.

I went inside to my spot. You know… I almost lied to Lee About the stash thing and all! But, I knew by the look in his eyes not too. I didn't feel like I should betray his total trust. So, I didn't… Something has most for sure come over me. And, it is really bugging me fucking out.

When I came out of the bathroom I just piled onto the bed full of squirming girls that are laying all over it! There is just enough room for me to lie still on the side of the bed. When, I looked up!

There… lying on the ledge that goes around the basement wall. Is, _JOC-ELYN_ looking down at me! I froze in my spot. And, with the stupidest look on my face. She signed to me to hush by putting her finger across those wonderful lips that set me on fire. Then she climbed from the lurch and crawled across all the people to right on top of me and did this.

She held me down with one arm. And, reached into her back pocket with her knees digging into my sides… She pulled out that 4x6 card I had posted. Handed, it to me. And, kissed me Really Hard! I felt my toes stiffen. Along with other things!

She said: "oops! _mmmmmmm!_

My brother will be here in just a few minutes, you almost missed me again! She kissed me _HARD_ again. I started to melt! She squeezed the inside off my thigh. Lifted herself off the bed and said: "Maybe later! Bye now." Then squeezed my balls.

She kissed her palm and blew me a SEE you later kiss! She walked out while I was still in shock!

The others in the bed started to applauded and scream. Patting me all over!

"God damn," one said. "That's better than TV!"

They reached out. And, started running their hands up & down my body! They had ahold of me. I tried to break free. I ran out into the street. She is gone! Her brother was waiting out front for her to take her home.

I could smell her all over me. I took in one Giant breath after another. I licked my lips for one more taste of her! I cupped my hands over my face just to breathe her in again! My heart is racing so fast I couldn't even feel it beat! Then, I will be damned, I passed out! Right there in the middle of Dickson Street. With a bag of dope in my T-shirt pocket hanging out.

The _New Fayetteville city police_ were cruisin up the street, with no good in their eyes! Terry and Rick ran up the street and grabbed me!

Terry said: "Just pick him up! Let's get the fuck out of here."

Into the YBR we went. All of those girls became my new moms for the next hour. It was the _wounded duck syndrome_ for Christ sake! They had all my clothes off. And, had me in the tub… Doing a Gang fuck on me!

They have the soap out, they are rubbing me all over. I had been out for about five minutes. These girls, at least 7 of them had been having fun with me in the tub. Washing me… And, stroking me… And, giggling like the little girls they are. I woke up with a hard on ten feet long. And, they were all over it! Switching off. One after another… After each one had fucked me to death! They let me up. I want to tell you something. When, 7 or eight girls hold down a guy with a ten foot hard dick and have their way. You ain't getting up till they are freaking done!

I stumbled over to Bonnie's. I was hoping she was there. She is. I knocked on the door. She opened it. And, I just fell inside. She helped me up. She had been working on plans for Friday night. She is in a *sheer* bed robe. And, as she helped me up, her naked breasts pushed against my back. I jumped and said: "NO MORE! NO MORE!"

She stood back laughing and looked at my Willy all red and swollen. She said: "Did Jocelyn do that?"

I said: "No, a bunch a nymph-os did! Seven or so of them! Took advantage of me while I was passed out… *PASSED OUT!*

What in the hell happened?

Well. Jocelyn climbed up on me and gave me that card with a super kiss.

Bonnie said: "No shit, that's great! So, why are you fucking 7 or so nymp-os then?"

She had to go home with her brother after lighting my fuse and leavening the fire. I got there too late I guess.

She said: "So, how did those girls get ya?"

Well, I went to the street after her. And, I passed out.

Bonnie is laughing: "I wish I could have been there for that."

She took off the rest of the clothes I still had on. Walked me to the bed… took off her night gown. And, crawled in… Held me till I was sound asleep… She lay there too. She fell asleep and never woke up till I moved the next afternoon.

I was a bit mixed up when I woke up. Bonnie is curled up breathing soft next to me. She opened her eyes and reached out for me, pulled me over.

She said: "See! She didn't shut you down. You are glowing Don. I can feel her. And, smell her on you."

Shower time.

I said: "NO! I want to smell her as long as I can."

What's next? I'm somewhat beat up! But, it HURTS so good! I'm just a bit scared too.

Wednesday afternoon in FederalVille… As, Teddy Jack Eddy called it… I was supposed to be somewhere? But, I couldn't remember where. I asked Bonnie what the plan was.

She said: "I should find Terry, Rick, Tony and the others. We can all meet up at my house around 8: 30. Or so!

I said: "ok" and I was off to the Grayhouse.

When I got there, Jerry Montgomery, and that *Windy Austin* guy, are on the porch talking. He was there to see Mac about the Gaybellie show they were doing Sunday.

I said: "You guys are on that bill?"

Windy said: "Shit Jack! *DON.* Jack. *DON.* Ok… Don."

"We are the closing act!"

Now, in most venues that is a shit time slot. Most times you are playing to the clean up crew. Or, the chair folders, just, ask Jimmy! Oh, you can't! He dead!

Oh well... put, on Woodstock and listen to what he says! Windy went on. And on, And on! About how great they are and all! He always does that. I looked at Jerry cringing like a lemon on his every word!

I said: "Fuck all that crap Windy! I don't give a fucking dog shit about you. Or, those powder puffers you fucking play with!"

HEY...Jerry!

He said: "What the fuck do you fucking want Don?"

WHERE is Terry?

"OVER AT FUCKING TED'S HOUSE...DON!"

I said: "What is the fuck wrong with you asshole?"

Windy is laughing about some shit. When, he fell down the stairs to the street. I love that 3rd step! That broke the tension.

Jerry said: "Terry is at Ted's house doing laundry."

Sorry man: "I have not found a place in my heart for that Windy fucker yet. He was driving me insane."

I said: "Well, don't tell the asshole. But, we are the closing group at Gaybellie. They have been moved to Matinee."

Jerry: "That should piss him off real good!"

I said: "You bet man, I can't wait!"

Now, at Gaybellie, the last act is *"THE ACT"* Everyone waits to the last minute to leave, the next day is school! So, the last band is the one everyone remembers. The people that will make the call will be at the EAR Friday night. To, see if we got the right stuff... As Bonnie's Guests.

Now, let me clarify something. *"Tribute Band."* Bonnie is way ahead of her time.

Like I said: "That was unheard of then. There were more people into C. S. N. & Y, Than that tired Joe Cocker shit! It is *VERY* lame!

But, you can't tell Windy nothing!

I told him he would make room for people like us. Way back when I first came here. Now, he has to deal with it!

A year or so ago we were. *Those, idiots at the* WALL. Now, we are replacing them for the Top Spot. If all goes well Friday night that is. Well, that is just icing on the fucking cake as far as I'm concerned!

Now, it looked like I was going to get the girl. And, the band too! I was so fucking stoked! Looking good so far!

My Dad said to me one time: "Look under the blanket before you climb in son. As, there might be a set of teeth under there! You never know who is going to STICK it to ya next!"

My dad was great that way. Always knew just what to say in a time of want.! Cool dude for sure! Miss Ya Dad. Everyday!

I took off walking to Leverett Street across the campus about a mile or so. As I walked up to Ted's apartment. There is Rick sitting on the stoup with Ted's one string guitar. He is playing "*Dear Prudence*" over. And, over again on the one string, sounded pretty good… So, I joined in.

I walked up as Jimmy White (*racecar Jimmy*) came down the stairs. And, out to Ted's sports car. There was a line of cars coming in both directions. He didn't care. He floored it. And, shimmied thru the oncoming traffic… Horns blowing… And, fingers being flipped! We are laughing so hard. We, were about to die.

Up from North Street is, *OH SHIT IN THE BED!* JOCELYN. And, Debbie Sue!

Oh, Shit!

Rick said: Calm down. And be cool asshole. You are just making a fool of yourself. Cool it man!

So, I sat back with the one string guitar and froze. Debbie Sue came up the steps along with Jocelyn. Debbie said that Patty is home.

Rick said: "How ya know that?"

Because her car is in the driveway And, Terry is unloading it as we speak.

I was still in shock. Looking at Jocelyn… When, she came over and looked into my eyes. As, she rested her forehead on mine, She exhaled right into my mouth. And, as I exhaled, she kissed me! After about a five minute Frencher, I'm so dizzy. I'm, about to pass out again.

She stood up and wiped her mouth and said: "God damn…that tastes fucking good! Give me another taste! Another… And, another!" Rick and Debbie Sue are just watching all this, smiling one of those, ain't they cute smiles on their faces!

At this time… Mike Boyd is at the street in the Snakeç honking at us too…"Come the fuck on!"

We went down the stairs to the street.

Debbie said: "Jocelyn and I have business on Dickson Street." She had some secret meeting she needed to attend. And, Jocelyn is going along as muscle… That ain't NO shit!

My heart fell to my feet. What? When ya gonna be back?

Jocelyn slid her hands under my shirt and scratched me all the way down. Brought freaking blood!

She said: "I gotta go with Debbie" We will see you guys later. That's where we were going when we saw Patty. We will be there soon.

I watched her walk off with Debbie. Was I dreaming?

If she looked back at me, I would know for sure. Just as I thought that, she stopped. And, TURNED around, And Ran back to me...

She said: "One more!"

Was I really kissing this beautiful girl? I could taste her in my mouth. Smell her on my clothes. And, I was bleeding! So, I wasn't dreaming. Or, speaking out loud this time...

Rick is smiling as we get into the snakeς and off down the street.

We pulled into Patty's. There is Terry sitting on her car playing guitar under the acacia tree.

She is waving at us as we crossed the street and into her yard. I went over and hugged her real hard. Kissed her softly on the lips and said: "God dang I'm glad you are back."

Terry said: "So am I. (hint hint, nudge, nudge)

She hugged him. And, sucked about half his ear off... And, then kissed him hard and said: "Man u taste so good! I been missin you too! I really have missed you Terry"

Wow! Looking like we are all in freaking LOVE! Spring! Love! Oh sweet spring in the Ozark's. I know why *Little Abner* had a hard on all the time! Believe me Droogies.

Those girls with Huge tits in the cutoff shorts and sun dresses in all those Hillbilly pictures are for sure right here in River City! Thank God for bringing me to this *Headless Horseman* Town.

As this is to be our first rehearsal at Patty's house, it's going to sound different... A whole new set up. I wanted to see how we were going to deal with it. It had been almost two weeks since Patty left. We had only played together that few times. The last week or so... Rick has been Third harmony. Instead, of the root monotone like before... It's going to be a real hoot to see how this will turn out.

We all went inside. Terry sat down at this big round table in the dinning room. Ok so far... Patty sat down in his lap kissing him. I found my fav spot. The corner! I could keep an eye on the front door. And, the table at the same time!

Patty has a Giant front window. So, you can see anyone that comes up before they see you!

Ok, not bad!

I looked over. Terry had turned Patty around in his seat. Her panties are around her left foot. The front of her sun dress is open. Her breasts are squeezing out from the sides as Terry picked her up with one hand deep in her crack of her ass. He handed me his guitar with the other.

He said: TAKE FIVE. Or... as a matter of fact *TAKE A FUCKING HOUR!*

I'm looking around at everyone. Nobody even moved! It was like nothing was happening. Nobody even noticed. But, I did. It's great. Everyone is happy now... Almost!

I was wondering when Jocelyn was coming back. As, Bonnie drove in, in a ball of dirt! She jumped out and ran inside the house and said: "Where is Terry?"

He is in the other room putting it to *Peppermint Patty!*

He is? Too fucking much! I just saw Debbie and Jocelyn on Dickson Street. They got into that Don Garimin guy's car.

I felt my heart sink! Don Garimin! Don Garimin! That asshole! I I asked: "Where did they go?"

Off with that guy somewhere!

Somewhere!! Where the fuck is somewhere???

Bonnie grabbed hold of me and said: "Not to worry man, they both got in! Key words here: Both got in! Get it!"

"Oh yeah" Got dang it! I can't take much more of this. I have to figure out how to get this guy OUT of her life for good!

Ok... Bonnie said that she had a plan for tomorrow morning. We are going to that Damn Concert & swimming area at *Savoy* about noon, so be ready to go when Mike gets here.

Mike? Why Mike?

Bonnie said: "I have to meet with a guy from *Nashville*. About an investment I am about to make. I need his advice.

Nashville? What is that all about?

Oh, that's just something I am working on. Don't worry about it, work on this right now! One thing at a time...

Rick and I went thru a couple of the songs we were going to work on later. Maybe... If Terry ever comes out with Patty that is! She was some Horny bitch as she put it! So, was Terry I assure ya!

I guess it is a sure thing that Terry and Patty had something a going mano! Rick just smiled and we tried *"Carry On"* again. I was ready to play. But, now I was worried about Debbie and Jocelyn out there with that Garimin guy! Shit, I didn't need that. I wished Bonnie never mentioned it. I had it all locked up I thought. More tunes. That's the ticket! Play more tunes.

Well, Debbie and Jocelyn never came back: I heard that Debbie had run off with Tony to the Grayhouse. Jocelyn went off somewhere with the Garimin guy. Oh well.

Terry and Patty came out of the room smoking a cigar. Not a cigarette, a cigar. She brought them back from St. Louis with her. They are "Havana

Cubano" #6 her dad gave her. Man they are sweet. Cigars rolled on the thighs of Cuban honeys.

We sat down and ran thru the song list we made the night before just like it was a show. Non stop from open monolog to closing songs "Ohio" and "Find the cost of freedom" Bonnie has the whole weekend down to a solid plan. Now, it's up to us.

After Terry and Patty joined the practice… the harmony was so fucking PURE! I wasn't thinking about Jocelyn for a minute. I'm in Music heaven. I remembered what it was all about. I was so glad Patty was back for two reasons. I think you know what they are.

Those cigars were like fucking dope! I was so freaking high I could hardly move anymore! I was wasted…

Patty said: "The last one we passed around had *Santa Clara Smooth* in it!"

"Santa Clara smooth?" What in the hell is that?" We were all stoked up to hear this deal. *Santa Clara Smooth* is heroin! I looked over at Terry, he looked blue. Really, blue! I thought he was ampin or something! But, it was the sodium light through the front room window to the table and reflecting off of Terry and Patty. Who now had her panties off again! And, she is on her knees giving Terry one hell of a blow job. Off to the bedroom they went again! We didn't see them again till 9 am.

Tony had since came over from the Grayhouse after walking Debbie to her house about 3 blocks away. I ran over to him and said: "Try this cigar Butt Buddy."

Tony said: "No man, I don't smoke, you know that."

I said in a low register voice I am famous for: *TRY THIS MOTHA FUCKER!*"

He said: "Well, what the fuck is it?"

Rick said: "It's a Cuban sweet cigar man. Loaded with Santa Clara *soft*… No man! That's *Santa Clara Smooth*! No shit! Try it! You gonna dig it the most!

We sat him down with the whole cigar roach, as we talked and bullshitted a bit more. We looked over. And, he is just floating about three feet above the cover of the couch. He looked like that *caterpillar* at the gate of wonderland! Smoking a hookah… And, giving directions… He was fucking TRIPPING jack. Don. Jack. Don!

What in the fuck is going on here?

He said in a very soft whisper: "Who the fuck are you guys? What in the fuck is…? *ON THIS FUCKING CIGAR?*"

He was up. And pissed spitting, And, screaming. You fuckers!! Then… down he went. Fell like a fuckin stone. Tony has a low tolerance for downers.

Later in this story! He has a bout of <u>714 sicknesses</u>! I'll leave that for later. They ain't been invented yet! What about *MTV*? *What's an M T V?*

Thursday morning, 9:30 am. Bonnie walks in the door, comes over and brushes the hair out of my face and gives me a kiss on the lips ever so softly.

She says: "Good morning beautiful. Let's get up. Have some coffee. Get the rest up and moving. The coffee will do it." She was right, as soon as the coffee started to boil. And, smell of Eggs & Bacon through out the house, everybody started to stir.

Patty looked like she had been drug through a wood chipper. She walked butt naked to the bathroom and never looked up. Started the shower and out came Terry. He had a Shit Eating grin from ear to ear.

Rick and I looked at each other and smiled. Tony came stumbling out from behind the couch where he fell an hour or two back and never moved. Rubbing his eyes and about to puke. What we didn't know was... he had dropped a hit of mescaline last night. And, was so stoned from the cigar he couldn't talk. It took him 20 minutes to work up the words to say what he did before he passed out!

He said: "He could hear every word we said all the rest of the night." Classic heroin story if I ever heard one.

We all had some coffee and toast.

Bonnie said: "How many got swimmin suits? Show of hands"

Nobody had a swimming suit!

"How about cut offs? No...no one?"

The only pants I had. Were covered with patches... As, was everyone else's... That will be a problem Saturday at Savoy.

She said: God damn it. Come on... we got to make another stop!

We went to the *Duncan House* and she put everyone in cutoffs and t-shirts. She said: "Don't keep them, There loaners! They belong to Mike and Jimmy."

What is so fucking important at *Savoy* this am? She told us that we needed to become at home with the place that will be the ticket. If we go swimming there, we will feel at home Saturday.

We looked at each other. And, realized why Bonnie was in charge of our careers so to say at this time. She knows what she was doing. I never asked her how. She seemed so happy while she was busy. Or, having something to look forward too!

She is moving us all out the freaking door to the Snakeç and her Mustang.

She said: "Don, you ride with me. Terry and Patty in the back..." She told Mike: "I have to stop along the way, so follow me and just turn when I do."

Mike said: "OK" and away we all went.

I said: "What do you want us to do?"

She said: "That we should not think about the show, just swim! It's a great place."

She reached out, took my hand from the consol and squeezed it. She looked over at me. She asked: "Do you feel better?"

I said: "NO! Jocelyn ran off with that Garimin fucking guy last night."

Bonnie said: "Not to worry! Just cruise along, It will all be ok darling."

Terry said: "What's this crap?" You will see her later. Get Ur mind on the caper. It's Sneaky time!" Yeah! Sneaky Time!! I love Sneaky Time!

I asked Bonnie why we were wearing cut offs. Why don't we just get naked like always?

She said: "We will be at a Christian camp where straight children will be. You can't wave your winky at them. And, not expect some trouble. Besides, I have you talked up as real nice guys! Which of course you are!"

Don't get me wrong. Mind your manners while we are here. Don't mess up what I've worked on to happen. This hunk a shit concert don't mean nothing. It's the people I have coming to see you work together in an outside festival setting. And, pull it off the same as you will sound tomorrow night at the EAR. They will be in the audience watching. Can I count on you guys?

Terry and Patty had stopped making out in the back. And, moved up to listen… Patty, who acted like she didn't like Bonnie at first… Had formed a bond with her… As, everyone does! They are good friends now. Sister's.

Patty says to Bonnie: "You are really on our side aren't you?" She reached around the seat from the back and squeezed Bonnie's left breast. I saw it. Terry didn't.

Well, Well. Well. My sweet lady Bonnie is a *Switch Hitter*. That's OK with me of course. To each his, Or, her own I always say. But, now I know how come Bonnie is so fucking intense in the sack. She is great on both sides of the fence.

She looked over at me when she knew I had seen. Shrugged her shoulders… Took a hit from the Doobie and smiled. I winked at her with an, I approve nod! She is very impressed.

Remember old Larry Stapleton? Things had changed here. And, were fixing to REALLY change right around the corner… All I had to do was hang on. And make it thru the next 4 days till Monday. Then as a Monday morning quarterback. We can talk about what had happened the last 4 days. See what we can do. And, not do. Now that we have an idea of where we are going with this…

Or… is it worth the time we will have to spend to be ready to make a move this coming fall. We had all summer to figure that out and make it count! We set Debbie's 16ᵗʰ birthday as a début date for our up coming road show, whatever that may be. We needed to make it all the way.

About this time we pulled into a Mom and Pop store just outside of town. Bonnie said: "Wait here, Ill be right back." She went inside. And, I saw a hand come into view in the front and only window. Then pull down the shade and turn over the CLOSED sign.

We are parked where we looked like we belonged there. We just waited to see what was next. 15 minutes later, Bonnie came back out and jumped in the car, burned rubber back on the highway. I looked over at her. She looked back and said: "What?"

I Looked at Terry and Patty. Nobody said a thing. I will leave it at that. You can make up your mind what it was she did.

She is in a different mood when she returned. All business! No Fucking around! A harder side of Bonnie I had never seen. Wow! Far-Out man! Dig it! What had happened?

We pulled into the *"Savoy Christian Center & Jump for Jesus Gospel Music Pavilion."* That's what it said: *I call um like I see um.*

We got out of the cars. And, to my total surprise, there is Don Garimin and Jocelyn. He had picked her up to go swimming. *Savoy* is actually closer to Farmington than Fayetteville is.

I saw them disappear up the cow trail. I ran off and followed them up the trail just out of sight. I didn't have a clue what I was going to do. I had to freaking do something. I'm shaking inside and shivering at the same time.

Bonnie had seen them too, she took everyone to the little church to show it to them, then to the outdoor stage and seating area to take a look at the lights and sound system that is even now being installed at the sight. This concert is a real deal around here every year.

They walked the whole mile up to the summit and onto the little beach where ya get in your inner tube and float back down. Then do it again. I waited around the bend on the bank till they started down. What I was going to do, I still didn't know. I figured it would just come to me.

She is in the water first. I watched those *Beautiful Breasts* go instantly hard. Her *nipples* are about to poke through her t-shirt. I swear I see one sticking through a burn hole the exact same size.

He started in. But, the water is 58 degrees, it's cold so. It takes him a minute Ur two. By this time, Jocelyn, is all ready down the river and rounding the bend where I am standing.

So, what the fuck do I do? As, she rounds the bend into the pool here, She dropped off of the tube to get all the way wet. She was only wearing a white bottom and t-shirt. Wet, the bottom didn't even exist! Oh my GOD! Instant hard-on!

There I am. With a super Jimmy standing on the bank! So, I just… jumped in, came up in the middle of her tube. She came up real slow like she was a *gator*. She came up with hands first, grabbed the tube, and then grabbed me!

Pulled herself up to where her head is resting on my lap and her legs are flopping around in the water. Those shorts she is wearing are absolutely non existent. Her perfectly shaped creamy white ass is molded into those linen white shorts. Her firm stiff nippled breasts are drilling holes in my legs. She keeps doing a Butter Fly stroke with her legs to propel us along in the current. When she does that, her buns are carved in stone as they part with a pop. And close again. I'm going crazy watching the mussels of her thighs stretch and ebb. *And she knows it!*

She said: *"Don…* (kiss) (kiss) I needed a ride home last night when Tony and Debbie ditched me. I had to be home by 10 pm."

Or, I would not be able to get out again in time for this week ends fun. Games. and, <u>Wholesale Debauchery</u>…

She said: "She wanted more than anything. To, share the experiment with me all the way to the end. Whatever that meant!"

I have this wave of *feel good* coming up all over me. I can't explain the feeling! If I could see my own Aura, I'm sure it is *Crimson Red* and steaming.

I turned when I heard that *Garimin* guy running down the trail.

He had gotten out of the water, it is just too cold. What a pussy! Hell, I've paddled out at *Huntington Beach* next to the pier in <u>January</u>. When the water was 47 degrees… No wet suit. I stayed out riding waves all day! <u>What a pussy</u>!

He saw her and I floating along. He got ahead of us at the next bend. As we approached it, Jocelyn spread out her long beautiful legs and almost brought us to a stop. Pulled me down… And, stuck her tongue down my throat till I chocked… Then she looked at him as she pushed her hand down my cut offs and licked her lips at him! He got the message, he just climbed into his VW. And Blew!

I asked: "Why are you guys here?"

She said: "I was going to tell him. You and I are doing our thing! But, you just up and fucking did it freaking for me Man!" I pulled her over to me. I said in her ear as I hugged her tight: "I know this is all happening kind fast." She said: *"No Shit Don!"*

She pulled herself the rest of the way up. Kissed me so sweet and soft… My, heart just STOPPED! She sighed and laid her head on my chest, we just floated the rest of the way to the dam. As I held her, I couldn't help but say to my self:

"You Lucky Son Of A Bitch!"

I told her: "I can't think of anything but you! Your smell, Touch, Everything that is you"

She said: "Well Don...I am stranded here now! How about you guy's take me over to *Farmington*, and, I'll meet you all at Patty's house after I get my brother to take me to Debbie's. To spend the week end... Her mom and dad are on vacation in Florida till Tuesday."

Her mom got permission for me to stay with Debbie Sue over the week end. So, she doesn't get lonely. That means we will be able to spend the entire week end with you and Tony. Ain't that great!

I said: That is *Great!* It sure the fuck is!

I needed Jocelyn for to *hold onto* the next four days. She is just what I need! We took her over to her house in Farmington. We cruised back down 62 to Fayetteville... Then over to Patty's house

Waiting there... is a guy that Rick and Mike ran into on their way back. His name is Fletcher. He is a dealer at the Grayhouse. *New guy...* I had met him in passing.

He is from *Bella Vista*, up on the border with Missouri. Lots of caves and caverns up there. Some of the very most famous ones! He has a 1958 *English Ford Lorry.* (Van) Little sucker...

Bonnie said: we need a break from practice. She is looking holes through old Fletcher there. New Meat I guess.

He said: "Let's go to the *"Blowhole"* and *cool off."*

The blowhole! What in the fuck is the *Blowhole?* At the same time Debbie and Jocelyn came up and in the door. We have arrived!

Debbie said: "Now...the evening can begin!"

I grabbed *Jocelyn.* Gave her a kiss... Sat her down next to me...

The *Fletcher* dude said: "We should get started on the way, if we planned to get there by midnight☾." We took along some *hot dogs* to eat. As, no body had any dinner, we just forgot about it some how.

We are going to cook them up out there. And, *Dine El Fresco!* And dig the place. *Fletcher* went on to describe the place.

"It is an outcropping of a cavern. On the other side of the mountain, the water fall goes out, then falls 200 feet. As it falls, it pass's this caves other opening.

The air it sends through the ground to here is 38 degrees year around. It's the only out door air conditioned park in the freaking world. We will sit around the camp site. And, eat dogs and party. Break up the night before the *Big Concert Tour... Day #1.*

All the way there, Jocelyn is on my lap. We are just a kissing away and not noticing anything except the wet spot in our crotches. I don't believe that she is looking for any <u>Oscar Meyer</u> hot dogs. She needed a foot long all night sucker. "Her words!"

So, I knew long before we arrived at the "*Blowhole*" what was going to happen to me. It seemed like *1000 miles* to the freaking place. We were squirming around. In the spot where we were squeezed in along with 10 other people… In this rolling friggin phone booth!

As the lorry stopped, Fletcher opened the back doors and we all just fell out. Everyone's legs are so asleep. We are marching around like *Spaced Cadets* on the "Terra five space ship" on friggin <u>Mars</u>!

What's next? Now what?

We all followed Fletcher over to the first camp table. Closest to the Blowhole itself, the place is deserted… It's pretty big. Not everything is by the Blowhole itself. The water fall came around the bend to some other more private camp sites.

All I can see is her! No one had eaten a thing. We didn't care. Or, even notice that we were just walking away from the rest of them. They didn't notice either. We walked arm in arm around the place for about 10 minutes. Then we saw a patch of grass all by itself in a clearing.

The place is drenched in *Blue Moon light*. Fire flies are everywhere. She has a thick blanket under her arm. I asked: "Where did u get that blanket?"

She said: "Bonnie got it from her car as we left Patty's. She just gave it to me."

Well, I guess *someone* noticed us walking away. Jocelyn led me over to that clearing. I spread out that quilt, I guess it was. It was too thick to be just a blanket. It was silky smooth and very cool to the touch.

She walked over to the stone bench. Then, took off her shorts… She unbuttoned her shirt. And, it fell open. She reached behind and took it the rest of the way off.

All of a sudden in that bright Blue Moon light… I'm looking at *soft creamy white skin* over the frame of a <u>Goddess</u>. She stood up.…came over to where I'm just flat gapping at her like a love struck kid! I had to drop to my knees. Before, I passed out again. That's all I needed to do.

I was also worried about my *sexual performance* too. I'm so worked up! I hope I don't just. Blow it. Before we even touched…

I have my pants off. And, in my hands, I'm barefooted. I never wear shoes! Not even to this day. A boot every now and then or a thongs! But that's about it.

I'm kinda famous for being able to go with the flow as long as any girl I've ever been with would want too, before we cum.

My Dad taught me about "<u>Slow Roll and Boil</u>."

He said: "The only problem a woman has with sex is… Just when she is really getting into it…that's it, Wham Bam Thank You Ma'am. No way son! Treat her like a *fine wine!* If you hurry the thing, you will miss the sweet climax. And, end up with sour grape juice!

My head is spinning as she walks over. She put my head next to her waist then pulled me closer. Her smell is making me *delirious*. Then after a tight hug. She dropped to her knees and we were face to face. In a snake like embarrass. Now…you in your dirty mind, thinks it was jack hammer time don't ya! Well…not so fast me Droogies!

We sat cross-legged naked looking at each other with erotic surges & Urges…burning their way thru our bodies. Coursing through our veins to our overly enlarged genitals. We would just shiver every now and then. And, sigh! We talked for about an hour or so, about everything under the sun. Moon... And stars…

Then we lay down on our backs. And, watched the stars for awhile… Talked some more. She wanted to know what I had in mind on this band thing. I lit a joint and we took deep hits. Blew them into each other… In a number of places!

I exhaled a mushroom Cloud. And said: "This Band thing…this band thing! A Life of MUSIC! Sound's good to me Ralph!" "What?"

She moved up and into my arms. Lay her head on my chest looking from the side. Her face is so hot on my chest. I noticed right away she is squirming around. I could still hear everyone at the Blowhole.

I think we have been here awhile now. When, I noticed my hands are crawling up her leg. To the split of her Most Wonderful Bottom… My fingers follow it all the way up her back. As, a wave of *chills* followed them till the bell rang at the top! She sighed real deep. She turned to me. She did the same.

I took her in my arms. Kissed her so deep I could feel her in my soul. Our bodies responded by curling up around each other like that statue. You know the one. I feel like *we* are one.

I feel her breasts against my chest. I dropped down. Behold in the moon light. They are so fine. I just swallowed them both! I have my hands around the small of her back. I followed the *Treasure Trail* to a where it is so wet, warm. And, sweet!

I just had to taste the pie. It's like an Explosion💣 went off in my mouth. Then all through the rest of my body! I've been told in later years. That when you are so in tune why your mate. The body fluids you exchange in foreplay. Are like sex speed to your *brain*. If you move through foreplay to fast, you are done when those kick in. That's not good. I thought I would not even make it to our first touch. There is so much of her to cover… 5 foot 8. 110 pounds of *WOMAN!*

I had worried for nothing. It is real clear. We are in no hurry to stop anytime soon. I'm kissing the inside of her thigh. When, she pulls me up to her.

She said: "It's… *Time!* I can't stand it any longer! I *HAVE* to have it NOW! She pulled me down hard on top of her. Reached down with one hand… Rubbed the moistness around with the other… Inserted me in all the way to her cervix… Then, clamped down!

Her nipples are so big… I'm sliding down to get one in my mouth. When, she wrapped her hands around me. Locked her legs around my back… And, pulled me in. she is just squeezing me till my breath is gone. She held me there for what seemed like for ever. She is squeezing. And letting up… Then, squeezing again… It felt so freakin good. I could not pull back. I just wanted to go deeper. and, deeper.

Our First Time! Dig it! Our grasp lightened, we started to move up. Then down. Slow…all the way out.…all the way in! She has a hold on both of my butt cheeks. She is pulling them apart. Tickling my balls! She sent shivers out the top of my head. Like a Lava Lamp blowing up!

I went back down south for a bit. It's like an Ocean of warm fluid of love. She tastes so Fuckin good… I had to stay awhile longer. I'm on my knees with my face between her legs as she wrapped them around my neck. She is almost doing a reverse hand stand when she grabbed me. Looked right in my face with these *Crazy Wonderful* eyes and said: FUCK ME!…Real hard!…*I mean REAL HARD!*

So, I looked at her. She has *fire* in her eyes.

I said: "WHAT?"

She said: "ENOUGH talk. Let's do it HARD. *Now!*"

So far, Jocelyn is the only woman I have had any kind of feelings for, other than sexually. I have been in that Funny kinda of love every since I first saw her. She is the only woman that has just knocked me down dizzy. She, just flat *FUCKED* my lights out!

Most of these woman are not going to take NO for an answer! Some of these girls are pretty big! They get this look in their eyes like, like that girl in "Anger Management" that throws the chocolate cake at Adam Sandlers face, because he won't make love to her, and then she throws him out! Well: that is how these women work.

Jocelyn on the other hand… Is so fucking Kind! She has an air of mystery to her in every move she makes! It's like she knows what I am going to do. Before, I do. Smart, and even though she is soft, calm and very young.…with those *freaking lips!* God… I love those lips! She will turn in a New York minute. Too, cutting you to ribbons!

I leaned over. And started to suck on those very lips…

Jocelyn has a *birthmark* on her Beautiful Top Lip! A pink *Strawberry* birthmark that turns BRIGHT red when she is Mad. Scared… Or, HOT!

I'm kissing her tongue with mine. Darting in and around hers… I reached out and pulled her to me, our bodies connected from head to foot.

Here I'm in a love embrace with the most *Strikingly Beautiful Woman* on the freaking planet. In *love!* Not, lust! It's surging thru my body, when it turned to full tilt boogie! I say not Lust because. I have been almost stocking her for weeks! I tripped over my feet and heart every time I saw her. Or, even thought of her! *I'm in love.*

The love making felt very different than before. More honest, And. full bodied. Instead of *My* feelings and need's, I'm more interested in hers. I could tell by how her body sucked mine in, made it part of hers.

Nothing like it had ever happened to me before. I'm noticing she is starting to get a little ruff! She is making the most erotic sounds any woman had ever made with me. Most times these girls I play around with are on top screaming FUCK ME. FUCK ME. FUCK ME ALEX!

"Who the fuck is Alex?"

OH MY GOD. FUCK ME ALEX. FUCK ME ALEX!

Not Jocelyn: She held me in her arms so soft and warm. That I felt things that the *crazy girls* covered up by making to freaking much noise! "Who… the fuck is *ALEX?*"

We are locked in a powerful embrace. Holding each other so tight, I could feel *her hard nipples grow even larger.*

They are like hot steel! We are soaking wet. And, trembling in a scissor lock, Legs wrapped around each other like we are doing *partner yoga!* I do believe we went all the way through the Zodiac of positions. And, made up a few more…

Then we closed the last page on the *Kama Sutra.* Right there under that *Blue Moon.* In the middle of what turned out to be a *parking lot.* The river runs right by our spot. But, I could hear the folks at the Blowhole partying down. We had been going at it for almost *TWO* and a half hours. No one had bothered us. Or, so we thought that is! Dig This!

Again she said: "Just fuck me as hard as you can! Harder! Harder!" I'm in motion. And, locked in now… When that happens to me… The sex takes over and I start pumping at a direct speed. From tip to the balls in and out! My cock swells to twice its girth. And, the head gets rock hard.

The pink edge gets these Huge nerve bumps around the tip like a *pink edged daisy.* I have a thrust that goes on. And on, till, she just can't take anymore and her cervix tells me that it is time to start the *flood!*

She said: "I am about to *faint* with passion. I read that in a *romance novel.* But, never thought it was true, till now!" She went limp right then in my arms.

She said: "Don't stop. I…_Surrender_.

I'm close to an Atomic Explosion💣 but, I just had to keep going deeper. Slower, she has tears coming down her face. She is grabbing me by the back of the head. Slamming my face into hers kissing me harder. And, harder! She is starting to scream more. More, more… "Oh Shit… Harder, Harder, Faster, Oh, my Yes! More, More, More… She screamed in my ear:

FUCK ME DAMN IT. FUCK ME. She _SCREAMED!_ Oh…shit!

At the exact same time as I thrust a hard….hard push!

We both just stiffened up into a full body lock. And, shook together!

We just held on for dear life. I'm cuming so hard. It feels like a _river_ coming out of me in hot. _Hot bursts…_ Our mouths locked in a love you for fucking ever kiss. Breathing like animals through our noses…

She said: "FUCK ME SOME MORE!"

I'm still so hard it was no problem. It's like we had just started.

We pounded. And, pounded another 30 minutes or so… Then again together we saw the _fireworks_ show of our lives. I'm afraid that we would be bruised the next day. Our pelvic bones pounded hard for at least 3 hours there under the full BLUE moon. She is so thin, I'm afraid I hurt her.

She said: "Don't worry about me… _Keep fucking!_"

I have her legs in the air. I'm tasting the pie again. She sighed and finally she shot out about two gallons of cum. She just melted into my arms. It flowed over me and onto the quilt. It's like hot butter.

She rubbed it all over us with her body, she lay back in my arms and we lay there till we heard Bonnie coming around the corner.

Saying: "Duck… _And Cover_, I am coming in!" We didn't even move. We just lay there soaking wet and trembling. Bonnie's quilt is soaked.

Sorry about that! Bonnie says: "Not to worry!"

Jocelyn is laying there spread eagle. Breathing heavy… trying to catch her wind! And bearings!

The smell of sex has Bonnie wet. I could see how wet her panties are under her mini skirt. She is shooting me the biggest beaver I ever saw.

She said: "Come on you two. Get your clothes on. It's time to head back to Fayetteville!"

I slide my fingers across her still erect clit. She moaned. And, hugged me as we stood up… We kissed one more good one.

We walked on a bit more.

She said: "I want more! I have to have more, Now!"

Bonnie walked back to the Blowhole. We fell right there in the path kissing. I'm still so hard I'm about to explode again. I'm sucking her clit so hard. I'm getting a blister on my chin.

She has a death lock on the back of my head. Then she let go and pulled me over on my back and shoved my cock up her so far it disappeared. She started pounding up. And, down. More... And, more, I just grabbed her, turned her over and raised her legs over my shoulders. Then sunk my cock in her farther than I ever thought was possible. She came alive, squeezed me. And, pulled on me... pushed my hands to her tits and I pinched the nipples so hard, I could feel it.

She said: "Bite them."

I grabbed both of her ass cheeks and spread them apart, shoved my cock even deeper and bit her nipples almost off! She screamed. "That's it! *FUCK ME HARDER!*

Then she went limp. Then she shot more cum all over me. I shot so high above us, it showered us both.

We fell into each others arms. She grabbed my cock and shoved it back in, clamped down on it. Her, cervix just sucked it dry like milking a cow. When I slowly pulled out, I came again. Hard... and, good! I was just sitting there twitching and cuming over. And over!

She said: "It's going to be a long drive Home. I can't wait till we get back to Patty's. Hard on! Yes mine!"

As we walked, she put my fingers in her snatch. We walked slowly. She is still so hot. She burned.

She said: "See... I could do it again here. Right, now! I swear to freaking god. I want you again...right now!

Well, everyone is waiting on us. They all knew what was going on. Hell: they all most likely watched and fucked just out of sight from us. Or, they could have fucked on top of us. Didn't matter... We only saw each other in that blue moonlight.

We sat at the very back of the lorry as most of the others drifted off. We slowly fucked under the quilt all the way home. I was still hard and wet as we went into the back room of Patty's house and shut the door.

She said: "Let's do it all FUCKING night. I started at her feet. And, kissed her all the way to her red lips. She inserted me again. We fell asleep with me still inside of her. Oh god! What a wonderful Woman! I had just been _LOVE FUCKED_ I like it! I like it a lot!

"Don't let the past remind us of we what we are not now. I am not dreaming! I am yours. You are mine. You are what you are!" C S N

At around 9 am. Came a pound on the bedroom door! I opened up my eyes expecting to be on the floor in my bag with Spanky biting me to wake up and let him out before he craps in my headphones! If I had headphones that is!

Spanky said: "I am holding up a very special <u>crap</u> for when you do!" But,

I noticed I'm lying with a Perfect Angel wrapped around me! Lying face to face with her… I leaned back a bit. Then, looked her over in the daylight streaming through the window to the bed… She is still half asleep.

As she awakened, she stretched out like she was a kitty waking up from a nap in the front room window. Oh my god! What a LUCKY son of a Boogie Woman was I! I had to pinch myself. Twice! Then, she reached over and pinched me too! She lay a *Good Morning kiss* on me that would have floored *Sinatra!* She stood up. Walked over to the dresser where her clothes are.

As she walked across the room, I watched her from the back. It was pure *Playboy*® stuff! She knew I was watching her. She walked with so much feeling: it knocked me back with a full sigh.

She turned on one foot as she slid on her shorts. Up they went over all that Soft White Smooth Creamy skin. Then, up to a "*SNAP.*" She reaches out for her shirt, slid it on. As her arms were over her head, the morning clear light shimmered on her midriff. I knew why I'm so deeply in love with this creature of the times! I'm already planning how I will KILL myself if she ever leaves me.

Debbie Sue crashed through the door as Jocelyn opened it! Into the room she spilled, Doob in one hand. And, a *Dr. Pepper* in the other with a Wild look on her face.

She said: "Jocelyn! Where the fuck have you been? You didn't come home last night!"

Jocelyn said: "Sorry about that. I was busy!"

Debbie said: "I should have thought to check here first."

Where did you guys go? One minute you all were here, then gone! Jocelyn: "It was a spur of the minute deal. We just split man. Calm down! What did you do? Debbie said: "*I fucked old Tony's balls off* for about 3 or 4 hours… Why?"

Jocelyn said: "*Well, that's what I was doing with ol Don-o there!*" They are in the kitchen having coffee. As, I heard *Peppermint Patty* retort from her and Terry's bed: "Well: I was fucking ol Terry's eyes out in here!"

Rick and Dianna had gotten together somewhere in the night. Dianna chirped in: "I am well fucked by Rick in here too!"

She said from the livin room: "Well! I guess we are all…*FUCKED!*

The place broke up!

I was pulling my pants up when Debbie came in. pulled um back down. Then, Jocelyn tackled me!

Debbie Sue sat on my shoulders as Jocelyn took a ping pong paddle and started beating my ass with it. I was hollering in pain as Debbie let me up! That feels real good! I said.

She laughed at me: "You pervert!"

I sprang to my feet pulling my pantaloons up at the same time. Jocelyn came around behind me with my t-shirt: she pulled it over my head. As, my head popped through, she kissed me real, real Hard.

She said: "I'm so warm inside. I feel funny. I knew you were the one when first I saw *YOU*! That's why I'm so Happy today!

She leaned in more to my left ear, SHE whispered: "I have to go with Debbie now, I will be in your arms the Entire time I am gone. As to the I Love You from last night, I think I LOVE you too! We will see!"

"*WE WILL SEE!*"

Softer she spoke: "I am so very glad You Love…Me! I can't wait till next I hold you close!" With a kiss on my ear, A squeeze of my boner… She and Debbie were out the front door. And, GONE! Daddy <u>GONE</u>!

I'm sitting on the bed as Terry. Then, Rick walked in. They looked at me. Then, each other and nodded… Rick came over. Threw a Black Cape over my shoulders, I stood up and did my best *James Brown* out of the room. It was a classic!

Got damn folks! I tell you me <u>faithful Droogies</u>. I was so damn hung up on this I could hardly think straight. When Bonnie came screaming down North Street. Then did a complete circles into the driveway that any Stuntman would be jealous about! She jumped out of the car… ran inside the house right past me.

She stopped on a dime! Then turned around with this *Double* take look on her face, Came back over to me. Wrapped her arms around me in a bear hug, and then kissed the *livin* shit out of me for 5 minutes! She is licking my face. And, sucking my lips as I looked at her and said: "Wow! What in the fuck is going on?"

She started jumping up and down, laughing and crying at the same time! She kissed me again, then spun me around, pushed me inside. As she is pushing me from behind she say's: "Come on Don!…*SHIFT IT!*"

Terry and Rick are there on the couch watching Monty Python. She just turned off the TV and kept jumping up and down! I grabbed her and said: "Calm down and tell us what's going on."

Patty is dressed and in there now wanting a big <u>kiss</u> from Bonnie too! So… damn if Bonnie didn't lay her back in a dip, then *French kiss* her till we all had Hard-ons! Patty dropped to the floor. She is out of breath and sweating!

Bonnie said to Patty: "That good enough?"

Patty just slowly nodded. Then, lay back on the floor. And swooned! Terry said: "Shit Bonnie! What did you do to her? She was fine a minute ago!"

We all fell back laughing! I'm so happy! There is nothing that could change this life. It is exactly what I had dreamed of, all coming true at the same time.

I felt that something was wrong though, I couldn't put my finger on it! Anytime before in my life so far, went to shit. If, I even looked happy!

I had to remember, up till now. Everything I loved in my life had just up and left me broken hearted with no reason! I wondered in the back of my head when she would up and leave me Too! My brain did a _DELETE_ as I thought that. Then removed it from my brain…

Even if she ever did leave me in the future, Everyday with her now would be worth ten then. Now, everything is _Horasho_ for sure. That in itself made me leery. I still had my guard up at all times. But, the shell is getting thinner! I'm _BEAMING_ in love with LIFE. And, a Wonderful Girl!

Bonnie is catching her breath from damn near kissing us all to death! She said: "I have a _Recording Talent agent_ From Nashville. He is going to be at the show tonight!"

She looked right at Rick and said: "SO, DON'T SUCK!"

He is a big record executive from Nashville, here to listen to this guy in town that wrote a bunch of country songs named Frank Woods. He wants him to write for them. _Acuff - Rose Publishing!_

Terry said: "Shit Bonnie! I have met this guy I think. Is his name Bob Risby?"

She flipped out, then kissed Terry: _Bingo!_

Terry went on: "I met him one time at _Pepper Jingle Factory._"

She asked if Terry thought he would remember him.

Terry: "No….I don't think so. We were recording as studio fill in artists. He said hi in passing. Big fat guy right?"

She Replied: "Yup! That's him. Well, great then."

What are you all going to do the rest of the day? Everyone looked at each other with a. _I don't fucking know, look!_

She said: "I want all of you to stay where I can find you at a moment's notice! Ok?"

She is looking right at Rick.

Rick said: "Bonnie, why every time you look at me like that, it's scolding me!"

She walked over, sat down on his lap, kissed the shit out of him! Dianna is shocked!

She said: "When ever I can't find someone. Or, I need something done. You are the first one I can not find!"

She kissed him hard again! Looked at Dianna, Asked, if she wanted a big sloppy kiss too. To all of our surprise she said: "YES… I think I do!"

OK… Bonnie went over and curled up in her lap and ran her tongue down Dianna's throat. And her fingers in her pie... Dianna is melting in the chair. When Bonnie let go of her... She is panting and trying to catch her breath. She said she felt the Baby move! Now that I think about it! That is when Dianna told all of us she was pregnant. What a magic night!

He opened his eyes then said: "OK Bonnie, leave my girlfriend alone. Whatever you say... I will try and be more responsible."

Bonnie stood up, looked at all of us. Then said: "Well, I guess you all are just my *Cross* to bear! I gotta run you Beautiful Room full of U S D A Prime Sexy MEN. Plus, Girls... She kissed everyone on the way out.

As she hit her Mustang to get in, we were all floating around watching her. kinda dizzy! She looked at us then winked! I love you all. Be where I can find you all! I'll be back at 3 pm, we need a last run through.

Oh, that's right! Your Instruments are in my trunk. Get um out now and practice good while I am gone. Our guitars! What the fuck? I didn't even notice they were gone. That will get me in later years! I lose my first MAR-TIN® that way. But, that's later down the road.

Patty had to go somewhere, Terry went with her. Rick caught a ride to Byrd's news stand with Mike to take Dianna. To make sure she would be at the show tonight. If he hung around there, Pearl would run them off. Because, Dianna stood around Drooling all day and not working! That is what he planned to happen, and it did. They would show up at the party in her Bonneville. I was the only one there now, all of a sudden I felt totally alone. I almost lost it there for a minute! I was once used to solitude. Now, it scared me.

Spanky is tearing at my pantaloon leg.

He said: "Come on man, Get it together! Come on... I'll take you for *Walkies!* Will that help ya out a bit?"

I closed the door to the place. We walked off up Leverett Street. Didn't know where we were going, didn't matter. I was Stoked for sure! What was about to happen next you would not fucking believe!

I just needed to walk. And, think about all of this! I'm noticing that I am a bit scared about tonight. Couldn't put my finger on it though!

As I walked, I was deep in a personal conversation with myself and old Spanky here. I decided I must be going in the right direction! Crazy as it is, it felt so fucking right! Oh well... I'll just go with it all and see what happens.

Chapter Thirty Six

"Welcome to the Twilight Zone! That's it...just ahead!"

About then, I'm at the WALL. It's deserted. As, it would be at 10: 30 am, I sat down. Looked down to the other end of Dickson and dazed out. I could have sworn I saw myself and Tad in front of the *Palace Drug* watching that car fire as Frank sat in front of the payphone on his VW.

I snapped back… as, this *totally strange* boy and girl caught my attention walking down the *Grayhouse steps coming my way*. They are looking at me. Then talking in clips & whispering to each other. Then, they point at me. And, shake their heads.

Now, I'm most defiantly interested in this action! I'm right back in STREET MODE! They came over, Sat down next to me. These two are right out of a "<u>*FURRY FREAK BROTHERS*</u>" comic I swear to god!

He is dressed in *Crush* Blue Velvet pantaloons, had to cost at least $200.00. He has on a Sony & Cher fluffy vest and more beads than at *Mardi Gras*.

She is dressed in a totally see-through sun dress. Bare footed. And, long, long blonde hair. I have never met "Two real Hippies in my life" But, here they are! I looked at the two Huge, Plump, round tits under that dress. And… the taper down to her full blonde bush at the crossroads! Her legs are so long I lost sight of them about ankle way down.

Her old man is watching me almost *Rape* his old lady with my eyes. As she pushed her breasts straight out, They popped the buttons to full naked view! Right there on the WALL at 10:30 am for Christ's sake!

They are on both sides of me now. She leaned into my face with her sweet breath. She said: "Lonely honey? *New in town?*"

My jaw dropped to the street. I thought… New in town! What is this all about? I played along.

I said in a road weary half scared voice: "A…. Yeah…sure! I been a hitch a hiking for about 26 days. I found my way here after a guy I met on the road told me this place is OUT OF SIGHT MAN! So, I made the turn at "Ohio" and here I am!" That's a tale I've heard more than once me Droogies.

She asked: "Are you hungry?"

He put his hand on my shoulder and said: "Need a place to crash tonight?"

Now, just what are these two up too? I wanted to see where all this was going. It is keeping my mind off of Jocelyn, kinda! Oh… What Fun!Ψ

But, these, two are up to something! I ain't no *New Guy*! Remember about the, "Leave for even a minute and all has changed upon your return!"

Everybody knows ol Spanky and I. Except, these two dummies. He is sniffing them both over. *He is not impressed!* He stays between them and me. Would not let them any closer now…

He is growling at them! *Real loud!* And mean! *Grrrrr Roof!* Showing his toofs and snarling. He looks at me with a: "Want I should bite the Holy shit out of the two of them just for grins Boss?" I gave him the NOT YET look.

Spanky said: "Ok Boss!" Then took up his flanking position… And, we were ready to play with these two idiots'! I love the *Sneaky Shit* the MOST!

He went to bite the guy anyway. As, he reached out to help me up!

He said: "What's with the mutt?"

I did retort: "Mutt?"

Oh no! Here we go! Spanky walked over to him, grabbed his bell bottom and him. Drew blood!

The Freak said: "*GOD DAMN IT MAN!! YOUR DOG JUST BIT MY ASS!*" I said: "*Well, Stand Off!* He doesn't seem to like you very much for some reason."

He said: "Shit! I'll butcher that piece a shit! Keep him away from me!"

I'm just about to beat the fucking shit out of him. When, I pulled back and acted. Weak and stupid… It worked.

He said: "Come on man, I got a meal and bed for ya up the street here. But, your fucking dog will have to stay outside, they don't allow dogs!"

I said: "Where we going?"

She said: "The Grayhouse" I almost gave it away laughing. I held it in, this is getting better by the fucking minute.

We went up the stairs from the street. The guy tripped. And, stubbed his toe so bad on step #3. It's bleeding all over the place! *I love that step!*

We went up on the porch and inside. The place is empty. Most are still in bed. I'm up early after all. As they are showing me around the place and telling me the rules! We went up the stairs to the second floor landing.

They are showing me the bathroom they used to have a tie-die factory in. I almost lost it again! (Tie-Dye Factory! <u>No fuckin way!</u>)

They are telling me this and that. Still, showing me around and telling me I could get a room then pay later if I was broke. As he is telling me that, she had reached down the front of my pantaloons. And, is squeezing my cock and balls… She even stuck her little finger under, and *UP MY ASS!*

She said: "There is other ways to pay the rent!…You Know."

Man… I'm having a hard time holding it in when of all people *Lee* came out of the House Mother's apartment, and down the steps!

He said as he slapped me on the back: "How's it going Don?"

I said: "Great Lee, how about you?"

He says: "Better now! I have to go to the VA."

I said: "I know… Bonnie will pick you up there at 2 pm."

He says: "That's great! I am looking forward to the show tonight. And, the concert you guys are playing tomorrow!"

I said: "We are closing the last set at Gaybellie Sunday night. You coming and hanging wiffs us back stage!"

He said: "Wouldn't miss it for the world!"

Then he asked: "Who are your Little friends here?"

I said: "Shit Lee… I don't even know their names! They are trying to rent me a room. And, give me a free meal or some shit like that!" We both broke up laughing! They are scratching their heads. Lee asked them what was up.

The guy said: "Ahhh… Well. Ahhhh…"

They said: "A guy rented them room 2d."

We broke out laughing again!

The guy asked: "What's so fucking funny?"

Lee looked him in the eye and said with daggers shooting from his eyes. To, the guy's eyes! "That's Don's room. Has been for over a year! What the fuck are you two doing in it?"

She said: "well, Then, I guess the bag and duffel are yours then!"

I asked them: "OK, what do you two want?"

Lee and I had the front exit blocked. I saw. And, heard Terry, Tony Mike, and Rick coming up the back stairs… They entered the landing and felt the vibes. Terry pushed through them to my side. Then, looked them over… Looked at me and said: "Who the fuck… are these *Clowns?*"

Now remember that Terry is a big assed biker-looking dude in a sleeveless levy jacket about 6 feet tall and mean as hell! Rick and Mike are pounding their fists behind them. Tony has *momma* out. And, in his hand… These two are now sweating profusely. Trying to figure out how they had gone wrong when the girl said: "Hi there you all… my name is *Anna*. And this here is Buck!

He said: "Howdy y'all!"

Rick said: "Shut… the… Fuck… Up!…Asshole!"

We all looked at each other and Terry said: "What do ya think we ought to do wiffs um?"

Well. They, look like a bunch a *Yankee Queers* to me! We all started to do our best parts from the restaurant scene in *Easy Rider*® as she pissed herself!

He is promising us the sky if we would not fuck um up! They didn't know what they were doing! We had no idea the *Hells Angels*® were in this town!

We looked at each other....we ain't no *Angels*!

We are even worst! We are... "*The Gavence Family Travelers!*"

She looked like she was about to explode. She said: "*Shit!*"

He said: "SHIT... Fuck! We have heard of you on the street! We didn't mean no shit! Really, we didn't!"

I asked: "Just what were you two planning to do with me?"

Anna here wants to *FUCK* your brains out! We were gonna feed ya with drugged food. And, then she could have her rather different way with you!"

I said: "Anna...is that right?"

She said: "Yes Sir."

Why didn't you just say: "I want to fuck out your brains? You are a Wonderful looking girl, why did you do it this way? You two are not cops are you? You have to tell us. Or, that's entrapment!"

But, we will just *KILL* you. And, then dump you in the pit! Don't come into this town playing these Dangerous games. This, ain't San Francisco Motha fucker!

Lee said: "Shit! Lets just bump um off now... I'll stack um in the cubbyhole till dark. Then, we can just dump them outside of town. We grabbed um. They freaked right the fuck out. Started crying and all that shit! We pushed them into the bathroom. Rick went and got a Giant butchers knife from the kitchen. Went into the bathroom where we had um cornered.

He said: "Those are some Big Tits you got there honey!"

Lee said: "Need a new tit purse do ya?"

Rick said: "*My Nam tit bag is worn out! I think I'll get that big left one. The Nipple is a bit bigger.*" He grabbed her, and then ripped her dress apart, and her *Giant Tits fell out!* He grabbed the tit and put the Razor knife under it. Then, he was about to cut it off! When she passed out right there on the stairs!

Mike grabbed the guy. And, started to drag him down the stairs... He is kicking. Scratching like a bitch! She has more balls than he does! He is on his knees begging Mike to spare him. He says: "Oh I'll spare ya all right! Shut the fuck up."

Chapter Thirty Seven

"There is a power out there! Get in touch with it. <u>Move with it!</u>

"Almost….cut my hair. Happened just the other day. Could have said it was…kinda long. But, I didn't. And I…wonder why. I just have to let my <u>freak flag fly!</u>"

David Crosby

The girl Anna, if indeed that is her name… Is coming to now… She staggered to her feet. She saw Mike dragging Buck down the stairs and screamed at the top of her lungs: "<u>POLICE</u>! <u>POLICE!</u>" "Murder."

I grabbed her. Put my hand over her mouth and said: "You can scream all you like. Nobody will care!

She is screaming through my hands not to kill Buck! "Please… don't kill him! We will never do it again! We will leave town right now! I swear to god! Please don't kill us!" What a fucking scene!

I'm freaking the fuck out! Lee shot a hole in the stairs with *momma!* Everyone froze! Her eyes are so full of fright… they are about to bug out! She passed out again! Mike and Rick dragged her over to my room. Then, lay her out on my bag. We pulled the Buck guy into the room, sat him down facing the corner and told him *NOT TO FUCKING MOVE!* We stood there till Anna came to again. She started to scream again as she woke up. Just, like that girl in chainsaw 2.

Carol had just come up the back stairs. Rick told her what was going on! She came in the room. The Anna girl calmed down a bit! Buck is looking over his shoulder. It got real quiet. She calmed down some more.

I stood up and said: "Hey there… we are doing a show at the *Ear* tonight. Would you two like to come?"

They looked at each other.…waiting for the catch!

He said in a trembling voice: "What?"

I say: "You can have my room here. It's paid for till September! It's all yours! We are having a big assed Party over on Lafayette Street about 5 pm. Food. Booze, And good Drugs! You two can meet everyone there. Anna looked at Buck. She then looked at her dress. She had done a bit more than pee on her self! They were expecting to get killed. And, now we were treating them real nice! Something was not right here.

I helped her up. Carol had gone to her room and brought back a pair of jeans and a t-shirt for her. You can shower. Then, come into my room and get dressed. Put on your makeup."

She said: "I don't have any makeup. We don't have anything!"

I said along with Lee: "You do now!"

She said: "What?"

I said: "Welcome to our family! You now have us! You have made the right connection. Just, the wrong way... You won't have to play those games any more."

Buck came over and hugged me a bit too hard for my liking. Then I knew what they were all about! They on the spot became close family friends for many years to come.

The Buck guy is wiping the shit from those *Crushed Velvet* Pantaloons! Lee came back in the room and gave him a pair of boots, jeans and a t-shirt. They were even the right size. I took those bells and shit canned them. While I was in the hall, Mike asked me if I had any idea who they are!

I said: "No!"

He said: "God Damn it Don! These people were gonna slit your throat motha fucka! You think you should give them another chance to do it again? We might not just be walking up the stairs next fucking time man! You and Terry are *VERY IMPORTANT PEOPLE* to this family! You need to exercise a bit more freaking caution"

I said: "Take it lite Mike! Everything's all right! I love you my very groovy brother! I saw through their shit before they ever said a word to me. I was just going along to see what happened next. To keep Jocelyn off of my mind!"

Mike said: "You. And, Jocelyn... I'm hip man."

He had some kind of "LOOK" on his face when he said that.

He went on: "Look: you just can't let them... *YOU JUST CAN'T LET THEM IN!* You don't know what. Or, who they are man!"

By this time Bonnie has pulled in and snuck up the back stairs like a black cat. She tippy toed up behind me. Giving Mike the *Shush* sign! She crept up and as light as air, she licked the back of my neck all the way around to my face. Then, stuck her tongue in my mouth, sucked mine out and bit it! She whispered in my ear Ever so softly: "*Who...you fucking with now?*" She could feel in the air that something very serious had just gone down here. I needed a kiss from someone! So, I just sucked her tongue out of her mouth. And, bit her back! "Ok! What's going on here?"

We walked back up stairs, there is most everyone sitting on the landing. Smoking, a Cheech and Chong special... Everyone looked pretty stoned and laid back.

Bonnie said: "Who, are these delightful people?"

Rick went over and put his arm around Bucks neck and said: "This here fella is Buck."

I went over to *Anna*. Who is sitting crossed leg on the floor. The jeans that Carol gave her have no crotch. She had no panties. Figure it out! She is throwing a wonderful big blonde *BEAVER* to us all. I lifted her to her feet. Then because I thought I had it coming. Plus, I wanted to see what Buck would do. I took a taste to this girl's mouth with all of my tongue. Then, kissed her hard! She wrapped her arms around my back, locked her hands together and pushed those Giant tits into my chest. Then, she lifted her right leg around me, kissed me back even harder. Buck is just standing there with a dumfounded look on his face. He didn't look the same in the jeans. He looks more like us now.

Bonnie spun him around and stuck her tongue all the way down his throat. She said: "hold up here, I need to give this guy the once over."

Then, after patting him down real good, she stuck both hands down the back of his pants and stuck her finger in his ass. She said: "Just checking your oil daddy-o" Then she did it again. Anna is still kissing me when Lee said: "Do I gotta pop another shell? Cool off!! What a freak out Man!"

Buck and Anna went to their now *RENT PAID* room for a nap. She is still real shook up. He kinda knew he had it coming. Anna seemed to love him a lot. I'm confused as to why she wanted to Rape me. Oh well, what the hell.

Bonnie grabbed my hand and pulled me around. Come on Don, we need to make a run right fast here. She said: "Rick"

He replies: "Yes my love"

She says: "Would you all wait here for a few?"

"Ok Darling!" She kissed um on the Cheek. And, down the back stairs we went to the Mustang®. She cranked up _Gunns and Roses_! Ah, Ha!! Just checking to see if you are awake! She cranked up *Blue Cheer*. As we drove up Center Street, She pulled over behind the Carwash. She put down the top. She said: "Scootch over here" She started licking my lips, and then sucked my bottom lip almost off. As, I sucked her top lip!

I ask Bonnie: "Why do you have me sitting here behind the carwash *sucking my lips?*"

She said: "They are so Fucking Soft! Damn it Don! Most guys have hard, ruff lips! All chapped and split!"

She swooned down to me again. Sucked on them again! They are just so Fucking Soft. I just can't help myself."

I said: "Ok! Their soft, why are we sitting here?"

She snapped: "Oh! I have given it a bunch of thought!"

I said: "Bonnie, come on"

We are going somewhere to make you the fucking best musician you can be. I can't do it for all of you though. Even though you are so Fucking Insane about Jocelyn… I feel we still have something that will always be with us too! I told you just before I took you to her house in Farmington. I will still Kiss you and Hug you anytime. As I will love you from aside, for the rest of my life! Then she just flat kissed me hard, she licked her lips and went *mmmmmm*. Then licked them again, reached over and wiped mine, then licked her finger. She said: "*I love your taste.*"

Then she cranked up the car, turned right on Center. And, up to the square. She parked on the south east corner, we got out. We walked up the street into *Guy Singers* music store.

I asked her: "What is this all about?"

She said: "Close your eyes love!" She walked me into that old as hell wooden floor store from 1923. Then, over to the counter, the guy walked up saying: "Hi Bonnie! Its here and waiting for you."

She said: "Take it out, hand it to this Wonderful Man!"

She held down my blindfold till he had handed me what felt like a guitar. She kissed me on the lips then whispered in my ear: "Don't let me down, I want you to reach for the *Fucking Stars*, I want to help you get there."

She took off the blindfold. And, I about dropped the guitar! It's like each and every Christmas I have ever had all rolled into ONE! She had bought. And, completely paid for a <u>MARTIN D-18</u>, with a hard shell case… With my name on the sound bar inside! I walked over and opened the case. I put it in there so very careful! I sat down on the seat there with tears in my eyes. I said: "Bonnie…god dang woman! Who are you? I can't let you do this."

Don't matter lover, its done. Here is the sales slip in your *REAL* name. My REAL name!

She said: "That's right Mr. Buford."

Nobody has called me Mr. Buford since California. Nobody!

I asked: Bonnie, How do you know that?"

She said: "You told me in your sleep."

I said: "My sleep!"

When we did that red and fucked like little minks after that heavy duty acid trip. Well, you may think you passed out from exhaustion. Now, I don't like telling tales out of school. But, you opened up for over an hour! Crying and choking. I had to hold you, kiss you and scratch your back to keep you in the bed. You were so wobbly. You kept falling down and hitting your head. You had this Hard as a rock boner, it would not go down.

So, I just got on my knee's and slipped you in. I just sat there feeling that sucker swell up and pulsate. That thing was so far in my cervix, I could feel it at my fallopian tubes knocking on my belly button! You just talked and talked for along time, then drifted off to sleep. You told me everything in your life since you were three years old and why you are here. Then you just STOPPED talking. Your breathing got real short. I was worried there for a minute. When, your cock got even harder. You were snoring and sound asleep. I had a Shaft of Steel up my Pussy.

Now, I could have just lifted off of you and left it at that. But, I am a Sex Crazy. Hard Fucking... Deep pushing... _Selective Nymph-o_... I just pounded up and down till I could not take anymore. I just Surrendered and fell faint. Then I lifted my legs as far as I could get them. And, not fall over. Then, shoved that thing as far up my keg as I could get it... I just sat there and creamed for a fuckin half an hour or so. Till I flooded the bed there...

As I lifted off of you. I wrapped my hand around your cock to see how long it stayed hard. I was still holding it when I woke up. When I let go... Down, it went.

You rolled over still snoring till I woke you up! That is the longest time I have every had great sex all by myself. EVER in my life! One orgasm after a fuckin nother for 6 hours! I lifted off of you an hour or so later a _Totally Satisfied_ Woman. For the first time in my life, I got it all at one time!

Bonnie: "Are you sure that is a true story? It sounds made up to me!"

She looked at me very profound. She said: "Well... I was pretty stoned. I can't attest to all those facts. But, it's true it's a story."

I said: "I don't remember _ANY_ of that stuff going down around there!"

"So, you pretty much had your way with me while I was passed out."

She said: "You Betcha Buckeroo! Ha! I would do it again too! In a snatch fillin heart beat!"

I stood up. Grabbed that MARTIN® and we walked out of the store to her car...

"Listen Don. I want you to say I signed for you. And, you gotta pay payments. Is that ok?"

Would this have anything to do with the love we have shared?

Yes. But, not the sex part... I said: "No Strings attached?"

God damn it... I am wet! See what you do to me! She wiped her panties off a bit, slid her fingers across _MY_ lips. And, then sucked it off... Um!

We took off for Patty's house to meet with everyone else. As we drove I looked at her, she looks some damn Happy. I could feel her stoke as we drove. I am not sure she has ever done this Band Manager thing before.

But she is for sure Born to do it! She is an <u>Inspiration</u> in my life to this very day. Even before this book. I think of her everyday. I still do! I love you Bonnie. I'm looking for you now.♥ I think maybe you are still out there. (Hint#2)

As we pulled into Patty's house and stopped, Spanky jumped over the back seat right onto my left nut with his back leg as he sprung out of the window to the ground.

I said: "Hey Bitch! Watch the snuts!"

Bonnie jumped out. Inside, she went. I got out. Grabbed, my new MAR-TIN, in I went.

I'm concerned about how I'm going to explain it. Shit! I just walked into the kitchen. There sitting in his spot at the table is Terry. Strumming a Brand *New Gibson Heritage*® Very GROOVY for sure! I smiled ear to ear! I never even asked! Terry looked at the MARTIN. He Nodded & Smiled. Then motioned me over…

We went into "*Suite Judy Blue eyes*" the room went deadly silent. All you can hear is those two guitars Harmonize. Our vocal harmony just rang with them. We are all awe struck after that song. Lay, back with jaws agape. Goose bumps the size of Turkey's.

Mike said: "UN FUCKING believable! *Son - Of - A - Fucking -* Bitch"

He said: "Do you have. <u>ANY</u> idea how great that fucking sounds?" I'm in the chills so freaking hard, I just could not speak! We went into "Country girl" then straight into "Déjà vu" then "Find the cost of Freedom" & "OHIO" That became our signature songs after awhile!

Remember the radio station way back on page one? Go figure! I knew then that song meant something to ME. I could feel it that day! *You can't stop something that is in the air!* George M. Cohan *said* that! NO SHIT! We got it!

Everyone is just melting for Christ sake! Bonnie is literally crying with deep sobs of Joy. She stood up, nose running and said this: "Listen you all, I want you to know how much I Love Each and Every one of you."

As she said that, *Debbie* Then, *Jocelyn* walked up behind her through the front door. They both started crying too. They didn't even know why! They hugged her real tight. The three of them just broke down right there. Hugging, and, choking on their tears.

Jocelyn said: "Hi Bonnie. Why are we crying here? You look so Wonderful, you are glowing."

Debbie Sue said: "<u>YEAH</u>!"

♥Bonnie brought them up to speed then continued: "I just know in my Heart that this is meant to be! Not just the Band. Not just the fact that all of you are in loving affairs both personal. And, with this here group of mysterians we call The *Gavence Family Travelers*, along with this very dynamic group of wonderfully talented musicians from around the country that have found their way here to this *Cosmic* gathering."

"I see a Wonderful Future for us all! Although the Fortune we all seek may not be the one we are about to make happen. Still, the rewards will be sweet from now on as we work towards our goal."

Then she went around to each and every one of us. Whispered something special in everyone's ear that we have all kept to our selves to this day… She kissed every one of us, Women included. She kissed Patty real hard, longer than the rest of us.

Terry said Again: "Bonnie… get your own girl!"

We all laughed, so did Patty. I will share her words now. The words she said to me were these: "I'll lick you all over for a dime! She paused then whispered softer: *Ok, for free then.*" It's a little before 5 pm.

Bonnie said: "Pack up everything, let's get!"

Off to the Pre-Party we go!

The excitement is building to a peak of total Freak Out! I need some calming down for just a short! I'm in shock!

Jocelyn takes me back to the bedroom, and then lays me down. She curled up next to me for a minute, pulled real close to me with all of her most wonderful long body.

She said: "I want you to kick their ass off tonight! I don't mean just get up there and play your songs! I want to see a *fucking show* from you guys that will hair lip the fucking Pope!

"No bullshit! I Will Kick Your ASS if it is not just *FANTASTIC!*"

She kissed me with a Bolt ⚡ of extra power I needed. She wiped the tears from my eyes. And hers! Then, rubbed them on her lips… Then kissed me HARD again! She stroked my hair and the back of my neck. And, then kissed me Harder… Put her hands on both sides of my face, looked straight into me for a second. I could see her eyes talking to mine. *They shimmered like Diamonds ♦ from the candlelight behind me.* Her breath is so sweet, it smells like Woman! I am Hypnotized on the fucking spot as she hauls off and kisses me even harder. If that is possible!

She pulled back with a *starved for oxygen* inhale look on her face. Her face is so red, I thought she would explode. Then she slapped the *DOG SHIT* out of me and said: "YOU GOT ME BUSTER!" Her eyes got wider, they pooled as she smiled, a stream of tears runs down the side of her Angel face as she kissed me again, then lifted me up and pushed me out the door to Mike's wagon we went. Me Droogies, I am stunned!

Mike laughed and said: "bout time! Let's get a goin! Up & *AWAY!*"

Mike pulled out onto North Street and off to Lafayette Street. We all sat in the front seat. Mike looked over at Jocelyn. Then me and said: "You two look so right sitting there" Then he gave me that Freaked out Look again! But, still said *nothing!*

We pulled up to the party, there is at least 100 cars lining the street on both sides. We got out, started down the path to the back yard. The smell of great Barbeque is wafting up and out of the pit. Rick is the <u>PIT MAS-TER</u>. Bonnie had bought a quarter beef. Rick is doing what Rick does best. The stereo is jamming hard! Bonnie's Mustang stereo hooked up to those same Speakers we used at that fake festival we put on. That reminded me. Scotty. And, Davie! The guys that are looking for us because of that! I forgot about that.

Jocelyn brought me a Tom Collins from the well stocked bar. There's a big assed Red, White and Blue banner that read. "We love you *Morison Smith Band*" under that it read: Good luck on your "*Crosby, Steal the Cash & Run Tour 71*" Bonnie had gone all out for this party. She goes all out for everyone she loves. We are so lucky to have her. She sure loves to FUCK! Just thought I would through that in here. One Hell of a woman for *fucking* sure!

The food is about ready when I noticed Buck & Anna. Anna is helping clean and serve the food. Buck is busy doing what ever Mike and Rick tell him to do.

Everyone is here, plus about fifty or so well dressed people I had no idea who they were. *Slumming!* They are Rich friends of Bonnie's. She is showing them a good time to tonight. She hopes to get some money out of them to help the cause. It is a pleasure to watch her work the scene.

"It's my back yard… my back gate… I hate to start my parties late. Here comes the party cart… ain't that great! Don't worry baby, you ain't late! As you always COME on time." Dire Straights!

She took Jocelyn and me inside where it is quiet. We sat down. Jocelyn reached down in her *black felt stiletto spiked boot*, pulled out. Then, lit a joint… Bonnie has some crystal lined out. We did them. She is now going to haul all these folks over to the Ear.

It's about 7:00 pm. First show is eight o'clock. You guys stay here and relax. Then walk over at around 7:50. This is very important! *Jocelyn*, I am putting you in charge of this one. See to it that Terry and Patty walk in first. Then Rick and Dianna… Then you two come down the steps slowly, you holding onto Don, *Bob Dylan* style. Come down the stairs like in that Dylan picture I showed ya. OK? I will have the Baby Trooper® on ya all the way to the dressing room. *I'll take care of the rest.*

I want you not to know what I have planned there till you walk in! That's very important. OK Jocelyn?

Jocelyn said: "Not to worry! Got the curry. It's a done deal. Chicky Baby!"

Terry and I are talking over the sets. Rick and Patty are practicing Harmonies. We are for sure in good form. Ready to make it. Or, break it!

Jocelyn gathers us all up. Locked up Bonnie's… We walk hand in hand to the Ear. We stop on the corner under the *Weeping Willow.* Kissed a long kiss… Jocelyn says: "If you only knew!"

She said again: "We will see.…what we will see!"

I hugged her to me, said again in her ear: I love you Jocelyn. I really love you so. I just can not explain it."

She said…again: "We'll see!"

We walked on. I thought… "What is this *we will see* stuff? Not what I was wanting to hear.

To some folks these are "The words of Death" Kinda like when ya want to be with a girl the rest of your life. And, you tell her so!

She says: "Well, *I just want to be friends.* OK!" Or, you say: "*I love you* to a girl. And, she says: "I know."

Those words are *THE KISS of Death!* I felt a shiver run up my spine. I don't have time to worry about that. I have a *Fantastic* show to do.

She stopped me at the doorway. She let the others go down the stairs. She straightened my shirt. Brushed my hair back *OUT OF MY FUCKIN EYES!* Then, we went down the stairs.

The place is raising hell! Howling… And, whistling in a *standing ovation!* We have not even played anything yet.

We walked through the crowd. Camera's *flashing.* People applauding! Into our dressing room we strolled. Sat down… And, started to tune up… (And… Freak the fuck out!)

It's about 3 minutes till Showtime. I looked at everyone. Patty looks so very cool, she always does. She is dressed in all black. With snow *white* tennis shoes on, with bright red laces… She is also wearing a *Raspberry Beret* and a giant gold medallion on a *silver chain* around her neck to her belly button. Her hair is Coal black. Perfectly straight to her waist, Cut in a perfect straight line. With over sized dark glasses on. She looks like Morticia Addams.

I am wearing a Brand new pair of *light blue corduroys'* with a button down shirt Jocelyn made for me. And, a pair of Beatle boots Bonnie had left over from the *English invasion* that just happened to fit. She has the Mop Top wigs that everyone had just after they hit the shores too. I didn't need them now. Or, back then.

I was after all.…The very first kid in JR. HIGH. (*I.e. Eva D. Edwards Jr High. Covina Califorina 1963*)Thrown out for Blue Jeans, And, Long Sandy brown hair past my shoulder blades. Before, the fuckin *Beatles* ever were heard of around here Bucko!

Surfer... *South Bay!* Terry is in a pair of <u>*White Peasant Pantaloons.*</u> Patty had them in her closet. He also is wearing a turtle neck sweater made of *blue mo-hair.*

Rick looked a bit *shaky,* that's Rick every time.

I heard Bonnie get up on the stage. She introduced us this way.

Chapter Thirty Eight

"The start of a Cosmic Journey down a Rabbit hole"

"Ladies and Gentlemen."

Here tonight. 2 shows only! *After a long run around the country!* Here are... Don - Terry - Patty & Rick.

"The Fantastic Morison Smith Band"

The "Crosby, Steal the Cash and Run" Tour 1971

We walked out in the spotlight. The four of us hand-in-hand to the stage. Took our seats... The lights go from *white to* many colors and effects. The PA system is sounding wonderful. These two new guitars are filling the room with the wonder of the music. Softly reverberating from every corner!

We started with "Carry on" Patty featured as lead vocal. She sang like a *Perfect Angel.* We all melted in our seats. She is such a great vocalist. When she sang the solo, I almost could not play. I'm rushing so fucking hard.

Jocelyn is looking right into me smiling so big it filled the room! I grabbed her heat. And, got my shit back together...

Patty didn't even ask the next song. She just went into it "Helplessly Hoping" We went into "Longtime Gone" and, directly into "You Don't Have to Cry"

We did a *Twenty* minute version of *"Country Girl"* Then, into "Lady of the Island" Nobody has made a sound in the room since song one.

After we finished "Wooden Ships" The place just fucking erupted into crazy laughter and applause. Everybody is whistling. And, hollering *Encore! Encore!* We are so fucking High. We are shaking. We are for sure *Scared Shitless!*

I had never in my life felt that from an audience anywhere! Jocelyn is clapping so hard. And, screaming so loud! Hers is the only voice I can hear! She is screaming. GOOD SONG! GOOD SONG! MORE! MORE!

Everybody but me got up and left the stage. The spot light centered on me.

I said: "I am going to sing a feeling. To the *two* most special women on this here earth. Next to me *MUM* that is! They know who they are." I went into *"GUINEVERE"* They both looked at each other. They moved across the room to the front and sat down. Then hugged each other as I sang to them… They both had tears in their eyes as I sang. They hugged each other harder. Then sighed, looked at each other Again.

Jocelyn said: "He is doing it!"

Bonnie asked: "*Doing what Jocelyn?*"

Jocelyn said: "*A Kick Ass Fantastic Show*!"

They both came on stage. *Kissed* me softly on each cheek… Then, they walked off stage hand in hand. I went into "*Four and twenty*" the stage spot flickered off as the Trouper Spot closed in on my guitar. And me! The place is so quiet. I'm kinda scared to be sure. I'm Dizzy. And, *stoked* at the same time…

All of a sudden, the place went nuts! You know… like when you listen to a hard rain coming your way! I guess I had hypnotized them all. Or, some shit! I walked to the dressing room.

Terry took the stage. He opened with "Pre Road Downs" Then, into "Down by the River" He did a song he wrote for *Patty*. Then, called us all back to the stage for a couple a more songs!

Before we started, *Patty* just stood up. In, "a cappella" She sang "Everybody I love you" As she got to the chorus. We all joined in. The place came unglued.

We started playing at the bridge. We went right into "*Sweet Judy Blue Eyes*" Then we stopped and spoke a bit. Terry started by *thanking everyone* for coming. And, then thanked *Pastor Bob Williams* for allowing us to use this place tonight. Without even one sermon!

The place fell apart in laughter.

Pastor Bob said: "Everyone needs to go to *Savoy* tomorrow night. And, hear a full show there. He has about 100 tickets with him. They are gone with more promised. In less than 15 minutes!

We went back to the singing. We went into "Ohio" Then, "Find the Cost of Freedom."

After that, we closed the show with Terry and me as a duo. We sang "Teach Your Children" Then kissed the room *goodnight* as we stumbled thru the crowd of screaming adoring new fans!

I noticed *Windy Austin* behind the bar watching us leave to the dressing room. He came in and looked at us. He said: "*I fucking hate you all!*" Turned around and left! We all looked at each other. And, then broke up laughing. Did that really happen?

I'm holding Jocelyn in my lap where she had parked herself. With, a *death lock* around my neck! She is laughing and *crying* at the same time. Hugging, and, kissing me all over my face. (Kiss. Kiss) licking my lips. Sticking her tongue in my mouth… And, pulling mine out. Kissing me harder and harder… She is breathing so hard. I thought she would pass out. Then, she did! What a fully packed. Firm girl,…Woman!

I gave her some real good *mouth to mouth*. We laughed. And, laughed till our sides ached. Everyone is coming in and out wishing us the best and wanting to know when we are going to write and release an album?

God it felt so fucking good. *Maybe to good!* I looked at Terry. Made reference to the *Windy* deal… Terry just shrugged his shoulders and snorted! As he flipped him Off!

He said: "Fuck the Dog if he can't take a Fucking Joke, I'll kick his fucking ass!"

Jocelyn is sipping wine/LSD. Spilling it in my lap as she danced. She would laugh out load and say: "*What a fucking show ya all!*"

Then Swing around. Lay one on me. And, go to licking my face and lips again. Kicking her feet. And, squirming around, grinding my knee into her crotch. Rocking back fourth. Screaming some more, She is for sure having a real good time. I watched her as she reveled! Lover, Gal/Pal, Beautiful! Those Lip's! I reached over and turned her head. *KISS!*

30 minutes later, we went out and did it again to an entire new audience. Same thing happened all over again. After… we all sat in the dressing room smoking the Doobs that had been thrown at us at the end there. Everyone wanted to know what to do now. We are so fucking high from the show we were damn near Hyper for Christ sake!

Bonnie said: Hell: "Let's go finish the food, drugs and booze at my house!" Everyone got up and away they went.

Jocelyn and I are sitting there kissing and sucking on each other when She said: "Don"

Yes Jocelyn.

She went on: "I don't want to go back over there tonight. How about we just walk back to *Patty's* house, just you and me… Ok?"

I put my guitar in Bonnie's car. She looked at me, gave me a kiss. Then she said: "Thank you Don! I am so fucking proud of you. I'll never forget this night!" a fuckin fantastic show!

I told Bonnie: "Jocelyn and I are going to walk back to Patty's house."

She said: "I know where you are going, It ain't Patty's house Buddy. She has something *special* planned for you my dear!"

She looked at Jocelyn and they both winked. She drove off. We started walking towards the campus.

She is holding my hand so tight. *Lords of London* would have been scared of a break! Dig it! We stopped there in the street kissed a passing kiss. Then started walking again, her hand is hot and sweaty. She has a little shiver to her. I asked if she was cold. She hugged me tighter.

She said: "I ain't cold Don! I ain't Cold!"

We walked up the *Walk of the Graduates*. So, many wonderful things have happened to me right here. It's a very magic spot for me. We walked around the back of OLD MAIN. Down these old stairs, to, a basement door there in the dark

She said: "Debbie and I found this broken piece a wood here. When… you push it, like this! She pushed it "SNAP"— The door opens! WOW!

Jocelyn… It's 2:30 am. Is there no one in here?

She snapped: "I ain't never seen no one."

Where are we going?

She went on: "I have something I want to show you. Come on. And, be quiet!" We started up the creaking back stairs to the third floor. She has a joint of Columbian Red Bud. *She lit it!*

We walked thru the scary dark BLUE moonlit halls. Ghosts… are jumping out from every corner. We stopped at the end of the hallway. There, is a big 100 year old wooden table. About 8 feet long and 5 feet wide… About a foot thick down to giant legs! There is a big window that the *BLUE* moon is shinning through. She climbed up on that table. She is *silhouetted* by the moon light. She took off her shorts and threw them at me. I caught them. Rubbed them all over my face… Took in her sweet smell… She took off her top by lifting it over her head. And, dropping it to the floor…

She stood naked in that big window. Then, spread her legs and arms. She said: "I am yours!"

She then lay on her back on the table top awaiting me. I striped off my clothes, climbed onto the table. I stared kissing her toes, working my way up to her lips. About half way… I got *bushwhacked!*

I lay on top of her. Kissing… Licking her face and breasts… She is directing something all the way home. It felt like he was on fire! We rocked back and forth, up and down, on the table, off the table, Into the hallway, down the hall, on the hallway bench, in that big window as people were strolling below on the sidewalk three stories down. We are hitting it so hard. We were making a bit too much noise.

We heard a door open down the hall. A guy and two girls came out of the stairwell. And, right in our direction. They turned on the light, came in the room. We are under the table by then. With our clothes, there is a drop curtain around the table so they couldn't see us unless we made noise and they looked. So, we lay there quietly and listened a minute or two.

We are still hooked together as we start kissing and slowly fucking again. Even though these people are right there, we could not stop. I don't know how to this day we didn't get caught. It seemed to add to the feeling! About then they got up, turned off the lights, walked down the hall and out. We slipped our clothes on still jerking with passion. We are no way close to done yet. We felt it might be time to move.

We left OLD MAIN. We went to the *Planetarium*. I striped off her shorts and shirt. Lay her down on the steps out side In the BLUE moon light. In full view of anyone whom might walk by.

She rolled me over. She is on top for awhile. We made love about everywhere on the campus. And, then walked to Patty's… We opened the door….no one is here. We didn't wait. We striped and hit the bed. Fucked ourselves to sleep.…

About sun rise, she slid her hands to my crotch and rubbed me awake. *I need more!*

I asked: "Did it wake you up?"

She said: "I just woke up wanting more. So, Here!"

She jumped on top of me. We helped the sun cum too!

Back for a nap again. Then, we did it again! I'm lying on my side looking at her as the front door opened. She woke up again. She looked at me and said: "I want to tell you something"

She pulled me close, guided me back in. She is slipping in and out of pleasure trying to tell me something. As, she moaned and moved! She had me right where she wanted me. She is not letting go.

Finally she squeezed my arms so tight. She fell on me. Reached around and tore three holes down my back! She stiffened. Tightened her legs and shook! She poured out on me. She tightened up again. More hot liquid poured form her. I knew she finally *came hard!*

She rolled over next to me still shaking and hugged my neck so tight I chocked. She is so out of breath. She could hardly talk. She is going.…Oh my god!

She opened her eyes. And, just melted me on the spot with the look she gave me of approval! She is nodding her head up and down. With sweat running off her like rain! I need a shower! *Join me?*

I am already there!

I got the towels. Plus, the Doob.

Does that thing <u>EVER</u> go down?

Nope! Not when in the *presence* of such a sexually charged electrical beauty like you! She is smiling. And, glowing at the same time!

Chapter Thirty Nine

"Heavy Drugs. Zelda.
And <u>RUFF SEX</u>"

Terry and Patty are here now. They hit their room and did the same thing. We could hear the bed pounding on the floor, Patty screaming FUCK ME! FUCK ME! FUCK ME HARD NOW! God Damn Son Of A Bitch that feels so fucking good!

That sent us to the shower. Of course, we couldn't hear that and not be turned on again. So, we scrubbed. Fucked. Scrubbed our shower away. I have never done so much savage fucking in my life. I just could not get enough she couldn't either.

It's about 10 am now, we couldn't sleep anymore. *It's to hot!* I decided to get up and get started on the concert stuff for today. We are going to head that way around 3: 30 pm. As, we are to play at 6 pm. We put on clean clothes. Waited for Bonnie and Mike to arrive… We are making out on the couch when Bonnie came in and said: "Everyone ready to go?"

Terry and Patty came out of the shower. *Got dressed…*

Bonnie and Jocelyn are chuckling about something. Looking at me and blushing! Bonnie's Nipples are so hard. They are about to Rip through her Tit-shirt. They blushed a bit more and went about their tasks getting us ready. (kiss)

Terry and I are talking about the night before. Rick and Dianna showed up and joined us. Dianna went off with all the girls. They did girl stuff.

Mike gave me *THAT LOOK* again.

I said: "<u>WHAT</u>?"

He looked at Terry.…Then, shrugged his shoulders.

Then said: "It would all come out in the wash."

Terry looked at me with an *"I don't know what his problem is Look."* Bonnie and Jocelyn grabbed me. Pulled me in the living room…

She said: "Which do you like better?" She has two posters made up for *Gaybellie.* And for next weeks *Ear* shows, And the Swinging door. We decided on both.

She gathered us all up like a *mommy goose* and away we flew. As we drove out 16 West, Bonnie showed us something she received last night.

She has this funny looking bottle with a turn crank on the top!

She said: "I have this full of two grams. And an 8 ball at my apartment for after."

I said: "Alright: the crystal!"

She said: "No my Handsome Man! It's… _Cocaine!_"

I grabbed the little screw top bottle and said: "Is that what that is?"

I had heard a bit about that in the _Navy_. But, I never thought I would ever see any! She passed it back. Told us to _twist_ the top and fill the little bowl in there. Then, like a nose inhaler, _Toot_ it up one side. Reload it. Then, do the other.

Terry, Patty and Bonnie are in the front seat. Jocelyn and I in the back. That _coke_ hit us right off. The next thing I knew. We are fucking right there in the backseat. We are pumping Coke Hard. As, Bonnie looked in the rear view and said: "That Shit Grabs a hold of ya don't it!"

Patty and Terry are going crazy too. Bonnie just laughed as we sped out the highway.

Bonnie said: KILL THE RICH!

Even though the stereo is _screaming!_ The car is full of _kissing_ and _sucking_ sounds! Wow! This stuff is fucking Fun. Bang, bang, bang, _bang_. Dig it! Suck. Lick. Chew. Pound… Feels like Heaven!

This Coke stuff is weird me Droogies! You can fuck, and _Fuck_ and Fuck. And, keep on _fucking!_ It always feels like you just started.

Bonnie said: "We are here. Pull up your pants and shorts. Look _respectable_."

Now, I don't know about you! But… after I been making _love_ for over 48 hours! It's kinda hard to look respectable! That cocaine stuff is kicking my Ass! My whole face is numb. It's a different kinda high!

I'm so FUCKING Horny I can not stand it! I told Bonnie. Jocelyn and I are going to go sit in the chapel, its over 200 years old.

Bonnie said: "Ok" And, ran off with Zelda. Who has arrived with Mike and the others?

Zelda took Bonnie inside the chapel and kissed her Cocaine hard! Bonnie is so _Horny_ after driving us there. They locked the bathroom door and made love for 15 minutes or so. It's quiet now. I'm looking at Jocelyn. Looking at me with this most _loving gaze…_ She took my hand. Held it close then looked me in the eyes.

She pulled me closer and said: "_I Love you so very much Don!_"

I tried not too. But, I couldn't win. I wanted to know _absolutely_ for sure!

When we make love… I feel like I have never felt. It's like you complete me. Inside, and out! She squeezed my hand harder.

She said again: "_I just flat LOVE you, I will go anywhere with you._" She kissed me on the forehead, hugged me to her chest. _I love you… I love you!_ I Love You!

She looked around the chapel. As, though it were full and said: "_I am In Love with This Man, No matter what!_"

I'm floored as you would expect! I'm totally speechless. I wanted her to say that so bad it hurt. Now that she has. *I can't speak.* I just reached out and held her close.

After what felt like for ever, Rick and Dianna came in all smiles. Looked like they had tried the *Coke!* They are all wet. Their clothes are not on right. And, then in came Patty and Terry. Also wet.

I asked: "Been swimming"

You know it! Says Terry.

Rick retorts: Swimming… and Fucking like the little fishies!

The stage manager came in. called us stage side. The announcer called us out. We walked out. I looked at the crowd. *All blue hairs and Jesus freaks.*

I should have looked out the Damn Window. Terry looked at me like, What Now?

I started playing "If I had a Hammer" Then "Lemmon Tree" Then, "Hang down your head Tom Dooley" We did our best Smothers Brothers show stuff. And, jokes along with a bit of FIRESIGN THEATER and SOUPY SALES jokes. And, a bunch more *Folk Music…*

We got a *Ten Minute Standing Ovation* and $160 from the gate. We gave half to Bonnie. And, Half to Patty! It isn't much. But, they both deserved anything we can give them. With out them, this would not be happening! *Our love to them both to this very day!*

The show was such a success. It changed our idea of what kinda band we should be. This is getting better by every passing minute. Plus, in *LOVE* too! What more could a guy ask for! A week end of Hot Sex… *That's, what!* Dig it!

"Stay seated while the ride is in motion!"

The Pastor thanked us for saving his show. Asked us back at *Christmas…* And again next year! We agreed… packed it up. And, even signed a few autographs!

Jocelyn is so proud to be on my arm! She made me shine! I reached around her waist, pulled her close in the back seat then started *French kissing* her. And, sucking those *Wonderful Lips* all the way to Bonnie's apartment…

I had held her so close. We are both wet from sweat. Bonnie parked the car and we went in the front door. Everyone is already out back and in the dug out cave under this old house where slaves used to hide on the railroad.

Bonnie said: "For us to come in the bedroom. She has *6* big honking lines of crystal. Mixed with the *coke*… she has an eight ball left. Should she break some out? Or, save it for *Gaybellie* this afternoon!

We all did one more line of blow. Then, a big line of crystal…

I said: "Save it!"

It will be a longtime. Before, cocaine comes to town to stay. About 1… Or, 2 years yet! So… we didn't see much more of that stuff. But, every now and then for awhile it seemed!

I'm looking forward to the next day. As is Bonnie!

The last two shows were just showcases. This one we needed to pull off great.

We found the three of us tooting the Coke and drinking Coors, smoking lumbo and sitting around the spool table talking about how we almost got fucked tonight. No body expected to see what we did when we walked out from that stage wing! I knew as I walked out that what we had prepared was not going to cut it! These people would think that "Crosby, Stills and Nash" is a *law firm* for Christ's sake!

"Ditto" Jocelyn said!

Bonnie asked: "Don. You are amazing! How did you know what to do?"

Terry and I know songs from 10 years ago. Being from *musical* families, long before we ever met… Or, this band thing ever came up. I thought of the song. And we just played it.

Patty is so damn good. Turned out she is *classically trained* as an opera singer. But just isn't into it!

She wants to sing *Rock and Roll*. That's why she is with us. She can fill the note where ever it is needed. When you work with *Troopers*, you can't go wrong.

People are starting to wonder what happened to us. When Terry and Mike came in and said: "Where the fuck you assholes been?"

We been right here.

"Terry said that people are leavening, he closed it up outside. Patty is ready to go too." He looked at me to see what I wanted to do as *Zelda* came in.

Bonnie said: "Terry. Here are my keys. You guys can drive my car back to Patty's. And come back in the morning." Rick and Dianna joined them.

They climbed the step from the screened in porch. And, out to Bonnie's car, down the road they went. It is quiet now. Bonnie went and broke out some more of that *Coke*. Rolled three bombers. We all sat crossed legged on her king sized bed. Tooted. Smoked, and talked.

Talk is starting to get steamy! Bonnie commented on how *Wonderful* Zelda's Pussy had swollen from the Coke stuff.

She went on to say: "I sure could lick a bunch more all over that *Bright Pink Pussy*. If she liked."

Zelda said: "You mean, this here *Hot Bright Pink Pussy Right Here* Bonnie?"

Bonnie said: "That one will do it!"

I looked at Jocelyn and said: "What do you think the two of them have in mind?"

Jocelyn said: "I don't know! I'll bet it includes the two of us though, don't ya think?"

By the time she said that, Bonnie had her thumb in Zelda's ass hole, reaming it out real good with her fingers. The other hand in her dripping wet Pussy.

Wow! I had not seen *Zelda* completely naked before. She is a stunning German girl. She sat there with her heels up against her buns. And, looked at Bonnie thumbing her asshole and stroking her pussy... And, she just flat exploded. She pulled Bonnie's shirt off and slid off her shorts. *They both* looked at us!

Jocelyn slipped off her shorts and her shirt. Then she reached over and unsnapped my jeans. Bonnie pulled one leg. And, Zelda the other... I fell out Stone Hard pulsing. The veins are sticking out so hard and full. I thought it was about to explode. Here I'm with three of the most beautiful women on earth. Their eyes are burning a hole me.

Bonnie reaches out and fondles Zelda's Huge tits with her free hand. Her Nipples are rock hard. Then Zelda is in Bonnie's lap pushing her legs apart. She buries her face in *Bonnie's dripping Pussy*. Reaches up and squeezes her tits almost off.

Jocelyn and I are creaming on ourselves watching this. Bonnie can't stand it anymore and turns around 69. They just cut loose all over the bed. I grab Jocelyn. Pull her to me, hold her around the waist. She showed me the front door. I slid right in and I'm right at home getting with it. The four of us are rolling all over each other moaning and groaning. Sweating... Sticking to each other just flat *fucking hard!*

Bonnie came up for air! She hollered *Snoot Time!* She got the mirror, made 4 Huge lines laced with crystal. We tooted it up, had a drink. And, what ever else anyone had to do at the time, back to bed. Bonnie is there waiting for the three of us. *She has another pile of coke*. She wants us to lie down next to each other feet at the bottom of the bed. We did.

She came over. She climbed between my legs and said: "I'll do you first. Because, it takes longer to sink in on the head of your dick."

She spit on me, rubbed a finger full of coke all over it, she licked her fingers and moved over to Jocelyn. She reached out, grabbed her ankles, spread them all the way out to my lap.

She filled her middle finger and rubbed it all over her inside and out. She rubbed another finger full on each of her nipples. She moved over to

Zelda who is creaming all over watching us. She poured a giant pile on her tongue and licked all over Zelda's pussy with it. Inside and out!

Then she had me put a pile on my tongue. And, licked it all over her! We mixed in a pile of pussies. A dick. *6 tits! Four butts. 4 pair of lips.* I'm in catbird heaven… We all did anything each other asked for. Then Zelda went in the big bath tub with Bonnie. Jocelyn and I just fucked each other in every hole we could stick it in. or, suck on! I was licking every part of her when I noticed the sun is up.

We could hear Bonnie and Zelda Screaming and Creaming in the tub. So, I pulled Jocelyn back to the bed and did it again! We are speeding our brains out. We had ended up doing more speed than Coke on the last toot! We just could not get enough fucking and sucking. We all took a break.

We are going to hit it again one more time when Terry and Rick pulled up with Patty in Bonnie's car. We scrambled for clothes. The, place is a wreck! Dick and Pussy juice is every where. The place stunk of *Raw Hot* on-going *Dirty Sex!*

Bonnie and Zelda are out of the bath cleaning up the place.

Bonnie said: "You two stink of love! The bath is yours. *Get in there.*" She threw us some towels. Our clothes and shut the door. I watched Jocelyn climb in the tub. I stopped her as she was about to sit down. I climbed in and she sat down on me. *I slid right in.* Along with warm water and her sigh, we are doing it again.

She said: "You know Don. I have some of my stuff upstairs."

I did know that Of Course.

I said: "That right?"

Jocelyn says: "I also have the key. And, she is gone till Monday."

We dance out the back door Naked. Then, up the stairs totally naked… I have a *blistering hard on.* That anyone who saw us going up there would have applauded! *REALLY!*⇒We lay right down in bed, started going even harder.

I feel a wetness dripping under my nose! *Shit!* I have a *Motha Fuckin* nosebleed from the Coke stuff, the Crystal. Or, both!

I said: "I have not had a nose bleed since I was 8 years old fer Christ's sake!"

Jocelyn lay me on my back, put a cold washcloth on it and waited. It stopped, we resumed our love making.

We could hear all of them down stairs talking. Asking, what happened to us, I heard Bonnie say. Man… Bump, Bump! Can't you hear um?"

"Hear what?" asked Terry.

Bonnie says: "They're up there!"⬆ She points over her head. "They have been up there Fucking Hard for over an hour now."

I guess that was our cue to pull up our pantaloons. Then, come on downstairs. And, get with it. We got dressed. She puts on clean clothes.

I say: Lucky, You!

We walked downstairs and into Bonnie's. Terry has the guitars out, he is strumming something he has written in the few hours we been apart. Amazing! He is such a talent! I feel like he and Patty are a godsend to me. They are both so talented. I can't help but learn from them.

We all joined in singing along to a song we had never heard before that he wrote an hour or two ago. I grabbed my guitar and laid down the most perfect solo lead I ever heard...*until then!*

Patty went in her room to what we would come to call the _Magic Closet._ (Every time we turned around, Patty would pull everything from an Auto Harp to Mandolins and Banjos out of there). She can play any instrument on this or any other planet. Where did this wonderful group of mysterians come from? She laid down the most perfect rhythm with the auto harp.

This is getting almost scary!

Mike speaks out: "Nice song man!"

I looked at Terry with this *Goofy* look in my eyes as he said: "What's with the Goofy look in your eyes?"

I asked: "Did you just write that"

He said: "Nope! We just wrote it." Rick said: "We should play that at the concert."

I agreed! We went through the song a few more times. We figured it out, had it ready by time to leave.

The whole time we were working on that song. Jocelyn never moved more than a foot from me. She would have been closer. But, my *turn coat* dog Spanky. Is now protecting her too...

Nobody told him to do that. He just took it as his *new job!* I love that ol Doggie Me Droogies! Just try to get any where near her if you are not me. And, you must deal with the WRATH OF SPANKY! Nobody wants that!

I guess we will have to keep our clothes on for awhile till the concert is over. Then all bets are off. After all, we ain't finished up yet!

We get to the fair grounds...they let our cars through into the *Horse Arena* being used as a staging area for the talent. There's the *Windy Austin* Bus sitting there. We sat in the car awhile making out and petting heavy. We smoked another joint or two. Windy is pacing around their bus, cussing about getting bumped back to matinee! *I love it.* After all...I tried to warn him! But, _No_... he wouldn't listen! Just kept on... And, on about it! *I knew this is what it would come down too.*

Chapter Forty

"It's serious I guess! Terry shows his <u>colors</u>"
"OR! The fight is ON!"
"OR... John Lennon. <u>Dead!</u>"

Terry looks at me and says: "Look at that poor little *Windy* guy! Ain't that a fucking shame!" As he flipped him off.

He said: "I hate that *pompous ass hole*, he said to me one time when I asked him about his band: *"Don't come here with that posh talk, you nasty little twit!* Like he is Joe Cocker... Doing that Phony Shit cover song *"A little help from my <u>fuckin</u> friends"* I'd bet <u>John Lennon</u> is rolling over in his frigging grave, and he ain't even dead yet!"

When he said that about John Lennon... I felt this *wind go through my soul!* It was very weird for sure me Droogies!

Then, I looked at Terry and said: "Man, you really hate that fucker don't ya?"

He Snapped Back: "<u>YES!</u>"

We climb out of the car a bit later after some good *cheap thrills* in the back of the Snakeç We had lost track of time. Mike is *banging* on the wagon saying: "Zip up, we are on in a few."

Windy had gone on stage 30 minutes to go. *Windy and the boy's* "<u>Rodeo</u>" are doing the same lame Joe Cocker deal! Jerking around like an idiot!

We are shown our dressing room. We went there to tune up and wait our turn. Jocelyn went to the burger booth. And, brought back about 30 hamburgers Bonnie bought. Even though we are still <u>flying</u> on the crystal from the hit we just did! I ate 4 of them before we were called to the stage.

Windy and the boys finished up to a *Luke warm* thank you. They were off. The guy announced us.

"Now you bunch of assholes!"

"To wrap it up for another *wonderful <u>Gaybillie 1971!</u>*"

"Here they are... The K K E G "Band of the Month!"

"The Fantastic *<u>Morison Smith Band!</u>*"

Out we went. Everything went like clockwork! We had them eating from our hands. Song after song, they wouldn't let us go! We sang more songs then we even knew. Remember Ears and Ogre from K K E G fm

92.1? They are here with a remote TRUCK! Their station has become the number one radio station in the 4 state corners. They made a real big deal about us. It was just *fate* I guess that they knew Debbie and Jocelyn so good. They also were good friends with Ann and her evil twin <u>Joyce</u>. They recorded some of our show and played it on the air the next day. Windy was so pissed! I'm lovin it!

I told him way back when: "That he would be making room for me and mine real soon."

He just laughed back then! *He isn't laughing now.*

We have done three killer shows this week. To, sell out venues. They played *matinee* at Gaybellie. Got bumped to make room for us!

That is all thanks to Bonnie Of Corse.

She said: "Hell lover, I gave the guy making the stage list a sleeve job!"... <u>REALLY</u>, I did!

I could feel the juice drip to my bare foot. That's how much I'm spotting! Her shorts crotch is dripping wet! I could not wait till we were back at Patty's, she could not either.

We did it all the way back in the back seat again. I guess it's kinda dangerous though. *Zelda* is in the front seat eating Bonnie out while she is driving! Zelda has her feet on the roof, she is butt naked. Bonnie has one hand *all the way* in her. And, steering with the other... She is fisting Zelda so hard. She almost kicked out the *windshield!*

We pulled over to a side road and turned off the lights. Zelda and Bonnie took over the inside of the car. While Jocelyn and I jumped on the hood, we all just fucked in the *BLUE* Moon light till we could try and drive home without fucking each others lights out. That was not easy.

We got back on the road. And into town. Bonnie dropped Jocelyn and me off as Zelda is still eating and licking on her breasts. Fingering her pussy as they drove off to her place... I could see Zelda's ass in the window as they made the street.

There is no one in the house. We lit a candle in the front room so we could see any shadow. I picked her up, sat her on my face and swallowed all her juices in. I took her smell as deep in me as I could get it. Lay her down. And, <u>*Just Fucked the socks off that little pink beavered vixen!*</u>

Then... we just passed fucking out in a full love embarrass. Again! My balls are hanging to my feet. My dick is 8 inches longer after this *FUCK-ING* weekend!

What will this Monday morning bring. After this week end, what could be next? *I can't wait!*

The next few months will be intense. I can not wait to get started.

I slid out of her as she said: "What do you think the painter will brush for us next Don?"

I said: Wow Jocelyn… How…*Extemporaneous*."

She said: "Extemperfuckinwhat?

We slept till a few hours later. *What a weekend!* Hell! Let's do it one more time! That's what we did.

She said: "How *Extemporaneous!*"

I said: "Yeah."

I awoke Monday morning from likely the most _POWERFUL_ wet dream I have ever had in my life! So far! But, the dream is real! I opened my eyes expecting to be at the Grayhouse, in my room in the back, when Jocelyn moved ever so softly on my chest. I could feel her long eye lashes on my skin. They felt like *Butterflies wings*. I wrapped my left arm around her waist, tickled her side over to the top of her most wonderful full firm and round ass. I followed the seam down to her thigh, and then tickled my way back up her spine to her neck. She shivered. And, stretched out in all four directions at once… Turned her head to me… Opened her wide oval eyes, pulled me down to a kiss… Those soft… Puffy lips just drive me crazy! To this day when I think about those lips!

She kissed her way to my ear and whispered, "*I LOVE YOU SO VERY MUCH!*" You just.…*Take my breath away!*" (Kiss… Kiss.)

I turned her over on her back and lay on top of her between her legs. I looked her in those eyes and said: "Jocelyn. You are the most Beautiful woman on this or any other earth in the universe. Everything from your hair… Too your feet… Is that of a Goddess! Your taste, And, smell are *Ambrosia* to me. I need a *LONG* drink of your love now."

I dropped down and took her in my mouth and buried half of my face in her loving heat! Her legs shot up, she tightened up like a rubber band. I kissed her thighs and licked them, worked my way up to her again and said: "You never have to worry about any of that shit ever again. That part of your life is over and done! I love each and every inch of you. Inside, And, out!

She reached under me… guided him home. We just melted together as one... Again! As we made love, she talked in my ear of all her plans and dreams for her life. Again, she didn't want at a *young age to waist away* with a *high school sweetheart* and hate it the rest of her life."

She said: "I want to travel… make music. And, children who will never have to live the way I have. I feel you so deep inside me. I know love is with us both. I have made out with a few boys so far, never made _LOVE_ though till now. All, they wanted to do is get my clothes off. Stick it in. Pull it out and say… See ya round honey! I have never been stalked by a *future lover* before! You scared me at first! I didn't know what you wanted from me. Besides, sex. But you never came on to me! So, I didn't have a clue. Debbie said you were a friend of Tony. Terry. And Rick, But, that was about all she knew. I thought I knew what love was before. I never expected it to… oh my!"

She stopped in mid-sentence. Started moaning louder and louder… Her insides are clamping down on me, so is her outside. Then, she screamed! She started going faster. And, faster! She stiffened and hugged me so hard I couldn't breathe. She held on… squeezed… _stopped breathing_, turned red. Swallowed… And, choked a little… Held her breath then squeezed even harder. Held it for what seemed like forever. Then… just screamed bloody _fuckin_ murder. And, fainted right away!

I could not get out. Not that I wanted to mind you. She has a death grip on me. She is breathing so deep. The look on her face is pure _ecstasy_! Her eyes roll when she opens them, tears are streaming down her cheeks. She pulled me to her face, locked her lips on mine and started sucking. Then we started breathing the same air. Her out into me… And, back again. I'm getting Dizzy! Then, I came harder. With, more love and passion than any other time in my life! And, still she would not let go.

Stanley is like in her cervix. She is milking and drinking the stuff! She is locked on the thing. As she kept it, it would not go down. She would not let go! _She is on fire_! So am I, me Droogies! _UN be leave a bull man!_

She pulled her self up. Then, curled up around me… She had me in a scissor lock. Her arms are around my chest, her nipples are so hard and hot they burn my skin. She kissed me again. I kissed her back hard. She put her wet tongue in my ear, gave me a sloppy wetty.

She said: "_I love you Don_, I really, really do! I have waited all my life to be free: there is no one in Farmington I can trust! Or, call a friend. Everyone at school hates me! All they want to do is fight me! Most think I am to tall and skinny. My _birthmark_ drives me crazy! Everyone that looks at me… is looking right at that! You have one too! Don't it bug you?"

I hugged her and said: "Jocelyn…(Kiss) I don't even notice it."

We came so hard together. We both passed out again. We just lay there in each others arms in shock!

I told her that: "The people in your life so far. Are not the ones? There is a much larger life for you! _Debbie_. And _Karen_! The three of you were together to survive till now, the three of you can now loose your _chrysalis_ and fly high. And, _FREE_." (Kiss… Kiss…)

This entire family thing we have goin on here just blows my fuckin mind! All of us have come together at this wonderful time for some reason that we may never know. I plan to just go with this where ever it takes us. It just feels. Too right!

I told her that she was very special! Talented. Smart and *beautiful*, they are all jealous. I will take her anywhere she wants to go in the world! NOW! I don't want to wait till we are 65 years old in a damn motor coach traveling around looking over the country. I want to do it *now!*"

I want us to pull off the road to some *Indian mesa in Arizona*. And drive. Or, climb to the top and fuck like bunnies! Anywhere we see we want to go. We will go. NOW! Not later!

Then... when we are old, we can write books about it. (Like I am doing now at 12: 01 pm. July 24th 2008) She, unclamped me from her love. She slid me out. Slow. Rubbed me all over her...

She said in my ear: "I am so happy now. I have waited *all of my life* for you! I am not going to let you get away now. *I love you so very much!* I love you!" Wow! I guess the girl *Loves me!* I Know I *LOVE* her!

Then she buried her face in my shoulder, we just broke down. She cried awhile longer and I just held her so close. She wiped the tears away with my hand and I licked them off.

I kissed her so very soft...I told her she and I are one now. That is just the way it will be no matter what! Or... what anyone has to *say about it!*

Not to present a bummer here at this so tender moment. But... we must remember that this young lady is all of just 16 years old, I think... going on 17. But, she is a mature woman of any age, her age meant nothing me. I'm all of just turned 21. So, I didn't see how her age made that much difference, it didn't matter anyway.

There is no one going to *separate* us! Ever! Real James Dean kinda shit man!

I told her that and kissed her again. She smiled. And, took a deep breath... Headed for the shower... I followed. We shared a shower and some hot water for our souls. I hadn't noticed how long all that took. It is now 12:30 pm. I could hear Bonnie's Mustang gearing down North Street hill. Her Laker pipes are beating the shit out of the air, her stereo is kicking ass! She came in the bathroom *naked*, got in the shower with us. She rubbed on Jocelyn. Then, me!

She said: "You two look so damn good together... you look so happy and unafraid. Like you could take on the whole world with one hand! You two know how much I care for... LOVE you?" She hugged us both and showered with us.

Bonnie finished up and we are alone again. Jocelyn had a few more things she needed to vent.

She looked at me again and said: "My hair looks like shit! Everyone calls me JOC! Or, ARLOW."

She stopped with a *choke of shower water* and said: "You call me *JOC-ELYN!* Why?" She is rubbing the water from her eyes as my heart sank even deeper. I actually feel weak! Watching her is just moving...

I started to answer. But, I could see she isn't done opening up her thoughts to me. I didn't want to stop her. I don't think she has ever done this with anyone before. I didn't ask.

She just kept talking about all her life's problems. I thought id let her get it all out, add my 2 cents afterward. I was taking in EVERY word she is saying. Like I was a dictation machine... I want this information. It is her. I want to know everything there is to know about her. So, I never let her feel misunderstood. Or, *NOT INVOLVED* in every part of our lives.

I continued to listen and gaze at her naked beauty now sitting crossed-legged between my legs.

She went on: "I am a *skinny bitch* with no butt, I can't go back to Farmington to live. Or, do a normal life there. Because, I can't stand it there!"

My *Dad is wonderful,* He is the very greatest! I know he wants to be free. He watches us out by the *Volvos* tripping. And, smoking dope... He wants to join us. But, as long as my Mom is there... he doesn't stand a chance. It's not her fault. She is just a southern woman with a heart as big as her pride. So, he has to put up this big front.

My sister *Juli* is so very cool. And, collected... She is the strength of our family, I know that! No girl could ever ask for a more *wonderful sister*. My brother John is so caring and thoughtful of all of our need's, he go's a bit heavy about things from time to time. I love them all more than anything!

But, *it's my time now!* I can't waist it: it won't come back again ever! You are only young one time! And, I don't plan to waste any of it!

I don't like my voice! And, nobody else does either. Every time I come to town and hang out with Debbie. And Karen we, have to get chased around by assholes that just want to drill us. And, drop us. They have hurt girls I know! You just gotta watch out for yourself.

Everything here with you seems to be what I'm on this earth to enjoy. With you, *YOUNG* means everything. I'm confused sometimes. But, all of this seems so fucking right! I have NEVER been so happy in my life! She kissed me hard. I love you. *Let's do it ALL!*

Jocelyn got out of the shower first. I'm rinsing off to do the same when Bonnie grabbed me.

She said: "We have some fish to fry about four o'clock. Make sure Terry and Rick are here too."

She leaned over and said: "*I love to look at you naked!*"

She put both hands. One, on the other from bottom to tip...

And said: "That's right, you should be in porno."

She squeezed my ass. And, damn if she didn't stick her middle finger through the door! I jumped a bit.

She said: "Just checking your oil! Now, get out of here before I forget I am a Lady!"

I stepped out of the shower and Jocelyn said: "Bonnie… you are the very best. Thank you for helping this to happen with Don and me!"

Bonnie said: "You have him now… you better hold on to him. You ever let go… and he is _mine!_"

Jocelyn said: "I hear ya Bonnie!"

Bonnie did retort: "You don't mind when I hug and kiss on Don, do you?" She went on: "He is yours… I tried to get him away from you! But, that wasn't going to happen! After I saw you two at the _cross_ ✝, _I knew!_ You don't know this. Because, you were not there! But, Don was crazy with heat and love the rest of that night. And, he was inconsolable about it! I knew once I showed him where you live he would not be any good to me anymore. Not just because he would be yours! But, because _I love you_ too! I would never do anything to hinder the love you two have. It is so powerful we all can see it beaming out of you both."

Bonnie told Jocelyn: "I have to tell you this. We were all tripping our asses off. It was so intense, and a lot were a bit too high. Paul had left two racks of Reds for us at Tim's house. Don was down at the WALL trippin and playing with Spanky, Some weird game about _Dog Revolution_. Or, something weird like that! He was so high, I was scared for him. I took his red. And, mine. Went to find him… He was spaced out so far… he said that Spanky and a new friend were standing on the WALL preaching. I told the guys at the house. I would find him. And, take care of him. Jocelyn… I took him home to my apartment and I FUCKED his brains out for 6 hours straight! I even _RAPED_ him for two more hours after he passed out!

He didn't stand a chance! I was not taking NO for an answer! I fucked him so long. And, so hard! He stopped breathing for about 3 minutes. I thought I had killed him. I was freaking out, when he opened his eyes and asked for _YOU!_ He stood up. And, fell down. Hit his head on the end of the bed. And, was out again… I am sorry! But, he was still so _hard._ I squatted on him another 20 minutes! I am sorry. I _RAPED_ him! I could not help myself. I knew the minute you two were together. He would be off the market. I told him. I wished he loved me. But, I knew it was not true. Inside, I love him very, very much! But, he only has eyes for you! I had to get just a bit of his color and strength before it was too late. Do you hate me?"

Jocelyn said: "No! But, <u>DON'T DO IT AGAIN!</u>" Ψ ψ ♥

The girls & I are all out of the shower now. I have made coffee. Terry and Patty are also getting up. Rick and Dianna had gone somewhere else for the night. The five of us are the only ones home. We sat down for breakfast. The girls made Eggs and stuff. We sat down to talk and figure out what Bonnie has up her sleeve for four o'clock.

She said: "That Bob Risby guy is back in town, he is at the MOUNTAIN INN, he has a tape recorder with him to record any songs you may have. Plus, a cover song as a *voice track for comparison.*"

He is most interested in *original songs*, you guys got any. Yeah, A couple! Well… work um up! I'll pick you all up at 3:30. She leaned over. Kissed Jocelyn, Told her she *loved her.* That she is very lucky to be in such a wonderful love affair. With such a wonderful man! As, is he to be found by you!" (Kiss…).

She looked at me. Sighed, and, kissed me.

Bonnie said: "She loves you so deep. I have never seen a *love* so bright and strong! You take good care of her! She is priceless! *I love you both so dearly.* See ya at 3:30." Then she was gone!

Terry said: "What's with Bonnie?"

He looked around for Patty. She has slipped out. And, is with Bonnie for some reason… *I knew why she was with Bonnie!* I didn't tell Terry that Bonnie has a giant love crush on ol Patty there! She wants to suck every hole on her till she screams!

Terry said: "Bonnie has desirers on my girlfriend Patty!"

I say with reassurance: "Well, I don't think you have anything to worry about. You got her good, no doubt!"

But, Bonnie is quite a lover! Patty most likely has never been kissed by a woman before. And, wants to try it again! I don't believe you have anything to worry about! Patty is a <u>Cock Hound</u>! Bonnie ain't got no Dick! *Take my word for it!*

When I was at her apartment. the night of the Super Acid trip, she took me home and jumped me!

Terry said: "We had a hunch about that when she took your red and never came back and you didn't either!"

I say: "I passed out! I thought I had *died.* I don't believe I was breathing for a bit. There was nothing I could do about it! I was paralyzed! But, I think Bonnie RAPED me!"

Terry say: "What?"

Me: "That's right! She said she Raped me for almost two hours!"

Terry said: "Are you freaked out about it Don?"

"NO… Not at all! I have never had a woman want me so bad after I had fucked her lights out for 6 hours. That she had to *Rape* me for two more. It turns me on!"

Terry informs: "You know! Some women secretly hope to be raped! They would never go out and get so sexy dirty on their own. They fantasize about it!"

I say: I guess so. But, Bonnie just flat <u>RAPED</u> me. It just makes my Dick HARD thinking about it! So much, I want it to happen to me again! The thought that someone FUCKED me for TWO hours! With, out my permission… Is just mind boggling! Bonnie has so much love to give. She has to work <u>*overtime!*</u>"

Terry helps: "Well Don, just hold the memory as a *wonder* of the world! Leave it at that!"

I approve: Oh well… Let's not *dwell* on the subject. Dig it! We are supposed to be ready with a few songs for that Risby guy.

Terry says: "What do you have in mind? Where is your guitar?"

We grabbed our guitars and went right into "COME TOGETHER" We used that to get a bit of *FUNK* into the mix. Terry laid this way cool kinda country. And, kinda… rock tune out. He went into the *chorus* to show us how to sing it. And, he realized that the damn song should start with the chorus. So, we worked out an open along with the *Harmony lines.*

Patty is fixing Dinner when Bonnie arrived. We are still working on the tune. She just went in and grabbed Patty by her crotch and squeezed her womanhood and said: "What's up Cakes? Don't worry! I was just checking your oil!"

She turned with a Snap! Then, smoothed her way over to the table doing her best "*Betty Davis*" and, ran her hands up Terry's back! He almost dropped the guitar! She had dropped her hands in the back of his pantaloons… and then!!! She… Pulled out a hand full of *ass crack hair!* Terry shot through the <u>roof</u>! With, a… "*Yee Oww… Son Of A Bitch! Motha Fucker!* God damn it Bonnie… What in the fuck are you fucking doing!"

I'm sitting there with my hand over my mouth about to fall back and out of my chair it was such a shock. And, so motha fucking *FUNNY,*

Everyone is on the freaking *flipping floor!* Bonnie, is standing there <u>CALM</u> as could be with absolutely <u>No expression</u> on her face! She is standing at PARADE REST with one hand in front of her. In her hand, is a giant wad of hair!

The room got deadly quiet to hear what was Bonnie going to say. I'm on the floor looking right at her as everyone else was. It just took a second. But, it seemed like an hour. She stood there staring at Terry jumping around with his hands in his pants. She waited for him to quiet down a bit.

She said: "<u>NICE ASS-FRO TERRY!</u>"

The laughter is so <u>loud</u>! Terry couldn't even hold it back! His Mad face went to *Crazy laughter* as he hugged and kissed Bonnie on the lips

And said: that will be a Ten buck deposit!"

She reached in her purse and put the hair in a coin snapper. Then, gave him the *Ten Dollars!*

She said: "I'll just let you WONDER what I'll do with it!"

Debbie and Karen had walked in with Tim, wondering what the fuck is going on here! The rest of us could still not talk. So, Jocelyn told them! Now, they is rolling on the floor too! We are all so fucking Happy. I looked around the room and sighed: "WOW! This feels so good, its gotta be right!"

As I look at everyone in convulsions on the floor! Writhing in side splitting laughter... Tony came in, he had that LOOK on his face, and the eye brow curled lip deal! He heard this all the way out in the street.

Debbie grabbed him... laughing so hard you could see her mouth working. But, nothing is coming out and she can't breathe, like the wind has been knocked out of her. She pulled him to the floor. Then, sat down on his chest, grabbed him by both shoulders and started body slamming him up and down to the floor screaming, laughing like a crazy lady saying: "God Damn it Tony! HA! HA. HA. It Is So Fucking...*FUNNY!*"

She is slapping his face side to side 7. Or, 8 times like the dog slapping the cat!

He grabs her. Shaking her... Getting, his *ass kicked!* As she calmed down a bit, she just stopped dead laughter. With, no expression on her face! She, grabbed Tony and just stared at him a second. Or, two... She is somewhere deep inside Tony with her eyes. She starts to shiver. She hauled off and lip locked Tony so hard, she busted his bottom lip!

We all were dead quiet watching this. Tony is bleeding pretty badly when she let up. A startled look went over her face. Then, she just broke out laughing again! Slamming Tony back to the floor... Tripping around the room... Slapping everyone on the back... Laughing out of control!

The room is going nuts again! Tony is bleeding all over the place. When, I said: "All Righty Then! Come on! It wasn't that funny!"

It was though! I looked around the room as everybody is retelling the tale. I got this warm feeling from my head to my toes. I thought. I was some what abused growing up. Mom in Texas, Dad in California... A different school every year or two. New *step bros & sisters* to break in every 2 years or so. But, through it all, my *Dad* and I were *BEST* friends. And, partners in crime... Fun & SEX... He had his girl friends stay weeks at a time in our home before he married AVON. If there ever was a man who was a *Professor of* Love, It's My Dad... He taught me everything I know!

I just watched how he treated them. I emulated that into my age group to fit MY times! These people were all mistreated too! We are now a family of *best friends* and New Lovers! I'm lucky as an outsider of sorts. To be allowed to even see these people let their hair down! Let alone become so much an apart of each of their lives. And, they mine to this very day! My Heart is swelling with Love and *Promise* for these, my lovers and family now!

Sounds like a street gang don't it! Well… if so. So, be it!

"Gavence Family Travelers will live on forever!

Bonnie broke in again and said: "You two, Come with me!"

The rest stayed and messed around. And, then the girls helped Patty finish the Dinner to have it ready to eat when we returned.

We found the Bob Risby guy. We talked with him a bit. He recorded our song then said: "I'll be back in two weeks. Be ready with 5 more songs. I like what you two have. Kinda, Everly Brothers gone *Furry Freak Brothers,* *I am interested.* See you later."

He thanked Bonnie. Gave her a hug! She took down some info from him. They went to the bar to talk more about other ideas she has. She is really getting the *gist* of the music business. She "*Get's It!*" We had a drink from Room Service, Smoked a Doob on the balcony till she returned.

She said: 'We will see!"

Down the hall we went into the parking garage. The car. And, then HOME! Bye bye to the Grayhouse I guess! Terry remarked.

Bonnie said: "Patty's is only temporary, you'll see. Things just keep getting better."

Bonnie drove to her place on Lafayette, ran in for a minute. She dropped off her briefcase and came back out with a sleeping bag.

I asked Bonnie: "What's with the bag?"

She asked: "You guys mind if I stay over with you all tonight?" Is Something wrong Bonnie?

She snapped: "Nope! I just don't want to be away from you people tonight. I have never in along time seen a bunch of people so damn right together! I need ya all tonight."

She burned rubber a few blocks. As, she is shifting into 2nd over Rainbow Bridge she looked in the rear view mirror. Her strawberry blonde long hair swishing my face in the seat with Jocelyn behind her… Her eyes *shockingly* blue in the rear view. Almost Cobalt and glowing!

As, she looked at me and said: *EAT THE RICH!* Bonnie said that a lot. I wonder what she means.

We blew into the driveway. Stood around her car a minute as *ONY RAY* rode up on a ten speed. We motioned him over, invited him to stay! He came on in. We looked at the Dinning room. It's like a *FRENCH* restaurant for Christ sake! Candles… And, fine *China.* Crystal glasses all set with two empty seats. For, who ever might want to join us! Like *ONY RAY!*

Jocelyn came over, hugged me real hard as she is jumping up and down saying: "Well? Well? *What the fuck?*"

I said: "Oh! — The Risby Dude… Nothing for a few weeks."

She said: "Well… that's ok. Come on in here. Let me buy you a Milk Shake.

Patty said: "Dinner in 15 everyone."

There are people everywhere in the house but our room. It's the coat room of sorts. She backed me in there. And, backwards on her back. Pulling me down on top of her, Man…she is HOT!

She wrapped her legs around mine. Her arms around my back, she stuck her tongue 3 feet down my throat going, umm… oh, that tastes good! Breathing hard she said: "Lets go eat! I want to sit with my Very Best Friends and life long Sisters. And beam with pride. As, we listen and watch you guys practice after dinner!

Only problem is. Karen. Debbie and I, Have to leave and go to our folk's homes for the night! Give me all of your clothes, I will wash them.

I said: "I'll be here naked!"

She says: "GOOD! That will keep you here. And, not at the WALL!" When you coming back?

She said: "I will be back tomorrow night. As, soon as I can get a ride to Debbie's."

I said: "Hell, Mike and I will come get ya!"

She said: "*NO!* I ain't ready for you to "Meet the Parents" just yet! They are not ready for you. I don't want anything to happen where I get grounded. Or, some shit like that."

I said: "What are you doing about school?"

She responded with: "I just Fucking QUIT! I don't need their shit!"

I snapped back: "No one should quit school in their senior year!"

She said with a bit of steam: "<u>Don't start that shit Buster!</u>"

I just saw Jocelyn get mad, I had never seen that before! I never want to see it again! Even though it turned me on a bit!

I heard Terry, Patty and Rick singing "OHIO" in the other room.

I stood up and said: "Sweetheart, I will be counting the minutes and seconds till you return. Can you call me?

She said: "Yes! I will do that the minute I get there. Let's go join the others" as, she kissed me. We walked into the room. She sat down at the table as I did. I could not take my eyes off of her! She is so beautiful. She sits down next to me and I melted. She grabbed hold of my arm like it's a *shotgun* and smiled at everyone in the room as she turned her head to me with a sigh!

She said: "Well… we gonna eat? Or, starve!"

We all toasted the ladies for this wonderful meal!

Writer's note:
At *No* time in these years, were any of the families involved with the SALES. Or Distribution of contraband!

Our crowd *did not* allow that to happen with in our ranks. Knowingly! If we found anyone with in our close circle doing that! They were OUT! The horse was NOT allowed at all! As, I can not speak for those that came and went in the Fayetteville scene, we did not let that influence our way of life! Having said that… We did believe in the barter system when it came to *cannabis*. 20 pounds of Tomatoes… For, one pound of pot! Was, most times the rule, you can take it from there.

Now, where the hell was I?… oh yeah!
Ψ Hell, I already miss her! We sang "All Most Cut My Hair" Now, it's time to eat. Man, that Patty can fucking cook. She worked all day on a Giant Turkey and all the fixings! We ate. Talked… Listened to the stereo… Laughed… And, talked… All are so full and content. Then, we all just fell back for about an hour after dinner and groaned!

Jocelyn and I went in for some HEAVY making out.

When Tim said: "Come on girls. Time for the bus to leave!"

He has his mom's car. And, is taking everyone home… We threw in our dirty clothes, away they went and out of sight! My heart dropped to the bottom of my feet, I just gave in. This last week has been so hard on me. My body is buzzing. I need a full 10 hours of heavy sleep. I went to bed.

Bonnie came in my room and said: "*NO STRINGS ATTACHED!* Can I sleep with you? Pretty. Pretty. Pretty please?" I opened the sheet and she climbed in. Before I could say *Goodnight* to her, she is on my shoulder and sound asleep! I followed her. I dreamed some *heavy duty dreams* that night. Not only was I so worn out, I was weak. But, I am sure I was doing a bit of detoxing too!

I woke up bright and early. Bonnie is already up and in the shower. I went in there to *wee wee*. She asked for a towel, I opened the door, she pulled me in. *Stand Still!* She started washing me all over.

She washed me and said: "I want to talk to you! This Bob Risby guy is just a guy. I don't want you to pay a lot of stock in him. If he comes back, so be it! If not… *forget about it!* We are on our own time table."

She is washing me between my legs, doing a real damn good job Too! She grabbed my balls and clamped down on them.

She said: "How can those do so much? And, still be so full!"

She massaged them awhile. You don't pull away from Bonnie. When she has hold of your balls… She won't let go!

I played with her giant tits till she let go!

Like I said: "I love to see you Nude! Now, get out of here. And let me *bang* myself to finish. Get out of here while you still can!"

I'm drying off in the hall. As, she screamed a few times, slapped the shower wall and sighed hard. The water went off. And, out she came.

Ok, I have to go do some business! I'll see you all around 9 pm. You all take the day off. And, then off she went. We all are sitting in the living room listening to *Frank Zappa* and smoking a joint. Talking about this and that… Just the four of us… Rick. Terry. Mike and me… All the girls are out and doing their thing! Patty is at School. Debbie is at School along with Karen. Jocelyn is at home in Farmington. There we were with nothing to do! We did that until 11. Or, 12 o'clock.

We are kinda expecting the Ladies to return sometime tonight. When the phone rang…

Patty answered: "Oh, hi Jocelyn!"

"Me Too!"

"Yes, he is sitting right here… Do you want to talk to him?"

"We are practicing at the table as we speak"

"YES! - UM! I know what you mean - Well, He is walking around in some kind of <u>PURPLE FRIGGIN HAZY</u>! - That's about right I guess - I know he LOVES you too! I see the way he looks at you… Sweet heart, you positively *GLOW!* - Me either! Well - Here he is — bye Jocelyn. I love you, see you in the morning."

☎ I heard that! The morning! I took the phone. The *millisecond* I heard her voice I melted. I put down my Guitar. Stretched the 100 foot phone cable to the back yard…

I lay there on the pic a nic table. We made *MAD* phone love for over an hour. Her phone is in a doorway that splits her kitchen from the living room. She can talk there after 11 pm or so. Everyone is in bed on the other side of the dog run, can not hear. The library door, And, the sewing room door are both a DEAD give always. And, afforded her time to pull her pants up if need be!

There is a fireplace in the kitchen. I would imagine her face in the fireplace glow as we spoke. I had my pantaloons around my ankles by now. And, I am doing the Slow Jerk as she moaned in the phone. Talked, <u>Extremely Dirty</u> telling me what she is going to do to me.

She said: "I am going to shove a *baguette* up your ass. Then, eat it out the other. Then, butter it. And, eat it again!"

I said: "I'll take the *buttered baguette*, lay my 5 pounds of meat right down the slice. Then, pump it full of LOVE juice!"

That's when we both *GAGGED!*

She said: "That's about enough of that *Buckaroo!*

I did the best I could to *French kiss* her thru ma-bell®. As we hung up till it be morn. I went back inside. Tony wanted to know the POOP. I told um they would be here at 10 or so in the morning. We were supposed to be going on some sort of a big <u>Celebration PICNIC.</u>

A what? *The plot gets even thicker!*

A pic-a-nic that Bonnie has all cooked up for the big concert week end passed. Terry and Patty had *LOVE* in their eyes! They departed for the MASTER bedroom. It was great! Had its own bathroom and everything Man! With a hose pisser!

Tony is reading "*The Hobbit*"® on the couch and listening to Jazz. Rick and Dianna are at the Grayhouse, they are not expected back tonight. Bonnie and Zelda are at the PARTY pad. Doing, what ever it is they do when they are alone. That Scrambles my mind just thinking about it! I was ready to crash out for the night. I couldn't wait till morning came. A pic a nic… a picnic! *That sounds great!* What is a Beaver Lake?

What's the "beaver" part about? I could smell Jocelyn on my pillow. I lay there and drank her in a few times and I was sound asleep. *SNOOZE OUT!*

As I drifted off… My last thought was "*Beaver*" I don't get it.

I remember waking up a few times as the *Garbage Truck* slammed outside the window above my head. It's been real Hot all night. I'm soaking wet by the time the sun is coming thru the window there.

I love that window. It would start this beam at Jocelyn's feet. Then, widen right up her body as she lay there sound asleep. After about an hour she would be in a beam of light a few feet wide and her entire creamy body. Foot to head!

I'm feeling the Heat of the sun on my ass and between my legs! I have one leg pulled up about to my chest. I for sure am *NOT* leaving anything to the Imagination. When I woke up a bit, opened one eye, and then kind of looked around the room in a morning haze. I scanned the room from one side to the other and lay my head back on the pillow with a sigh. I was laying there alone as I thought.…What the Fuck!

I slowly turned around, hopping I was just seeing things out the side of my eye when low and behold! There sits Bonnie, Just below her is Zelda! Zelda is sitting crossed leg on the floor with both of her hands between her legs pushing the back of her head into Bonnie's booger!

Bonnie, is sitting against the wall with her legs wrapped around Zelda.

She has Coffee in one hand, a cigarette in her lips and a camera in her other hand! She says: "Thanks for the show. I'll lay some copies of the pictures on ya when I get um developed."

Terry asked as I came through the bedroom door: "Hey Don. What about that Risby guy? You think he is for real man?"

I replied: "Well... Bonnie does! So, that's good enough for me. Besides, we need to try writing a few songs to see what happens. We know where we want to go with our sound. Let's put it to theory."

I could not believe the *Vernacular* we are using now when music is concerned. Just a year ago, we were just trying to figure out how to play "Down by the fucking river" for Christ sake! Now, we are actually doing it the right way. With structure, and phrasing, Measures, Timing and Harmony so fucking sweet, it would melt butter!

We thought we were ready...

Bonnie & Zelda came in from the store.

She said as she rubbed my ass with her hands: "Feel better Don?" Then she wet her middle finger, stuck her hand down the back of my pants, and then rubbed it into my asshole with more of that cream. Mamma will make it all better!"

Then she said to the group: "Ok, you think you are ready! *Ready for what?* You only know the songs that you knew all along! You guys are not ready for anything! Thursday, I am taking you guys for new clothes!"

New clothes... what!

She went on: "I can't have you three running around in these *facokata* bullshit jeans! If you would have not saved the day at Savoy, They were going to throw you all out for the patches on your clothes and crotch areas! I told them they would lose their best act if they did! Then, it would be a *bummer show!* They were gonna bums rush you guys!"

So... the clothes gotta go!

I said: "I don't need no special clothes in the closet. To, play rock and roll Bonnie!"

She said: "You can wear them right now. I need that 6 month old look to them. You guys can achieve that in a week or two. It's a *look* I am trying to get here. Not slobs! When they go beyond where I want them to look! *Not new.* But not old! I will get you more. Ok?"

Hey Terry: "Here comes Mike Boyd down Leverett."

Great! As he puts up his guitar! I followed.

We all went out front. Mike pulled in, handed us a fatty he is burning, and then stepped out. Picnic I hear.

That's right.

10:15 am. I'm looking out the front door to see who would show up next. When here comes Debbie Sue from her house on foot. She is alone and carrying all the stuff she and Tony would need for the next two days. She see's me. A giant smile came over her otherwise deep in though face. She is a bit out of breath as she dropped the bags just inside the front door and collapsed on the couch with a swoosh!

IT IS TOO FUCKING HOT! It's only the first of freaking May and its 86 degrees out there all fucking ready! I swear to god, it gets hotter each and every freaking damn year! I just can't understand it. Every time I... Hey Don!

Yes Debbie.

She says: Ah... whew!... Jocelyn has taken a Cab from Farmington to Karen's house. She is supposed to be staying there for a week to keep Karen Company while her dad is on the road!

I said: "Hey Debbie."

She got up. And, came in the kitchen where I'm washing the breakfast dishes before we all took off. She wrapped her arms around my waist then laid her head on my back.

She said: "Do you know how in *love* Jocelyn is with you?

Well Debbie, if she is only 10% as much in love with me as I am with her! *That's good enough for me!*

She went on: "Well Don... she is absent minded these days! Jocelyn is NEVER absent minded. She just walks around looking at something out there. She follows the little animals around. Kicking at the rocks on the street."

She says that you: "Take her Breath away"

The minute she sees you, she only thinks of one thing.

We are talking it over. About Terry, Tony and you! And me! She just has an *urge* to climb inside of you every time she thinks of you. Or she is near you. When she is with you inside her... she has never felt the connection with any other boy.

Jocelyn told you all of this.

She said: "Its like your parts are custom made. To just fit perfect! She said her insides grind. And, roll when she thinks of your love! She feels a vacuum when you are not there."

I'm Amazed Man! Is she talking about me?

I said: "Are you sure she didn't just *eat a bad bagel?*"

She replies: "No... it's like she would tie herself to you if she could."

I turned around. I have my arms around her shoulders as she talked straight through my eyes to my heart! She pulled herself up on her tippy toes. Whispered in my face *very* close, Nose to nose, Eye to eye...

She said: PLEASE... DON'T HURT HER! If you are not true in your confessions to her, *Stop now*. And, tell her it's all a game."

I walked her to the table, got her a Dr. Pepper. I sat down, took her hand in mine, kissed it softly and held it there.

I said: "I love Jocelyn more than life it self! She looked into my eyes…

"She said: "She could believe me for now! If I ever hurt Jocelyn in any way what so ever! She would see to it I never would forget about it… _Ever!_ I can see that you are in love with her. She has some problems you don't know about yet! That, I will leave it to her to tell you about… You may be called upon to muster more involvement than you want to give!"

I say: "Debbie… What will be, Will be! I am only interested in one thing. The life I want to spend with Jocelyn! How ever that is achieved! Is the way it will be!"

She is looking down at her bare feet. Shuffling them around on the cool linoleum floor, I lifted her head in the cradle of my hands and kissed her nose. Told her she had absolutely nothing to worry about!"

She smiled. And, gave me that _Debbie_ laugh. Then,…SLAPPED THE DOG SHIT OUT OF ME!

She said: "OK then! I'll be watching ya!"

She jumped up and out the front door as Jocelyn flew out of the car side door, ran into my awaiting arms! She knocked me to the porch steps and started kissing me all over my face.

Saying: "_God I've missed you!_ I can't stand it! Hurry in here. I want to show you something! She pushed me into the bedroom, pulled my t-shit over my head, grabbed my pants from the back, UN snapped them and pulled them down. I kicked them off. She already has the sun dress she is wearing un buttoned and off her shoulders. As it hit the floor, she jumped to me and wrapped her legs around my waist, her arms around my shoulders and planted a _French kiss_ on me that they are still talking about in _love land!_

She hopped down and backed me to our bed. Then, pushed me down… I'm rock hard now. She is too! Her nipples are like search lights, calling to my mouth! As I lay on my back… She climbed me, sat down on me and went _bug fuck nuts_. "NVTS" <u>nuts</u>! She is like a pile hammer… lifting and falling with full force to my hips. (Hey… _How do you turn down this jack hammer?_) She went faster. And faster, moaning, pushing. Scratching my shoulders, getting tighter and tighter… She went off like a _volcano_! Screamed… _All Right Mother Fucker!_ She jumped all the way up… Then just dropped on me with all of her weight… Folded up in a pile on top of me… And… _just shook!_

She sat down on me so hard! I knew that Jimmy is deep inside her <u>cervix</u>. I could feel it twitching and pulling on me. We kissed still hooked up for about ten minutes.

As, Terry bangs on the door, He says: "15 minutes! And, the train is pulling out... *On Time!*"

She pulls off of me, rolled over. Melted into the bed for a minute! She said: "This wave of <u>HORNY</u> came over me about 2:30 this morning from a deep sleep! A wet dream about us in the back of Bonnie's Mustang®. I want to do that again soon! I like the way the tuck and roll wraps around the back. And, up to the front!"

"I love you so very much Don! It's more than I thought! I couldn't eat. Or, sleep the whole time we were apart. I never want to be away from you that long ever again! I want to stay with you from now on. Starting today! Is, that ok with you?"

I'm about to cry! I reached out... grabbed her and just looked at her!

She said: "What! Are you alright?"

Tears are on my face as I said: "*Oh yes my love! I am very all right indeed!*"

We fell together and kissed. Then, got up and wiped each other tears. Rubbed them on each others lips... Then we pledged our eternal never ending love, opened the door. And, went out to the others!

Debbie saw us come out the door and said: "Just a little quickie me Droogies?"

Jocelyn did her best pirate and said: "ol One Eye was hiding in the cave captain!"

They laughed. And, high fived... Walked out hugging each other to the car... Debbie is kissing and whispering in her ear. She would blush, giggle and look back at me. Then, giggle some more! I had never felt this before ever!

Chapter Forty One

"Something strange... This way comes! That ain't no shit!" We walked out... Applause rang out!

There… in the driveway is one hell of a line up for freaking sure man!
"Let me see here."
Tony and Debbie… Jocelyn and I. Terry and Patty… Zelda and Bonnie… John Palamisano. Mike Boyd. Buck and Anna… Rick and Dianna will join us from the News Stand later. They are already half way there.
We have everything from food. To, a rather large drug collection!
Two kegs of beer.
Two cases of Boot Leg COORS,
Assorted Reds and bird eggs,
Some crystal And ½ ounce of blonde hashish!
Two bottles of Jack. And more wine than a wino could drink in a year! All the implements of camping… And *Orgy gear known to man!*
We also have a <u>*scary foggy night*</u> coming up at this place called Beaver Lake. I don't know y'all… I Never been there…
Zelda says: "It's the <u>3rd largest man made lake in the world!</u> It dams the Mulberry and the Arkansas Rivers just south of *Eureka Springs* (*Aint that where them thar Hillbillies live?*). It's like that *Deliverance* movie that just came out with Burt Reynolds. They flooded about 20 towns down there. At, low water levels in the late summer. You can see most of them. And, dive the rest."
Bonnie jumped in: "That's right Dildo Breath… Streets in downtown parts still have stuff still on the *store shelves. Cars* parked out front. Its dam *spooky brother!* That's where we are going? *No,* we are going out by a little town named GOSHEN!"
I said: "Land a Goshen!"
Mike said: "How <u>*original!*</u>"
I say: "Well sir… I try to abide."
We will go through that town and over the bridge. Down to the lake!
Bonnie said: "There is my friend's summer camp there."
I said: "*A summer camp?*"
She chirped: "No beautiful"

She moved like a playboy bunny across the driveway and to her car.

She went on: "You see… this guy. And, his girl friend are _Nudists!_ The gate is ¼ mile up the winding road from the house and party area."

John jumped right in Thar: "You mean we can strip. And, stay naked the whole time we are there?"

Bonnie says: "YUP! That's right man!"

She explains: "There is a party barge and an outboard motor boat too! It's not very big! But, a motor boat at best! The house is two stories and faces the bend in the lake. The big floating party barge has a smoker and grill. Plus, a wet bar! _Stereo_ and these benches that are built to fuck on…" They are out under the stars along the beach. They are just the right high off of the sand, for some solid penetration for sure! Around the rest of the grounds here and there are more of those benches under trees, rock over hangs and ponds. There is one on the summit. That as you make love, you can see _all the three state lines."_

Mike hollered: "Let's go! I'm Already Naked! And, ready to ROCK!

We are at the house now, it is Stunningly Rustic looking. Big A-frame two story house with a guest house… An, outdoor spa on the screened in porch… Plus, one in the front yard too! I won't say there were hot tubs. Or, anything like that. More like old cast iron tubs they found in Carolina that seat two.

Each has a pump made from old water cooler air conditioner pump. They are heated. If you want to start a fire and boil the water! She laughed! There is a natural sauna, an old Indian steam lodge you had to fire up your self."

All part of the _experience!_ This looked like a great 48 hours ahead! We all stood there in awe… jaws agape.

First thing Debbie Sue did. Is pull her shirt over her head… Her two _melons_ fell free to the world. She reached her arms up to the sky to let the lake breeze cool her. Her Shorts hit the ground. She turned to me and pinched my ass. Then, winked at Jocelyn…

Jocelyn reached down and pulled off her _Daisy Dukes_ then jumped on me. And, just laughed out loud!

Patty is tall in the saddle. And, looking so fine in her nakedness… She is a bit shy! But… it didn't take her long to catch on. Zelda and Bonnie are naked. And, running for the beach and a cold Coors! _John Palamisano_ is nude with a strapping hard-on. Chasing Bonnie! Terry and Mike went to see what made the place tic. Tony and Debbie are actually _Fucking hard_ on one of the FUCK benches! Just buns up _intercourse!_ Right there in front of god and everyone. Jocelyn and I are naked in a love knot, kissing hard and rubbing against each other.

I picked her up. She straddled my hips, locked her ankles behind me. I got a rush of pure vibe and almost lost my step and fell. It's like in the Fuck flicks. Where, they are going crazy when they just freeze up! Look at each other with fire in our eyes. I was just flowing. She was too! We are so wet, we needed a towel.

As we walked to the house and inside, Bonnie came over and hung a dish towel on my still rock hard jimmy and said: "Put that thing away buster and give us a hand." I cant! It wont go down.

We are all still naked as j-birds. We went about setting up camp for the weekend. Then, we sat down to do some serious drugs and drinking to get into the proper mood for this affair.

I'm waiting for Mike to roll a bunch of joints. Bonnie is making lines on this Huge mirror she found in her bed room! It's about 5: 30 pm now. Still plenty of light and fucking heat!

This place has no a/c. no place did then! What I liked about it is the humidity. Right here it's about 99% all the time. You take a *cold shower…* you step out… And you are covered in sweat before you can towel off. I like that! It makes *Jocelyn* and me *extremely greasy* and *sticky to the touch*. It's like pouring baby oil all over us. Best part is… its body fluid! I just lick her off from head to toe and start at the top again then work my way down.

She tastes like *Motherhood, Love, Children, and Life.* WOMAN! I taste her like she is food! When she cums, I have to drink her inside me, I suck and suck her empty to get each and every drop! From the start of her wetness along those inner thighs, to, her flood of life at the apex! I just feel *electricity burning* in every gland and fluid pump in my body till the flood starts!

(God damn man: "I gotta stop a second! I am spotting up my typewriter here!")

We found our bedrooms. Like we will ever use them. We settled into the living room… We turned it into a studio. Write songs! Yeah… Sure! Fuck like Bunnies? Yup!

We set the place up so we are in a circle looking inward at each other to write and work up these new songs for the Bob Risby guy. We have pretty much decided to work on that goal. Our next goal is to find our own <u>House</u>.

Terry. Patty and I. Went right to work on song one…

We have an old Wallensak® *monophonic* tape recorder. Wasn't much! But, its sound is <u>REAL good</u>! One microphone that was actually hard wired to the recorder itself. 20 Foot cable on it, nice phantom powered 48 volt condenser microphone. Get's real hot after awhile… A couple of rolls of reel to reel tape… And we is set!

We have everything on the table a guitar player would ever need. Bonnie saw to that! Picks. Even finger ease! Extra strings that we use all the time... A bottle of guitar polish, to keep these two brand new high class guitars in shape...

The girls all disappeared to the Giant Kitchen. Bonnie and Zelda gave them all a dish to cook for dinner in an hour. They went right to work. John and Mike are gathering firewood for inside and out for the night. Bonnie went out on the porch and rang the *triangle dinner bell!* Everyone came a running. They had set a Wonderful table with about everything to eat they could make fast. Everyone sat down at the table.

I said a few words: "My friends... family. And, lovers! We are here tonight to celebrate our first full week as the *Fantastic...*"MORISON SMITH BAND."

She goes on: "Everyone did their job perfectly! We used *TEAMWORK* to reach our goal... we reached it! Now... we have to find which fork in the road to take. We have a lot of family business to do before the end of May. I know that this weekend everyone will share each others love. Both, body and soul! We are totally alone. And, free to do and act any way we want. From total whack out! Too, solid fucking non- stop for 48 hours. It's up to you....*Anything goes!* Anything! Orgies, Solo. Groups, what ever... Let's eat. Fly. Fuck. Swim. Fuck."

Mike hollers! "You said fuck twice!

She answered: "I like fuck! It's my favorite one for sure"

Now, in closing! Everyone howls! I want everyone to line up right here... Jocelyn last!

Now this is a sight to behold for sure. I wish I had a camera. 13 people standing NUTS & CUNTS TO BUTTS naked in a line... And, they don't know why!

I said: "Walk by and stick out your tongue. Tony is the Doctor. He is putting a hit of ORANGE WEDGE ACID on each tongue. Watching it dissolve under your tongue before you could pass. Then, Mike gave you a cannon ball of fine Wine and a *joint* of your own to smoke while you wait to get off.

When you dissolve acid under your tongue, it's trip time in less than 10 minutes... And, hard tripping 30 minutes later! Everyone is counting down... and finding where they would hang all night. And, talking... We built a *big tripping fire* in the fire pit. Fun night ahead! Did someone say something about an ORGY? Well? *Did they?*

We had a most wonderful Dinner. The sun is down. The night sky is jet black without NO moon. First *new* moon after the Blue moon of last weekend that was so damn good to all of us! What a time for all of us to find each other. And, fall so hard in love.

We all are moving out to the party barge for the trip. John and Mike had their set up ready and going with a great fire there too. We stayed at the pit and played music. The rest wandered back and forth from the barge.

Jocelyn came up. Wrapped one arm around me… and started massaging my groin. And, tickling my inner thighs… She leaned in and stuck her mouth over mine and said into my mouth: "*I am getting off on that acid!*"

I had noticed that everything had a tail! I looked in her eyes and the pupils are gone! She has two warm scared black voids in the middle of her eyes and the rest are bright white. Her eye lids are gone too! Up inside her head somewhere. Orange Wedge is heavy on the *strychnine!* It has to travel from *Berkeley* to get here. And, a lot of *preservative* is needed. Hence… *strychnine!*

So, I knew the trails and sparks and swirls would be in vivid bright day-glow colors all night. And, I would guess into tomorrow night too. By this time tomorrow night we will be starting to crash. Or, just keep getting higher. It's hard to tell with Orange Wedge. We will just have to see.

We are *snorting crystal* so we don't miss one second of this rather expensive acid. 5 dollars a hit… As, compared to 50 cents for *blotter*. And 1.50 for *window Paine!*

Orange Wedge borders as close as you can come to Owsley STP. With out the psycho babble! Some here have never taken anything as strong as this acid is. I am a <u>veteran traveler</u>. I can direct someone else's trip even while mine is too intense! This is going to be one hell of a weekend for sure! It's getting kind of *Spooky*. As a ground fog formed around the beach and the house grounds, *Temperature* and *dew point* matched about dark.

The fog is now coming off the water surface. And, crawling the holler to us… The fires are dancing on the fog. I knew I was getting real fucked up! I saw a cat crawl out of the boat and work his way up to my feet.

He said: (Now, this is a cat talking folks!) "You Don't Have Any Idea What The Fuck You Are Doing Do You? Your bored stiff aren't ya! You need some *ADULT* supervision!"

He sat down on Jocelyn's lap. And, looked her in the face, She is jaw dropped stunned. Looking right at the cat… He is licking his lips!

He said: "I'll bet you taste real damn good little girl! You know, I am a PUSSY too! But, I have four legs… Better to scat with! I have some advice for you young lady! Keep a close eye on the brown hole tonight" She said: "The what?"

He (the cat) looked around like *Red Skelton's*. "Clem Kadiddelehopper." And whispered: "The brown hole is everywhere"

She looked over at me. Then back to her lap and he is… Gone!

She had a *super blank* look on her face like those kids in that pink Floyd video. She reached out for my hand, grabbed it and pulled herself over to me then curled around me.

She said in a low smooth voice: "Wow! Did that really happen?"

She looked right through me and ducked! Looked off like something flew over my head and then over hers. *Bats!* Everyone would be seeing those fuckers soon enough. I knew that! I have a slight problem when I take real good *cosmic acid* like this. My Willy grows about two feet long. Hard as a rock! And, just stays that way for the duration! Doesn't matter what I do, It's just hard!

Jocelyn has already locked onto it with a death grip! She is getting off real hard! The fire I built is ready to lite. I took an *old broken mirror* I found in the dumpster back in town. And, broke it into big pieces. There is a concrete stump in the middle of the fire pit. That is so you can lean firewood against it for a taller flame, more like a bonfire would look. So, I leaned those mirrors against the concrete and the fire wood around that. That way... when the flames are dancing, you will be able to look inside the fire to the mirrors and see yourself burning! Wow! Ain't That Great!

They are thick old glass mirrors. I figured they would not crack or melt too fast. They never even chipped! Down on the barge is a room for dry goods, coats and such. It's kind of a little A-FRAME with felt roof paper tacked on it for water shed. The acid is affecting the other males here the same way!

We nicknamed the acid "*MOST-BONERFIED!*" Every guy has a blistering Hard-on! It is affecting the girls too! Their first set of lips are swollen like giant pillows. I was petting her snatch with a soft tickle up and down the outer lips from the bottom to the top. We are lying right next to Tony and Debbie. You could see me rubbing her. But, to each his own! Is the way of the night! I noticed that her outer lips are swelled up 6 or 7 times normal. She is dripping wet.

Bonnie leaned up in her lawn chair and hit the flash light at her cooder! Low and behold her too! Debbie and Zelda all looked and pawed at them selves to see. Sure enough! They are all swollen too!

So, let's see...

I said: "Super hard Wang's that are not going down anytime soon. "

We all looked around... Every Johnson is burst hard! The girls showed off between their legs around the fire pit! They pointed a wet cooder at each of us drooling! *This is like LSD Spanish Fly!*

We started discussing this thought!

I said: "Now... take the combo of drugs we are doing here tonight! Ok! The best acid money can buy. Pure China White Crystal Ice. Allrighty! Lumbo Red, Mucho booze, Ect! Looks to me like we should combine these cocks and cunts into a *viable activity!*"

There is a vibe in the air. We felt that someone was watching from the forest line. I wasn't sure if there was. Or, wasn't! But, the way she hugged me close, made me hope there was. We are kind of spreading out to our own little make out spots. We had our blanket laid out on the Beach. It isn't a real *natural* made beach. Bonnie's friend hauled sand all the way from Galveston, Texas to here. *I felt right at home on it!*

The Lake is so smooth. It is a mirror of the stars. It's hard to tell where the Lake stopped and the sky began. I had my hand between her legs stroking her, tickling around the cheeks of her butt to here delta.

She would shiver and say: "I am so fucking stoned! So stoned!"

As she gazed from under my wing out to the lake, we were watching Hundreds of fire flies dance just above the water. At least, I think we were when we heard a SCREAM in the night that a Horror movie director would pay for! It echoed from the cliffs and across the water then back again and again!

We are all Naked, Erect. And UP! Looking all around to see, or, hear what in the fuck that *banshee yell* was! I knew I heard it. Everyone did! My Wang is throbbing up and down with the excitement! It just would NOT go down. I think we hit on what we now have. Called Viagra! I wouldn't know. As, mine is still hard from the… (oh! Ok! Sorry bout that! Ok!…I'm going!)

Now! Where was I! Oh yes! The <u>BLOODY SCREAM</u>…

Tony came running up the bank and said: "Something just grabbed Debbie! Before I could get up! It grabbed her and *poof!*" They was gone Jack!"

Terry is standing at *attention* with Patty wrapped around him with sockets for eyes! We found out later. That, *Patty* was a poser! She wanted to be a part of our crowd so fucking bad. She only said she had done acid! Never before! This is some HEAVY DUTY ACID! We all did twice what you should do! To make sure the weekend was a great time!

With the *speed* it's going to be *Impossible* to just shut your eyes. Smoke some lumbo and Mellow out! No Fucking way Man! We had done so much of Bonnie's Crystal all day to get us here. We are blasted. Speed in the acid. The booze, Plus, the other *potpourri* we had taken. Or, will take before this weekend is over. Would have to stand as *world book* kinda stuff Man!

Tony Wailed: "Hey motha Fucker!…Shut the fuck up! What about <u>DEBBIE?</u>"

Everyone is so hung up on what I was saying. We totally forgot about DEBBIE! We all froze. Did a double take at each other then broke out in an *uncontrollable* laughter fit! I'm laughing trying to question Tony at the same time when he broke up too! He fell to his knees laughing like a *Jack Ass*.

He said looking to the sky: "I have seen the light! And it is I! *WOW!* Save Debbie's ass God! Debbie… Forgive me!"

As he is breaking up laughing! I'm tripping so fucking hard, I can see in the night! I am off my fair madden, to find thee my love. Laughing like a *Doggy in the alley* on bushman's night behind the bowling alley. He did his best stage left exit. And fell all the way down the hill over each and every rock there was.

It was like he rolled this way and that way. So, he wouldn't miss not one rock! I noticed as I'm watching all of this. Jocelyn has turned over on the blanket. I'm sitting across the small of her back tickling her shoulder, neck and head. Blowing up her spine to the base of her skull with a shivering warm breath…

As I leaned up to work down from the neck, the head of my jimmy drug along her back! I felt this explosion in the back of my eyes. I went straight up.

Tony said! "Hey! Hey! Snap to man! What about Debbie! WHAT about Debbie! Come on you guys!"

Debbie… I gazed into space as Jocelyn reached back and dug her finger nails into the side of my leg. She is shaking!

She said to Tony: "Man, it's like I have this… in my eyes… look out Don!…Still there!…Oh shit!…*DUCK SUCKAS!*"

Tony shook me! Shook me again! Let's go! And, he went!

Oh shit! Jocelyn has turned over under me and is looking up reaching out drawing lines in the air around my face mumbling, drool is running back down her face to the blanket. I snapped back to the world for a minute because that scared me. I leaned over and slowly kissed her then licked the juice away with my tongue. I blew my breath into her nostrils and petted her hair back away from her face. She is crying.

She said: "I want to give a million dollars to the ahhhh."

Now get this!

"She said: "I want to give ah… *One million dollars* too… ah… too… <u>The National Find Debbie Fund</u>! She is out there some Fucking place."

Then in her Nakedness, she jumped up and said: "Follow me Droogies!"

She ran off… *Buns flapping* into the night… Or, the lake, hell who Fucking knows! I fell over backwards and hit my head. Knocked myself out for 35 minutes! *I think!* While I was out, I am told that *Jocelyn* did indeed also disappear!

Bonnie went off looking for them. She is now gone too! John is Fucking Zelda on the alter, that's what we named the fuck bench on the summit! So we knew where they were. Women are vanishing in the dark left and right. <u>AMAZON WOMEN</u>! Tuff girls!

Just *GONE* in the mist… Eaten as it were… by the Monster in the Fog. Creeping out of the Lake! The Big *Creeping Crawling Cock* is on his way! <u>*Bow Wow on the Prowl!*</u> Through the fog just for you!

Don't worry Baby! It's all the same in their eyes. Ok, here we go! Debbie has been missing over an hour now! Who knows what Big Foot long cock sucker has a hold of her! Bonnie is also missing. And, looking for Debbie! Jocelyn Has vanished into the **haze** also! Well, its time to rally the troops, and start looking!

Terry is coming up the hill bare footed Johnson swinging and says that he was taking a wizz. And, now Patty is gone! Mike and John come running down the hill looking for Zelda.

We got 5 women. Totally naked with out even shoes on, in an *extreme sexually excited state*, lost out there in the forest!

Tony said: "We should spread out. Look around. Then, get back here in 30 minutes to report."

I said: "Not to go around hollering their names out! That's just a give away as to where YOU are! Just sneak. And, listen to every sound. Let your ears be your eyes! That's what I did in country! And, I am here to tell you now!"

Ok: we will stand in each direction of the compass and walk straight into the bush! Back here in 30! Move out!

We are naked. And barefooted heading into the forest in pitch dark looking for 5 stoned out of their minds woman with dripping vaginas… Eyes so wide they are not there. *Night vision!*

Well… I let the others do the hunting, sounded made up to me! I had an idea where these women had gone. I didn't let on! I am a sneaky bastard when it comes to 5 naked women lost in the woods. Here is my plan!

I'm tripping so fucking hard. I am seeing four of everything that IS there, and 20 or so of what is not! But, for some reason I could think of this fun and great plan. Made me wonder if they really did pump LSD into our food and water in Nam… I sent all the other guys in the wrong directions with no way to ever come around to where I thought the booty is hid! It is becoming a Treasure Hunt of sorts!

I could hear the others going off on a Snipe Hunt. I wouldn't see them again till sun rise! When we first got here… I took my look around walk like I do every where I go. I found a little cove around and down the mountain side to where a stream came out of the side of the mountain and made a nice clear *warm swimming hole* with a small waterfall. water is warmed by a hot spring, it's making the foggy mist. Nice little pebble beach warm from the day. And, perfect water eroded stone rock in the shape of a big couch with just a thin layer of water going over it. The rocks were Hot when I was here earlier. So… they should be *real nice and warm now.*

I built a fire. But, didn't light it… I Drug an *ice chest of assorted* drinks and dope in there. Three quilts and pillows from the living room.

I showed Jocelyn and Debbie where it was. Told them to pass the word at dinner… Then all slip away one at a time. Disappear with an air of mystery! Hence the <u>BLOODY SCREAM</u>! Like Halloween for Grown up's! Did I say that?

Anyway, Debbie Sue is a trouper! I knew it the second I first saw her falling down the GRAYHOUSE steps. So, long ago… I love her in my own special way. And, she is such a wonderful person! So full of life, Piss and vinegar! She is *LOUD* and <u>obnoxious</u>! Set in her ways. And, out spoken to the point of violence! Always there to *back up her family and friends…* No matter if they are right or wrong! Great people for fucking sure! A credit to the family… This! Or, any family!

My *nelson* is still so hard! It's starting to get *sore* from all the up and down when I run or walk. I found my self just grabbing it to hold it down. Don't hurt as bad. That thing just will *not go down.* It's got everyone! But, who's complaining!

I came around this part of the bank that drops down about 6 feet to that pebble beach cove. I could see the fire smoke in the fog going along the water about a foot above it going the other way. The fire is dancing in that smoke and fog. The fog muffled their voices and laughter till I was right on them!

My *hard-on* broke the fog a few seconds before the rest of me arrived. They are all there having drinks and Tripping so hard I thought they were cross legged floating 3 feet of the ground. Real Zen kinda stuff. Jocelyn came up and took my hand. Her nipples are so erect. They are *bright red* in the fire light! She rubbed them across my chest and ran her hands along my body from my neck to the crack of my ass. Then between my legs till she had both balls in her hands, squeezing them softly!

She said: "Let me buy you a milk shake buddy."

She led me over to the middle of the pack of ladies and sat me down on the thickest quilt right in the middle of their circle. Started rubbing me all over with Hot Baby Oil Bonnie brought! Patty came over, sat crossed legged, placed my head in her wet moist lap. She stroked my brow! Debbie is tickling my left leg top to foot. Bonnie had charge of the other! Zelda has my left arm. Jocelyn has my right.

Jocelyn is tickling my chest and stomach. Every part of me is being done by a beautiful girl at the same time. As they are all petting me. Jocelyn is getting nasty right there. They one by one went and found their mates and brought them back here. Except for the sex noise that is always loud when the people doing the fucking are doing the tripping. We went at it for over an hour! I think!

Then we wandered around hugging then falling, fucking, walking, falling and fucking some more! Right in the dirty rocks and sometimes mud and water! I sat her up on a warm bed rock and stood all the way up straight and buried her in my face. I'm standing at eye level with that pink little tight *cooder!* Unreal! A whole new view! No matter how much we all fucked so far! Plus, everything we are tripping on! These *cocks and pussies* will not go down!

I'm *peaking* every half hour or so. Harder each time... So, is Jocelyn! When we would see something scary, I would grab her or her me and just shove it in! Dry was not a thought at all, both sexes are flowing out their cooders, its fluid non stop. The girls are literally pouring down their legs! I tried to catch as much of it as I could in my mouth! But, a bit may have got away! It tasted sweeter and thicker than normal. Each girl had their own flavor! Tasted Hot! And Sweet! It was hard to tell who was who a few times there! God, what a <u>fucking</u> night! <u>WHAT</u> A fucking night! Dig it Droogies!

Patty is getting real high. Maybe too high for a first timer! She had me fooled. She was doing fine an hour ago!

Terry said: "That, the more he fucked her, the more spacey she got." He said: "Man, it's like her face goes blank and she stares out into space, she just goes limp on me! She is still fucking... and getting off. But, it's like she is in a Trans! What is she doing now?"

I asked: "Sitting crossed leg with her fingers up her cooder, thumb on her clit rubbing it!"

She said: "I can't stand you out of me right now." So, she will sit there rubbing her self till I get back and slide in her.

I say: "Sounds hot to me Terry. Why don't you just go right back over there and pick her up by the crack of her ass Terry style? And, shove your pulsing hard cock ten feet in her juicy pink, hot inflamed swollen dripping cunt. And, spinner her around on it by the ceiling fan on medium."

He drew a check in the air, turned and said:" Yes sir mister Captain Sir!

He walked right over to her sitting on the bench. Grabbed her by the crack of her ass... Flipped her over on the bench top... climbed on and shoved it home. She SCREAMED like a virgin getting her hymen broke the first time. In, dire wonderful sweet PAIN!

She screamed again: TERRY, MY GOD! She then went deadly silent. Wrapped around Terry light a snake... Then she started chanting: Fuck me daddy, Fuck me daddy, Fuck me daddy!

This set everyone off! I looked around and noticed that Bonnies friend must have thought of this when he built these fuck tables. Each one is almost with in sharing distance of each other. Everyone is so turned on by Terry and Patty... dicks are pumping! And, girls are swooning. And, surrendering their love and passion!

Jocelyn is <u>LSD</u> tight from the *strychnine* when we first started the night. She now is sopping wet, loose and IN charge! Taking it deeper and deeper each time, then pulling me all the way in and holding me by the ass so I couldn't pull back. She pulled her legs over her head to the sides of her face and arched her back then moved me to my knees and said: *Not that fast!* <u>Slow</u>, *easy*, that's right. out-*in*-out... *oh yes, that's it.* Keep doing that till I say stop!"

Every leg in the place is in the air, *cooders are getting slammed!*

That old flapping sound two bodies' make when cunt and cock and pelvic bones smash together. Are bouncing off the rock walls! I'm noticing I'm peaking again. When her insides felt like they are binding up, putting a strangle hold on my Willy. When, it started to really hurt. I looked at her. Her face is clinched in <u>ecstasy</u>. She is Cumming so damn hard, she is almost in convulsions, squeezing me so hard, she has cut off the blood. I couldn't get out. Or, in, I'm stuck! Again, if I died now... it would be ok.

She is still grinding down on it to get it as far in her as she could! Then she just fainted into my arms breathing hard. She is out cold and shaking, pouring sweat! Her heart is pounding. She is cooing something about her grand mother crawling up her leg with a .45 Smith & Wesson in her hand. She shot up with me still hard and in her.

She said: "God Damn It Don... where is Debbie Sue?

From a bench five feet away Debbie says: "WHAT!"

She says: "Oh! Ok, I was just looking for you: I thought you were still missing."

As she said that, she started pumping on me again, we are going hard again. She started chocking me. She is actually squeezing my *Adams apple* back to my tonsils. She is almost *pile driving me*. When I noticed I'm loosing consciousness, she is pounding me so hard: she is driving me down on the rock, chocking me harder. As I was about to pass out, we came together and she let up on my neck slowly as if she were loosening the band around the arm of a junky shooting up.

I felt this heat fill my brain and my whole body EXPLODED! Every inch of us is on fire. And, in UN controllable convulsions! I tried to pull out to see if I still had one. I could not pull out! She would NOT let up or get off of me. I'm tripping so hard I am about to *FLIP* out! She slammed her mouth on mine. And, started breathing for both of us. A half hour later I came too. I had just passed out with her still slamming away on me, never lost that boner.

Jocelyn: "I can't breathe!"

She took her hands from my throat as she said: "Just lay still, don't move... it will pass"

Pass! What will pass?

She said: "You are paralyzed"

I swear, I can not move! I tried to get up again. But, I could not move. So, we just lay there and freaked out for about 20 minutes. Shaking and convulsing! I thought I felt her kind of pulling me deeper as we lay there motionless! She is almost passed out again. She isn't doing it!

If we were still in the heat of passion, I most likely wouldn't feel this. It's so faint, it feels like her uterus and cervix are working together to pull my bubba farther in unconsciously. Her body is doing it!

It grabs me with a gentle sucking, squeezing at the sametime kinda motion. Then, her hips started to move around me. She is still spaced out! It's like her body is lining her up for a cum shot to hit home!

Then her legs came up, they wrapped around me, pulled me in even more. She all of a sudden opened her eyes. And, then shot her arms around me. She pulled herself up to me, hugged harder. And, then sighed in my ear! She held me there for 5 minutes or so. Then as fast as she shot up, her whole body let go. Most times when she does that... A gallon of fluid flows out of her.....not this time! _NOTHING_ at all!

I felt this wave of fright with delight come over me.

I said out loud: "I think this woman just got _PREGNANT_ Man!"

Terry said as he is pumping Patty hard and furious: "That was fast!"

I just started to get this warm great feeling over me when I stopped and said to myself: IT'S THE ACID!

I spun around fast. Looked at her sleeping... She is flush red, smiling from ear to ear, curled up with her hands between those beautiful legs in a fetal position. I'm told that position helps conception. She looks like the Angel she is. I knew... she is _knocked up_! Oh well. So, be it.

I put that thought in the _very back of my head_ and moved along! If she was, she would tell me soon! Till then I didn't want to think about that. So I didn't!

We lay there another 20 minutes or so. Then, John and Mike came running by screaming bloody murder yelling: Rape!

I looked at Terry and Patty watching too.

I said: "RAPE! Are those two getting raped. Or, reporting?"

We hadn't worn any clothes now since we arrived. Seemed it was getting on in the time department. Rape. What the hell is this all about? What have these buffoons done now?

I'm still tripping hard. The crystal had me back up and running again. Seemed everyone had kind of, _come too!_

Where did those two Rape victims go? We all had gone off to fuck in different directions at about the same time last night. Bonnie and Zelda have a plan they are going to lay on us. They will share it around the camp fire just after dark tonight.

She said: "The folks who own this place are also into "Leather and Lace." Anyone here besides me and Zelda know what that means?

We all looked around... Patty knew! Bonnie saw Patty's hand up giving some kinda secret sign or some shit like that! Bonnie's eyes grew bigger... she invited her to the stage! Let me run down this PARTY PIT here.

(HOLD UP! I gotta light a joint! Puff, Puff! There we go man! Where was I? Oh, yeah! Puff, Puff, Puff, What? Oh! Hey... What about the RAPE? The what?) Puff.. Puff...

Hold up man! Let me run down this *PARTY PIT* here. What about the fucking Rape!

Hold up Terry: "I feel that they need to know about this wonder in the woods!"

You know, that is where we spent most of our time. The house is great! We went there to eat, wash and drink. But, we are tripping and speeding, absolutely NAKED. We didn't do much washing up except dips in the lake or tub. I didn't even know where my clothes are, didn't care!

This PARTY PIT is half on half off the water. It is a 100 foot around in a perfect circle deck of redwood. With, a large *pentagram* in the middle 13 feet in circumference exactly... That caught my attention. On the beach end is a half circle cook station with a bar. With, a changing room and a small stage,

Listen to this STEREO we are listening too. On each end of the half circle is a BIG assed wooden box made of cedar that is fiber glassed and locked with a Huge padlock. Under the *BAR* is another big box.

Bonnie says: "The key is in the house hidden behind the fridge, hanging on the cooling coil! Put it back as soon as you unlock the boxes! Don... Don... *HEY DON!*"

I'm standing there with a goofy *LSD* smirk on my face looking at Bonnie from head to toe.

I said: "WHAT THE FUCK DO YOU WANT BONNIE!"

She said: "*STOP A MINUTE MOTHER FUCKER!*"

She kneed me in the snuts, pushed me down, and sat down on top of me. I felt her hot wet pussy on my stomach.

She wrapped her legs on me and said: "DO I HAVE YOUR ATTENTION NOW?

OK! I pulled her down, kissed each of her stiff hard nipples, sucked one for a minute, she calmed right down. She is laying on me. I'm scratching her back and her beautiful ass up then down.

I said: "Ok now sweetie?"

She said: "I need you to listen to what I am trying to tell you, it's very important!"

She got up, she said: "Stop Fucking with me Beautiful'

As, she wrapped her hands around my ass then stuck her finger in my asshole...again!

She said! "Just checking..." I beat her too it... "Just checking my oil, I know."

Do that prostrate thing a little Bonnie. *She sunk her thumb just inside and found the gland and massaged it.* (i.e. G-Spot) As I was about to blow... She leaned in to me and whispered in my ear: "When the sun comes up" (she blew warm breath) Yes Bonnie! She pulled me closer and before she spoke she looked around like agent #99.

She said in a whisper: "Your ass is getting a bit Gamey! Kinda sandy too! Everybody has a super bad case of the LSD dirties! At sunrise... let's all go skinny dipping to wash um up a bit, what do ya say? Then, I have some plans for this day and night I'll lay on everyone, OK?"

I said: "Yup!"

We are looking behind the fridge now, she leaned in to get the key, and it's hard to reach. She had to lean in on one leg and raise the other.

She is having trouble.

She said: "Give me a hand lover."

She put her foot on my shoulder, her cooder in my face. I'm holding her up there as she fished behind the fridge. Her mussels around and in her woo woo are working hard. Contracting then opening and closing over and over again... I swore it breathed & winked at me. And, then spit in my eye!

She is kind of faking it a bit. She is doing all of that twitching, watching me out the side of her eye.

She said: "Got that fucker!"

I said: "You sure did!"

She said: "Not my pussy, the key!"

I said: "I knew that."

I helped her down. She fell into my arms. Then, onto her feet again... She held me, looked at me then said the most unbelievable thing I had heard her say so far...today.

I want to ask you a most likely loaded question. What's that Bonnie? She says: Well... I mean ah. Well... ah like. *Does Jocelyn*"

I said: "You will have to ask her."

We are back at the *PARTY PIT* again. She took me over to one of the boxes on the end, gave me the key.

Terry said: "Where is John and Mike, What's with the Rape?"

I said: Oh Yeah! The Fucking RAPE! How the fuck do I know?

Bonnie said: "Shut the fuck up about that rape shit!"

She turned back to me: "Now, be Fucking careful here. *Barton NEVER* tells anyone where that key is. I'm looking at Jocelyn squirm around on the quilt motioning me over there.

Bonnie says: "Hey… you hear me Don? I had to go with him and Jana to the *TORTURE* pit out there to deserve this key!"

OK… Let's stop here a minute. I should have known something was up when I heard Bonnie say… <u>*TORTURE PIT*</u>… I didn't even catch that, my dick is twitching. Looking at Jocelyn as I listened kinda to Bonnie…

She went on: "So, don't fuck me up! I put YOU in charge!"

I took the key, opened the box, inside is a VOICE OF THE THE-ATER® folded horn *model A7 speaker.* Same on the other side… The fronts came up on hooks then off, loaded on the back. In the box under the bar is a *1000 watt, 500 watt per channel* Peavey CS-1600. A <u>24 channel EQ</u>, A new fangled deal called a CASSETTE DECK. Never saw one of them critters before. WOW!

I just said Critters! HA! *I am country now!*

Bonnie slapped me again, real hard too!

She said: PAY - A-ATTENTION ASSHOLE!"

Ok! There is a Reel to Reel. An 8 track player… A tuner… A Duel-Twin 1200 turntable, Four Neumann U91 microphones and stands, plugged into a 6 channel Peavey® board.

NICE system for sure!

We will play a few parties. Then, a Wedding later down the line here!

Anyway, Bonnie said: "You are in charge of this stuff. Anything, anything happens to it! Zelda and I gonna Rape you!"

I didn't know that was in my future at the time. It won't be Fun this time buddy, you got me! YES, BONNIE KISS, KISS. Good! Here! She kissed me, then handed me the key!

We could have used it all last night too! But, nobody was into a stereo last night. We were busy making our own music. As Bonnie and Zelda went to the house, she turned, then walked backwards and told everyone she had something to tell us all at sunrise. So, gather everyone up. We will be right back.

I have to check and see how come Zelda here, has an itch inside her fallopian tubes. I'll be right back! So, Jocelyn… Me. Terry and Patty went out in the Bush to hunt everyone down.

We found Tony and Debbie inside each other in the boat. We walked over to them, sat down and watched them awhile.

I remarked: "Wish I had a camera. She is wrapped around him like moss on the North side of a tree in winter!"

She has him down. She is looking backwards doing *Jumping Jacks* on old Tony's wobble stick! He is screaming and creaming. She started slapping the cat shit out of Tony, grinding down on him like he is a stump being ground out! As she did that, she looked around at us not missing a move!

She said something that just dropped all of us to the ground in uncontrollable laughing fits!

She said in a swirling head matter of fucking fact point of notice voice real loud! "I am so **STONEDIDER!** (I.e. Stone - did- Ur) I can't freaking stand it! Tony... Tony... *DO IT FUCKING NOW!*"

They both shot off like a ROCKET on pad #9 at Kennedy! Then she slapped him again and SCREAMED: "I AM IN LOVE WITH THIS WONDERFUL MAN!"

I hollered: "Furor Bonnie... and her Storm Trooper Zelda wants us at the PIT! We will see you there. Something, about a torture pit... Come on now!"

What about the fuckin Rape asked Terry again?

What *FUCKIN RAPE?*

As we walked looking for John and Mike, I asked Jocelyn what in the hell did Debbie say.

Jocelyn said: "I think she said, <u>STONDIDER</u>. *Yup*, that's right!"

I asked: "She ever said that before?"

"Nawh! That's Debbie. She just makes shit up when it suits her: she's real Far-out that way. *I sure do love her...* we are sisters for life you know!

I said: "No Shit. But... I don't think that is what she said. Stondider... That's it! Sure she has never said that before!"

NOPE! <u>NEVER!</u>

Come here Don... She sat me down, said she wanted a bit of hands on her. She lay out spread eagle on the bench there. The sun is coming up. The bench is still warm from the day before.

She said: "Climb up here and tickle me all over a minute. Take your hands: rub them everywhere and then some."

We have been <u>*HEAVY TRIPPING*</u> so long... It is starting to feel normal! I started at her neck... licked petted and tickled each and every part of her. We are both dripping and twitching after about 20 minutes. We had a long, quickie and lay in each others arms now in the lake and watched the Sun clear the mountain top.

It's first Rays felt warm and good. But, just a few minutes later... it is sultry! The LSD dirties are worst in the heat. *Believe me!* As the sun is on us hot now... I looked at myself... Bonnie is not kidding. I looked like I was in the <u>NATIONAL GEOGRAPHIC</u>® for Christ's sake!

I told the rest who were all coming from the woods too, that we are to meet here. Then wait for Bonnie who will be here in a minute. *Its band meeting time!*

She and Zelda came down the walk. I had one of the only three 8 track Tapes. I found it in there on the stereo. It's turned up a bit. But not loud!

Bonnie came down, Zelda is carrying a big hand full of towels and a bucket of <u>ALL I N ONE</u>® *Hippie soap*. That's right! Right from *Woodstock*, Where Bonnie bought a case of the stuff! Everybody on the other end of the pit... Please, pay attention. This won't take long.

We all moved to the half that is over the water, kind of a boat dock too.

She said: "Every one in the water! Its only waist deep, imported sand from Galveston, TX. With a closed in bottom!"

I asked Bonnie: "just how rich are these people?"

She said: "So Rich... *Nothing shocks them!* Still though...*No richer than you will be if you stick with me!*" We all applauded.

She went on: "Ok, I want to run down the events of the day after a wash... so let's have some fun. Lets all get INVOLVED!"

Zelda started washing Debbie and Tony from top to bottom!

Tony said: "Zelda, I'll do it myself thank you!"

Zelda grabbed his arm and wrenched it behind him, then picked him up by his shoulders and said the first <u>FULL</u> sentence I have heard her say so far!

She said: "*YOU CAUSING TROUBLE BUDDY?*"

Tony froze, noticed she had a hold of his roosack with the other hand she is lightly twisting it!

He said: "No Ma'am. Wash away!"

Debbie is in Ecstasy! She is groaning and moaning as Bonnie washed every part of her most <u>beautiful</u> body!

Debbie is a Stunning young woman! Every part of her is just the right size to fit her *wild personality!* God was very good to her, she knows it too! Bonnie had moved to Jocelyn and me. We knew better than to even move. She and Zelda washed us bare handed. They felt and squeezed. And, probed! She fingered us both here and there, up this crack and down the other. Bonnie is singing: "I painted her. I painted her. Over her front and down her back... every Nooky and every Crack. I painted her."

Jocelyn then grabbed me and we floated away. As, Bonnie turn around and said: "NEXT!"

She let go of Zelda, they walked off toward Terry and Patty who are sitting there watching all of this in wonder. And, hopping they would not be included, *Especially Patty!* Her Nipples are so hard on those Giant tits. She is panting and scratching holes in Terry! He didn't seem to mind though. I don't know what Zelda did to her. But, I want Zelda to teach it to me!

Jocelyn snapped back and jumped me, almost drowned me! she shoved it in to scratch that itch and blew like *Krakatoa!* (I.e. Crack-A-Fuckin-Toe-a).

I'm watching Patty and Terry get the treatment, when Terry just lost it. Hauled Bonnie out on the deck, and shoved his bubba root deep in her with her legs in the air over Terry's shoulders! Kicking like she is swimming.

Patty has tackled Zelda and has most of her arm up Zelda's cooder, her tongue rapped around her throat!

Bonnie flipped Terry over and started pounding up and down on him like a cheese grader. I noticed Jocelyn and I are on the bench watching them and phone polling again too!

Tony is pounding Debbie's beautiful white creamy body! She is limp like a rag doll moaning his name and pledging her love for ever and chanting that she is... SO DAMN STONIDIDER, Over. And, over again! Terry came and so did Patty... Zelda and Bonnie turned their attention to Mike and John. Then, fucked their brains out while the rest of us got out... Dried off and took our seats at the party pit round table.

Bonnie and Zelda are still drowning those boys as they SCREAMED OUT... HELP. POLICE, *HELP!*

All is some what quiet now. The breeze is starting to come off the lake. The sun is all the way up. I guess so! Its 3: 30 pm. 3:30! What the hell! You and Jocelyn passed out here about 10: 30 am.

Bonnie and Zelda went to their room and fucked till about 20 minutes ago, everyone seems to have taken a short break! The acid is all gone now. So, is the speed? I'm hungry and tired as hell! We had another night to go here, I figured we would all hit the house and just crash, and then head back tomorrow! Oh no ya don't! Bonnie has a whole night planned! It included the trip home and the rest of tomorrow into the night.

Jocelyn and I went to the house, found our room and lay down just for a minute, we were out! Rick and Dianna sat down, woke me up.

I looked at them and said: "Where did you two come from?"

Rick replied: "We got here an hour or so ago, what happened to you two?"

I responded with: "Shit... I guess we just passed out."

He said: "Well... come on, let's get started."

I say: "Started on what?"

Bonnie is ready for us to get moving.

Jocelyn and I walked outside with Rick and Dianna. We stopped at her *Bonneville*. Dianna striped off her clothes. Now... I looked at Jocelyn. She... looked at me. No one has EVER seen Dianna Nude before!

Dianna has these two great big round firm sticking absolutely straight out... up and tall... creamy white, soft big pink nippled tits! Her full tapered waist went straight down to a perfectly shaved pussy like I had never seen in my life. I was shocked. Dianna naked with a shaved cooder, my dick got harder!

Jocelyn grabbed it and said: "God Damn Dianna! You are fucking most beautiful!"

Bonnie came up behind Rick, Stuck her hands between his legs from the back, grabbed his swinger now meaty, and pulled it back up the crack of his ass and stuck her finger in it and said: "*Don't worry honey, just checking your oil, its great!*"

New blood! We are all used to looking at each other now. We had seen us all in every sexual position. In, and out of the dirt! <u>New Nakedness</u> is refreshing! Here's the rub, and why we are all shocked!

Dianna didn't come, because they knew it was going to be a *naked* affair! Most times they bow out and hit their room then have private sex! This is the first time any of us had seen Dianna naked. She is stunning! I could not stop watching her. What a Southern beautiful girl!

A True..."<u>SOUTHERN BELLE</u>" for fucking sure!

We all are walking to the house now, carrying a whole new batch of supplies Dianna brought from the Restaurant.

Bonnie is down at the PARTY PIT with a bunch of stuff on the main spool table all laid out and ready for our <u>BAND</u> meeting! She turned on a microphone, backed the music down.

Called us all over there: "Ok... This thing on? (Tap- Tap- Tap) Everyone grab a seat, this won't take long."

We all sat down and she went into it: "I hope everyone is having one hell of a good time!"

We all howled!

She went on: "Ok... we have to go home in the morning! Dianna & Rick are here now. Along with new supplies... Welcome to you all!"

We howled again!

She went on: "You know the rule here... No clothes on anyone. If ya won't strip, Ya don't stay! *That's the rule.*"

She says: "As before…. anything goes. Anything! Ok, the whole band is here. I want you all to play with these microphones here, *practice* live on the PA. So, you all can get used to that sound….all the time! We only have 4 microphones here. So, do the best you can!"

I said: "Bonnie"

She sweetly responded: "Yes love."

I said: my *dick* is still so hard, I can only think of sticking my Stanley the Penis, in ol Jocelyn here. How we gonna practice?"

She zoomed back with: Ok, here it is. I stopped at a friend's house before I picked you all up. He is a rep for *Columbia Records*. He gave me a free copy of the "*Stones*" new album here.

She pulled it out, read the cover: "Its… ah… is that right?"

She turned it around. And, held it up…

She, pointed at it and said: "BROWN SUGAR! I'll take this 8 track tape here and put it on the stereo after the meeting! I want Terry and Don to learn the song—-ah—- She, ran her finger down the list! Ah… shit…"

She said: "*JUST A DAMN MINUTE!* Ok, what the fuck! Just a minute! I think I may be a little fucked up here! No Shit!" Dig-it! ♥

She reached down… stuck three fingers in her *pussy*. Then, her thumb on the clit… Fell backward on the deck… Legs in the air! And, banged herself for a minute or two then blew! Ah…that's better!

She said: "DON…Close your legs for a minute! Ok, Thank you! Now… where was I?"

She said: "Oh man…that felt GOOD! *Shwew!*" She pinched it again then continued.

She said: "Ok… I have a ¼ ounce of *fresh Crystal*. I want you guys to know. And, play for me this song here, WILD HORSES by dark. Ok! I have a *Temple Ball* in my purse. An ounce of GOLD cola bud! I also have a Gallon Jug of *THUNDER BIRD*® wine. With, 15 hits of ORANGE SUNSHINE in thar! After dinner, we will have a half once glass a piece! That's all! Then every 2 hours all night we will have another. *TOGETH-ER!* Its ORGY night! No running off in the woods tonight."

Chapter Forty Two

"The Prelude to...
Halloween for Grown ups"

Now, I'm intrigued... This sounds like fun!

Bonnie went on: Me, or Zelda will come and get one of you at a time. Take you to a very special place! Special indeed! The people that own this place... Built an "Outdoor Den" Of torture, and bondage!"

That's where the *"LEATHER & LACE"* comes in! Don't ask today where it is, we will not tell ya! You will only be shown when we come for ya!

We don't care if you guys and gals got a HOT COCK up your BUTT! You pull free and come with us! If you don't! The punishment will be quite severe. I assure you!

"All the dope, other than the bottle of acid will be on the honor system! All out on the table IN THE HOUSE! We haven't messed that place up yet to bad! So Party OUTSIDE, So, we don't have to spend too much time tomorrow cleaning before we go home! Terry... Don."

We shot up *dicks flapping* to attention! "You guys put up the *MUSIC* stuff after you all play the song and a few more at the little show tonight. OK? I don't want the stuff fucked up. Or, broke... Its *ORGY* night! And, we will not be paying attention to static gear! So, put um up!"

I said: *"ORGY? YEAH!"*

She said: "What's wrong with that! If ya don't want to join in the mix, just watch and fuck each other! But, when we come for you... *All bets are* off."

"Here's the rub ya-all," "You can never tell what happened in there... ever! That's the rule. If you don't abide, you can't come back here again! That's the rule."

I agreed to it before they gave me the keys! We *NEED* to be able to come back here business wise. Get it Done! So, help me out here! I knew that Bonnie and Zelda just wanted to have their way with us all! I had no idea what awaited out thar in the soon to be DARKNESS!

She said: "Listen Don... Mick Fleetwood has brought together so many artists in Fleetwood Mac it's unbelievable! He said in an interview, that he had each and every one of them many times!"

I said: "Is that what you have in mind Bonnie?"

She clipped back with: "No Don! Here is what I have in mind for to-night! A sex filled *HALLOWEEN* for grown ups! They got everything out there built into an altar, the owner built it for just this reason!"

I accused: "Bonnie... you say these people are Nudists!"
Kinda!
Are you sure they are not a <u>Coven</u>.
She grabbed me, put her hand over my mouth: "Shhh!"
I said: "There is a *Pentagram* on the party deck circle. Those... what is it you call them... FUCK BENCHES! They look a bit like love <u>*sacrifice*</u> alters to me. They are in a circle too! Bonnie... what are you up to?"
She said: "Don... you are to FUCKING smart for your own good some-times, you asshole! I love you so much! Yes, it's a Witch and Warlock S & M rack, that's all I can tell you. I assure you Don, you and Jocelyn will dig it the most! After you go thru what we have planned, nobody will be bitching. Or, tell what happen EVER! You'll see!"
Then she winked and ran off with Zelda to prepare.
The girls had prepared a Buffet for the night! All cold foods that won't spoil down at the outdoor bar, we can munch on that all night. We all just did a HUGE line of Crystal to wake back up.

"NO sleep till BROOKLYN!"

That's the rule in a *SPEED* run! As we would be speeding so hard, Trip-ping on *sunshine*, we won't be very hungry! Bonnie won't let us forget to eat tonight! She is going to watch every one of us eat sometime before dark!
She said: "That what she has planned for the *orgy* will require a lot of REAL energy, not fake! She doesn't want anyone *dying* on her and Zelda. While we are out here in this <u>most free and wonderful place</u>, I am intrigued! So, is Jocelyn! Even more now... We can't wait!
Something heavy duty is going to happen to each. And, every one of us tonight for sure! Everyone kinda has a job for the next few hours. We had a song to learn!
Bonnie put the album on. <u>BROWN SUGAR... *She turned up the vol-ume, WAY...* WAY</u> Up!
I said: "Isn't that kinda loud?"
She snapped: "Nope!" Ain't nobody can hear it. I want to hear you guys out that PA soon." Off she went. She looks up at the road every few min-utes or so. Like she is waiting on someone...
We are hearing this "Rolling Stones" album for the first time. It has only been out a few days we were told. We snorted. And, smoked... Petted each other heavy as we listened... Then, played it again!
We are swimming, fucking, eating and drinking. Having a great after-noon! We had the song down and the vocal was... Ok! We went up, sat down at the mics. We sounded pretty good doing the song.

We played it four or five more times. Bonnie called everyone to the kitchen in the house! It was like in _THE TIME MACHINE_ and the _Morlocks_ blew the air raid siren and in the people went! Or, Jim Jones in Guyana! Time fer some cool-aid folks! Grape Thunderbird I think!

As we entered the door, Zelda had a cup of tomato soup you had to drink and chew up a piece of _buttered garlic bread_. She is not taking any chances! _What is up their sleeves!_ It's getting _SPOOKY_ around here!

We didn't know what they were up too, The _MYSTERY_ made it even worst! Or, better… depending on how ya looked at it!

You would drink the soup and eat the bread and a multi-vitamin. Then Bonnie _administered_ the ounce of wine _LSD!_ She made you rinse it around in your mouth under your tongue and gargle with it! It's obvious, at least to me. _Something is up here!_

Remember the _Witch girl in California_, with the wax Poof/Balls that wrenched my dick almost off? Well, she filled me in on a lot of this Witch stuff. Some of it is _WAY OUT THERE!_ But, I figured Bonnie would not HURT any of us. So, what the hell! HALLOWEEN for grown ups!

Shit… everyone knows how big I am on DOPE and _GHOSTS!_ Shit man, _NOBODY BIGGER!_ Especially if there is SEX involved!

We have all passed thru their line now. We are all back sitting at the PARTY PIT. _Stereo jamming!_

I have Jocelyn lying on top of me. Kissing me all over my body! I'd grab a taste and suck her delta as it would stick itself in my face. She is having a great time! It's about 6 pm now. And, Bonnie wants to hear the song sang to her! Then we can sing as long as we like. And, then move along to the next step!

Chapter Forty Three

"Who is in the Rolls Royce at the top of the road?"

The scene is getting *surreal*, as the acid started coming on. Bonnie and Zelda have the gig at the bar. And, administered another glass of the acid/wine to everyone.

I noticed that Bonnie was signing me to hit the stage again and play that song for her now. Wild Horses... I looked up the road where she is walking. And, there is a *Rolls Royce* sitting there. From that spot you can hear the stage perfectly.

I said: "Terry, Come on everyone... Let's play the song for them.

Everyone looked up the road to where Bonnie is talking to a Guy & Girl. They are sitting on the Rolls listening. We went into the song...

Bonnie hollered down... Play it again. We did.

We sounded REAL good there in that little valley/holler. They got in the car a minute. Then Bonnie got out. They left and she walked on down.

She said: OK! You all passed the first phase of the audition.

I said: "Audition"

She said: "YUP! That's right. You guys can be the <u>house band </u>if you like. Money will be discussed later. You have one more test to perform. It has to do with tonight. I'll tell ya more after all of that stuff has run it's course.

Anna came bouncing down the trail with those *BIG* tits swaying from side to side. She went around *French* kissing everyone. Turns out, she, and Buck have a real great relationship. She can fuck anybody she wants and so can he! Not bad I guess... if ya have *shit for brains!* But, works for them. She got to us, stopped and curtsied! May I *French kiss* your boy friend Jocelyn? And... then you please? She didn't wait for an answer. She just did it and skipped away. Kissed Jocelyn for at least 2 minutes...as she pushed and squirmed to get away fom her.

Zelda had Buck down: she is sucking his rather large dick. I can't believe he and Anna thought he was going to get that dick in me. I still was blown away by that whole scene. It would have hurt for sure! No doubt about that!

Bonnie called everyone to the PIT. And, we sang to her and pledged our love for her as our sole salvation and savior! She stood up after the song and pulled her pussy lips apart. Then, pissed like a man at least 8 feet in front of her! She said that was the way she marked her territory! And we

are hers! She applauded and said: _LET THE GAMES BEGIN!_
Remember everyone… When we come for you… _YOU GO!_
Everyone one agreed and waited to see what would happen next! I knew that nothing would happen till 10 or 11. And, then it would end at 5am, the darkest hour of the night! I could have talked Bonnie into a peak I think. But, I didn't want to spoil the fun!

Jocelyn said: "What if they want to _FUCK_ me?"

I said: "FUCK YOU?"

She did retort: "Yeah: you know, get down on me. What, do I do? I am not queer!"

I clambered: "No shit! Well… They say we are all a little Queer. If I was a girl, I could not help myself. You would be every bit as beautiful to me even if I were a girl too! It's this way Jocelyn. Bonnie asked me awhile ago if you were a switch hitter, asked me if you went that way."

She asked: "What did you tell her?"

I said: "Honey, I told her you don't swing that way that I know of. But I couldn't speak for your deepest secret fantasy's sweet heart. So she would have to ask you your self."

Jocelyn said: "Ok, I'll try and play along! You promise you won't let it go too far? They won't hurt me will they? You wouldn't let them hurt me?"

I responded: "Well… I have no idea what is going on here either! You will be out there on your own with them. If you don't want any thing new to happen to you for what ever reason. You do not have to go! After all… it's just a game sweet heart."

I kissed her worries away.

She said: "Well… ok then, I'm counting on you Don! Don't let me get hurt."

I told her: "You never have to ever worry about that my love!"

We went back to kissing and sucking till something happened! Far Out Man! I trust Bonne. So, I wasn't REAL worried! But, I'm not sure about that Zelda! She scares me from time to time.

She said as we pulled apart: "I have to go clean up a bit in the little girl's room. I am really getting off on the Sunshine. I'm seeing all kinds a stuff now. I'll be back soon."

It is dark now. Terry came over as Patty followed Jocelyn. He sat down. John noticed that Bonnie had brought down a whole carton of eight track tapes! He pulled out "_DAYS OF FUTURE PAST_" and cranked it up! The perfect tripping music _reverberated_ from the lake and the rock faces around us. We are really alone! No roads around the top to see. Or, hear down in, _Wonderful place!_ We are really digging it.*

Terry asked: "Do you think that Bonnie has ever _KILLED_ anyone?"

I said: "There will be more! But listen Terry…_Never forget!_ "_The Canary_ *sings. But, the Eagle flies!"*

Terry snapped with a chuckle: "What in the fuck is that supposed to mean?"

I say: "Shit… how do I know. I'm trippin!"

I reminded him: "Don't forget also… that I was a cock teaser at <u>Cucamonga Roster Rama!"</u>

Jocelyn asked: "Wow Don. That's cool… What was it you did there?" Me: *"Shit Jocelyn, I used to enrage them little buggers!"*

She had just swallowed a big mouthful of *Dr. Pepper.* Her head seemed to be spinning in circles. Out her nose came the *Dr Pepper.*

So I said: "Naw… Naw… I'm just bull shittin ya." Jocelyn asked, "What was it you did to enrage them little buggers Don?" I told her, "I used to dress up like a big egg and sit on them! It really freaked them out. Then into the cock ring! Hot damn, up and down, blood everywhere! You gotta watch u self now though! They don't allow that no more man. You gotta do it green."

I asked Terry: "Remember the night of the Big blue acid Trip at Tim and Tony's. When I never came back?"

He replied: "Yes I do!"

I said: "I stopped breathing for almost 3 minutes! Bonnie did kill me! I was out cold for over two hour's! She *Raped me then!"*

He was shocked as he said: "While you was fucking knocked the fuck out?"

He looked around and back again then said: "So… oh shit I don't fucking know!" I don't know what they want of me. I'm tripping too hard for this! Don, I am so fucking stoned! I keep seeing these faces coming down from the trees at me! I just saw a *freaking something* go right through *YOU!"*

As I looked at Terry, there is three of him! One in clear bright blue, bright red, bright green! His lips move… and, then I hear his words. The trails are so intense: I am not sure which figure to watch. So, I try to watch them all.

SHIT! I just fell down. I didn't even know I was standing up! Hell! I didn't even know I was walking! As I lay there, I saw Jocelyn coming down from the house. The, house light is framing her. She looks like she is floating toward me not even touching the ground. Terry is saying something to me. But, he is just an echo in the back ground getting farther… and, farther away. Even, though he is right here!

Jocelyn floats over to me and sits down with her legs around my back to my front locked. She wrapped her arms around my chest and lay her head on my back. She is burning Hot! Like she has a fever! Her crotch is hot and wet. Her nipples digging into my shoulder blades… She feels so good!

I wondered where she was while I was talking to Terry!

Debbie and Tony came out next. Sat down around the FIRE pit where we all were congregating!

Jocelyn said: "Terry and I should go up to the house and drink our next glass of wine, everyone else just did. Bonnie is for sure setting us up for something here. I'm scared Don."

As Terry and I walked, I said: "Frasier is gonna knock the chip off of old Clay's smart ass shoulder!"

I was trying to get a bit of reality going. We are all starting to really trip and we are going for more! That's *three times* now, we were afraid of the Bonnie deal coming up! None of us had any idea what was going to happen to each of us! But, we couldn't wait to find out.

We got to the house and looked back at the Fire Pit. It looked like a Devil Worship deal with it all lit up and everything running. We didn't turn it all on last night. But, I must have been seeing the future! As the Devil says at the Cross Roads: "You ain't seen nothin yet!"

I watched Debbie and Jocelyn talking. I could see *Angels dancing above them*, shooting little *Day-Glo arrows* into their Hearts. They just fell back and laughed and laughed.

Oh Yeah! Bonnie had my hand and she pulled me in the living room. It's dark in here. Except for a *crystal ball* in the middle of that big mirror lighting a whole bunch of lines of Crystal!

Bonnie said: Remember that cocaine stuff?"

I said with excitement: "YES!"

She said: "Half and half. I saved an eight ball of that stuff."

She said: "Everyone does not know this, Just US! Keep it that way!"

Listen: "I am going to close this door as we all head down there to the pit. You and Jocelyn, Terry and Patty, can come on in and help yourself"

She pulled me over to the day bed in the room. I have a Giant Hard-on again, won't go down. We all have um again.

She lay me down, lifted her left leg, and then slid me in. *I just let her!* I could tell the night is going to really be something here! I think she has got herself into something Bigger than she thought. The night would tell. She is setting us up for sure.

She is really laying it to me now. She is shivering. She drops on me. I feel the tight lips of her cervix, she sighs a Hot relief breath in the air! She swallows my dick with her love and lifts off of me. Then, leans over and kisses me she says: "Thank You for helping me tonight! It will get Very *Heavy before dawn!* But... just go with it. *You will be glad you did.*

Bonnie.

"Yes my LOVE"

I was very serious: "Are you going to HURT anybody tonight? I won't be able to let you do that you know! You, Raped me!"

She hugged me: "Don, are you upset about that?"

I said: "Bonnie... _You have Raped me two times!_"

Her mood shifted gears. She got all serious. Tears started running down her faces. She sat down. Put her head in her hands. Really started crying out loud...

She said: "I never wanted to hurt you. I swear to god! I just want you so fucking bad. I couldn't stand it! I was the one that brought all of you people together. I love you all so much. We are a family... A family!"

She is crying Harder now: "I didn't mean to hurt you. I am so sorry! Please... don't Hate me. _Please!_"

Well, I been around the LSD bend a few times and I know when the acid is shifting gears and setting a persons emotions inside out, just to ruin their trip. I had to turn this around. It is my fault!

I picked her up, lay her down on the day bed, spread her legs and shoved it in. I slowly moved in and out. Ever so easy and soft! She pulled me down, reached around and grabbed my sack and almost pulled it off. She whispered to me: Oh man... that's right where I need it! More of that... Nice and Slow!"

She seized up more and her vagina started to pull inward, I started to see the Pleasure in her eyes, Hot sparks in the dark of the room. Then I pushed in all the way... and she came.

She just let all the last couple of days fall out of her. She let go and fell back. I had not cum. I'm so Hot. I could not cum! There is no way I was _Cumming till morning with Jocelyn._ I plan to Trip Hard on this very good clean acid and mix with everybody. _It's Orgy night!_

Well, I feel much better now Don.

She kissed me then said: "Thank You, let's join the others!"

We did a Giant line in each nose, rubbed it on both of us and out the door we went! Everybody is at the PIT now. The Party is in full force. What a Fucking Trip. Fucking Far out man! I am HARD and it won't go down. All night to Fuck! Dig It Man! _HEAVEN!_

The girls are all locked up at the bar laughing and carrying on! They have Zelda laid out on the bar. Patty is Jamming a 14 inch black Dick up her pussy, they are all screaming when she doubles up and yells in _German!_ She has a Butt plug in her ass on high vibrate. And, clothes pins on her nipples! They are all just laughing and laughing!

All the guys are deep in bullshit conversation about anything and everything. But, most of all about this _Secret Bonnie deal._ We walk up and sit down on the blankets. Everyone comes over. I am sitting there crossed legged: Jocelyn lies down in front of me and stretches out with her head in my lap. We are all in a circle feet pointing in, everyone can see everyone and anything they are doing, the blankets surround the fire pit in the middle.

There are *twinkle lights* in the trees. I think! They all twinkle independently, they look like stars & fire flies. The trees are Huge. And, have colored flood lights in them pointed up into and out into the sky! The fire flies are everywhere. And, I can see *Creatures in the woods* that is now pitch black and full of eyes looking back at us. And, mystery!

Bonnie breaks the silence and says: "Ok everybody. There is one more glass of wine left for each of you."

Zelda brings them over, walks around the circle passing them out. Hold for a toast! Everybody waits.

She continues: "Tonight we are all going to find out who. And, what we really are! Some of you might not like what you find out. Each of you will confess alone with just us!

Nothing will ever be repeated about what happens in there. If you repeat it! Ok! It's not a secret! But, be Warned! It will be very eye opening and very shocking! When each of you rejoins the group, you will be changed for ever. Plus, more in tune with yourself and others! These woods are full of Demons tonight. That have come here to keep you from the right path! Have complete opened minds to *RECEIVE!* Don't fight it! Except what ever happens tonight as Real! But remember… your head tonight. As, you may need it real bad before dawn!"

We all had our Wine. And, Zelda put on some of that sitar crap.

Hell… tonight it sounded REAL good, it just grabbed me.

Bonnie said: "Also, this is an <u>ORGY</u>! Everyone is *fair game tonight*, EVERYONE!" She is looking at Rick and Dianna… they nodded their consent!

They are still Naked. That's a good sign. So, LET THE NIGHT BEGIN!

Anna came over and spread my legs. rubbed my Cockhead… Kissed and sucked on the tip like a straw awhile. She went, UM… and moved along!

Jocelyn moved up on me and grabbed on, curled up against my body to protect what is hers! I kissed her. We just went to making out. Kissing mostly… It felt so good just to suck those oh so wonderful lips. I could taste her so strong! She took my breath away. I reached around her as she sat back and took each breast in my hands.

Chapter Forty Four

"The Machine... Violent Sex... LSD & <u>Zelda</u>"

I'm massaging them. And, blowing on the back of her neck as she started to shiver... We noticed Bonnie and Zelda disappear down a path I had not noticed. (I guess they pulled one on me)

They are dressed in *long sheer see thru coal black capes.* They, have their hair up with... that's Right! With *pointy hats on*, with a bag in each hand, with a finger wrapped around a small torch!

Everyone is piling up. Rubbing and stroking each other, kissing and rolling around on each other. We are hallucinating so hard, it appeared there were many more of us. Anna screamed, then jumped into the middle of the bunch, spread her legs and started pumping herself with that 14 inch Dick!

Buck came over and pulled it out of her with great trepidation and replaced it with his. Squatting over her... He, pile drove her hard and fast till she is screaming, hollering blood murder! I mean. It's is a good damn thing you can't hear this place from outside. The cops would be on their way for fucking sure! SHIT! *Fucking Bats!* Duck you suckers... Bats everywhere! Tony and Debbie are balled up next to Terry and Patty. It's getting about 10: 54 now. Things should start getting real strange anytime now. I felt like a kid at the Forth of July show. Wait for it to start.

The Acid has hit real hard, the speed and the day catching up.

Writers note.

"I don't know how involved any of you Droogies (You... My readers) were in this life style. But, the more drugs you would do. And the longer you went without sleep. The high became almost in *REAL TIME!* Sometimes we would just smoke dope and stay up 3 or 4 days. And, get just as high on the third day! Just thought id through that in there." Anywho... Where was I? Oh Yeah...

Everything will shift gears as your trip goes on. The Sex will become *Deep Tripping* and *Discovery* with <u>violence</u> nobody really expects. Did I mention: VIOLENCE? *Nobody gets hurt!* Right!☙

The love and sex will not reemerge till we all start to crash. Or, come down a bit. Then you become very emotional. You actually FEEL the pain! It's UN real for sure! I Love it!

It will be all MYSTERY & Magic till dawn or so. With hyper/Passionate, hard pounding, abandoned, uninhibited, Raw, *LSD* way the fuck out there sex... just who am I fucking and who is fucking me kinda thing! Or, none at all!

As we are leaving in the morning, I know there would be no crashing out. _No sleep till Brooklyn!_ I noticed we are looking each other over in a total freak out. Like the guy on the deserted island. Seeing his shipmate as a *walking hot dog on a bun with mustard...* When we noticed that Mike is no longer with us!

As Mike... And, John's dates are putting on this shindig tonight. The two of them were stag. They had been running the stereo. And, the Bar till Bonnie and Zelda come for them. Or, back to them. Which ever comes first. It's for sure. Mike is gone! It's under way... who will be next?

I found my self laying on Jocelyn. Just, looking up at her looking down at me and smiling!

I said: "What are you thinking about?"

In her sweet voice she said "What? Oh... I'm just looking at your face. You are so bright blue in Aura."

I said: "Good!" with a giant smile on my puss.

She asked: "Why is that good?"

I told her: My Aura is Bright Blue when I am Very Happy. Or making love with you. Or, playing Music."

She is reaching over me and running her hands down my chest. She licked her finger and stuck it in my belly button. Snapped it with a POP... Then, she leaned over me and her nipples fell into my open calling mouth. I suck down on them hard!

She reached my cock, grabbed it with one hand, the balls with the other and started stroking! She did that till my suction grip gave away on her tits and she sat back up! She pinched my nipples till they were hard and erect. Then sucked on them... Kissed me...

Whispered into my mouth""*I LOVE YOU DON!*"

I reached up around her back and held the kiss a long time till we floated away into the cosmos. I heard someone walk up behind us.

Bonnie tapped Jocelyn on the shoulder.

Mike walked in and sat down! Bonnie led Jocelyn down the path, she looked back at me with a *scared look on her face* and they were gone!

I looked around the pit. Everyone is kissing and talking. Hugging, petting... Talking... Fucking... Sucking... and all that!

I went up to the house, there's Patty. She is grabbing smoke and more beer for the bar.

I'm worried about Jocelyn. What are they doing to her? I looked at Mike with a, WHAT'S it all about?

He looked over at me with a *way blank look*. And, says in a faint voice: "*NO WAY MAN!* I ain't got nothing to say!"

It's a bit past Eleven thirty now, *very Spooky!* The music is down and sweet. I want to hold Jocelyn. I sat there talking to everyone and watching some Fuck slow and some hard. It's still making me Hot. Even after the two days of *non stop speeding*, fucking and tripping, No sleep and very little food... A lot of smoke, *speed* and more booze! We are about as far out there as anybody could possibly ever hope to get!

There is a fog coming up and over the dock right up to me. It covered me like a blanket and enveloped me! There are Hands coming out from the fog. I couldn't see their faces: they are grabbing my ass, cock and balls. Hands everywhere Rubbing and Stroking every inch of me! Just hands... nothing else! They went from rubbing and stroking. Then, went to my mouth and held it open. A pair of lips... *Just lips* wrapped around my cock and started sucking! Hands are running up and down the insides of my legs and arms. And, then caressing my entire Torso at once... I could feel my Heart being squeezed into my throat. Beating Wildly and Irregular! My feet tickled like they were asleep, my head is spinning. I looked down at my crotch... the head of my dick looked at me and turned! The Cum hole spoke like lips. Where is Jocelyn? I want Jocelyn! As my dick said that! Jocelyn tapped me on the shoulder...

Hey there Buddy: "She kissed me Warm and all the way to my Soul. She is totally calm. Dig This!

She moved around me real slow. Like she is floating! Her Nakedness shown in the firelight as she hung her arms straight out from her shoulders and started dancing to the new Stones record!

She would move up and shake her womanhood against my face. And, stroke the back of my head. Put both hands on the side of my face and grind her pelvic bone hard into my lips. She is about to back me over. When, Zelda taped me on the shoulder.

She looked at Jocelyn and said: "Good Job Sister. We will bring him back soon. *Straight Up.*"

She stood me up and walked me backward to the path.

We disappeared into the trees. Down this damp path she is leading me. We got by the water and she stopped. She took my Cock in her mouth and clamped down. She squeezed both Ass cheeks hard and pulled them apart. She bent me over a tree stump and poured warm oil down the small of my back around the crack of my ass. Then, with both hands she massaged it into the entire area.

She put warm oil on her hands and massaged my cock. Then, my balls then both! Then reached around, And again on my butt... And, around my asshole, she licked up my stomach to my mouth and kissed me, I could taste vegetable oil, with a hint of Jasmine oil, valerian root extract, the earth sour taste of mescaline powder and Crystal.

She left me alone there for a few minutes. And, then returned with Bonnie! Bonnie came to me, She took my hand and led me to this round open area cut from the solid forest.

You could not see it from out side, even a foot away from it! In the middle of the circle is a fire pit like the one at the house. Up against the backdrop of a stone out cropping and small dug out cave is a "*Machine*" of some kind.

All around the circle are these statues of demons and gargoyles, all looking to the center of the platform the machine is on! Looked like a lot of people are an audience in front of the platform form time to time! It looked like a Water Wheel. Only this Machine looked kinda strange.

Around the tree line are torches with oil flames. They threw an eerie dancing light everywhere in the place. To the left of the machine is a bath tub looking thing, not very deep. About 6 inches in all… But 8 feet long and 6 feet wide! It has a drain at the foot that opens and closes.

I could see a flame under it to warm the stone. It's also full of the same fluid that Zelda had rubbed on me. I could feel my skin starting to crawl from the drugged oil she had rubbed on. They are waiting for it to take effect. I'm laying in that shallow tub looking up just tripping so very hard I almost did not know what was going on! Catatonic I think they call it.

Then the oil on my body started to take over my ability to resist. Any move made on my person. Or, any part of me there of! I'm feeling dizzy and weak.

Next thing I know. Bonnie and Zelda had taking off their capes and moved to tub side. Zelda does not look the same, she looks evil and *mad*! I blew it off to all the fucking drugs I'm on. *That may have been a mistake for sure.*

They have their hands on each leg and the buttom of my feet. Zelda the left, Bonnie the right… They basted my legs up to my waist then back to my toes, they oiled and sucked each toe at the same time. The clear fluid is full of speed, natural stimulants and cocaine.

I'm starting to Speed heavy. The mescaline is on the fringe. And, I knew their plan was for it to take hold about the time they are done with me! I'm speeding, spinning but I could not get up! A Little body movement, that is about it! They rubbed all the way up to my crotch and moved to my head. They basted me from dick to the top of my head and rubbed it in real good.

Bonnie said as she was rubbing around my face and ears and slicking my hair back: "I want you to open your mind to the possibility that we are all one! When you go back to the group, you will never be the same again. Nor will they! Now, we are going to help you up and over to the Machine there, then strap you in. You will let us strap you in. You will not resist! Is that *Understood!*

I nodded my head YES.

They helped me from the tub. And, over to the Machine, They stood me in two foot cuffs and strapped my feet in real good! Then they spread me eagle wide, they left me standing there with my hands tied into the straps. They went and got this long pipe, it has a bowl on the end where the mouth piece is. You put the dope. Or, what ever in the bowl, and, then blow it into your victim. Some folks have been held here against their will Bonnie says, some never leave here the way they came in! We have a mix of hash and coke we are going to blow into you. Is that ok Don?"

I said: "Let's get on with it!"

She said: "Ok, first we are going to crank the Machine here, is that OK too?"

I said: "Yes! You ol Witches... you old girls. Lay it on me!"

On each side of the Machine, There are two cranks each. One to truss the victim into mid air 3 feet above the deck... The other is too move the feet over head. And, bring it back again.

The other is to turn the entire rig over and back again. I am Impressed! Now, we are going to lift you to where we can perform the duties needed to cleanse you from all things bad! Then make you a forever member of the *Holy Court!*

I say: "What if I don't want to be a member of the fucking Wholly Court!"

Zelda slapped me in the face: "Be now you silent! Speak only when told to do so! Even if things turn unpleasant, neither shall you speak. Nor, wail! If ye do blunder and speak against thee master! Terrible fate will be fall you now. Or, then thee will see!"

Now sister... bring the cleansing tools from the waters of change! Let them cool from their blistering cleansing heat!

As they reach body temperature. Insert the tools of change! Zelda bowed and backed away. Giant Tits swinging... She turned back with a stainless steel platter of what looked like surgeon's tools. Or, a EVIL chiropractor for Christ's sake... She rolled them from the pan and lined them in order. Using the adjoining table next to Bonnie... All I could do was watch as they prepared! Dig it! I am about to OD for fucking sure on all this crap they keep rubbing on me.

They are Deadly serious now. Holding candles chanting in tongues walking around me dragging their fingers on me as they circle the table... They stop and took up their spot on either side.

They Unlocked the Mechanism and started turning at the same time. First my arm started up to the top stretched as far as they would without coming off. Then, the legs start pulling to the sides. As they did, the whole thing lifted me off the ground three feet! I'm now strung spread eagle in this spider web. I could not move in any direction at all!

I started to Panic when I remembered... I could not move. Bonnie floated over. The Mescaline is hitting along with the Strong Acid! Mescaline has the *Best colors of any space drug* there is. It's loaded with natural strychnine. On buttons... you have to cut out the little nubs first!

Oh, Shit Fuck...it's the girls, Take it easy! I tried to move again and no good.

At this time Bonnie unlocked this Nasty device and slid my rock hard cock into it and relocked it! Zelda had turned the Machine to where I was now facing down hanging in mid air! I felt her and Bonnie Rubbing more oil from my head to my toes again. Then, they took up spots on either side again. Still facing down, I could not see anything but their cooders and legs. They were busy up there. When, Zelda took a hold of my left butt cheek and Bonnie the other. They spread them far apart. Zelda took her fingers on her other hand and pried my asshole open. While putting some heavy jelly on and in it... Then Zelda let go!

Bonnie massaged my asshole a bit to get the KY to melt. When it was warm to her finger... She inserted it. I wasn't ready for what was next!

It is obvious they have done this to everyone so far, or so it would seem. And, they are not gonna stop till they get us all. When they left me there a minute or two as they moved on...

I felt this wave of *Surrender* come over me. Slow at first from the middle of my body out in both directions till a wave broke at both ends! I'll be *damned* if I didn't lose conciseness.

They turned me back over and drained me out into a slit in the rock that ran off to the lake. I'll bet there is some stoned fucking fishies out thar!

As I started to come too, they turned the Machine to where I was upside down. The thing around my Dick is getting real warm. It had been hanging all this time and had stretched him a couple of inches longer.

Zelda came over and stuck a clean water supply up my ass and rinsed. *THEY ARE PERFORMING LIKE A COUPLE A NURSES IN THE E ROOM.* Bonnie took off the Dick thing. And, greased Cocaine was applied! Bonnie stood in front of me. At, belly button high with her tongue licking me and sucking on me everywhere!

Zelda is behind me standing about nose high at the top of my ass. I'm empty in both areas now. No chance of a boo boo!

Just how sick is this action?

Bonnie swallowed my cock in her mouth. She sucked. And, sucked... Rubbed her tongue around the swelled head so fast it burned.

She felt my head starting to swell and took me out of her mouth and pointed my cock head at her face and jacked me off till I came hard in her face. She held it. And, sucked it dry again... Kissed Zelda and shared it! They said: "One down. And, 7 to go!"

They turned me over and stood between my legs. Took turns pounding me... I stayed Rock Hard no matter what they did. I'm about to cum again. Zelda pulled it over to her and jammed it in her cunt as far as she could get it. She started to strangle me! Hands on both sides of my throat... Pushing my Adams apple through the back of my neck...

Bonnie is going around the circle and chanting. Zelda is laughing and squeezing my throat harder. I'm loosing my sight as she bore down ever more. I could not move a mussel. She pounded me so hard. I've pulled a mussel in my back. She froze as she pulled me out. And, I shot again all over her face. She rubbed it in her and my face.

Bonnie had taken my balls into her mouth and is moving them around with her tongue as I woke up for being strangled. She is *jacking me off* over her head so hard. I though she would pull me off!

Zelda has her tongue *in* my ass. Nasty Girl! Chewing on my actual asshole flesh... Yeee Owe! I didn't even care! (What are ya laughin at?)

Bonnie had gone over to the table as Zelda reached between my legs and pulled my *cock backwards* and stuck the tip in her ass! I felt my head enter her ass and a flood of pleasure came over me I can't explain to this day! I didn't know I had a three foot dick! Maybe I just thought it was my dick. Could have been left over from someone else. But, something was most different from the back.

She held it in there. And, rubbed the shaft with coke oil... She let go and my cock popped out of her ass and hung there shaking.

My balls are all the way up inside of me. Bonnie pressed them back into my sack. She lowered the rig to just above the deck. And, turned me on my back... She straddled my head between her legs and started to raise the rig. She cranked till my head was at her cunt. She said: EAT, OF THY MOTHER'S FLESH!

She lowered her body till she is sitting on my mouth. I sunk my tongue around her clit and vacuum locked it! She stiffened and wrapped her hands around my neck and pulled me in more.

Zelda sat down on my *cock* and started pumping up and down. She is saying over and over. I knew he would feel this good. *I knew he would.* Bonnie turned her head a said: "Don is about to make me explode. I can't stand it! I'm gonna cum so fuckin hard! I'm about to pass out!"

Zelda said: "We can't get him to give in."

She had her hands over my ears. She thought I couldn't hear them. Bonnie said. "He is a *Class A Fuck* for sure my friend! I am burning. Let's keep him twice as long!"

What will we do now? We used up all our tricks! He is in a Trans... look!

I knew what I was supposed to look like, so I played along.

I stopped breathing, my head fell, and I dropped my breathing to nothing! All Navy training to survive a bunch a gooks chasing ya, they flipped out! Bonnie grabbed a butcher's knife and cut the cotton ties and I fell to the floor. Slapped, the floor with my elbow like it was my melon! I lay there playing the best *possum* you ever did see. Time for them to get back some of their own medicine...

I slowed my heart beat to almost nothing. As, Bonnie listened to my chest, Zelda held a piece of glass under my nose. No fog. Bonnie flipped out! Zelda looked shocked. What did we do Bonnie?

We may have pumped too much stuff in him and he over dosed on us here! What in the Fuck we going to do!

Shit Bonnie... Don't fucking ask me!

Zelda said: *"This is the second time you have killed him Bonnie!"*

Bonnie snapped: "Oh... is that fucking right? What, were you doing earlier when I pulled you up from strangling him for 5 minutes!"

When she said that, Zelda is fucking me so hard. I wasn't playing possum no more.

Before Bonnie pulled her back... she slugged me in the face twice! She is a violent woman.

Ok! Ok! Ah shit Zel! What are we going to do!

Bonnie cradled my head in her lap and started rocking back and forth crying and shivering how she didn't mean it! Please Don, don't die! Please don't leave me. Please. Oh god.

She said: "I have killed the coolest guy in Fayetteville!"

"Oh shit, I am a dead woman! They will lock me up and throw away the Fucking key Zel!" "God damn... what am I going to do"

Zelda said: "Well, let's put him in the lake and sink him!"

Zelda! For Gods Sake: "This is Fucking Don here we are talking about! You can't dump this man in the Fucking River! She slapped the dog shit out of Zelda. Get your shit together!"

It is a fact NOBODY could find this place, nor could you see. Or, hear anything going on in here... that's the idea! They carried me over to that bath deal and started trying to revive me. I am still playing dumb… Kinda! I had them fooled. Because, for the first time in 8 hours, my cock is limp! It's getting cool. And, in the light I looked *blue*.

Zelda thought if she jacked me off. I might wake up… No good.

I was out now! They left me lying on the bath thing and walked over and sat down with their backs to me.

He ain't cold yet… said Zelda. Lets fuck him some more!

Bonnie snapped: "ZELDA… Shut the Fuck UP! Oh My God: I am fucked!"

We have been here way to long… these girls had a bunch more people to make it through before they are done tonight! So, as they are crying on each other. I creped up behind them and put a hand on each shoulder.

Scared them so bad. They are almost pulling their own tits off!

I flipped Bonnie over and shoved my cock in her hard. She lit up! I had my entire hand in Zeldas pussy opening and closing it. I pumped Bonnie till she pushed me out. And, blood was coming down the crack of her ass. She screamed, bit me on the arm and drew blood!

I knocked her down with my fore arm and shoved my dick in again. Pumped… And, thrust in farther! I have a tit on one hand almost twisting it off. She is bleeding. And, screaming. Rubbing my ass cheeks… When, Zelda pulled me off of Bonnie. And, decked me with a left hook!

I woke up. She was jacking me off hard again. I grabbed her. She pulled away and got on her knees. Put her head on the ground. Pulled her asshole apart…

I ran at her as fast as I could and jammed that thing in there. She screamed bloody murder! (I'll bet she did!) She grabbed my ass and pulled me in harder!

I pulled out of Zelda. And, stood on top of Bonnie… I held her head down with the side of my foot. Went down on my knee and fucked her tits! (JESUS CHRIST O MIGHTY!)

She is still *bleeding from her pussy and ass.* I wiped some off and licked it. (No Man: you didn't do that!) It tasted warm. And, salty! Sure the fuck did Jackson. I spun around and stuck my cock in her mouth. As, Zelda tripped me! Then, _Black Jacked_ me in the side of my *melon* just above my right ear, I'm "*Knocked the fuck out!*"

She pulled me off of Bonnie. They dragged me over to the bath thing! Bonnie said: "Lay him face first over the dragons back there.

When I came too, they were taking turns sucking the fluid from the end of my dick. Bonnie climbed me again and sat on me. Threw cold water in my face… I came too! She had my legs back around my head. She had a hold of my cock from the _inside!_ (No fucking way!) And is stroking it inside me… Then, Zelda tears at me with her finger nails…

I could feel a _climax_ coming up my spine! It's like lava. Burned all over me!

I broke away from both of them, turned and knocked Bonnie out cold with one sucker punch to the jaw. Then I Swung around and caught Zelda with an upper cut and she went down and out! I pulled them onto the deck and laid them next to each other. They is "knocked the fuck out"

I kneeled between Bonnie's legs, pulled her up and shoved my cock in her and just FUCKED the shit out of her, literally till she came to! She saw the look in my eyes and realized I had knocked her cold and was monster fucking her as she awoke.

Her puzzled Raped look turned to pure pleasure. She wrapped around me like a vine. She couldn't get enough. She sunk her nails into my back. I didn't notice at the time how tore up it was. And, she is cutting me in half with her legs. Then she stiffened up... _she came hard!_

Zelda is still out as I pulled out of Bonnie and stood over Zelda. I had a special get even planned for her! I pulled her legs over my shoulder. Shoved my cock all the way up her ass till I hit oil! Law Zee Mazziappa! I had both hands in a death grip on her tits as she came too!

She tried to get up from me. I shoved her back down pushed her leg over her hard and literally squatted on her ass and shoved all 21 feet of pulled back cock in her and started humping up and down with the pile driver! _Anybody know how to turn this Jack Hammer Off?_

All the way in... All the way to the head almost out... And, jam it back in again! I pumped. Pounded... till she exploded! My balls looked like cantaloupes.

She grabbed me. And, super strength came over her. She slammed me hard to the floor. Knocked me almost the fuck out! She put a couple of pillows under my ass, jacked me straight in the air!

Then she stepped over me, squatted down and shoved my cock up her ass. (Naw... she didn't!) She started literally jumping up and down on me. With my Nasty, Dirty. Shit dripping feet right the fuck in her mouth. I shoved my toes in her nose. Used her jaw as a foot step up as I _pissed_ in her face! (Did he say: "PISSED in her face?")

(I do believe he did sir.")

(... OH!)

Bonnie wanted more... she tried to cut in. And, Zelda knocked her off the deck unconscious to the ground. She strapped me by my neck to the post, then ran over to Bonnie and turned her over, lifted her ass in the air, shoved that 14 inch 4 inch around rubber cock right the fuck up her ass and bent it around, shoved the other half in her cunt! (Bull Shit) and said in her face: _You Got Knocked the Fuck Out!_

I pulled Zelda off Bonnie. And, buried my mouth into her pussy and shoved my cock into Bonnie. We did that awhile and Zelda fell off satisfied. Each person was supposed to get 20 minutes or so. This had gone on at least 2 hours now. I turned Bonnie over on her back and stood flat footed at the edge of the table. I slipped him all the way in and leaned over onto Bonnie and her tits pushed out the sides. I took her head in my hands, pulled her into a hard *French kiss*.

Every time my cock would enter her cervix, I pushed my tongue and a full breath down her throat! I could feel an earth quake coming from my brain down my spine and into my balls. I swelled. And, swelled... I pumped and pumped!

Bonnie is bleeding more. And, screaming louder.

I'm throbbing and throbbing, shoving deeper and deeper, she just scissor locked me then screaming. Cum and blood ran down my balls and my leg! (Are you shittin me?)

She pushed me out and grabbed my Dick. Started sucking it harder and faster... And, harder, Chewing on that sucker! I didn't even fuckin care!

I pulled it from her, she opened her mouth and I filled her entire mouth... she choked. She is crying. And, begging me to stop! As, I pulled and held her down with my knees, *I filled her mouth again till she gagged!*

I held her head up so she had to swallow it. She stopped breathing, Coughed and spit up blood & cum. (Man: you are a sick motha fuckin puppy Jack!)

Then she wiped her eyes. It's all over her face. (OH Pa-lease!)

Her eyes are burning where she rubbed it and what ever in her eyes.

I picked her up crying hysterically. I slapped her down to the deck again. Picked her up... And, slapped her again harder...

She screamed: NO! DON'T HIT ME AGAIN! *Please: don't hit me again!*

I carried her crying over to the table and lay her down. I licked and sucked her breasts nipple hard again. She melted, pulled me down as I slide in her again, (Again?)

She whispered in my ear! *WHAT A MAN! FUCK ME HARD: YOU* BRUTE! *I love you Don, No one has ever done that to me before.*

Fuck me one more time please, Fuck me one more time! Please. Please. Please.

I slowly slid back in, with the love of a virgin. She turned herself over to me right there. I slowly fucked her to another *smooth climax* and satisfaction!

Zelda is still knocked out as Bonnie walked me back to the group. She didn't blindfold me. She hugged me all the way to the clearing! She turned to me before I stepped into view of the others. She went on her knees and sucked me hard again!

She said: "I have to send you back to her the way I found you! Don, I love you very much, what happened in there is nobody's business!"

Listen Don: "We really put Jocelyn through it man! We did things to her only she can tell you about, she never gave in, and it was all you. Wish Don was here. Wish Don was here. She is most _definitely a woman sexually_ and deeply in love with you! What happened in there? Stops there!

She grabbed my now hard again cock and said: "Agreed?"

I slid him back in her and pumped her two or three more times as I kissed her. Then, walked back to the others!

Terry disappeared next!

Jocelyn looked at me in the fire light: "God damn Don!"

She started to cry. "They beat the _wholly shit_ out of you!"

She is wiping Bonnie's blood from around my mouth. She thought it was mine! She noticed I had a swollen eye. She kissed it. And, laid me on top of her... We rolled over in each others arms and held on! We listened to the others talk. Patty had told her tale. It was nothing like mine.

Jocelyn said the same.

She squeezed my hand and said: they really put it to her. What did they do to you?"

I can't tell ya! Just lay on me. And, kiss me over. And, over again... Deeper, and deeper, we started breathing in and out of each other. I didn't even care!

We passed out in each others arms. As, we woke from our nap... they were taking Tony. The last one of the night! Sunrise would be in an hour and we would be heading home.

Bonnie drug her ass by us and said: "Breakfast by Buck and Anna in 30 minutes, Clean up! Your clothes are in the house. Bus leaves for Fayetteville at 7 am."

"Gather everyone and get ready to eat and go home!"

Alright!... _What a PARTY!_

Well... this party is a total Freak out! I'm sitting thinking about what had happened the last 48 hours. As, Terry came up with my clothes...

Don... Hey!

I looked over as he sat down. Jocelyn brushed off your clothes and sent me with them. They are cleaning up and getting ready to lock up, we are about to leave.

Terry sat down and we talked a bit about the night.

He said: "Don, I got what I wanted last night!"

Oh yeah: what's that?

An answer... And,...you know!

I said: "Oh, that's right."

He said: "Well... I am not going to lay it out here. Let me tell you this though, the way everyone else sees it, you got the ass end of the thing!

They had you in there over two hours, the rest of us about 20 minutes! I looked Terry over as the sun was coming up. He looked pretty good for what he had been though the last 48 hours. Not just what they did to him out there. But, the whole weekend was a learning experience for all of us!

I said: "I think they pulled my back out kinda bad!"

"Why's that?"

I say: "Well... you will have to help me up, as I can't get up."

Terry said: "Don!"

I answered: "Yes"

"They did more than pull out your back!"

He went over to the bar, got a small coke mirror and brought it over. He held it in front of me. I could not believe I was looking at me!

My left eye is black as night. The whites of the other are *blood red*. My right eye brow is cut open. I have dried blood around my nostrils. I have a fat bottom lip, a scratch across the top of my lip and forehead! I have a patch of hair gone on the side above my ear where Zelda clipped me with that Black Jack. Jack!

I started to put on my T-shirt as Jocelyn came up! As I leaned forward to pull my shirt over my head, She, Screamed. Dropped, the glass of OJ she had for me. She stood there with her hands on her face in *Horror!*

Terry is shocked! He stood there jaw gapping, *Eyes wide open!*

I looked at them both, as Jocelyn started *screaming:* "WHO FUCKING DID THAT TO YOU? *WHO THE FUCK DID THAT TO YOU? TELL ME NOW!"*

She has a hold of me saying: *TELL ME NOW!* Come on shit head! *Tell me now!*

John, Patty and Mike have shown up. Mike says as I am looking all over the others: GOD DAMN IT DON! WHO in the FUCK DID THAT TO YOU?

I said: *WHAT? WHAT!* I couldn't see my back of course!

But, EVERYONE IS FLIPPING OUT OVER IT!

We could here a ruckus at the house. Where, Jocelyn has stormed off too!

Terry is doing his: "I AM GOING KILL SOME FUCKING BODY!" I had not seen him that mad since the night I met him at the GRAY-HOUSE.

He kicked in the door, walked in the living room, then the kitchen where Bonnie, Zelda and Anna were.

Jocelyn has Bonnie by the hair... she is beating her on her back and shoulders. Then… she tripped her to the ground, dropped her knee to Bonnie's chest like a W W F wrestler!

Straddles her shoulders with her knees… And, she is slamming Bonnies head to the dirt floor! She is yelling at Bonnie! HOW COULD YOU FUCKING DO THAT TO DON? *WHY DID YOU DO THAT? YOU FUCKING BITCH!* Slamming… And, slamming her head on the dirt floor!

GOD DAMN IT BONNIE, WHY! She is crying hysterically! I picked her up off of Bonnie. She turned and looked in my eyes and cried harder and ran to Debbie and out the door they went with Anna in tow!

Terry took over now. The others are standing around Bonnie and Zelda in the middle of the circle! I was still in the dark. I'm more interested in Jocelyn. When, Terry grabbed Bonnie and picked her up with his Giant hands and held her up. And, he is shaking her!

He caught my attention as I was turning to leave after the girls when he said: "How… *in he FUCK*… could you two fucking ass holes do that to my LEAD VOCALIST?

My fucking *FRONT* man!

He said: "How in the HELL is he going to sing and perform tonight? Why did you two do this to him? Why in the fuck DID you do that! You two beat the fucking shit out of him! Is that not enough? ARE - YOU - TRYING… *TO KILL HIM FOR REAL?*

He slammed her to the floor. And, grabbed Zelda! "You are the cause of all this shit! Bonnie never acts this way till YOU FUCKING COME AROUND!"

He slapped the dog shit out of her. He let go. And, she fell to the couch. She has her hands on her face! She could not believe Terry was so fucking upset!

I said: Sing tonight! Sing WHERE?

Terry is in control: "DON… DON! Shut the fuck up ass hole! Why did you let these two do that to you! *WHAT IN THE FUCKING HELL IS FUCKING WRONG WITH YOU?*

I said: "Fuck that shit Terry!" "*SING WHERE?*" I can't even see! For Christ's sake I can't play no fucking where! What in the fuck are you talking about?"

Bonnie and Zelda saw their chance to escape! Zelda grabbed Bonnie. They ran out the back door into the woods. And hid!

I said: "Terry! Calm down man! Come on, please. Please! Sit down and talk to me. Where am I singing tonight?"

He says: "Don." He has tears running down his face.

What man!

He said: "God damn man. They fucked you up really bad."

Terry... I have my hands on his shoulders.

He said: "Don, they fucked you up bad man!"

Come on Terry... Forget that shit!

I'm telling Terry to forget it. But, I'm going crazy to know what the big drama is!

Terry explains: "Well... first Don. It's not *Monday*. It's Friday!"

He reached up and turned me around a bit. I still had no t-shirt on. I dropped it as I came in here. Some how you thought we were here on the weekend. I was going to tell you it is Wednesday asshole. But, I forgot and it didn't seem to matter anyway. We were leaving this am and you would figure it out then.

Bob Risby will be at the show tonight. He expects 4 original songs from us. We were supposed to write them before Friday. Remember."

I say: "NO: I don't remember. Terry listen: I will do the show tonight as if nothing had happened out of the normal. And, you will be very proud. Terry... I swear to you! No matter what happens to me anytime at all. I am a *TROOPER*. The show must go on!"

I put my hands on my face and said under my breath! "*Who will help the widow's son?*"

He looked at me and said: "That we didn't even have one song to play for him."

I told him I had a note book at home (Patty's), with a bunch of song poems I wrote while I was in the service and alone far away from home. Some fun... some tragic...

We can knock out some rhythm lines when we get home. And, fake it a bit, we should pull it off! We can bury them in our other cover songs we do, they will seg together. Ok?

He said: "Will that work?"

I say: "If we make it work, and if it's meant to be. We can do it! Let's get ready to go home. Ok? Come on."

He said: "Don, I wanted to comfort you! You have comforted me!"

We shook a hand shake of *BROTHERHOOD*, he helped me up.

He saw my back again and was pissed all over again! GOD DAMN IT. SHIT. GOD DAMN IT. SHIT. SHIT!

He is spitting as he cussed! I took his hand and said: "come on man... we got bigger fish to fry!"

MAN... I want to see my back. But, on the other hand I didn't! I looked over at the cars.

Everyone is ready to go. Bonnie and Zelda had snuck back from the woods and are crying by the *Mustang®* with their heads down. Kicking rocks around the driveway...

Jocelyn came over to hug me and console me. She reached out and started to put her arms around me! She stopped at my shoulders. She looked into my eyes, hers are Huge and they're pooled with tears. That is it!

She said: "You don't even know do you?"

I said: "Know what sweetheart?"

She just crumbled down into a cross legs sitting position and cried harder.

Terry said: "Come on man....I have to show you something."

He took me to the bathroom by the bar. It has a big mirror in it.

He said: "Get a hold of yourself! Look at your back!"

I looked... My jaw fell, my eyes bulged out of my head, and I turned where I could see all of my back. Then, dropped my pants... From the back of my neck, All the way down to the top of my legs. Are cut and deep scratches all the way down!

I looked like Indians had strung me up and skinned me! I couldn't feel it. Because, they had made a plaster of the oil they used, it had so much coke in it, I didn't even know I had a back! I sat down. I had a look on my face like. How the hell could two girls do that to me? I thought how bad that is going to hurt by the time the back car seat rubs that stuff off and it becomes irritated.

Tears are running down my face now. I could not believe that those two did this to me! Ok, we beat the wholly shit out of each other.

That was ok. I was so very tired. I had been Raped! Then, beat up by Amazon women. Killed... And, drugged, ECT! All I wanted now is Jocelyn! Where is she?

(I know what you are thinking. Oh! Shit, this is fucking strange. But, I can handle it!)

I started to walk out the door. I got Dizzy and couldn't continue. Mike came over. Where that hair is missing is one hell of a wallop! The skin is broken. It appeared that my skull is cracked.

That's where Zelda caught me with the BLACK jack, I told them! Mike said: "Don has a very bad concussion here. I think we should take him to the hospital. Don... can you walk now."

I stood up the best I could. And, passed right out on the floor... Hit my head again...hard.

When I came to... Jocelyn is petting my head and stroking my forehead with a cold towel! Bonnie is pouring tears from her face. Zelda is holding Bonnie. Rocking, back and forth crying. Looking at me hard! Everyone is walking around looking at them with anger in their eyes.

I asked: "What... What... ah what, what."

Bonnie screamed out! GOD DAMN DON! *DON'T FUCKING DIE!*

She fell to the floor in a fit. Zelda stood up and screamed, ran out the door. Bonnie crawled over... she took my hand and prayed to the lord not to let me die!

Terry took her from me as she was screaming. *She loves me, don't die! Don't die, please. I am sorry!"*

He got her outside... it's just Jocelyn and I now. She stopped crying, held me and said that she would never let anyone do that to me again. So... come on and don't kick it on me.

We just started. You can't go now, I love you. I love you don't die!

I assured her I was not going to die any time soon!

She said: "You talked! Alright!"

He talked in a complete sentence! She hugged me hard! I wrenched with pain! She shot off of me.

She said: "oh god... I am sorry! Here let me."

I stopped her and said: "Help me up dear."

She did, we walked out to the car. Everyone is standing kicking the rocks around and mumbling. As I got closer, they all erupted into applause! Bonnie is still crying and Zelda is shaking uncontrollably. Zelda could not look at me. I knew then *SHE* did this to me, not Bonnie!

I do believe that German woman is in the Hitler family. Zelda Ann Hitler!

I have a whole new respect and understanding of old Zelda there! I knew Bonnie would never turn on a friend. She would take the blame to her grave! I walked over to Bonnie the best I could. I took her in my arms and looked deep inside of her! I didn't say one word. She is frozen with fright! Her eyes were *turgett with fear.* That I would never love her... Or, want her around anymore. Not that I would knock the shit out of her.

She figured our love affair and close friendship would be over.

I leaned in and took her mouth on mine and kissed her with so much love she just fainted away in my arms. All of her fear poured out of her. I kissed her again and held her to my face. And, rubbed her face with mine... I love you Bonnie! I told you I did! No matter what!

Our embrace broke with a sigh. And, a pledge of our never ending love and forgiveness!

Jocelyn came over with tears running down her face and hugged Bonnie. She said: "I'm sorry for being so mad at you."

Jocelyn whispered in her ear: "I know you didn't do that. But, you could have stopped it. Why didn't you?"

She said to Jocelyn: "When I saw that Zelda had almost strangled him to death. And he was UN-conscience. I pulled her off of him. But she had already done that. She told me. Don is already dead... What would it matter? If we just pushed him off in the lake. I was shocked! But, what could I do Jocelyn… she, had already done it."

Bonnie said: "He didn't tell you what we did to him."

Jocelyn said: "No! That was the deal.

Bonnie walked to the Mustang. I walked over to Zelda. Everybody is watching this one. She looked at me kinda from the top of her eyes as she looked down in shame.

I say: "Zelda." She looked at me.

I'm rubbing my sore jaw where it met the ear and said: "You hit hard there Zelda… Kinda like a man! Are you jealous of me? Or, all of us! We have a new understanding now… Bonnie loves you so much. She was ready to take the fall for you. Bonnie is most special to me. And the others! We love her more than… she even knows! You did this to me. I am going to let this go."

We were all a bit to stoned and caught up in the moment. Besides, I got a few hits in on you last night that shook your base woman! I'm a big boy! I knew what I was getting into. We still friends? She smiled that smile of hers. There is Murder still in her heart!

She looked up: she is ready for me to knock the shit out of her for tearing up my back. I looked around at everyone. They are shocked too! I said to everyone: Listen people… the last 48 hours have been something from a dream. Some of it I am not sure we really did." Everyone laughed! Mike said: "Well, that shit on your back ain't fucking nothing man!" Mike could always be counted upon to announce a misdeed!

I said: "I hold no grudge against Bonnie. Or, Zelda! They did what the ton of drugs told them to do! I don't know what happened to the rest of you. But, my experience was an eye opener! I will never be the guy that drove in here Wednesday. As, Terry told me it really was! I have changed, as the rest of you have. Zelda! You hurt me pretty bad you know. I don't know if I can forgive that. But, I am willing to try. Ok!"

Everyone stood and were screaming: _GAVENCE FAMILY TRAVEL-ERS FOR EVER!_

Jocelyn is hugging Bonnie and me. John is hugging Zelda. We, all were just HOLDING EACH OTHER. And, laughing. Crying and going on! Bonnie broke and wiped the tears she said: "WE should haul ass out of here and go home! We have a big night ahead, we gotta go now!" I was reminded of this James Taylor song as I walked to the car.

"Late last night so far away. I dreamed my self a dream. Well, I dreamed I was so all alone. Isn't it nice to be home again. I said: Welcome home, didn't we miss your smiling face. Well, the sun was nice in L.A. _SUNSHINE!_ Isn't it nice to be home again! I Said: isn't it nice to be home again."

All the way home no one said a word. Jocelyn had her head on my chest. She is sleeping now, holding my thigh in her grip. My, hand in the other... She is not going to let go.

Bonnie looked at me in the rear view mirror. Our eyes met. Her eyes are still crying and showing her sorrow for what they had done. I reached her hair and petted it! She smiled in the mirror as into town we rolled. I passed out from the concussion. I should have gone to the hospital that morning. Now, at 59 years young, I have a burning head ache there often! Navy thinks they did it. I will just let them think that! Dig it! What do those assholes know anyway!

We just rode to town and thought about what all had happened. And, what we were expected to do in a short few hours! I leaned down and kissed Jocelyn. Oh so soft and long. I was just kissing her and kissing her, I started to drift away as we drove listening to the sax solo in the song as I awoke for just a minute.

Bonnie turned into the driveway and stopped the car. We are all half asleep. I cracked my eye... she is looking at me and still crying! I opened my eyes. I looked at her. Her lips curled, her eyes widened. She whispered to me: I am so sorry, my heart hurts Don. I can't get the pit of my stomach to stop quivering. Don! I thought we KILLED you. I was going to start—Jocelyn moved... Bonnie turned around.

She said: "Are we here?

She looked around as she stretched and rubbed her eyes. She reached so softly, so not to hurt my shoulders and back and kissed me.

She said: "Come in side my hero, I want to wash you all over. Then kiss you dry!

She took my hand. Helped, me out the door... I got Dizzy again, had to sit down. She looked at Bonnie. Bonnie ran around the car, they helped me into the house. Mike had the door open. And, Terry helped me to our room. God damn it! He said as he left the room.

Bonnie is outside the door still crying!

Terry went in his room... shut the door & threw a chair against it!

Jocelyn says: "Don, I will be right back with some juice for you, will you be alright?"

She lay me on my stomach... my back is on fire now!

Jocelyn went out the door and shut it. She took Bonnie by the hand. Walked her into the empty living room... Everyone, but us had gone home. Patty is with Terry. And, we are alone.

Jocelyn sat Bonnie down then said: "Bonnie, I think it would be better if you would go home now"

Bonnie looked up at Jocelyn crying. Looked into her face, and then spoke with her eyes to her. "If anything happens to Don, just KILL me please."

She spoke: "God Jocelyn."

She bowed her head... I am so very sorry!

She hugged Jocelyn she said: "Please, don't hate me. I couldn't stand it! I love you all. You people make me whole. You all give me a reason for fucking livin! I never planned anything like that to happen. I'll suffer the rest of my life for hurting him!

She handed the rest of the ¼ ounce of coke to Jocelyn. About an 8 ball...

She said: "If you don't take him to the hospital. Mix this with instant tea and lightly pour it down his back. I have to go now. I will see you all at the EAR." With that... She ran out the door. And, burned rubber all the way up North Street...

Jocelyn sat back on the couch and cried to her self, she cried a few minutes then wiped her eyes and went into the kitchen. Then, into the room... I'm writhing in pain now. The last thing I was thinking about was the EAR! We went into the shower, I stood there as she washed me all over a couple of times, she patted me dry and I felt better. She poured a bit of the coke tea water over my back and it got cold and stopped hurting. She kept a hand towel in a bowl of the stuff and ice water.

I felt the love and motherly instincts come from her. All I could do was look at her work on me. She didn't leave me... she, held my hand, smiled at me and stroked my brow. I'm kinda sick I guess, the drugs have all wore off. I'm on my own with a very important show tonight that could not be cancelled for any reason, except Death. I thought about that! I'm wasted!

As Jocelyn kept working on me. I knew she is tired too. I sat the bowl on the floor. Then, pulled her down next to me and held her oh so close. Then, kissed her softly I said: "What did I ever do to deserve an angel in my life like you."

Then we passed out for a few badly needed hours of sleep.

Now... this is fucking way out there what happened next.

She came back in the room and said: "Its 2: 30 pm. I hate to make you move. You have to get a show ready for tonight."

She had broken out all of our gear... she had it laid out perfectly, ready for us to work. She banged on Terry's door, got them up.

Patty said: "Yes Love... lets feed these two MEN."

She agreed: "They went to work... so did we."

My guitar playing is off. And, muffled... I couldn't seem to push down the strings. My left hand just wouldn't work for some reason.

Jocelyn FREAKED The Fuck Out!

She said… "Ok, that's it! Let's take him to the hospital."

They helped me to the car. And, up to *WASHINGTON COUNTY HOSPITAL.*

They said: "I had been beaten up at the lake yesterday. I may have a concussion!

They agreed and treated me, gave me more Drugs and out we went. They did something to my back that took care of it. Still raw, But felt MUCHO better… And, clean, that was good! I noticed the E/room guys looking at me. They had realized what was all over my back. That Coke stuff is not a thing in town yet. But, they knew… I could tell.

Out the door we went. I felt a TON better now, real good as a matter of fact!

Bonnie said: "It's the *morphine sulfate.* We had a few hours left before 8 pm. Patty had finished the meal. We all chowed down. Then, back to the work. We went in my poem book and pulled out 4 good ones, added a rhythm line, the girls wrote them out on poster paper.

We had them down pretty good, we broke to pack up and go. Rick showed up. We showed the tunes to him. He caught right on. We loaded up and made like a baby. We headed out!

When we arrived at the WALL, it was packed.

Remember how… "Leave town and come back everything has changed" Shit!

Well… Everyone is buzzing about how I got fucked up Thursday night in a camping accident. But, I'm still going to play… they are so impressed!

They saw us coming and went into a full sized freak out! Everyone was worried about me! People I had never seen before were patting my butt. Saying words of love and encouragement to me!

Girls are kissing me. And, squeezing my sack… There seemed to be a riot down the street.

I asked: "What's that all about down there?"

Muffin… of all people stood up and said: "That's for you guys. The place is full. Waiting for you…

K K E G has a Mobile Truck outside on West Street. They are going to broadcast the first show.

I'm getting nauseous from the pain pills and the concussion. And, had to sit down… Everyone flipped out! Crowded around me wanting to do what ever they could.

Terry said: "Jocelyn! Let's get out of here!"

They put me in the car… we drove the block to the stage entrance and went into our *PRIVATE* dressing room. It is ours all the time. Nobody is allowed in there. Even if we are not there! Pastor Williams rule! Stay out!

The place is absolutely packed. Bob Risby came in the room and looked at me... what the fuck happened to you Don?

I said: "A couple of witches had their way with me last night."

Then he said something that got us all...

He said: "Oh, did Zelda get her hands on you? Looks like Zelda got her hands on you."

He walked over and lifted my shirt. "Yup! That's her trademark"

You guys know she is not in Germany now because of a murder charge there. She can't go back.

She completely _skinned_ a man there. She would have done it to you too! What stopped her? Bonnie had been listening to him.

She said: "I FUCKING STOPPED HER BOB! Why did you bring her to me?"

He said: "Bonnie, Nobody else wanted her! You two hit it off right away!"

The rest of us are totally in the fucking dark here.

Bonnie!

"Yes dear"

What is he talking about?

She said: "I'll fill you in later I am going to announce you in 8 minutes!"

Bob... come with me please.

They left the room... she is pushing him out the door as he is laughing at me. We all fell back and looked at each other. What in the hell was that all about?

Anybody have a clue?

Jocelyn said: "God Don! She was going to KILL you! Then dump you in the mother fucking lake! She tried to kill you! Kill you! Oh my god! Kill you! Oh god!"

She fell into my arms: "I don't know what I would do! She would have ruined my life, that fucking bitch! Ruined my LIFE! And, ended everything!"

I'm looking for anything else to talk about. As, I looked out the stage door the place is packed! If they sold booze here, they would make a lot of money tonight.

Out of nowhere I sprung up and said: "Nixon! Nixon! That son of an ass eating hog! Did you guys here about what he did? He had 13,000 war protester arrested at... Oh god!"

Terry asked: "What's wrong?" He jumped up and looked out the window.

I said: "Terry!"

He said: "What?"

I went on: "Did I ever tell you what my radio show icon name was?"
"What?"
He asked: "What are you talking about?"
Ah, oh— Shit! I'm pacing back and forth and shaking.
I said: "Yeah, ah…it was…oh shit!"
Mike asks: "What was it man"
Mike is about to grab me.
I said: "It was, *THE HOUSEWIVES BEST FRIEND!* Yea, that's right! Housewives best friend… housewives…best friend… oh… Shit!" And, I hit the ground.
Motha fucker! Mike and Terry picked me up. Put me on the couch. Rick!
What?
Stall Bonnie.
WHY?
Look asshole! <u>FUCK</u>! What happened?
He just started talking nuts, acting weird and fell over. Is he passed out? Hey! Can you move Don? I was looking at the ceiling. And, my eyes are spinning. I could not stop them. I thought I was going to puke. I turned over so I wouldn't drown and nothing happened. I went to stand up: they helped me to my feet. I staggered… and they caught me!
Terry said: "Don… you can't play tonight. We can't expect you too. I'm going to stop this before you stroke out on us. I am taking you back to the hospital.
Jocelyn came through the door… she started to say something and stopped as she noticed the shape I was in. Her eyes went wide again.
She, said: "What's fucking going on here now?" She started to cry and ran to me. "What is wrong?"
He started talking funny and collapsed. We, can't get him to respond here. I am taking him to the hospital.

Bonnie said: "Now, here they are!"
Don Morison. Terry Smith. Patty Hargrove. Rick Basham… "CROSBY, STEAL the CASH and RUN!"

Terry, Patty and Rick looked at each other.
That's right!
The place is going nuts waiting on us to emerge everyone is freaking out, not watching me now. I stood up, grabbed my guitar and looked at them with their jaws agape.
"Let's fucking go! Terry, you got that break in song two down?"

In an astonished voice with a blank expression on his face he said: "Yes."
Rick: "Don't fuck up!"
He said: "Ok, but I can't promise anything!"
Patty leaned over and I kissed me on the cheek.
I said: "I love you Patty. Thank you. Let's do the show!"
We walked out through the crowd and they came alive! Hooting and hollering! The Baby Trouper followed us all the way. Bonnie had the stage set in a backward V. That way... Everyone had a great view of us. We sat down and the lights fell.

The lights went soft *RED* and *Crystal Blue*. They are on Patty. We opened with "Linda Ronstadt's "Different Drum" The hit she had with the Stone ponies, who went on to be the *EAGLES!*

The place is dead quiet. The slight Reverb in her voice, made her sound like a *crystal velvet fog* across a snow covered pass in the mountains. She sang like the angel she is. So pure and clear... with the feeling of the *opera singer* she is trained to be!

We went into "Longtime Gone", then one we wrote. We had the place locked. No one in... no one out! No one moved through the whole First show.

As we played, I started getting weaker and weaker. I didn't think anyone noticed. I'm sure I could do one more show. We finished "Find the cost of FREEDOM" the last note rang in the room for what seemed like minutes! We are in the dressing room before the room came too!

The place slowly woke up... Cheering and hollering ENCORE! <u>ENCORE!</u>

Bonnie got on stage and said: "Thank you everyone. I don't know about you all. But, I still have goosers. Some of you may have noticed. Don is pretty beat up. He was in a bad wreak at the lake this morning and should be in the hospital. But, there was no keeping him from you!"

The crowd went nuts...

She went on: "Yes, Yes. I, agree! Now, he has relapsed. We are taking him home. See you all next time... and thank you all for coming! We love you all!"

People are starting to get up as I walked thru the door with my guitar. The room went silent, and everyone took their seats. Bonnie stood on stage with papers in her hand. She sat me down in my seat.

She just walked off and joined Terry and the others at the stage door. Terry is standing there with his arms crossed. He looked at Bonnie who had a... What the fuck look on her face!

Terry just shrugged. Bonnie joined the others. And, watched me to see what I was going to do.

I sat there. Looked around the room... And, into each person's eyes with mine... Even held a look on a few! I sat there another 2 minutes or so and started to strum my guitar.

"I've seen the needle and the damage done. A little bit of it in everyone. But, every junky needs the setting sun!"

They are stunned. Then, I did "Carry on" by my self. Then, into *Guinevere, Teach your children.* Then, 'OUR house...

Terry came out as I started, "Cowgirl In the Sand" and then we went into, "Down by the river."

Rick and Patty came out... we finished with "California Dreaming" and." If I had a hammer" <u>Music history</u> was made on Dickson Street that night!

We went to the dressing room. And, let Bonnie work the front as folks filed out! Jocelyn is standing waiting for me with her hands on both sides of her face with tears of JOY this time.

I smiled: "I like those tears better!"

She walked over slow and caressed me with her very *special love.* She says: "Don... that was *incredible*, it took my breath away!" Again!

She said: K K E G broadcast that ENCORE too! Ears and *Ogre* were completely blown away. They will play that all week. I love to watch you on the stage. There is pure truth in your face and guitar when you sing.

Risby said: "Great Fuckin show! I AM very IMPRESSED! I'll call you next week Bonnie... Again, *Great show guys!*"

There is a big after show party at the *Stone and Hill house.*

I said: "Do we have to go?"

We have to slide through. We left. And, cruised there... Went in said hi to everyone and rubbed the elbows of those Bonnie had invited. Then we left them all to Fuck! Drink, and have fun.

Mike took us home. He is as wore out as we are and just dropped us off in the driveway. Then, he went home.

Patty opened the door, lit the place up and put on tunes. We all came in. I sat down on the couch and just passed out right there. Terry and Jocelyn helped me to the bedroom. Jocelyn lay me down, closed the door. She lit two candles and turned me over. Pulled off my pants and my shirt... Then, her clothes! She sat across my legs as they were not tore up. As, she straddled my leg I could feel her warm moist soft inner thigh and her hair and lips. They felt like heaven!

She said: "I have to rub this stuff the doctor gave me on you now, tell me if I hurt you!"

As she softly smoothed the stuff on she said: "You were so fucking good tonight... I don't know how you save the day every time! You play guitar like it is part of your brain. You think... it plays! You make it look so fucking easy. You're singing hypnotizes me every time. I feel like I am moving closer to you from across the room. But, my feet are not touching the ground! I love you so very much Don. Our children will be blessed with your talent!"

I said as she worked on me: "If they have that from me. And, the artistic wonder and beauty from you! They will have great lives!"

She kissed my ear and whispered: "Sleepy time my wonderful MAN... *Sleepy time!* I will be right here holding you till you wake."

She slid her body against mine, we both passed out!

The place is dark and quiet for the first time in weeks. It feels so good just to sleep! Nothing else, just sleep. We had really been through something very strange in the last three days. I couldn't put my finger on it at the time. I hoped I would get an epiphany sometime. And, just go! Ah ha! That's what that was all about! Till then I guess ill just file it away till someday when I put it on paper.

Life is really hauling ass now, it seems to be coming closer to some kind of a lonely rail station in the middle of now where. The track is moving under me real fast. I can't count the ties any more.

I could hear the sounds of the night as I slept. I wasn't awake. But, not asleep either. I'm so fucked up. Jocelyn hugs me tighter and sighed in my ear. She is a sleep, though she licked my ear and kissed it. And. sighed again. Hugged me tighter, it hurt so good!

I didn't move. I am so in love with this woman. We melted together and sighed together. The rest of the night just slipped away. It was wonderful! Peace at last! Peace at last!

Saturday morning... around FUZZY o'clock! I got up to a hot room. I'm so Dizzy. I had to lie back down. I didn't make it though. I had to sit down on the couch to regain my footing! I'm sitting there with my head spinning, thinking what happened to me.

Ok... Did I get Raped? Or, did I want to get Raped!

I thought on. Maybe, I wanted to get Raped all three times. Maybe! Even in my Wildest Fantasy. Did I ever think a woman would? Or, could really try to kill me... And, then roll me off into the Fucking Lake for Christ sake.

I thought how close to *SNUFF* sex that is. Only thing missing would have been the underground Video of the affair. But, I am sure that's because VCRs were not available to the public yet!

Bonnie actually *DID* kill me, what a trip. Now, I still am not sure that Zelda actually KILLED me. I was playing that little game with them. But, fact remains that I can't remember about 25 minutes or so. Or, do I remember Zelda doing that to me. I don't remember Bonnie pulling Zelda off of me. I will tell you one thing I *DO REMEMBER* though! The pain I'm feeling... is a sensation I never will repeat!

I don't know how you girls can take all of that in the Pussy. But, UP YOUR *FUCKING ASS*! Five gallons of some kind of liquid, Come on!

We all have an ass.

Remember Zelda said: I Love to get royally fucked in my pink tight ass-hole. You gotta ass, I gotta ass, _and all gods' childrens gots a ass!_ Analyze that thought awhile!

Ok, your ass hole. And, my ass hole is exactly the same. My ass hole and my girlfriend's ass hole are exactly the same. Here is the question! If you girls like it in the ass so much, what is the attraction?

I'm stumped when it comes to some of the things they did out there in the woods. Where those devices came from, and, to who did they really belong?

What was that place _REALLY_ for? Who is this BARTON? And, what was his old ladies name again?

How did Bonnie get the permission to use the place to FUCK us all night long? And, then do what ever they wanted to said people with out thought of reprisals?

Don't think I went into the Sacrifice pit to get Raped. I wanted something different, even if that meant getting strung up. And, fucked in and out of every hole on my body with out being able to move... Then be able to cum hard, cum again and not really be doing anything but Grooving!

I was Tripping so fucking hard, I would not have been able to tell real from not! They could have run a snake up my ass. And, out my mouth! I would not have been sure it really happened. That's why they drugged us to almost killing a few of us.

I knew they wanted to Fuck each one of us that night, and they did! Fucked each and every one us real freaking good me Droogies! But, I have to tell you, it was me they were after. Or, should I say: "Zelda was after." _She is ravenous, Cunning, HIP._ She knew every move she made. A CAT on a hot tin roof if you will... Like she had done this many times before... And, she has no intention of stopping with us!

(End of Part one.)

Sex, Drugs and a Rock Band 70/71)

Join with us… as we Stake our Claim to the North-West part of town. And, get our own home. Have a ton more Sex! A whole bunch a Drugs! And, build a real money making band. And, get ready to take it on the road. Complete with Huge Breasted Woman in see through sun dresses. We start right out with heavy Drama. And, LSD fun. So join us in:

Sex, Drugs & a Rock Band - Book Two
The Next Logical Step

1971/1972

LaVergne, TN USA
18 December 2009
167542LV00001B/1/P